Environment & Development

Environment & Development

Essays in Honour of Dr U. Sankar

Edited by

K.R. Shanmugam
K.S. Kavi Kumar

SAGE www.sagepublications.com
Los Angeles • London • New Delhi • Singapore • Washington DC

First published in 2016 by

SAGE Publications India Pvt Ltd
B1/I-1 Mohan Cooperative Industrial Area
Mathura Road, New Delhi 110 044, India
www.sagepub.in

SAGE Publications Inc
2455 Teller Road
Thousand Oaks, California 91320, USA

SAGE Publications Ltd
1 Oliver's Yard, 55 City Road
London EC1Y 1SP, United Kingdom

SAGE Publications Asia-Pacific Pte Ltd
3 Church Street
#10-04 Samsung Hub
Singapore 049483

Published by Vivek Mehra for SAGE Publications India Pvt Ltd, typeset in 11/13 pt Minion Pro by RECTO Graphics, Delhi and printed at Saurabh Printers Pvt Ltd, Greater Noida.

Library of Congress Cataloging-in-Publication Data

Sankar, U., honoree. | Shanmugam, K. R., editor. | Kavi Kumar, K. S., editor.
Environment and development: essays in honor of Dr U. Sankar / edited by K.R. Shanmugam and K.S. Kavi Kumar.
Other titles: Environment and development (Sage)
New Delhi; Thousand Oaks: SAGE, [2016] | Includes bibliographical references and index.
LCCN 2015039346 | ISBN 9789351506492 (hardback : alk. paper) | ISBN 9789351506508 (ebook) | ISBN 9789351506485 (epub)
LCSH: Economic development—Environmental aspects—India. | Environmental policy—Economic aspects—India. | Sustainable development—India.
LCC HC440.E5 E477 2016 | DDC 333.70954—dc23 LC record available at http://lccn.loc.gov/2015039346

ISBN: 978-93-515-0649-2 (HB)

The SAGE Team: N. Unni Nair, Guneet Kaur Gulati and Ritu Chopra

Contents

List of Tables

List of Figures

Foreword

Professor U. Sankar is one of India's most respected teachers and economists. During the last five decades, he has not only distinguished himself as a great teacher of economics, but also contributed immensely to policy making in India. He has been instrumental in establishing the Madras School of Economics (MSE) along with Dr Raja J. Chelliah.

Dr U. Sankar has been a pioneer in the promotion of Environmental Economics as a discipline in India. He coordinated the Environmental Management Capacity Building Technical Assistance Programme funded by the World Bank and implemented by the Ministry of Environment and Forests during the late 1990s. Subsequently, he coordinated the activities of Center of Excellence in Environmental Economics set-up by the Ministry of Environment and Forests at MSE. During the past 25 years, he has made significant contributions towards operationalization of sustainable development in India. His contributions range from designing economic instruments for addressing pollution problems in specific industries, analyzing trade and environment interlinkages, identifying appropriate eco-taxes on polluting inputs and outputs, and prioritizing low-carbon growth strategies for fostering green economic growth in India.

Dr Sankar has also made significant contributions in the fields of development economics, public finance and policy. His critical enquiry towards pricing of public utilities and services has been very well received both nationally and internationally. His contribution on 'Economic Analysis of India's Space Programme' has been truly one of its kind.

This volume on *Environment and Development: Essays in Honour of Dr U. Sankar* contains sixteen chapters that cover the entire spectrum of Professor Sankar's intellectual contribution. The contributors to the volume are eminent economists from India and abroad who had an opportunity to work and interact with Dr Sankar during his long and distinguished career.

This volume consists of two parts: the first part has 11 chapters in the area of 'Environment' while the second part has five chapters on 'Development'. At a time when the focus is on sustainable development, the articles in the volume are of particular relevance in as much as they reflect the concern for environmental degradation. I am sure that this volume will be of use to economists, policymakers, government agencies, NGOs and other stakeholders interested in the field of Environment and Development.

C. Rangarajan
Former Governor, Reserve Bank of India
Former Chairman, Economic Advisory Council
to the Prime Minister
Chairman, Madras School of Economics

Acknowledgements

We are grateful to all the contributors of this volume who readily agreed to write in honour of economist of par excellence Professor U. Sankar. We are thankful to SAGE Publications India, for their excellent support throughout this endeavour. We are grateful to the reviewers for their constructive comments. We gratefully acknowledge the help provided by Sudha, Saraswathi, Jothi and Geetha of the Madras School of Economics in organizing the manuscript.

Introduction and Overview

K.R. Shanmugam and K.S. Kavi Kumar

Introduction

While India has registered an impressive average economic growth of 7.92 per cent since 2003–04, it faces many challenges in meeting the developmental needs of its billion-plus population. Several crucial sectors of importance from the Human Development perspective, namely, health and education, continue to underperform highlighting the urgent need for broad-based development. Further, the growing population, growing urbanization and the never satiating demands for higher and higher consumption pose serious concerns regarding the sustainability of the impressive economic growth. As higher demands of the growing population need to be met by the greater exploitation of existing resources, they tend to exert additional pressure on the aggregate resource base of the economy.

The natural question that arises to the contemporary policy-makers and social thinkers is: Whether the *impressive* growth rates of the economy can *last* and if so, how? The ecological footprint analysis finds that world's present demand on the biosphere is already 25 per cent more than the bio-capacity—the biosphere's ability to meet the demand.[1] For India, it is estimated that the total national footprints have doubled since 1961. It is also shown that

[1] The Ecological Footprint measures human demand on the biosphere in terms of the land and sea area required to provide the resources we use and to absorb the waste we generate.

the balance between India's demand on and supply of natural capital has worsened, leaving the country as an ecological debtor. This means that India is depleting its ecological assets, and its productive base more than contributing to its growth. As a result, the current global level of consumption is unsustainable.

Over the past five to six decades, the measurement of economic progress and associated macro-economic policy has largely been influenced by the information flowing from the System of National Accounts (SNA). The SNA based its assessment of an economy by focusing exclusively on the economic activities for which prices are available. Growth in the gross domestic product (GDP) symbolized progress—captured through raising standards of living, creation of jobs and improvement in quality of life. However, the economic progress—symbolized by GDP growth—has also resulted as mentioned previously in the degradation of natural resource base and environmental quality. Further, the economic progress has not been uniform raising concerns about distributional issues.

In an attempt to broaden the perspective of well-being beyond economic growth and income, the UNDP developed the Human Development Index (HDI). While the HDI added quality-of-life dimensions such as literacy and life expectancy to the income, it failed to satisfy the sustainability requirements. It has been argued that without focusing on over-exploitation of natural resource base, the HDI will not be able to capture the sustainability dimension of development.

There have been many criticisms of the exclusive focus on GDP growth since 1960s. One of the most recent comprehensive assessments was by the Commission on the Measurement of Economic Performance and Social Progress (known as Stigliz Report, Stigliz et al., 2009). The key dimensions of well-being have been identified as education, health, social interactions, political freedom, intra-household equity and present and future conditions of environment. Arguing that many of these dimensions enhancing human well-being occur outside the market, the Stigliz Report maintained that such transactions are not properly accounted in the conventional measure of GDP. While the Stigliz Report did not favour any single measure to capture the complex concept of well-being, it suggested that a measure of comprehensive (or inclusive) wealth can be a useful indicator of economic performance. Such wealth could include natural capital, social capital, human capital and man-made capital.

Various World Bank reports and more recently the Inclusive Wealth Report (IWR, 2012) defined comprehensive wealth. In economic parlance, sustainable development (SD) requires maintenance of intergenerational well-being, that is, to ensure that total well-being of the individuals in future generations do not decline over time. In other words, SD ensures that the future generations of individuals are at least at the same level of welfare as enjoyed by today's generation. Hence, intergenerational equity in welfare of the future generations lies at the heart of the SD. In this broader view of sustainability, an economy is sustainable if and only if it is dynamically efficient and the resulting stream of total welfare levels is non-declining over time (Stavins et al., 2003).

Arrow et al. (2010, 2012, 2013) follows a similar approach to define the sustainability as the non-declining intergenerational well-being over time. That is, the sustainability depends on the capacity to provide well-being to the future generations of individuals. The indicator of this capacity is called comprehensive wealth (the social worth of entire range of capital assets constituting the productive base of an economy), including both marketed and non-marketed assets. The sustainability criterion is satisfied if this comprehensive wealth measure is increasing on a per-capita basis.

The approach adopted by Arrow et al. (2010, 2012, 2013) is quite broad-based as it takes a comprehensive view of SD by considering the entire productive (capital) base of an economy. The capital base includes reproducible capital goods (e.g., roads, buildings), natural capital (ecosystem, minerals), population (its size and demography), intellectual capital (e.g., public knowledge) and institutions (formal and informal) that help in resource allocation. The authors acknowledge that market for several of these assets may not exist, and estimate the shadow prices for a number of capital assets.[2] For example, consider clean air as an asset for which market does not exist. Nevertheless, since clean air is one of the most important ingredients of life, it carries some value with it. In this sense, the maximum price that one would be willing to pay for an extra unit of clean air (i.e., to avoid an extra unit of pollution) is the shadow price of pollution. These shadow prices are used to estimate the value of the comprehensive wealth. Using this, it is shown that an economy's intergenerational well-being is dependent on its comprehensive wealth. In other words, intergenerational well-being would not decline over a specified period of time if and only if economy's comprehensive wealth was not to decline over the same period.

To infer whether a country is on the path of SD or not, Arrow et al. (2010, 2012) adopted the concept of comprehensive investment (net addition to the stock of comprehensive wealth, holding the shadow prices constant). This is equivalent to the notion of 'genuine savings' as introduced by Pearce and Atkinson. Genuine savings (S_g) refers to that level of savings, over and above the sum of all the capital deprecations in the economy. Intuitively, if $S_g > 0$, any nation must be adding to its capital base. If $S_g < 0$, the nation is running down its capital stock. As it happens, one cannot tell too much from the value of S_g at any point in time as the interest is in the entire consumption path, not just one point on it. However, if S_g is persistently negative, it can be interpreted that things do not look good for sustainability. If S_g is persistently positive, there is a greater chance that the way the economy is configured is sustainable. Recall that if (comprehensive) wealth declines, the present value of utility or well-being also declines. Hence the development path is unsustainable because wealth is being 'eaten into'. Moreover, additions to wealth (i.e., comprehensive investment) can be formally identified with genuine savings since genuine savings are defined as 'true' net national product that is not consumed. Hence, continued positive genuine savings is the criterion for determining whether wealth is increasing and hence whether the development path is sustainable.

[2] Shadow price is the maximum price that one is willing to pay for an extra unit of a resource for which market does not exist.

Sustainable Development: Professor U. Sankar's Contributions

Adopting SD as long-run objective necessitates a paradigm shift in the manner in which public decisions are made and implemented. It demands a shift in the approach from viewing ecology and environment as means for drawing inputs and sinks for disposing unwanted outputs of economic process, to living in harmony with nature—now and in future. Growing consensus on global climate change and the realization that existing global agreements (such as Kyoto Protocol) may not be sufficient to halt (or reduce) the harmful effects of climate change further emphasizes this need.

Now there is a consensus that sustainability has to be assessed in terms of economic, social and environmental outcomes. The existing information base for assessing government programmes is public expenditure incurred (an input), not output or outcome. This information is based on historical/actual costs and not on economic (opportunity) costs. Even the economic efficiency criterion is not met because in many cases costs are not minimized. For many environmental goods, the market prices even when they exist do not reflect the social costs because of market failures, institutional failures and government failures. Measurement of social costs and benefits involves equity issues, and measurement of environmental costs and benefits involves identification and measurement of 'external' costs and valuation of non-market benefits. Further, most environmental problems are cross-cutting in nature and hence their solutions necessitate an integrated approach.

Addressing these issues poses new challenges and also presents new opportunities. The challenges arise because operationalization of these items is not simply a financial accounting exercise based on conventional methods of budget preparation. Manifold reforms—legal, administrative, costing, valuation, institutional and monitoring—needed in this context require political will as well as reorientation in project management techniques. The opportunity arises because the issues can be looked at in a holistic manner (as against narrow sectoral approach) in the three tiers of government

(Centre, States and Local bodies) integrate environmental considerations in public policy-making and thereby initiate ecological fiscal reform.

Professor Sankar over the past two decades has contributed significantly towards operationalization of SD objectives in India. His contributions ranged from designing economic instruments for addressing pollution problems in tanneries and bleaching and dyeing units of leather and textile units, analyzing trade and environment inter-linkages, identifying appropriate eco-taxes on polluting inputs and outputs, and prioritizing low-carbon growth strategies for fostering green economic growth in India. Professor Sankar has also contributed extensively to the fields of development economics, applied economics and public finance. Some of his important contributions in this regard include proposing 'Acceleration of Growth through Globalization of Indian Agriculture', taking stock of 'Economic Reforms and Liberalization of Indian Economy', 'Economic Analysis of India's Space Programme' and prioritization of 'Issues Before various Finance Commissions'.

Professor Sankar has been instrumental in promoting the use of economic principles in environmental management and had coordinated the Environmental Management Capacity Building Technical Assistance (EMCaB) project funded by the World Bank and implemented by the Ministry of Environment and Forests (MoEF), Government of India, during late 1990s. Subsequently he coordinated the activities of Centre of Excellence in Environmental Economics setup by the MoEF, Government of India, at Madras School of Economics. He had contributed significantly towards the development of the 'Environmental Economics' curriculum in various universities and had edited a *Reader in Environmental Economics* (published by the Oxford University Press) in 2000. The Reader continues to be a classic reference book for the practitioners and students.

Professor Sankar's contribution towards promoting higher education in economics needs special mention as he strived hard to fight against several odds and established Madras School of

Economics (MSE) working closely with Dr Raja J. Chelliah. He had served as the first Director of the School and continues to provide invaluable intellectual support as Honorary Professor. His vision of promoting quantitative methods for teaching economics in southern India has enabled MSE to now stand as one of the premier institutes in India for higher education in economics.

Apart from rigorous theoretical and applied works, Professor Sankar strongly believed in contributing towards policy formulation. He had been one of the most sought after academician by various government agencies. He had advised several Ministries of Government of India, including Ministry of Finance, Ministry of Commerce, Ministry of Agriculture, Ministry of Environment and Forests, Department of Science and Technology, Planning Commission, several Finance Commissions and Indian Space Research Organization. Number of state governments had also benefited from his insightful advices.

As Professor Sankar is a multifaceted personality, his PhD supervisor Professor Arnold Zellner (2005) mentioned that,

> Sankar has been so active and successful in many different areas, namely family, research, teaching, administration etc. is the result of his strong determination, strength of character, fine intellect, willingness to work very hard and excellent judgment in choice of research topics and other matters ... When he attended my courses and served as my research assistant, I learned more about his great intellect, determination, willingness to work hard and his devotion to India and its wellbeing.

Dr Chelliah (2005) rightly remarked that:

> Dr U. Sankar is a man of many talents. His wisdom, personality and quiet dignity embellish his deep scholarship and many notable academic achievements. As a person, a scholar, a research colleague and a teacher he has endeared himself to the academic community of three generations.

Analogous to Professor Sankar's multifaceted personality, the contributions included in this volume cover a range of fields, sectors and issues of concern to India that broadly fall in the domains of 'Environment and Development'.

Overview of the Book

As discussed earlier, the pollution and the degradation of natural resources are adversely affecting the economy in several countries including India. In an influential study, the World Bank (1995) for the first time provided an aggregate economy-wide estimate of cost due to various environmental pollutions in India. It estimated the health impact of water pollution at $5,710 million and the agricultural output loss due to soil degradation at $1,942 million. The health impacts of air pollution were assessed as $1,310 million and the loss of livestock carrying capacity due to rangeland degradation was found to be $328 million. The cost of deforestation came to $214 million and the loss of international tourism was found to be $213 million. Overall, the results showed that the total environmental damage was $9.7 billion per year, or 4.5 per cent of GDP in 1992 values. In the opening chapter of this volume, Mani and co-authors provide a fresh estimate of such aggregate cost of environmental degradation in India and argue that it amounted to 5.7 per cent of GDP, equivalent to $80 billion annually in 2009. Such significantly high damages provide rationale for effective and urgent policy interventions.

Shanmugam's chapter deals with one of the crucial inputs in assessing the public life-saving programmes and the estimation of costs of environmental degradation, namely, the Value of Statistical Life (VSL), which in turn depends on the implicit discount rate associated with health risks. Synthesizing insights from various methodologies, he argues that the Indian workers discount future life years at a real rate of 3–10 per cent. This translates to VSL of US$1.45 million based on Indian data. It is worth noting that this value of VSL is far below the figures associated with the developed country studies, but is comparable with the VSL estimated in other developing countries. Earlier chapter by Mani et al. uses a slightly lower value of VSL (US$1.15 million) while estimating the cost of environmental degradation in India.

The chapter by Kalirajan and co-authors stresses the need for green economic growth in developing countries to address climate change concerns and argue that green growth cannot be achieved by the developing countries on their own. The authors emphasize the importance of technology transfer and capacity building in developing countries to move on to low-carbon economy, an argument that Professor Sankar had made repeatedly in his recent writings.

Investments in green economic activities are believed to offer the co-benefit through creation of 'green jobs'. Such employment opportunities are not limited to developed countries alone and could help in addressing poverty in developing countries. According to a Woods Hole Research Center report, India could create some 900,000 jobs in biomass gasification by 2025. Another 150,000 people might find employment in advanced biomass cooking technologies. These numbers do not include jobs generated in biomass collection and on biomass plantations (Holdren, 2007). Ishwarya and Brinda in their chapter while analysing the pattern of carbon intensity and labour intensity in India argue that the green jobs in developing country context should address additional perspective of environmental protection. Thus, the green jobs should not be restricted to those that reduce the carbon footprint, but include those that build the economy's overall resilience to effectively address climate related shocks.

The Indian textile industry covers a wide range of activities and uses a wide range of raw fibres, including natural fibres. As a sector, it provides direct employment to over 35 million people and contributes to 4 per cent of the country's GDP. The Indian textile industry is the second largest after agriculture in providing employment. The textile industry is known to use restricted chemicals such as azo dyes and formaldehyde. Natural resources such as water constitute an important input for the textile industry. Thus, manufacturing of all variants of textiles has an impact on the environment. Heavy use of natural resources such as water leads to resource depletion and the release of effluents and emissions contributes to the degradation of the environment. Badri Narayanan's study demonstrates the effectiveness of natural dyes in reducing the environmental burden and argues in favour of judicious mix of natural and environmentally less harmful synthetic dyes for sustainable growth of this crucial sector.

Two of the major environmental issues with global concerns include trade and environment inter-linkages and global climate change. Mukherjee and Chakraborty's chapter and Pattanayak and Kavi Kumar's chapter of this volume delve on these aspects. Providing subsidy to protect the interests of domestic firms is not specific to any single country. Such subsidies often lead to deterioration of domestic environment with, for example, free electricity supply to agricultural sector leading to over-exploitation of ground water, etc. Mukherjee and Chakraborty provide a fresh evidence for environmentally harmful impact of subsidies using the cross-country data. They further point to the limited role played by the trade restrictions under World Trade Organization (WTO) as a means of reducing environmentally harmful subsidies.

Global climate change negotiations are hampered by wide-ranging positions taken by various countries with regard to the sharing of greenhouse gas (GHG) mitigation costs. Several criteria are used for apportioning GHG emission mitigation cost burden include population, historic emissions and economic output that accord with several ethical principles. Pattanayak and Kavi Kumar's chapter argues that in addition to the existing criteria used for apportioning GHG emission mitigation cost burden, one may have to include the impacts and vulnerabilities imposed by the potential climate change. Such analysis, they argue, would lead to distribution GHG emission rights, that is, in accordance with the principles of distributive justice.

Valuation of non-market goods and services is an area that needs continued research and Haripriya and Kathuria's study and Sukanya and co-authors' study use different valuation methodologies to analyse distinct resources. The former study uses the hedonic pricing model to assess the willingness to pay (WTP) for reliable water supply based on the implicit effect of the resource scarcity on property prices/rents, the latter use contingent valuation method to assess the WTP of farmers to conserve minor millets. Haripriya and Kathuria have used information gathered from household level survey and estimated the aggregate WTP for improve water supply and quality in Chennai at approximately ₹950 million. Sukanya and co-authors explore the determinants of farmer's WTP to conserve certain varieties of minor millets through primary survey in Kolli Hills.

Use of economic instruments for resource management is another area of high policy importance and studies by Durba and Venkatachalam and Zareena and Amanat delve on this aspect. The former study analyses the existing institutional arrangements in the context of surface water allocation in the Malaprabha river basin in Karnataka. Arguing that the existing institutional approach adopted by the government has not resulted in effective allocation of the resource, it proposes a system of tradable water rights for sustainable use of water. Zareena and Amanat's study focuses on tiger conservation and demonstrates through a bio-economic model the efficacy of giving stakes for local communities in tiger conservation.

The last five chapters of the volume look at various development aspects to complement the environment development focus of the volume. The developmental topics covered include demographic issues by Jayaraj, employment generation by Kaushik and Dasgupta, fiscal policy issues by Rao and Srivastava, and sectoral issues by Prachitha and Shanmugam and by Balasubramanyam and Ahalya.

Jayaraj's chapter deals with the alarming issue of 'Lowness of the weight and the declining trend of female-to-male ratio in India'. It identifies the relative importance of discrimination in natality and excess female mortality in accounting for the 'lowness' of the sex ratio. He argues for providing for social security measure such as widow pension, and free health care for women in addition to improve the other infrastructural facilities like roads, hospitals, schools, protected drinking water, clean fuel and public transport.

Despite the impressive average growth performance, poverty eradication has been one of the persistent objectives of the country. It provides various income-enhancing programmes for poor. The chapter by Kaushik and Dasgupta estimates the impact of two such programmes—Integrated Rural Development Program and Public Works Program, using the NSS data for 15 major Indian states.

As it finds that subsidized credits programme has a negative effect, it argues for a re-evaluation of this programme.

Inter-state disparities in fiscal capacity and how lower fiscal capacities translate into differences in Governments' fiscal intervention in provision of services like education and health are of great importance. Rao and Srivastava's chapter analyses the inter-state imbalances in education for the period: 1993–94 to 2008–09 covering 28 states. They use the summary indicators of disparity like the ratio of maximum to minimum, the ratio of average per capita expenditure on education to minimum, and the coefficient of variation and show some reduction in the extent of disparity in the general category states while the disparity is higher in the special category states. They also show that some of the low income states slipped to below average in terms of their priority and capacity ratio.

India compares poorly in terms of health outcomes and is off-track in meeting Millennium Development Goal 4 (MDG 4). Therefore, there is an urgency to improve the health performance of the country. The chapter by Prachitha and Shanmugam assesses the performance of the Indian States in raising health outcomes, using the stochastic frontier methodology for panel data for the period 2004–10 and argues that the Indian States can improve their health performances without additional resources, but employing the existing resources efficiently and also by increasing their public expenditure on health and increasing the number of medical doctors/specialists in the community and primary health centres.

A general view is that the growth is necessary but not sufficient for promoting development objectives. Another view is that both the resource endowments and the structure of the economy are dictated by history and geography of the region. The chapter by Balasubramanyam and Ahalya illustrates various propositions such as comparison of productivity of labour, rates of return to capital invested and total factor productivity between firms located in two major cities in south India—Bangalore and Hyderabad. Particularly it has discussed the contribution of clusters to human capital formation in the context of the software firms located in Bangalore and Hyderabad.

These 16 chapters are offered as a mark of respect to the contributions of a great economist, Professor U. Sankar. We believe that the theoretical and empirical rigour along with policy focus that the analysis and discussion presented in these chapters showcase Professor Sankar's legacy. We hope that both scholars and policymakers will benefit from this collection of chapters.

References

Arrow, K., Dasgupta, P., Goulder, L.H., Mumford, K.J. and Oleson K. 2010. 'Sustainability and the Measurement of Wealth', NBER Working Paper No. 16599, National Bureau of Economic Research, Cambridge, MA.

———. 2012. 'Sustainability and the Measurement of Wealth', *Environment and Development Economics*, 17(3): 317–53.

———. 2013. 'Sustainability and the Measurement of Wealth: Further Reflections', http://www.krannert.purdue.edu/faculty/kjmumfor/papers/sustainability%20reply.pdf (accessed on 2 September 2015).

Chelliah, R.J. 2005. 'Sankar: A Profile' in G. Mythili and R. Hema (eds), *Topics in Applied Economics: Tools, Issues and Institutions* (pp. 23–25). New Delhi: Academic Foundation.

Holdren, J.P. 2007. 'Linking Climate Policy with Development Strategy in Brazil, China, and India', *Project Report, Woods Hole Research Center*, Woods Hole, MA.

Inclusive Wealth Report (IWR). 2012. *Inclusive Wealth Report: Measuring Progress toward Sustainability*. Cambridge: Cambridge University Press.

Stavins, R.N., Wagner, A.F. and Wagner, G. 2003. 'Interpreting Sustainability in Economic Terms: Dynamic Efficiency plus Intergenerational Equity', *Economics Letters*, 79(3): 339–43.

Stigliz, J., Sen, A. and Fitoussi, J.-P. 2009. *Report by the Commission on the Measurement of Economic Performance and Social Progress*, http://ec.europa.eu/eurostat/documents/118025/118123/Fitoussi+Commission+report (accessed on 2 September 2015).

Zellner, A. 2005. 'In Honor of Professor of Ulaganathan Sankar', in G. Mythili and R. Hema (eds), *Topics in Applied Economics: Tools, Issues and Institutions* (pp. 19–21). New Delhi: Academic Foundation.

SECTION I

Environment

1

Estimating the Cost of Environmental Degradation in India

*Muthukumara Mani, Anil Markandya, Aarsi Sagar, Elena Strukova and Gaurav Joshi**

Introduction

Economic growth is universally recognized as a prerequisite for development. A strong momentum in investment reflecting rising productivity, healthy corporate profits and robust exports has fuelled a buoyant economic growth exceeding 7 per cent a year in India for almost a decade. Economic growth has increased employment opportunities and allowed millions to emerge from poverty.

Economic expansion is also often accompanied by rising demands on the already scarce and often degraded natural resources (soils, fossil fuels, water and forests) and the increasing pollution footprint will negatively impact human health and growth prospects. In India's case, a remarkable growth record has been clouded by a degrading environment and growing scarcity of natural resources. Mirroring the size and diversity of its economy, environmental risks are wide-ranging and are driven by both poverty and prosperity. Environmental sustainability could become the next major economic challenge as India surges along its growth trajectory.

*The team acknowledges Dan Biller, Giovanna Prennushi and Michael Toman for carefully reviewing and providing expert guidance to the team at crucial stages.

This study provides estimates of social and financial costs of environmental damage in India from three pollution damage categories: (i) urban air pollution, (ii) inadequate water supply, poor sanitation and hygiene and (iii) indoor air pollution; and three natural resource damage categories: (i) agricultural damage from soil salinity, water logging and soil erosion, (ii) range land degradation and (iii) deforestation. The estimates are based on a combination of Indian data from secondary sources and on the transfer of unit costs of pollution from a range of national and international studies (a process known as benefit transfer). Data limitations have prevented estimation of degradation costs at the national level for coastal zones, municipal waste disposal, and inadequate industrial and hospital waste management. Furthermore, the estimates provided do not account for loss of non-use values (i.e., values people have for natural resources even when they do not use them).

Methodology for Valuation of Environmental Damage

Environmental damage means physical damages that have an origin in the physical environment. Thus, damages to health from air or water pollution are included as well as damages from deforestation. The term cost means the opportunity cost to society, that is, what is given up or lost, by taking a course of action. When goods traded in markets are damaged, prices and knowledge of consumer preferences for the damaged goods (embodied in the demand function) and production information (embodied in the supply function) provide the necessary information for computing social costs. Estimating social costs from reduced productivity of agricultural land due to erosion, salinity or other forms of land degradation is a good example. However, many damages from environmental causes are to 'goods', such as health, that are not traded in markets. In these cases, economists have devised a number of methods for estimating social costs based on derived preferences from observable or hypothetical behaviour and choices.

One example is the value of time lost to illness or provision of care for ill family members. If the person who is ill or who is providing care to someone who is ill does not otherwise have a job, the financial cost of time losses is zero. However, even in such a case the person is normally engaged in activities that are valuable for the family, and time losses reduce the amount of time available for these activities. Thus, there is a social cost of time losses to the family. In an economic costing exercise, this is normally valued at the opportunity cost of time, that is, the salary, or a fraction of the salary that the individual could earn if he or she chose to work for income. In summary, social costs are preferred over financial costs because social costs capture the cost and reduced welfare to the society as a whole. All costs are estimated as flow values (annual losses).

Unfortunately, information needed to estimate social costs for some categories is often lacking, particularly in developing countries, such as India. In such cases, one has the option of relying on financial costs, which generally do not capture all the social costs. In this study, financial costs have been used for a significant part of the analysis, but with social costs being reported wherever these could be obtained or estimated. In general, these financial costs are likely to underestimate social costs.

Cost of Environmental Degradation

This section provides a summary of estimated social and financial costs of environmental damage. A discussion of each environmental category is provided in the following sections. A detailed methodology of all the analysis can be found in Bolt et al. (2005).

Environmental pollution, degradation of natural resources and inadequate environmental services, such as improved water supply and sanitation, impose costs to society in the form of ill health, lost income and increased poverty and vulnerability. This section provides the overall estimates of social and economic costs of such damages, referring, as much as possible, to damages for 2009.

In some cases, however, the figures may be based on damages in an earlier year if that was the latest information available (see further sections for details).

The results are summarized in Figures 1.1 and 1.2 and in Table 1.1. Total damages based on years 2009–10 amount to about ₹3.75 trillion (US$80 billion), equivalent to 5.7 per cent of GDP. Of this total, outdoor air pollution accounts for the highest share at 1.7 per cent (Figure 1.1) followed by the cost of indoor air pollution at 1.3 per cent; crop land degradation cost at just over 1 per cent; inadequate water supply, sanitation and hygiene (WSH) cost at around 0.8 per cent; pastures degradation cost at 0.6 per cent and forest degradation cost at 0.2 per cent. The individual damages are shown as shares of the total in Figure 1.2. Outdoor air pollution accounts for 29 per cent, followed by indoor air pollution (23 per cent), crop land degradation (19 per cent), water supply and sanitation (14 per cent), pasture (11 per cent) and forest degradation (about 4 per cent).

In addition, India has experienced some damages from natural disasters (floods, landslides, tropical cyclones and storms). These are, however, not included in the earlier figures as they are not the result of anthropogenic factors, although such factors can

Figure 1.1:
Annual cost of environmental damage (billion ₹)

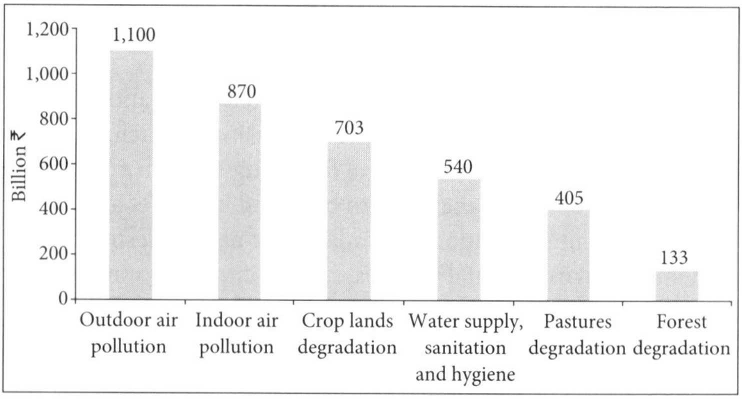

Source: Authors' estimates.

Table 1.1:
Annual cost of environmental damage: Low and high estimates (billion ₹ per year)

Environmental Categories	*'Low'*	*Mid-point Estimate*	*'High'*	*Mid-point Estimate as Per Cent of Total Cost of Environmental Damage*
Outdoor air pollution	170	1,100	2,080	29
Indoor air pollution	305	870	1,425	23
Crop lands degradation	480	703	910	19
Water supply, sanitation and hygiene	475	540	610	14
Pastures degradation	210	405	600	11
Forest degradation	70	133	196	4
Total annual cost (billion ₹/year)	1,710	3,751	5,821	1
Total as per cent of GDP in 2009	2.60	5.70	8.84	

Source: Authors' estimates.
Note: Author estimates are rounded to the nearest ten.

Figure 1.2:
Relative share of damage cost by environmental category (in percentage)

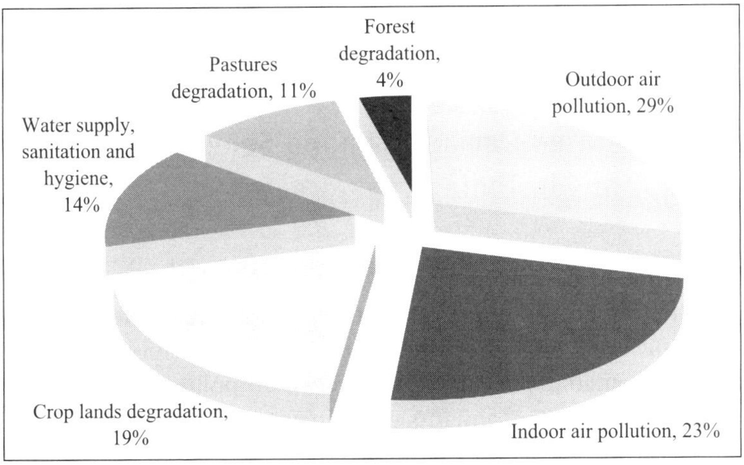

Source: Authors' estimates.

exacerbate their impacts. Over the period from 1953 to 2009, damages from natural disasters were estimated at ₹150 billion a year on average (in constant 2009 prices) and took the form of loss of life and injury, losses to livestock and crops, and losses to property and infrastructure.

Similarly, while India has been phasing out lead in gasoline since 2001, there are a number of other sources that are not controlled. This is probably due to the fact that some gasoline is still produced with lead due the presence of lead in pipes, drinking water, soils, food, paints and other products. Lead exposure could result in substantial mortality from diseases associated with high blood pressure among adults and IQ reduction and mild mental retardation. While some studies have suggested high levels of lead among urban population (both children and adults) in India, there is great uncertainty about current blood lead level (BLL) in the urban population as a whole (and the rural population). It is therefore necessary to undertake new studies of BLL in children and adults to provide a more accurate estimate of health effects and their costs taking into account the gradual lead phase-out in India.

In addition to the mid-point values, 'low' and 'high' estimates of annual costs are presented in Table 1.1. The 'low' and 'high' range estimates differ considerably across the categories because of the uncertainties related to economic valuation procedure or uncertainties about exposure to specific hazards.

Health-related Damages among Selected Populations in India

The damages associated with environmental health are estimated for different groups of the population. This mainly reflects differences in terms of who is affected by the different pollutants but also the availability of data. The outdoor air pollution losses were estimated for the inhabitants of cities with a population of over 100,000 (due to data limitations); inadequate WSH costs were estimated for the whole population of India and indoor air pollution costs were estimated for the households that use solid fuel for cooking (about 75 per cent of all households). These differences in coverage should be borne in mind when comparing across the different environmental burdens. In particular, coverage for outdoor air pollution is less complete than the others and thus the figures for that category are underestimated.

The higher costs for outdoor/indoor air pollution (other than lead exposure) are primarily driven by an elevated exposure of the urban and rural population to particulate matter pollution that results in a substantial cardiopulmonary and chronic obstructive pulmonary disease (COPD) mortality load among adults. As noted, the rural population has only been assessed for indoor air pollution.

Figure 1.3 gives the estimates of damage per person within the different exposed populations used to construct the figures in Table 1.1. We note that a significant part of the health burden, especially from WSH is borne by children under five years (Figure 1.4). These figures would suggest that about 23 per cent of all under-five mortality can be associated with indoor air pollution and inadequate WSH, and 2 per cent of adult mortality with outdoor air pollution.

Figure 1.3:
Annual environmental health losses per person of the exposed population

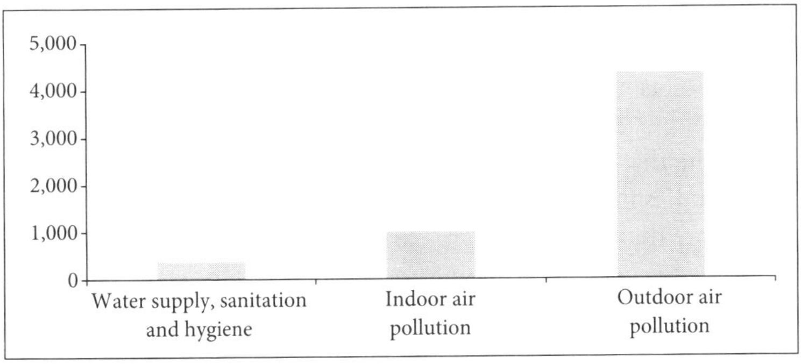

Source: Authors' estimates.

Figure 1.4:
Estimated share of annual mortality from different sources in India

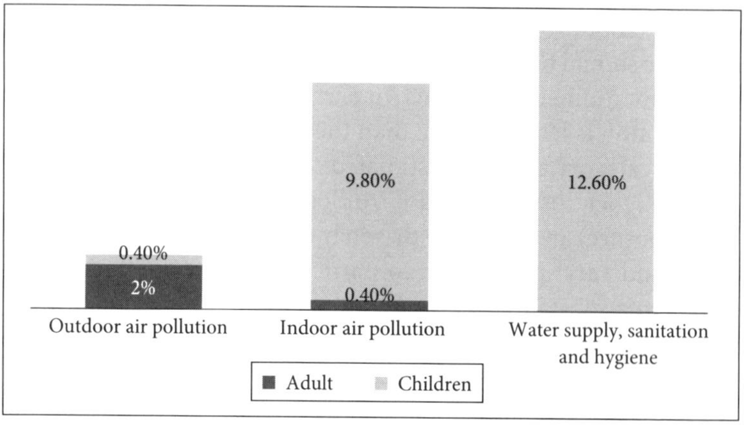

Source: Authors' estimates.

Environmental Damages and the Poor

While this study does not address the impacts of the losses estimated earlier on poor households (something that should be undertaken as a separate study), one can comment on how the poor are affected by the environmental damages. First, the losses related to WSH are likely to be concentrated among the poor who most often do not have access to piped water or sanitation. Second, the rural population is more affected by the water and indoor air pollution-related damages than the urban population. For the urban population, the distribution of impacts by income class is less certain. Some studies indicate that urban ambient air quality does affect the poor more than the rich (Garg, 2011) but the present study has not been able to confirm this point. In overall terms, however, it is very likely the case that the poorer urban population suffers more both from urban air pollution and inadequate WSH, and in general it is the poor who are included in all major cost categories (those who live in big cities and use solid fuel for cooking).

Other Categories of Damages

Crop land damages arise from the decline of the value of crops due to soil erosion, water logging, salinity and overgrazing. We derive a range of estimates due to uncertainty of crop and pasture profitability as well as the uncertainty of the level of degradation.

Forest degradation has arisen in India from unsustainable logging practices in some regions and general over-exploitation of forest resources. Although the country has gained about 7 per cent in overall forest cover between 1990 and 2010, there has also been a notable degradation in some forests. This results in loss of ecosystem services, including carbon sequestration, provision of timber and non-timber forest products, recreational and cultural use of forests, and prevention of soil erosion. The losses are valued using a range of techniques, which are subject to considerable uncertainty arising from the estimates of forest productivity and methods of obtaining values for the non-marketed services.

Finally, impacts of changes in fisheries were examined but it was not possible to value these in monetary terms due to gaps in the data.

Another way of looking at the role of environmental resources is in terms of the 'GDP of the poor'.[1] Natural resources degradation is more significant when compared with their income. One measure of the growth potential for the poor is in the share of GDP generated in agriculture, forestry and fishery, which made up about 17 per cent of GDP in 2010. To be sure, not all GDP in these sectors goes to the poor but a more significant part of it does go to some other sectors. Figure 1.5 summarizes the potential impact of natural resource degradation losses on the GDP and GDP of the poor (i.e., GDP in agriculture, forestry and fishery). In total, these losses amount to about 2 per cent of GDP and 11 per cent of the 'GDP of the poor' (GDP in Agriculture, Fishery and Forestry) in India. It should be

[1] Gundimeda and Sukhdev (2008) introduced a concept, GDP of the poor. This includes GDP only from agriculture, forestry and fishery, since these sectors reflect growth potential for most of the rural, predominantly poor India, making up 72 per cent of the total. The importance of these sectors for the poor is also discussed in World Bank (2006).

Figure 1.5:
Natural resource losses compared to GDP and GDP in agriculture, forestry and fishery in 2009

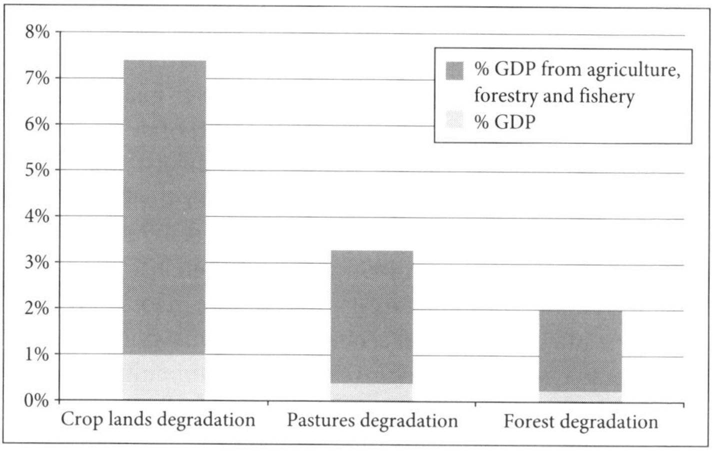

Source: Authors' estimates.

noted that while this is an interesting concept, this could also be an underestimation of impact of environmental damage suffered by the poor, as much of the health damage from pollution in urban areas is also predominantly borne by the urban poor.

Comparison with Other Countries

The cost of environmental degradation (COED) in India is roughly comparable with other countries with similar income level (Figure 1.6). Studies of the COED were conducted using a similar methodology in Pakistan, a low income country, and several low and lower-middle income countries in Asia, Africa and Latin America. They show that the monetary value of increased morbidity, mortality and natural resources degradation typically amounts to 4–10 per cent of GDP, compared to 5.7 per cent of GDP in India.[2]

[2] The environmental media included in the analysis include outdoor/indoor air pollution, inadequate water supply, sanitation and hygiene and natural resource degradation

Figure 1.6:
Cost of environmental degradation (health and natural resources damages)

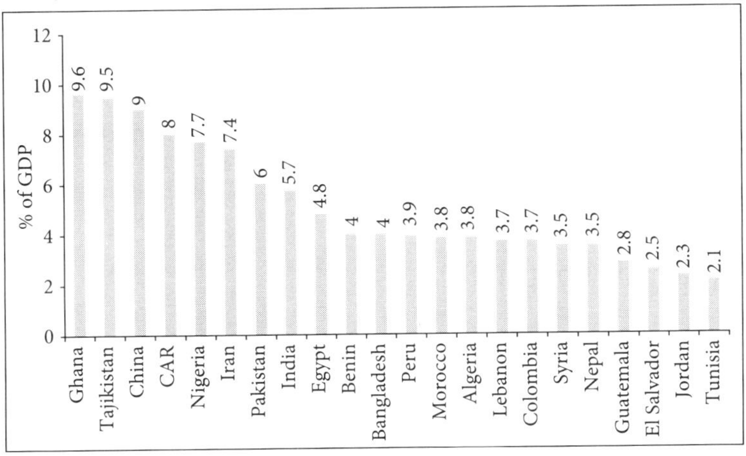

Source: World Bank (2012b).

Figure 1.7:
Health cost attributed to outdoor air pollution

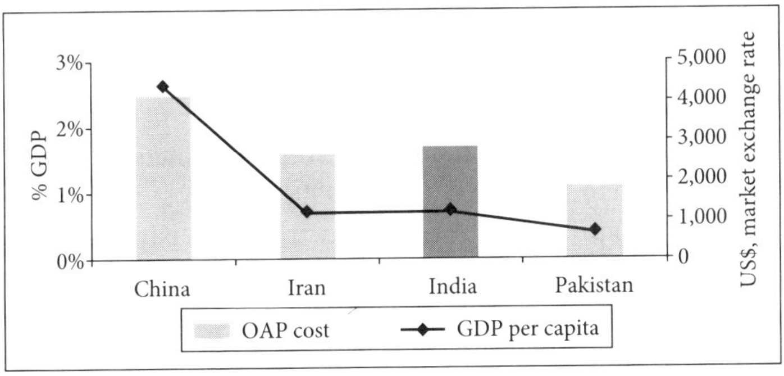

Source: World Bank (2005, 2006, 2007).

The situation also looks consistent across different countries if one compares only the health costs of outdoor air pollution (Figure 1.7). In all the selected countries, these vary between 1.1

(soils salinity/erosion, pastures degradation, deforestation and forest degradation, fishery loss). Losses from natural disasters were included in cost of environmental damage (CED) study in Peru and in Iran.

and 2.5 per cent of GDP. In India, the health cost of outdoor air pollution is estimated at about 1.7 per cent of GDP. The high cost of outdoor air pollution-related mortality in urban areas is the main driver of environmental health costs. A World Bank study on China (2007), later cited in 'China 2030' (World Bank, 2012a), applied a methodology for outdoor air pollution valuation similar to the one utilized in this study.

Urban Air Pollution

Particulate Matter

There is substantial research evidence from around the world that outdoor urban air pollution has significant negative impacts on public health and results in premature deaths, chronic bronchitis and respiratory disorders. A comprehensive review of such studies is provided by Ostro (1994) and Ostro et al. (2004). The air pollutant that has shown the strongest association with these health end points is particulate matter and other secondary particles with similar characteristics of less than 10 microns in diameter (PM10).[3] Research in the United States in the 1990s and most recently by Pope et al. (2002) provides strong evidence that it is particulates of less than 2.5 microns (PM2.5) that have the largest health effects. Other gaseous pollutants (SO_2, NOx, CO and ozone) are generally not thought to be as damaging as fine particulates. However, SO_2 and NOx may have important health consequences because they can react with other substances in the atmosphere to form secondary particulates. In particular, the evidence implicates sulphates formed from SO_2, but it is much less certain about nitrates, formed from NOx.

The focus of this study therefore is the health effects of all fine particulates (PM10 and PM2.5). This requires data on who is

[3] Also called total suspended particulates or TSP.

exposed, the health impacts of that exposure and the value attached to those impacts. Two distinct methods of valuation of premature mortality are commonly used to estimate the social cost of premature death, that is, the human capital approach (HCA) and the value of statistical life (VSL). The first method involves estimating income losses from premature death and was dominant in the past. But because this measure is not based on individual preferences and has other conceptual problems, it has been overtaken by both stated and revealed preference approaches to estimating preferences for reducing mortality risks. The monetary value of these preferences, or the willingness to pay, when divided by the relevant risk reduction yields the VSL. Because HCA almost always underestimates the VSL, HCA has been applied as a low estimate and VSL as a high estimate in estimating the cost of premature mortality.

Given the data limitations, we can only estimate impacts for the urban populations and in fact that too only for a part of that population. Only major cities have TSP and PM10 monitoring data. In this study, we focus on cities with a population of 100,000 and above only. Since the baseline population is from the 2001 census, there are many cities that have achieved a population of 100,000 since 2001 and have not been included in the study. This can be updated in the future.

Pollution data for all cities, where available, were taken from the Central Pollution Control Board's (CPCB) Environmental Data Bank website for the year 2008. Health damage estimates for PM10 were calculated based on observations for the year 2008.The study included 96 cities with monitoring stations and 223 cities with no monitoring stations (254 million people in total). The population for 96 cities with monitoring stations amounts to 186 million, or about 16 per cent of the country's population. In addition, there are about 225 cities with an average population of 69 million for which there are no data on PM concentrations. Since excluding them from the estimation of health impacts would be a serious omission, annual average PM10 levels were assigned to these cities based on scaling up of the World Bank modelling PM10 concentrations (taken from the World Bank Internal Research Database), using an average factor for the major cities.

The age distribution of the urban population was estimated using urban population parameters from the 2001 India Census. PM10 were transformed into PM2.5 to obtain values for the latter using a ratio of 0.5 based on evidence from India (CPCB, 2011). This ratio reflects the mean of the PM2.5/PM10 ratio for large Indian cities reported in this chapter.

Based on the current status of worldwide research, the risk ratios or concentration-response coefficients from Pope et al. (2002) were considered likely to be the best available evidence of the mortality effects of ambient particulate pollution (PM2.5).

Damages due to anthropogenic factors are measured from a baseline PM2.5 concentration, which we set equal to 7.5 $\mu g/m^3$ (as in WHO, 2002a). This is considered to be the level one would find in the natural environment. A log-linear function for estimating cardiopulmonary mortality associated with outdoor air pollution was applied.

The morbidity effects assessed in most worldwide studies are based on PM10. Concentration-response coefficients from Ostro (1994) and Abbey et al. (1995) have been applied to estimate these effects. Ostro (1994) reviewed the worldwide studies and based on that Ostro (2004) estimated the concentration–response coefficient for restricted activity days (RADs), whereas Abbey et al. (1995) provided estimates of chronic bronchitis associated with particulates (PM10). A linear function for estimating morbidity end points associated with outdoor air pollution was applied. The mortality and morbidity coefficients are presented in Table 1.2 based on these estimates.

The health effects of air pollution can be converted to disability adjusted life years (DALYs) to facilitate a comparison with health effects from other environmental risk factors. DALYs per 10,000 cases of various health end points are presented in Table 1.3.

Based on 2009–10 data, urban air particulate pollution is estimated to cause around 109,000 premature deaths among adults and 7,500 deaths among children under five annually. Adult mortality estimated above is consistent with Cropper et al.'s (2012) estimate of the annual mortality associated with coal electricity generation in India (about 60,000 people calculated at about 650 deaths per year

Table 1.2:
Urban air pollution concentration—Response coefficients

Annual Health Effect	*Concentration-response Coefficient*	*Per 1 μg/m³ Annual Average Ambient Concentration of:*
Long-term mortality (% change in cardiopulmonary and lung cancer mortality)	0.8*	PM2.5
Acute mortality children under five (% change in acute respiratory illness deaths)	0.166	PM10
Chronic bronchitis (% change in annual incidence)	0.9	PM10
Respiratory hospital admissions (per 100,000 population)	1.2	PM10
Emergency room visits (per 100,000 population)	24	PM10
Restricted activity days (% change in annual incidence)	0.475	PM10
Lower respiratory illness in children (per 100,000 children)	169	PM10
Respiratory symptoms (per 100,000 adults)	18,300	PM10

Source: Pope et al. (2002), Ostro (2004) for the mortality coefficients. Ostro (1994) and Abbey et al. (1995) for the morbidity coefficients.
*Mid-range coefficient from Pope et al. (2002) reflecting a linear function of relative risk. In the analysis, however, we used a log-linear.

Table 1.3:
DALYs for different health end points

Health Effect	*DALYs Lost per 10,000 Cases*
Mortality (adults)	75,000
Mortality (children under 5)	340,000
Chronic bronchitis (adults)	22,000
Respiratory hospital admissions	160
Emergency room visits	45
Restricted activity days (adults)	3
Lower respiratory illness in children	65
Respiratory symptoms (adults)	0.75

Source: Ostro (2004).
Note: DALYs are calculated using a discount rate of 3 per cent and full age weighting based on WHO tables.

with 92 coal burning power plants in India). Electricity generation is responsible for a fraction of PM pollution analysed in this study.[4] Estimated new cases of chronic bronchitis are about 48,000 per year. Annual hospitalizations due to pollution are estimated at close to 370,000 and emergency room visits/outpatient hospitalizations at 7,300,000 per year. Cases of less severe health impacts are also presented in Table 1.4. In terms of annual DALYs lost mortality accounts for an estimated 60 per cent, chronic bronchitis around 5 per cent, RADs for 7 per cent and respiratory symptoms for 25 per cent.

Table 1.4:
Estimated health impact of urban air pollution

Health End Points	*Total Cases*	*Total DALYs*
Premature mortality (adults)	109,340	820,049
Mortality (children under 5)	7,513	255,431
Chronic bronchitis	48,483	106,663
Hospital admissions	372,331	5,957
Emergency room visits/outpatient hospital visits	7,303,897	32,868
Restricted activity days	1,231,020,030	369,306
Lower respiratory illness in children	16,255,360	105,660
Respiratory symptoms	3,917,855,052	293,839
Total		1,989,773

Source: Authors' estimates.

The estimated annual cost of urban air pollution health effects is presented in Table 1.5. The cost of mortality is based on the HCA as lower bound and the VSL as upper bound for adults and HCA for children.

The cost-of-illness (COI) approach (mainly medical cost and value of time losses) was applied to obtain an estimate of the morbidity cost (see cost of morbidity in Table 1.5).

[4] Cropper et al. (2012) analyses direct emissions from coal burning power plants and applied annual average intake PM2.5 fractions. Ambient concentrations of PM2.5 are analysed in this report.

Table 1.5:
Estimated annual cost of health impacts (billion ₹)

Health Categories	*Total Annual Cost**	*Per Cent of Total Cost* (Mean)*
Mortality		
Adults	1,018	92.2
Children under 5	13	1.2
Morbidity		
Chronic bronchitis	1	0.1
Hospital admissions	3	0.3
Emergency room visits/outpatient hospital visits	8	0.7
Restricted activity days (adults)	46	4.2
Lower respiratory illness in children	14	1.3
Total cost of morbidity	72	9
Total cost (mortality and morbidity)	1,103	100

Source: Authors' estimates.
*Percentages are rounded to nearest per cent.

To summarize, the mean estimated annual cost of PM urban air pollution totals ₹1,103 billion or 1.7 per cent of GDP in 2009. About 90 per cent of the cost is associated with mortality, and 10 per cent with morbidity (Table 1.5). Measured in terms of DALYs,[5] about 54 per cent of the cost is associated with mortality and 46 per cent with morbidity (Table 1.5).

Water Supply, Sanitation and Hygiene

The main health impacts of unclean water and poor hygiene are diarrhoeal diseases, typhoid and paratyphoid. In addition, there are costs in the form of averting expenditures to reduce health risk.

[5] The sum of years of potential life lost due to premature mortality and the years of productive life lost due to disability (www.who.int).

Diarrhoeal and related illnesses contribute the dominant share of the health cost. We consider these in turn.

Diarrhoeal Diseases, Typhoid and Paratyphoid

WHO has proposed a rigorous methodology (Fewtrell and Colford, 2004) that links the access to improved water supply, safe sanitation and hygiene to diarrhoeal illnesses (mortality and morbidity of children under five) and other population morbidity-based on an extended meta-analysis of peer-reviewed publications. About 88 per cent of diarrhoeal cases globally are attributed to WSH (Pruss-Ustun et al., 2004). This is a conservative approach where malnutrition impact on early childhood diseases is omitted. If considered, this additional indirect impact would approximately double the mortality attributed to WSH (World Bank, 2010). However, a major part of these losses are in the form of acute respiratory mortality that was accounted for in the indoor air pollution section. To avoid double counting and be on a conservative side, we considered only direct impact of inadequate WSH.

Mortality for children under five and diarrhoeal-based child mortality are high in India. Baseline health data for estimating the health impacts of inadequate WSH are presented in Table 1.6. The Office of the Registrar General (2004) indicates that 14 per cent of child mortality is due to intestinal diseases. A baseline diarrhoeal mortality rate of 14 per cent of under-five child mortality is thus used for diarrhoeal mortality estimation.

For diarrhoeal morbidity, however, it is very difficult or practically impossible to identify all cases of diarrhoea. The main reason is that substantial numbers of cases are not treated or do not require treatment at health facilities, and are therefore never recorded. A second reason is that cases treated by private doctors or clinics are often not reported to public health authorities. Household surveys therefore provide the most reliable indicator of total cases of diarrhoeal illness. Most household surveys, however, contain

Table 1.6:
Baseline data for estimating health impacts

	Baseline	*Source*
Under-5 child mortality rate in 2006	52–82	NFHS-3
Diarrhoeal mortality in children under 5 years (% of child mortality)	14%	Office of Registrar General (2004)
Diarrhoeal 2-week prevalence in children under 5 years	8.9–9%	NFHS-3
Estimated annual diarrhoeal cases per child under 5 years	1.85–1.87	Estimated from NFHS-3
Estimated annual diarrhoeal cases per person (>5 years)	0.37–0.56	International experience (Krupnick et al., 2006)
Hospitalization rate (% of all diarrhoeal cases)—children under 5 years	0.15%	NSS (2004)
Hospitalization rate (% of all diarrhoeal cases)—children under 5 years	0.3–0.6%	
Per cent of diarrhoeal cases attributable to inadequate water supply, sanitation and hygiene	90%	WHO (2002b)
DALYs per 100 thousand cases of diarrhoea in children under 5	70	Estimated from WHO tables
DALYs per 100 thousand cases of diarrhoea in persons >5 years	100–130	
DALYs per 100 thousand cases of typhoid in persons under 5 and over 5	190–820	
DALYs per case of diarrhoeal and typhoid mortality in children over 5 and under 5	32–34	

Source: Ostro (2004).

only information on diarrhoeal illness in children. Moreover, the surveys only reflect diarrhoeal prevalence at the time of the survey. As there is often high variation in diarrhoeal prevalence across seasons of the year, extrapolation to an annual average will result in either over- or underestimation of total annual cases. Correcting this bias is often difficult without knowledge of seasonal variations.

In spite of all these difficulties, a reasonable estimate has been made of the number of cases and prevalence of diarrhoea in the population, along with the number of DALYs per 100,000 cases of diarrhoea. The figures are summarized in Table 1.6.

Table 1.7 presents the estimated health impacts from inadequate WSH, based on the parameters given in Table 1.5, including the assumption (from WHO) that 88 per cent of diarrhoeal illness is attributable to WSH. The estimation of the incidence of the disease in India was based significantly on the NFHS-3 survey, which provides data on diarrhoeal prevalence in children under the age of 5 years. It reports a diarrhoeal prevalence (preceding 12 days) rate of 8.9 per cent in urban areas and 9 per cent in rural areas. This rate is used to estimate annual episodes per child under five, and then total annual cases in all children under five. The procedure applied is to multiply the two-week prevalence rate by 52/2.5 to arrive at an approximation of the number of annual cases of per child. The prevalence rate is not multiplied by 26 two-week periods (i.e., 52/2), but multiplied by 52/2.5 because the average duration of diarrhoeal illness is assumed to be three to four days. This implies that the two-week prevalence captures a quarter of the diarrhoeal

Table 1.7:
Estimated annual health impacts from water, sanitation and hygiene

	Cases		*Estimated Annual DALYs*		*% of Total DALYs*
	Urban	*Rural*	*Urban*	*Rural*	
Children (under the age of 5 years)—increased mortality (thousand)	41	198	1,384	6,714	87–93
Children (under the age of 5 years)—increased morbidity (thousand)	57,831	178,898	20	63	1
Population over 5 years of age—increased morbidity (thousand)	149,836	344,183	177	406	11–6
Typhoid/paratyphoid mortality (thousand)	0.57		19		0
Typhoid/paratyphoid morbidity (thousand)	1,150		8		0

Source: Author estimates.

prevalence in the week prior to and a quarter in the week after the two-week prevalence period. The table provides estimates of DALYs lost to waterborne diseases. About 60 per cent of the DALYs are from diarrhoeal child mortality. Typhoid/paratyphoid deaths add another 20 per cent of DALY.

The estimated costs associated with the impacts identified previously are given in Table 1.8. The hypothetical value from which the estimates are based relies on the WHO methodology, which uses conditions in developed countries as the benchmark. The incidence rates for these illnesses are close to zero in those countries (0.3 per person/year as per Fewtrell and Colford, 2004).

The total cost is ₹490 billion. The cost of mortality is based on the HCA for children under five. The cost of morbidity includes the COI (medical treatment, medicines and value of lost time) and value of lost DALYs estimated at GDP per capita. We used GDP per capita as a proxy for WTP for one additional year of life, expressed in DALYs.

Table 1.8:
Estimated health impacts from inadequate water, sanitation and hygiene

	Estimated Annual Cost (Billion ₹)		
	Urban	*Rural*	*Total*
Mortality			
Children under age 5: diarrhoeal mortality	50	227	277
Children under age 5: typhoid			0.3
Persons over 5: typhoid			0.5
Morbidity			
Diarrhoeal morbidity	105	103	208
Typhoid morbidity[6]			3.3
Total annual cost	155	330	489.1

Source: Authors' estimates.

[6] About 25 per cent of estimated COI is from hospitalization and doctor visits, 70 per cent is from time losses for the ill individuals and their caregivers during illness.

Averting Expenditures

In the presence of perceived health risks, individuals often take measures to avoid these risks. These are usually considered as a cost of the health risks of environmental burdens. If consumers perceive that the municipal water supply or the other sources of water supply they rely on are unsafe, they are likely to purchase bottled water for drinking purposes, or boil their water, or install water purification filters. The estimated costs of these options are given in Table 1.9. The assumed hypothetical level of expenditure here is zero (i.e., no aversive expenses would be incurred if the water supplied was safe). The total amount of aversive expenditures for India amount to about ₹55 billion a year.

In summary, the estimated annual cost associated with inadequate WSH is presented in Figure 1.8, totalling ₹470–610 billion per year, with a mean of ₹540 billion. The cost of health impacts represents an estimated 90 per cent of total mean cost, with averting expenditures accounting for about 10 per cent. Health impacts include both mortality and morbidity, and averting expenditures include bottled water consumption and boiling of drinking water in the household. Annual costs by major category are presented in Figure 1.8.

Table 1.9:
Estimated total annual household cost of averting expenditures

	Total Annual Cost (billion ₹)	
	Urban	*Rural*
Cost of bottled water consumption	20	7
Cost of household boiling drinking water	4	3
Cost of household filtering drinking water	14	7
Total annual cost	38	17

Source: Authors' estimates.

Figure 1.8:
Annual costs by category (billion ₹)

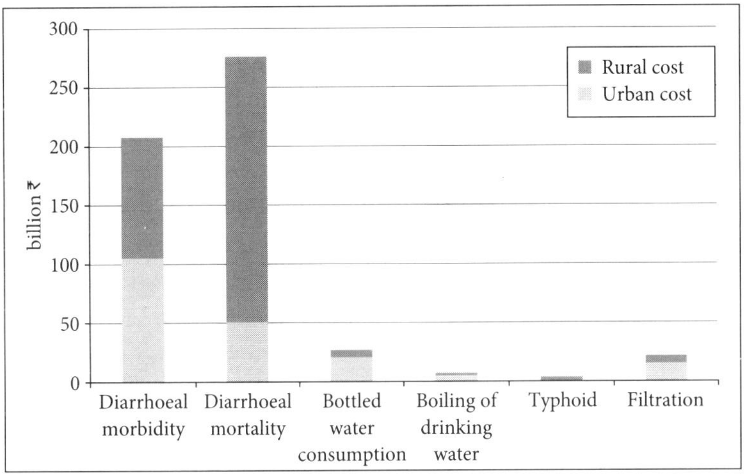

Source: Authors' estimates.

Indoor Air Pollution

WHO (2002b) estimates that 1.6 million people die each year globally due to indoor smoke from the use of traditional fuels in the home. The most common is incomplete combustion of fuels such as wood, agricultural residues, animal dung, charcoal and, in some countries, coal. The strongest links between indoor smoke and health are for lower respiratory infections, COPD and cancer of the respiratory system. Indoor smoke is estimated to cause about 37.5, 22 and 1.5 per cent of these illnesses globally (WHO, 2002b).

There are two main steps in quantifying the health effects. First, the number of people or households exposed to pollution from solid fuels needs to be calculated, and the extent of pollution, or concentration, measured. Second, the health impacts from this exposure should be estimated based on epidemiological assessments. Once the health impacts are quantified, the value of this damage can be estimated.

The odds ratios in Table 1.10 have been applied to young children under the age of five years (for acute respiratory illness—ARI) and adult females (for ARI and COPD) to estimate the increase in mortality and morbidity associated with indoor air pollution.[7] It is these population groups that suffer the most from indoor air pollution. This is because women spend much more of their time at home, and/or more time while cooking (with little children at their side), than in comparison with older children and adult males, who spend more time outdoors.

Table 1.10:
Health risks of indoor air pollution

	Odds Ratios	
	'Low'	*'High'*
Acute respiratory illness	1.9	2.7
Chronic obstructive pulmonary disease	2.3	4.8

Source: Desai et al. (2004).

The NFHS-3 reports that 90 per cent of rural and 32 per cent of urban households use solid fuels for cooking in India. The national weighted average is about 71 per cent.

To estimate the health effects of indoor air pollution from the odds ratios in Table 1.1, baseline data for ARI and COPD need to be established. These data are presented in Table 1.11, along with unit figures for DALYs lost to illness and mortality. The hypothetical level against which damages are calculated is a situation in which there is no exposure to indoor air pollution and the odds ratio is one.

The results of the estimation of health losses associated with indoor air pollution are presented in Table 1.12. Estimated cases of ARI child mortality and ARI morbidity (children and female adults) from indoor air pollution represent about 38–53 per cent of total

[7] Although Desai et al. (2004) present odds ratios for lung cancer, this effect of pollution is not estimated in this report. This is because the incidence of lung cancer among rural women is generally very low. The number of cases in rural India associated with indoor air pollution is therefore likely to be minimal.

Table 1.11:
Baseline data for estimating health impacts

	Baseline		*Source*
	Urban	*Rural*	
Female COPD mortality rate (% of total female deaths)	9.5		WHO estimate for India Shibuya et al. (2001)
Female COPD incidence rate (per 100 thousand)	79		
ARI 2-week prevalence in children under 5 years	22%	22%	NFHS-3 (2006)
Estimated annual cases of ARI per child under 5 years	1.0	1.0	Estimated from NFHS-3, 2006
Estimated annual cases of ARI per adult female (>30 years)	0.4	0.5	Estimated from a combination of NFHS-3, 2006 and Krupnick et al. (2006)
ARI mortality in children under 5 years (% of child mortality)	22		Office of Registrar General (2004)
DALYs per 100 thousand cases of ARI in children under 5	165	165	
DALYs per 100 thousand cases of ARI in female adults (>30)	700	700	Estimated from WHO tables
DALYs per case of ARI mortality in children under 5	34	34	
DALYs per case of COPD morbidity in adult females	2.25	2.25	
DALYs per case of COPD mortality in adult females	6	6	

Source: Ostro (2004).

ARI in India. Similarly, the estimated cases of COPD mortality and morbidity represent about 46–72 per cent of total estimated female COPD from all causes.

Table 1.12 also gives the DALYs lost to indoor air pollution. An estimated 8 million DALYs are lost each year. About 70–80 per cent are from mortality and 20–30 per cent are from morbidity.

The central estimated costs associated with the impacts identified previously are given in Table 1.13. Briefly, the cost of mortality is based on the VSL estimated for India as a higher bound and HCA as a lower bound for adults and on HCA for children under five.

Table 1.12:
Estimated annual health impacts of indoor air pollution (thousands)

	Estimated Annual Cases ('000)		*Estimated Annual DALYs ('000)*	
	Urban	*Rural*	*Urban*	*Rural*
Acute Respiratory Illness				
Children (under the age of 5 years)—increased mortality	19.5	166.4	662	5,660
Children (under the age of 5 years)—increased morbidity	7,570	47,925	12.5	79
Females (30 years and older)—increased morbidity	9,401	47,384	65.8	331.7
Chronic Obstructive Pulmonary Disease				
Adult females—increased mortality	7.5	53.4	74	363
Adult females—increased morbidity	39,000	202.5	127.7	455.6
Total disability adjusted life years—mortality and morbidity			942.4	6,889.3

Source: Authors' estimates.

Table 1.13:
Estimated annual cost of indoor air pollution

	Estimated Annual Cost (Billion ₹)	
	Urban	*Rural*
Acute Respiratory Illness		
Children (under the age of 5 years)—increased mortality	20	190
Children (under the age of 5 years)—increased morbidity	5	15
Adult females—increased morbidity	10	20
Chronic Obstructive Pulmonary Disease		
Adult females—increased mortality	99	485
Adult females—increased morbidity	6	15
Total	140	725

Source: Authors' estimate.

The cost of morbidity includes the COI (medical treatment, value of lost time, etc.) and value of DALYs estimated in GDP per capita.

To summarize, the total annual cost of indoor air pollution is estimated at ₹305–1,425 billion, with a mean estimate of about

₹865 billion (Table 1.4) or 1.3 per cent of GDP in 2009. About 68 per cent of this cost is associated with COPD, and 32 per cent with ARI.[8] COPD and ARI mortality represent about 90 per cent of the total cost, and morbidity about 10 per cent (Figure 1.9).

Figure 1.9:
Annual costs of indoor air pollution (billion ₹)

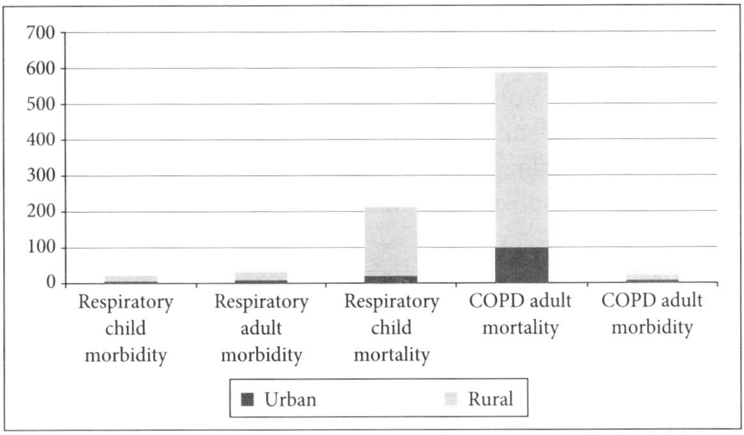

Source: Authors' estimates.

Taking another classification, respiratory child mortality is 77 per cent of the cost, and adult female COPD mortality is 21 per cent of the cost (Figure 1.9). ARI in adult females and in children represent 2 per cent of the cost.

Natural Resources: Land Degradation, Crop Production and Range Land Degradation

Major categories of land degradation in India are similar to those in other Asian countries. They include: (1) water and wind soil erosion and in particular, irrigation-related land degradation, including secondary salinity, water logging and irrigation-related soil erosion;

[8] Based on the mean estimated annual cost.

(2) pasture and range land degradation; and (3) degradation of forests and bushes and related loss of biodiversity (see Table 1.14 for aggregate estimates of land degradation in 2002). Land degradation eventually causes landslides and mudflows especially in the sensitive mountainous areas. Most affected by degradation is pasture land near villages as well as bush and tree vegetation. Common causes are ineffective land management and lack of alternate energy resources. Land degradation not only affects agricultural productivity, biodiversity and wildlife, but also increases the likelihood for natural hazards (World Bank, 2007).

Losses to crop lands and range lands include damages from soil salinity and water logging due to improper irrigation practices and human-induced soil erosion. In the absence of data on the annual

Table 1.14:
Land degradation in India (million hectares, 2002)

	Degree of Degradation				
Degradation Type	*Slight*	*Moderate*	*Strong*	*Extreme*	*Total*
Water Erosion	27.3	111.6	5.4	4.6	148.9
a. Loss of top soil	27.3	99.8	5.4	–	132.5
b. Terrain deterioration	–	11.8	–	4.6	16.4
Wind Erosion	0.3	10.1	3.1	–	13.5
a. Loss of top soil	0.3	5.5	0.4	–	6.2
b. Loss of top soil/ terrain deterioration	–	4.6	–	–	4.6
c. Terrain deformation/ over blowing	–	–	2.7	–	2.7
Chemical Deterioration	6.5	7.3	–	–	13.8
a. Loss of nutrient	3.7	–	–	–	3.7
b. Salinization	2.8	7.3	–	–	10.1
Physical Deterioration	–	–	–	–	116.6
Water logging	6.4	5.2	–	–	11.6
Total (affected area)	36.8	137.9	8.5	4.6	187.8

Source: indiastat.com

increase in salinity and eroded crop lands and range lands, the annual loss of agricultural production (crop and range land fodder) is estimated based on accumulated degradation. This estimate may be more or less than the net present value of annual production losses depending on the rate of annual increase in degradation. The losses are considered in this section and the next.

Soil Salinity and Water Logging

Soil salinity and water logging reduce the productivity of agricultural lands and, if a threshold salinity level is exceeded the land becomes unfit for cultivation. According to the conventional welfare economics, if agricultural markets are competitive, the economic costs of salinity would be measured as the losses in consumer surplus (consumer willingness to pay above market price) and producer surplus (profit) associated with the loss in productivity. These losses include direct losses through reduced yields as the land becomes saline or degraded. In practice, the calculations can be more complex as account needs to be taken of crop substitution to more saline-tolerant but less profitable crops and other indirect losses. Because of lack of data, the losses here are approximated by the value of 'lost' output related to the salinity, with some simple adjustment for changes in cropping patterns.

The estimated losses from saline soils were calculated under the assumption that such land is only used for wheat production (if it is used at all). This reflects the assumption that when soils are saline farmers will tend to plant crops that are more tolerant of this factor and wheat is such a crop, as opposed to pulses and rice. FAO estimates indicate a loss of yield of 5 per cent for wheat per unit salinity (dS/m) for levels of salinity over 6 dS/m. Taking these values and applying them to lands under wheat is the basis of the estimated loss of output.

The estimates indicate a net income from a hectare of land under wheat in 2009 as being in the range of ₹8,000–18,000 and total losses from salinity based on the above assumptions come out between ₹0 and 10 billion in scenario 1 and between ₹3 and 13 billion in scenario 2.[9]

In addition to the losses, we also have to account for the losses from strongly saline lands that could not be cultivated at all. There are estimated to be about 13 million hectares of agricultural land that cannot be cultivated, either because they are waterlogged or because they are highly saline. If we assume half of this area is saline, then the annual net losses from land wasted due to salinity are about ₹60–135 billion. In total, therefore losses due to salinity amount to between ₹63 billion and ₹148 billion. The middle of that range is ₹110 billion (0.17 per cent of GDP in 2010).

The losses due to water logging are estimated in a similar way. Then annual production losses are about ₹20 billion or 0.03 per cent of GDP in 2010.

The remaining waterlogged wasteland is estimated by Indiastat.com to be 7.5 million hectares. None of this area is deemed to be cultivatable. Given that the loss in annual profits for paddy production on one hectare is in the range of ₹15,000–24,000 per hectare, the annual net loss from land wasted due to water logging is about ₹83–143 billion or ₹113 billion on average (0.2 per cent of GDP in 2010).

Soil Erosion

In addition to soil salinity, land degradation caused by wind and water erosion is substantial in India. Two major impacts of this erosion are sedimentation of dams and loss of nutrients in the soil.

Soil erosion contributes to sedimentation of dams in India. This in turn reduces the capacity of dams and thus irrigation capacity. We do not have reliable data on sedimentation of dams and

[9] Information of the salinity level (slight, moderate, strong) was not available at the time of the study. Two scenarios were considered to address this issue.

reduction in the capacity of dams in India. Hence estimates of losses in crop production as a result of sedimentation could not be made.

As far as soil erosion and the loss of soil nutrients are concerned, this can be valued in terms of the costs of replacing the losses.

The estimated cost of soil nutrients (in terms of nitrogen, phosphorus and potassium) substitution is about ₹320–600 billion or ₹460 billion on average (0.7 per cent of GDP in 2010). Soil erosion is thus by far the most substantial problem of land degradation in India.

Adding up the three categories of losses arising from land degradation in India, we get a total of ₹715 billion or 1.1 per cent of GDP in 2010 (Table 1.15). Another way to express the loss is the percentage of GDP from agriculture, forestry and fishery, which are sources of income predominantly for the poor. Gundimeda and Sukhdev (2008) refer to this as the 'GDP of the poor' and the percentage of loss is about 6.4.

Table 1.15:
Estimated annual cost of crop losses due to land degradation

	Total Loss (billion ₹)			*% of GDP 2010*	*% GDP of the Poor*
	Low	*Mean*	*High*		
Salinity losses	63	110	148	0.2	1.1
Waterlogged land losses	103	133	163	0.2	1.2
Erosion losses	320	460	600	0.7	4.1
Total crop land degradation losses	480	703	910	1.1	6.4

Source: Authors' estimates.

Range land Degradation

Land use reported in India suggests that the main causes of range land degradation in India are irrational land use management practices leading to denudation of vegetation from range lands which, exacerbated by intermittent droughts, has resulted in many pockets of desertification. According to land use data from Indiastat.com, about 10 million hectares are classified as permanent pastures. At the same time, about 1.5 times more land, including that under miscellaneous tree crops and groves and cultivable waste land, is also used as pastures. There is a substantial share of degraded lands within all these land categories. Forest lands that are used as pastures are estimated in the next section to avoid double-counting. An estimated 60 per cent of livestock grazes in the forest area (Kapur et al., 2010).

The loss in yield is valued in two ways. In the first method, the reduction in fodder production is valued at the price of fodder. In the second method the loss of fodder is converted into a loss of livestock based on livestock feed requirements and a value is attached to the loss of livestock. In both cases, the hypothetical value against which losses are calculated is one in which original productivity prevails.

The estimated annual cost of range land degradation for the two methods is summarized in Table 1.16. The mean of two estimates is ₹405 billion at 0.6 per cent of GDP in 2010 or 3.6 per cent GDP of the poor.

Table 1.16:
Annual cost of range lands degradation in India

	Billion ₹	*% of GDP*	*% of GDP of the Poor*
Market value of fodder losses	400–800	0.6–1.2	3.6–7.2
Foregone livestock income from fodder losses	170–256	0.3–0.4	1.5–0.2.3
Mean cost	405	0.6	3.6

Source: Authors' estimates.

Forest Degradation

The cost of deforestation and degradation of forests is the aggregate social loss associated with degraded or deforested lands. These losses include, in theory, a wide range of local, regional, national and even global costs. Examples include direct losses of timber, fuel wood and non-timber products, recreation and tourism losses, indirect use losses (such as those associated with damages to ecosystem services, water supply and carbon sequestration) and non-use value loss associated with the loss of forests. This section examines each of these categories of losses with the available data.

India's forest cover is about 21 per cent of the total land area (about 69 million hectares). Dense forest constitutes only 12 per cent of the total forest cover area (indiastat.com). Although forest cover area increased by 0.1 per cent in 2007 (indiastat.com), the north-eastern mountainous states with the most dense forest, like Nagaland, Arunachal Pradesh, Tripura and Assam, continued to experience deforestation due to the widespread practice of shifting cultivation. This loss is especially damaging for hilly areas where destructive agricultural practices can result in total ecosystem destruction. Total deforested land averaged from 2006 to 2009 is at about 0.6 million hectares annually (indiastat.com).

Many sources reflect a substantial level of land degradation in India. Overexploitation of forest resources has led to the opening up of the canopy and an increase of shrub-covered areas. The degraded area grew from 19.5 to 24.4 million hectares in 2003 (3rd National Report on Implementation of UN Convention to Combat Desertification, 2003). From the figure of 2.4 million hectares and with annual forest deforestation assumed to be at the same level as in 2006–09, the total degraded forest area in 2009 would be estimated at 28 million hectares.

The estimated losses from the degraded forests are based on the use values attached to the forest in their non-degraded state. Previous studies have estimated the use values for two categories: direct use value and indirect use value. Under direct use value (i) timber, (ii) non-timber forest products, (iii) fodder, (iv) ecotourism and (v) carbon sequestration are included. Under indirect use values, (i) soil erosion prevention and (ii) water recharge are covered. No estimate has been made of non-use values from forests, nor has any account been taken of biodiversity values (e.g., from bio-prospecting) although these can be significant.

A summary of the values obtained, both in total and normalized in terms of rupees per hectare, is given in Table 1.17. The biggest source is carbon sequestration, followed by fodder and ecotourism.

Table 1.17:
Estimated annual use values per hectare of forest in India

(Billion ₹ except where indicated)

	Low	*High*
Direct		
Timber	17.2	17.2
Non-timber values	21.0	21.0
Fodder	94.4	188.8
Ecotourism	51.2	51.2
Carbon sequestration	266.8	339.5
Total direct	450.6	617.7
Per hectare (₹)	6,471.3	8,871.2
Indirect		
Soil erosion	15.5	15.5
Water recharge	6.4	6.4
Total indirect	21.9	21.9
Per hectare (₹)	314.5	314.5
Total use values	472.5	639.6
Total cost per hectare (₹)	6,785.9	9,185.7

Sources: Author estimates applying secondary data from GAISP (2005–2006), FAO (2009), Gundimeda et al. (2005), Gundimeda (2001), Pearce et al. (1999), 3rd National Report on Implementation of UN Convention to Combat Desertification (2003), World Bank (2006), World Bank (2012a), data from indiastat.org and www.indg.in

In order to value the losses, we assume that degraded forests provide between 20 and 80 per cent for most of the direct use values but none of the indirect values since indirect values are only associated with dense forest functions. In the case of sequestered carbon, a more precise figure is available: degraded forests are associated with 20 per cent loss of total accumulated carbon (Gundimeda, 2001), reported in the range of 21–59 tC/hectare in India,[10] valued

[10] We assume that degraded land would continue to sequester carbon up to 80 per cent of what it uptakes on non-degraded forest. Carbon issues are complicated and at the next stage

at a social cost of carbon US$20 per ton of CO_2.[11] The losses are applied to 29 million hectares of degraded forest and about 0.6 million hectares of deforested lands.

Based on these figures, the total annual losses from degraded forest land and annual deforestation losses are presented in Table 1.18. The resulting losses are in the range of 0.1–0.3 per cent

Table 1.18:
Estimation of annual forest value loss

(₹ per hectare, except where indicated)

Losses	*% Loss*	*Low*	*High*
Direct values			
Timber	80–100	198	248
Non-timber values	20–100	60	301
Fodder	0	1,356	2,712
Ecotourism	100	51	51
Carbon sequestration	20	766	975
Total direct		2,432	4,287
Average % loss		42	53
Total direct (billion ₹)		60.5	106.7
Indirect values			
Soil erosion	0–100%	0	1,783
Water recharge	0–100%	0	765
Total indirect		0	2,548
Average % loss		0	100
Total indirect (billion rupees)		0.0	63.4
Total degradation losses (billion rupees)		60.5	170.2
Total deforestation losses (20% carbon losses only) (billion ₹)		9.14	25.47
Total		69.7	195.6
% GDP		0.11	0.30
% GDP for the poor		0.60	1.68

Source: Authors' estimates applying secondary data from GAISP (2005–2006), Gundimeda et al. (2005) and Gundimeda (2001).

they should be carefully studied in the context of geographical location and other specific factors. This study attempted to provide indicative country-wide estimates.

[11] The same CO_2 price is applied in China 2030 (World Bank, 2012a).

of GDP. We should note that this is very likely an underestimation of the total losses as it excludes non-use value loss. Gundimeda et al. (2005) estimate that the non-use and bio-prospecting values of forests could be as much as 6–20 times greater than their use values. Due to the high uncertain nature of this estimate, we did not use it in this study.

Conclusions and Policy Implications

This chapter provides estimates of social and financial costs of environmental damage in India from three pollution categories—(i) urban air pollution, including particulate matter and lead; (ii) inadequate WSH and (iii) indoor air pollution—and three natural-resource damage categories: (i) agricultural damage from soil salinity, water logging and soil erosion; (ii) range land degradation and (iv) deforestation.

Until recently, most available studies have estimated the costs of environmental degradation for specific sites or industries. When government officials asked researchers a simple question about degradation—how large are the impacts of environmental degradation?—the response was often an emphatic 'Large!' (a rather imprecise number). Since 2000, however, the World Bank has conducted a systematic effort to measure the COED at the national and local levels in several countries (Croitoru and Sarraf, 2010). The strength of this type of work is that it actually quantifies in economic terms how large is 'large' and thereby gains the attention of decision makers and offers specific insights for improved policy-making.

The cost of degradation exercise undertaken here could be instrumental in moving the environmental debate beyond the ministries of environment to reach other sectoral ministries, especially the finance ministry. Over the past decades, COED analyses like this have had major impacts on decision makers in a number of countries in terms of influencing national policy dialogue, increasing environmental investments and strengthening the capacity of national institutions in environmental valuation. COED analysis also highlights the need to incorporate the results of the environmental valuation into decision-making at the sectoral and national levels, so that the environmental costs and benefits are mainstreamed into national and local planning processes.

Past policies and decisions have been made in the absence of concrete knowledge of the environmental impacts and costs. By providing new, quantitative information based on research under Indian conditions, this study has aimed to reduce this information gap. At the same time, it has pointed out that substantially more information is needed in order to understand the health and non-health consequences of pollution. It is critically important that existing air quality, health and environmental data be made publicly available so the fullest use can be made of them. This would facilitate conducting studies on the impacts of air pollution on human health. Furthermore, surveillance capacity at the local and national levels needs to be expanded to improve the collection of environmental data, especially data on various aspects of air quality. These efforts will further improve the analysis begun in this study.

If related to the GDP of the poor, which was about 17 per cent of the total GDP of India in 2010, then losses in the forestry sector are at about 0.6–1.7 per cent.

References

Abbey, D.E., Lebowitz, M.D., Mills, P.K., Petersen, F.F., Beeson, W.L. and Burchette, R.J. 1995. 'Long-Term Ambient Concentrations of Particulates and Oxidants and Development of Chronic Disease in a Cohort of Nonsmoking California Residents', *Inhalation Toxicology*, 7(1): 19–34.

Bolt, K., Ruta, G. and Sarraf, M. 2005. *Estimating the Cost of Environmental Degradation* (A Training Manual in English, French and Arabic). Environment Department Papers, World Bank.

Central Pollution Control Board (CPCB). 2011. 'Air Quality Monitoring, Emission Inventory and Source Apportionment Study for Indian Cities: National Summary Report', Available at http://cpcb.nic.in/FinalNationalSummary.pdf (accessed May 2012).

Croitoru, L. and Sarraf, M. 2010. 'The Cost of Environmental Degradation: Case Studies from the Middle East and North Africa'. Directions in Development, World Bank.

Cropper, M., Gamkhar, S., Malik, K., Limonov, A. and Partridge, I. 2012. 'The Health Effects of Coal Electricity Generation in India', Draft Working Paper, World Bank, Washington, DC.

Desai, M., Mehta, S. and Smith, K. 2004. *Indoor Smoke from Solid Fuels. Assessing the Environmental Burden of Disease at National and Local Levels.* Environmental Burden of Disease Series, No. 4, WHO.

Fewtrell, L. and Colford, J., Jr. 2004. 'Water, Sanitation and Hygiene: Interventions and Diarrhoea—A Systematic Review and Meta-Analysis', HNP Discussion Paper, World Bank.

Garg, A. 2011. 'Pro-equity Effects of Ancillary Benefits of Climate Change Policies: A Case Study of Human Health Impacts of Outdoor Air Pollution in New Delhi', *World Development*, 39, 6: 1002–25.

Gundimeda, H. 2001. 'Managing Forests to Sequester Carbon', *Journal of Environmental Planning and Management*, 44(5): 701–20.

Gundimeda, H., Sanyal, S., Sinha, R. and Sukhdev, P. 2005. *The Value of Timber, Carbon, Fuelwood, and Non-Timber Forest Products in India's Forests.* Monograph 1 of the Green Accounting for Indian States Project (GAISP).

Gundimeda, H. and Sukhdev, P. 2008. GDP of the poor, The Economics of Ecosystems & Biodiversity (TEEB) D1.

Kapur, D., Ravindranath, D., Kishore, K., Sandeep, K., Priyadarshini, P., Kavoori, P.S., Chaturvedi, R. and Sinha, S. 2010. *A Commons Story. In the Rain Shadow of Green Revolution.* FES.

Krupnick, A., Larsen, B. and Strukova, E. 2006. *Cost of Environmental Degradation in Pakistan: An Analysis of Physical and Monetary Losses in Environmental Health and Natural Resources.* Washington, DC: World Bank.

National Family Health Survey (NFHS-3) 2005–06 India. 2007. International Institute for Population Sciences.

National Sample Survey Organization (NSS). 2004. 'Morbidity, Health Care and the Condition of the Aged', *Report No. 507 (60/25.0/1)*, Government of India.

Office of Registrar General. 2004. *Report on Causes of Death: 2001–03, India.*

Ostro, B. 1994. 'Estimating the Health Effects of Air Pollution: A Method with an Application to Jakarta', Policy Research Working Paper, World Bank.

———. 2004. *Outdoor Air Pollution: Assessing the Environmental Burden of Disease at National and Local Levels.* WHO Environmental Burden of Disease Series, No. 5, Geneva, World Health Organization.

Pearce, D., Putz, F. and Vanclay, J. 1999. 'A Sustainable Forest Future?', CSERGE Working Paper GEC 99-15, London.

Pope, C.A. III, Burnett, R.T., Thun, M.J., et al. 2002. 'Lung Cancer, Cardiopulmonary Mortality, and Long-term Exposure to Fine Particulate Air Pollution', *Journal of the American Medical Association*, 287: 1132–41.

Pruss-Ustun, A., Kay, D., Fewtrell, L. and Bartram, J. 2004. 'Unsafe Water, Sanitation and Hygiene', in Majid Ezzati, Alan D. Lopez, Anthony Rodgers, Christopher J.L. Murray (eds), *Comparative Quantification of Health Risks: Global and Regional Burden of Disease Attributable to Selected Major Risk Factors.* Geneva: World Health Organization.

Shibuya, K., Mathers, C. and Lopez, A. 2001. 'Chronic Obstructive Pulmonary Disease (COPD): Consistent Estimates of Incidence, Prevalence, and Mortality by WHO Region'. Global Programme on Evidence for Health Policy, World Health Organization, November 2001.

WHO. 2002a. *Global Burden of Disease 2002*. The World Health Organization.

———. 2002b. *The World Health Report 2002*. The World Health Organization.

World Bank. 2005. *Islamic Republic of Iran: Cost Assessment of Environmental Degradation*. Washington, DC: World Bank.

———. 2006. 'Unlocking Opportunities for Forest-Dependent People in India', *Main Report: Volume I. Report No. 34481—IN*, Agriculture and Rural Development Sector Unit, South Asia Region, Washington, DC.

———. 2007. *Cost of Pollution In China. Economic Estimates of Physical Damages*. Washington, DC: World Bank.

———. 2010. *The Economic Impacts of Inadequate Sanitation in India*. Washington DC, Available at http://www.wsp.org/wsp/sites/wsp.org/files/publications/wsp-esi-india.pdf (accessed May 2012).

———. 2012a. *China 2030*. Washington, DC: World Bank.

———. 2012b. *Inclusive Green Growth: The Pathway to Sustainable Development*. Washington, DC: World Bank.

2

Discount Rate for Environmental Health Risks: A Comparative Study

*K.R. Shanmugam**

Introduction

Exposures to environment contaminants may cause risks to human life and health. To regulate these life/health risks, the government undertakes various policy proposals. The health benefits of these policies often have different time patterns of incidence. As resources are scarce, these policies need to be assessed for their financial and economic viability. The cost-benefit analysis (CBA) is highly useful to assess the policies with long time paths or the policies whose effects extend across generations (Clain, 1992).

In the case of marketable goods and services, their prices reflect social values as long as the goods in question are not rationed and there are no externalities. As the health benefits are non-marketed, the society's willingness to pay (WTP) for these benefits is the appropriate benefit concept. However, Moore and Viscusi (1990) argue that the WTP amount should reflect the society's rate of time preference with respect to health risks. Therefore, the economic analyses of life-saving policies require appropriate discount rate for comparing the long-term health benefits.

*Professor, Madras School Economics. E-mail: shanmugam@mse.ac.in

Economists in general argue that the long-term health benefits are very much similar to other benefits. If capital markets are perfect, the society's riskless rate of time preference can serve as the appropriate discount rate for all benefit components. In the absence of capital market perfections, the issue becomes more complex. Since the human health/life is less freely transferable across time than money or economic goods, there is no explicit inter-temporal market to observe. Further, many argue that capital market rates may not accurately reflect the trade-offs individuals make with respect to health status over the years. Thus, the debate in the literature is whether one can use the same discounting rate that is used for evaluating other benefit components or one can use a different rate for health benefits (Moore and Viscusi, 1990).

Many studies have attempted to resolve this issue empirically by estimating the discount rate for health impacts and then compared the estimated rate with market interest rate (e.g., Atmadja, 2008; Kula, 2004; Van der Pol and Cairns, 2001; Viscusi and Moore, 1989). These studies are broadly grouped into (i) stated preference studies and (ii) revealed preference studies. In the former, individuals are asked to evaluate the stylized inter-temporal prospects involving real or hypothetical outcomes such as health and life years while in the latter, rates are computed from economic decisions that individuals make in their ordinary life (see Frederick et al., 2002, for an excellent survey).

Early studies in the revealed preference category examined the individual's trade-off between the immediate purchase price of electrical appliances and the long-term costs of running them. Estimated rates from these studies varied widely across product categories and vastly exceeded the market rates. Another set of studies called labour market studies estimated the discounting rates from wage-risk trade-offs. They have used three alternate but equally plausible models: discounted expected life years (DELYs) model (Moore and Viscusi, 1988), Markov decision (MD) model (Viscusi and Moore, 1989) and life cycle (LC) model (Moore and Viscusi, 1990). The wage responses to the variation in life years at work environmental risk provide the direct estimates of discount rates that workers apply to their future utility in these models.

Interestingly, the estimated rates in these studies, ranging 2–17 per cent have a more plausible range than individuals' implicit discount range (17–300 per cent) for appliance energy efficiency.

In this study, an attempt is made to estimate the discount rate for work-related environmental health risks in India using all three alternative models—DELY model, MD model and LC model, and compare the results obtained from these models. This study also estimates the value of statistical life and the value of longevity at risk of Indian workers. The rest of this study proceeds as follows. The next section provides a brief review of the literature. The methodology, the data and variables used in the study are explained in the subsequent sections. Then empirical results are presented and explained. In the final section, the general conclusions and implications of the study are given.

A Brief Review of Literature

The discount rate is an important parameter in the CBA. It measures the relative values of various benefits/costs that occur at different points in time and is not surprising therefore that so much controversy has centred on this over the years. Indeed, the arguments about the rate of discounting and ensuing controversies date back to the 19th century (see Von Thunen, 1826; Bohm Bawerk, 1884).

One group of studies suggests the zero rate, meaning that the society values future the same as the present (e.g., Ramsey, 1928). The other group of studies recommends a positive rate. The basic argument for a positive discount rate is that individuals attach less weight to a benefit/cost in the future than they do to a benefit/cost now. This is because (i) the consumption today is preferred to the consumption tomorrow (the rate of time preference or impatience is positive) and (ii) a rupee's worth of resources now will generate more than a rupee's worth of goods and services in the future and the marginal productivity of capital (return on investment) is positive.[1] Although most economists accept this impatience principle, many argue against permitting a pure time preference (also called as utility discount rate) to influence the social discount rates, that is, the rates used in connection with collective decisions.[2]

In the most theoretical debates on the social discount rate, the background appears to be a Samuelson–Bergson type of social welfare function: $SW = f(U_1, U_2, \ldots, U_n)$, where SW is social welfare that depends upon the (income related) utilities of individuals in the society. The change in the society welfare is affected by the changes in individuals' income, that is, $\Delta SW = \Sigma^{n}_{i=n} \Delta Y_i$, where U_i is the *i*th individual's utility resulting from a change in its income Y_i. The conventional total utility function increases as income/consumption increases while marginal utility function decreases as income/consumption increases with constant elasticity. This diminishing marginal utility (DMU) of income/consumption is one of the reasons for giving greater weight to the present consumption as opposed to future consumption (Kula, 2004).

Many models that are developed to compute the social rate of time preference (SRTP) or the consumption rate of interest (S), including the one employed by Sharma et al. (1991) for India contain the notion of DMU. Based upon this, a linear formula for the SRTP can be expressed as: $S = m + \varepsilon g$, where m is a pure time discount rate (or myopic preference for consuming a good sooner rather than latter), g is the growth rate of per capita real consumption and ε is the negative of the elasticity of marginal utility of consumption (see Markandya and Pearce, 1988 for a lucid derivation of S). If the consumption grows, S (is positive and) rises

[1] For example, if we invest now ₹100 with a nominal return of 10 per cent, in one year's time we would get ₹110. If inflation is 4 per cent, this is equal to a real return of ₹6.

[2] Markandya and Pearce (1991) summarized these arguments as follows. First, acting on the impatience principle will not necessarily maximize welfare over the lifetime of an individual (Krutilla and Fisher, 1975; Stortz, 1956). Second, what an individual wants carries no necessary implications for public policy. For instance, in many countries, states compel individuals to save through the state pensions. Third, the underlying value judgement is improperly expressed. A society that places a premium of the satisfaction of wants should recognize that what matters is the satisfaction of wants as they arise. But this means that it is tomorrow's satisfaction that matters and not today's assessment of tomorrow's satisfaction.

above the private discount rate, m. With no growth in per capita consumption, $S = m$. S can be positive even if the consumption is falling as long as $m > |\varepsilon g|$.

One can obtain the opportunity cost of capital or social return on investment (ρ) by looking at the rate of return on the best investment of similar risk that is displaced as a result of undertaking the project in question. It is only reasonable to require an investment to yield a return at least as high as that on the alternative use of funds. This is the basic rationale for a discount based on the opportunity cost. Since there is a shortage of capital in developing nations (like India), such rates are usually very high and their use can often be justified on the grounds of the optimal allocation of scarce capital. However, a major criticism levelled against the opportunity cost discounting is that it implies a reinvestment of benefits at the opportunity cost rate and quite often this is invalid. Therefore, many past studies have applied the weighted discount rate procedure as advocated by Marglin (1967).

In the case of perfect market, the market interest rate is r, which is equal to S ($= \rho$). The social discount rate is simply the market interest that reflects equally the consumer and the producer rates of time preference. The SRTP for discounting consumption here is the demand side of inter temporal maximization while the supply side takes into account the capital productivity (Boscolo et al., 1998). In the presence of distortions (market imperfections, taxes, risk, etc.), the market rate is unlikely to reflect the SRTP or the social rate of return.

Therefore, many suggest the use of a risk-free consumer lending (treasury bill) as a proxy for the SRTP. Some others argue for the adjustment of discount rate (i.e., low rate). One such argument favours a very low discount rate in the case of irreversible loss/damage. Therefore, as indicated previously, various studies have attempted to empirically measure the time preference rate of individual that can be captured by a single discount rate and then compared the estimated rate with the market rate. Broadly, these studies are grouped into (i) stated preference studies and (ii) revealed preference studies.

Stated Preference Studies

The stated preference studies adopt four types of experimental elicitation procedures to calculate the discount rate. They are choice tasks, matching tasks, pricing tasks and rating tasks. In a choice task, individuals are asked to choose between a smaller, more immediate reward and larger, more delayed reward. In the matching tasks, respondents fill in the blank to equate two intertemporal options (e.g., $10 now = $12 in one year). In the pricing tasks, each respondent will specify a WTP to obtain (or avoid) an outcome occurring at a particular time. In the case of rating tasks, each respondent evaluates an outcome occurring at a particular time by rating its attractiveness or aversiveness. Interestingly, these studies have used real rewards, including money, rice and corn, and/or hypothetical rewards: monetary gains and losses, and aversive health conditions. Although there is no theoretical basis for preferring one method to the other, evidence indicates that they yield very different discount rates: negative to infinity (see Frederick et al., 2002).

Revealed Preference Studies

In the revealed preference studies, discount rates are inferred from economic decisions that people make in their ordinary life. That is, discount rates are estimated by identifying the real-world behaviours that involve trade-offs between the near future and more distant future. Early studies in this category have examined the consumer's choices among different models of electrical appliances that presented purchasers with a trade-off between the immediate purchase price and the long-term costs of running the appliance.In these studies, the rates implied by consumers' choices vastly exceeded the market interest rates and varied widely across product categories [e.g., Hausman (1979) found 17–20 per cent for air conditioners and Gately (1980) showed 45–300 per cent for refrigerators].

The labour market studies have estimated the discount rates from wage-risk trade-offs, in which workers decide whether to accept a risky job with a higher wage. They use three different models: the DELY model (Moore and Viscusi, 1988), the MD model (Viscusi and Moore, 1989) and the LC model (Moore and Viscusi, 1990).[3] The hedonic wage approach that rests on Adam Smith's proposition that 'risky jobs command compensating wage differentials' forms the basis of these models.

Hedonic Wage Model

The hedonic approach treats jobs as bundles of characteristics such as working condition, and levels of risk of accidental injury. Employees are described by the amount they require as compensation for different risk levels while firms (employers) are characterized by the amount they are willing to offer workers to accept different risk levels. An acceptable match occurs when the preferred choice of an employee and that of an employer is mutually consistent. Thus, the actual wage embodies a series of hedonic prices for various job attributes including accidental risk and other prices for worker characteristics.

Suppose there are *m* such indicators of worker's personal and job attributes other than job risk level (p), denoted by a vector c = (c_1, c_2, ..., c_m). Let *W* represent the schedule of annual earnings. Then, *W* (p, c) reflects the market equalizing differential function. Controlling for other aspects of the job will provide an estimate of the wage premium that workers receive for job risk. Thus, the theory considers both sides of the market and examines equilibrium

[3] Arguing that each of these three labour market models involves a different mix of compromises involving the theoretical realism of the model and the assumptions that must be imposed to achieve estimable equations, Moore and Viscusi (1990) conclude that no single model is dominant in terms of its theoretical and empirical properties.

risk choices and either wage levels or price levels associated with these choices.

The firm's demand for labour decreases with the total cost of employing a worker. As providing greater workplace safety is costly to the firm, it must pay a lower wage to offset the cost of providing safe work environment in order to maintain the given level of profits along the iso-profit or wage-risk offer curve. Figure 2.1 shows wage offer curves for two firms, with wage as an increasing function of risk, OC_1 for firm 1 and OC_2 for firm 2.

The labour supply is characterized subject to several mild restrictions on preferences. With a von Neumann-Morgenstern expected utility approach and with state dependent utility functions, $u(W)$ represents the utility of a healthy worker at wage W and $v(W)$ represent the utility of an injured person. Worker's compensation after job accident is a function of the worker's wage. We assume that the relationship between worker's compensation and wage is subsumed into the functional form of $v(W)$ and that workers

Figure 2.1:
Wage-risk trade-off

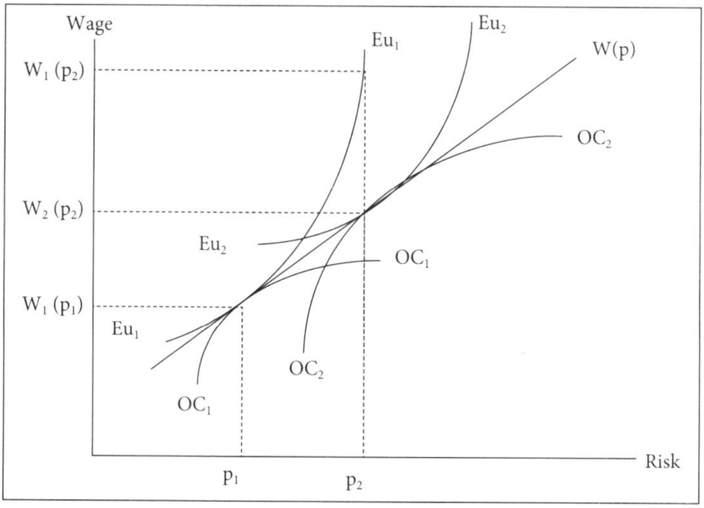

Source: Viscusi and Aldy (2003).

prefer health to injury [i.e., $u(W) > v(W)$] and that marginal utility of income is positive [i.e., $u'(W) > 0$ and $v'(W) > 0$].

For any given risk level, workers prefer the wage-risk combination from the market offer curve with the highest wage level. The outer cover of these curves is the market opportunities locus $W(p)$. That is, workers choose from potential wage-risk combinations along market opportunities locus $W(p)$ to maximize expected utility. In Figure 2.1, the tangency between the constant expected locus EU_1 of worker 1 and firm 1's offer curve OC_1 represents his optimal job risk choice. Worker 2 maximizes his expected utility when EU_2 is tangent to OC_2.

All wage-risk combinations associated with a given worker's constant expected utility locus must satisfy: $Z = (1-p)\ u(W) + pv(W)$ and the wage-risk trade-off along this curve is: $\frac{dW}{dp} = \frac{-Z_p}{Z_W} = \frac{u(W) - v(W)}{(1-p)u'(W) + pv'(W)} > 0$ so that the required wage rate is increasing in the risk level. The estimated value $(\partial W/\partial p)$ is a local measure of the wage-risk trade-off for marginal changes in risk. This is in fact the worker's marginal willingness to accept (WTA) risk as well as his marginal WTP for more safety and the firm's marginal cost of more safety and its marginal cost reduction from an incremental increase in risk. That is, it reflects the marginal supply as well as the marginal demand price of risk. It is noted that the estimated wage-risk trade-off curve $W(p)$ does not imply how a particular employee is compensated for non-marginal changes in risk.

In Figure 2.1, worker 2 has revealed a WTA risk p_2 at wage W_2 along EU_2. If risk exposure to employee 1 changes from p_1 to p_2, he will require a higher compensation to keep his utility constant. Thus, with large changes in risk, a worker's wage-risk trade-off will not be the same because the relevant trade-off must be made along the worker's expected utility locus and not the estimated market wage-risk trade-off (Viscusi and Aldy, 2003).

Since each point on the hedonic wage function $W(p)$ represents the slope of the expected utility curve, this function is used to estimate the welfare effect of a marginal change in job risk.

If all employees have homogenous preferences, then there will be only one expected utility curve, and the observable points on the $W(p)$ will represent the constant expected utility locus. Likewise, if all firms are homogenous, $W(p)$ will be approximately the firm's offer curve. Ideally, one needs to estimate the constant expected utility curve in order to estimate the WTP/WTA for risk reduction. However, most studies use the hedonic wage function as it is the locus of tangencies that is observable in the labour market data.

Basically, the past empirical studies on the topic specify some sort of the following wage equation:

$$W_i = \alpha + \beta_1 p_i + \beta_2 q_i + \Sigma_k \gamma_k X_{ki} + \varepsilon_i \qquad (1)$$

where W_i is the worker's annual wage rate, X is a vector of worker's personal as well as job characteristics variables. p_i and q_i represent the annual probability of work-related fatal and non-fatal injury risk faced by worker i (some studies allow the interaction between risk variables and other X variables), and ε_i is the regular random error term reflecting unmeasured factors influencing worker's wage rate. α (a constant term), β_1, β_2 and γ_ks are parameters to be estimated using regression method.

Let us assume there are 100,000 workers, and each of them face an annual probability of job-related fatal risk of 1/100,000 (=p). The estimated β_1 is the annual wage premium that an individual worker accepts for facing the given fatal risk. Therefore, the value of statistical life is: 100,000 * β_1.[4] Thaler and Rosen (1976) carried out the first empirical study to estimate the hedonic (quality-adjusted) value of life.

Currently, we have a hand full of studies to provide life value estimates for developed as well as developing countries. Table 2.1 summarizes the past (selected) studies on value of life and injury. The estimated life values differ vastly among these studies.

[4] There are two principal value-of-life concepts. The first one is the amount that is optimal from the insurance standpoint, while the second one is the optimal deterrence amount. In our case, it is a measure of deterrence amount for the value to the individual at risk of preventing accidents and a reference point for the amount the government should spend to prevent small statistical risks (Viscusi, 2008).

Table 2.1:
Summary of labour market studies on the value of life and injury

Study (year)	*Sample*	*Source of Risk Variable*	*Value of Life ($ million)*	*Value of Injury*
Cousineau et al. (1992)	Labor Canada Survey, Canada, 1979	Quebec Compensation Board	3.6	Not reported
Garen (1988)	Panel Study of Income Dynamics (PSID), USA, 1981–82	Bureau of Labor Statistics (BLS)	13.5	21021
Herzog and Schlottman (1990)	U.S. Census, 1970	BLS	9.1	–
Kniesner and Leeth (1991)	2-digit manufacture Data, Japan, 1984; 2 digit manufacture data, Australia, 1984; and Current Population Survey, USA, 1978	Year book of Labor Statistics; Industrial Accident Data; and National Traumatic Occupation Fatality Survey (NTOS)	7.6 3.3 0.6	77547 8943 47281
Leigh and Folsom (1984)	PSID, 1974 and Quality of Employment Survey, USA, 1977	BLS	9.7 and 10.3	
Liu et al. (1997)	Taiwan Labor Force Survey, 1982 to 1986	Labor Insurance Agency, Taiwan	0.135 and 0.589 (5 years mean is 0.413)	
Marin and Psacharopoulos (1982)	Population Census and Surveys, UK, 1977	Occupational Mortality Tables	2.8	–
Moore and Viscusi(1988)	PSID, USA, 1982	BLS and NTOS	2.5 and 7.3	–
Shanmugam (1996/7)	Questionnaire Survey, Chennai (India)	Chief Inspector of Factories	1.2–1.5	–
Thaler and Rosen (1976)	Survey of Economic Opportunity, USA	Society of Actuaries	0.8	–
Viscusi (1981)	PSID, USA, 1976	BLS	6.5	46200

Source: The values given in the table, except Liu et al. (1997), are taken from Viscusi (1993).
Note: Values of life and injury are in 1990 US dollars.

Dillingham (1985) argues that values vary either due to specification errors or the errors in variable problem. Viscusi (1993) and Viscusi and Aldy (2003) listed almost all the major studies and found that the range of value per statistical life (in 1990 dollar) was \$0.6 million to \$16.2 million in the United States, Britain, Canada, Australia and Japan.

Life Cycle Issues and Discounting

The hedonic wage equation (1) includes the probability of job-related death risk p (or injury q) as a measure of risk, which abstracts altogether from LC issues such as variations across individuals in the potential losses resulting from death (or injury). For instance, a young worker may face a more substantial loss from a given fatality risk than an old worker. That is, there may be age-related differences in proclivity towards risk-taking. A few attempts have been made to recognize the influence of life duration in unstructured models through job risk–age interaction term (Shanmugam, 2001; Thaler and Rosen, 1976; Viscusi, 1979). However, this approach does not capture changes in the life expectancy with age or the role of discounting. To overcome these issues, as mentioned earlier, three alternatives models have been developed. They are the DELY approach, the MD model and the LC model.

The DELY approach includes the expected discounted life years lost (ELYL) variable (instead of job risk) in the standard hedonic model to estimate the impact of changes in expected remaining lifetime on wages. Although this model is simple to estimate, its structure has no formal theoretical basis.

In the MD model, worker selects the optimal job risks from the wage offer curve where this risk affects the probability of death in each period. In selecting their optimal occupational risks, workers determine their life expectancy. The LC model recognizes that there is a probability in each period that the consumption stream may be terminated. Thus, the wage responses to the variation in life years at risk provide the direct estimates of the discount rate that workers apply to their future utility in all these models. The methodology section next explains briefly all these models.

Using the DELY and MD approaches, Moore and Viscusi (1988) and Moore and Viscusi (1990) found that the estimated rate of time preference was 11 per cent for US workers. Adopting LC approach, Viscusi and Moore (1989) found that the real discount rate for US workers was 2 per cent. Thus, in the labour market studies, the estimated discount rates have a more plausible range than consumers' implicit rate of discount range, from 17 to 300 per cent for appliance energy efficiency.

In the Indian context, Shanmugam (2006) estimated the implicit discount rate (ranging 7.6–9.7 per cent) for workers using the DELY approach. Utilizing the LC model, Shanmugam (2011) estimated the real discount rate that varies across regions ranging from 2.4 to 5.1 per cent. Using the consumption approach, Kula (2004) provides the estimates of (i) ε, the elasticity of marginal utility of consumption (using time series data (1965 and 1995) on per capita spending on food, per capita income and prices of food and non-food); (ii) the growth rate of real per capita consumption (g) and (iii) m, the mortality-based (pure) time discount rate (it is simply the average death rate for the study period) in India as 1.64 per cent, 2.4 per cent and 1.3 per cent, respectively. With these estimates the social discount rate ($S = m + \varepsilon g$) in India is computed at 5.2 per cent. Table 2.2 summarizes the implicit discount rates from the past (and selected) studies that use real or hypothetical outcome relating to health/life years.

Methodology

In order to estimate the implicit rate of time preference for deferred health benefits exhibited by the Indian workers in their choice of occupational risks, this study utilizes all the existing three alternative labour market models. These models and the empirical settings are explained briefly later. For more details, see Moore and Viscusi (1988, 1990) and Viscusi and Moore (1989).

Table 2.2:
Summary of (selected) studies estimating implicit discount rates

Study (year)	*Category*	*Good(s)*	*Real/ Hypothetical*	*Elicitation Method*	*Annual Discount Rate*
Chapman (1996)	Stated preference	Money and health	Hypothetical	Matching	Negative to 300%
Dreyfus and Viscusi (1995)	Revealed preference	Life years	Real	Choice	11–17%
Ganiats et al. (2000)	Stated preference	Health	Hypothetical	Choice	Negative to 116%
Johannesson and Johansson (1997)	Stated preference	Life years	Hypothetical	Pricing	0–3%
Loewenstein (1987)	Stated preference	Money and pain	Hypothetical	Pricing	–6 to 212%
Moore and Viscusi (1988)	Revealed preference	Life years	Real	Choice	10–12%
Moore and Viscusi (1990)	Revealed preference	Life years	Real	Choice	2%
Shanmugam (2006)	Revealed preference	Life years	Real	Choice	7.6–9.7%
Shanmugam (2011)	Revealed preference	Life years	Real	Choice	2.4–5.1%
Van der Pol and Cairns (1999)	Stated Preference	Health	Hypothetical	Choice	7%
Van der Pol and Cairns (2001)	Stated preference	Health	Hypothetical	Choice	6–9%
Viscusi and Moore (1989)	Revealed preference	Life years	Real	Choice	11%

Source: Shanmugam (2011).

Discounted Expected Life Years Model

The DELY approach includes the ELYL variable (instead of job risk) in the hedonic wage equation (1) to estimate the impact of changes in expected remaining lifetime on wages. Therefore, the wage equation to be estimated takes the following form:[5]

[5] It is noted that the injury variable is not included in the empirical estimation as it is not significant in most cases.

$$\text{Ln } W_i = \beta_1 \text{ELYL}_i + \beta_2 \text{q}_i + \Sigma_k \gamma_k X_{ki} + \varepsilon_i$$
$$= \beta_1 p\, [(1-e^{-rT})/r] + \beta_2 q_i + \Sigma_k \gamma_k X_{ki} + \varepsilon_i \qquad (2)$$

In equation (2), X includes other determinants of wages such as job tenure (or experience), education levels and dummy indicators for backward community (caste), supervisory status and union status. It also includes other non-pecuniary job attributes-whether job provides good security (or it has irregular work hours) or if it requires the worker to make on the job decision. Inclusion of these variables would control for a variety of job attributes, thus reducing the bias in the coefficients of the job risk variables.

Information on workers' age, sex and the remaining life data from life expectancy tables isused to calculate the remaining life of sample workers (T), which is used to define the discounted life years lost variable ($(1-e^{-rT})/r$). Weighing this variable by the probability of fatal risk (p) yields the DELY lost variable (ELYL).[6] Since this particular risk variable ELYL is a non-linear function of the discount rate parameter, equation (2) is estimated using the non-linear least square (NLS) method. The discount rate, r is computed in the estimation process. The discounted duration of life at risk is also known as the quantity adjusted death risk and is useful to calculate the quantity-adjusted value of life (QAVL).

The QAVL differs from conventional estimates of the value of life in that the trade-off is not between wages and death risk probabilities but between wages and death risks that have been weighted by the discounted number of potential years of life lost. Consideration of duration of life lost makes it possible to estimate the value of each year of life lost.

Life Cycle Model

The LC model assumes that (i) all life years are equally valued; (ii) job risks will reduce the life duration of workers; (iii) a worker's

[6] Future health risks are discounted at a rate of time preference r so that the ELYL of worker with T year of life remaining who chooses the risk level p is: ELYL = $p. \int_0^T (1-e^{rT})\, dT = p\, [(1-e^{-rT})/r]$.

state-dependent and time separable preferences is $U^j(W_j)$, where W_j is income in state *j*; (iv) there are only two states: State 1 is no accident state in which the worker is healthy and earns a wage *W* that increases with the job risk *p* (which is assumed to be a constant) and State 2 is an accidental/risky state where the worker dies if an accident occurs and earns no wage; and (v) the worker's time horizon equals his/her expected remaining lifetime, *T* that depends on *p* with longevity a decreasing function of *p* (i.e., $T_p < 0$).

Discounting the future utilities at a rate of time preference r, the expected discounted lifetime utility of a worker with *T* years of remaining life who selects a job with risk level *p* can be given as:

$$V = \int_0^{T(p)} U^1(W(p))\, e^{-rt} dt \tag{3}$$

The worker's problem is then to choose p in order to maximize his/her expected discounted lifetime utility *V*. From the first-order condition for a maximum, the following equation can be derived as:

$$\partial W/\partial p = -r\,(\partial T/\partial p)\,(U(.)/U_W)\,[e^{rT(p)}-1]^{-1} \tag{4}$$

In equation (4), the left side is the worker's marginal rate of substitution (MRS) between the current period wages and job risk that depends upon the expected remaining time (*T*), the discount rate (*r*) and the effect of risk on longevity ($\partial T/\partial p$). Taking logarithms on both sides of equation (4) yields:

$$\ln(\partial W/\partial p) = \alpha_i - rT + \varepsilon \tag{5}$$

In equation (5), the error term ε captures errors in the approximation: $\ln(e^{rT}-1)^{-1} \approx -rT$. These errors will be small for typical values of *r* and *T*.[7] The term, α_i ($=\ln(-r^*\partial T/\partial p^* U/U_W)$ is a function of the discount rate, the longevity risk trade-off and the utility function of the individual worker. Moore and Viscusi (1990) suggest that this term can be approximated by a vector of variables

[7] For instance, if $r = 0.1$ and $T = 25$, the approximation is less than 1 per cent of the true value.

Z that incorporate proxies for differences in tastes. The estimated parameter (r) on the longevity term will give a direct estimate of the worker's rate of time preference. This in turn will provide guidance in selecting the appropriate social discount rate for policies that affect health status over time.

Regarding the estimation, Moore and Viscusi (1990) suggest the following two steps (structural hedonic system equations estimation) procedure: in the first stage, the following wage equation is specified and estimated using the NLS method:

$$\ln W_i = \Sigma_k (\alpha_k R_{ik} p_i + \beta_k R_{ik} p_i^2) + \Sigma_m \gamma_m X_m + u_i \qquad (6)$$

where R_{ik} is a dummy indicator of the region of residence of worker i. The risk term p is entered as a quadratic term with both linear and squared risks interacted with one of the k regional dummies. Thus, variation in the implicit price of risk arises due to differences in region and in the risk level. X_m are other determinants of wages such as job experience and firm size. The NLS method is used to estimate equation (6). From this regression estimation, the estimated implicit price for the worker i residing at k region can be computed as: $\partial W_i/\partial p_i = (\alpha_k R_{ik} + 2\,\beta_k R_{ik} p_i)\ W_i$ and this term will become the dependent variable in the implicit price equation that is specified as:[8]

$$\partial W_i/\partial p_i = Z_i\varphi - r^* T + \varepsilon_i \qquad (7)$$

where Z, a vector of variables (dummy indicators for education levels, union status, backward community, private job and owing a house) and the discount rate r is estimated using the expression:

$$r = [\partial \ln(W_i/\partial p_i)/\partial T] = [1/(\partial W_i/\partial p_i)]\ [\partial(\partial W_i/\partial p_i)/\partial \mathrm{T}]$$
$$= r^*[1/(\partial W_i/\partial p_i)] \qquad (8)$$

[8] It is noted that since the observations with negative implicit price are lost in the log transformation, the wage-risk trade-off $\partial W/\partial p$ is used as the dependent variable and then the parameter on the longevity term T is transformed by dividing it by the implicit price term after estimation.

Since the endogeneity of T may cause bias in the OLS estimation, equation (7) can be estimated using two-stage least squares (TSLS) method.

Markov Decision Model

This approach assumes that the time horizon for both living and working is infinite. In each period, the worker faces a lottery on life and death. Let p be the probability of death and $1-p$ be the probability of survival. Let $p = p_j + p_o$, where p_j is the job risk and p_o is other risks to life. When an individual is alive, he reaps consumption x that is equal to his income in that period. Let $U(x)$ be worker's utility function. As the worker is assumed to be a risk averter, the first-order and second derivative values of U with respect to x are greater than zero and less than zero, respectively (i.e., $U_x > 0$ and $U_{xx} < 0$). The wage rate $W(p_j)$ determines the consumption level and worker selects his optimal wage–job risk combination from a schedule of available wage-risk combinations. As shown by Viscusi (1979), the wage-risk trade-off is positive, that is, $\partial W/\partial p_j > 0$.

Then, this model assumes that the worker's objective of maximizing discounted expected utility from the wage schedule $W(p_j)$ takes a time invariant MD problem:[9]

$$\begin{aligned}\text{Max } V = {} & (1-p)\, U(W(p_j)) + \beta\,(1-p)^2 U(W(p_j)) + \ldots \\ & + \beta^{t-1}\,(1-p)^t U(W(p_j)) + \ldots\end{aligned} \tag{9}$$

Equation (9) can also be written as:

$$\begin{aligned}\text{Max } V &= U(W(p_j))\,(1-p)\,\Sigma\,[\beta(1-p)]^{t-1} \\ &= U(W(p_j))\,(1-p)\,G(p)\end{aligned} \tag{10}$$

[9] In this structure, the utility of survival in any period t is weighed by the probability of surviving at least $(1-p)^t$ and the discount factor β^{t-1}.

where $G(p) = \Sigma\, [\beta(1-p)]^{t-1} = 1/[1-\beta(1-p)]$ so that the worker selects p_j to:

$$\text{Max } V = U(W(p_j))\,(1-p)\,/\,[1-\beta(1-p)] \tag{11}$$

The optimal value of p_j satisfies:

$$V_{pj} = 0 = U'(W(p_j))\,(1-p)\,(\partial W/\partial p_j)\,G(p) + U(W(p_j))\,(1-p)\,G'(p) - U\,(W(p_j))G(p) \tag{12}$$

Solving equation (12) for $(\partial W/\partial p_j)$ yields:

$$\frac{\partial W(p)}{dp_j} = \frac{U}{U'}\left[\frac{1}{1-p} + \frac{\beta}{1-\beta(1-p)}\right] \tag{13}$$

The previous equation describes the worker's MRS between wages and job risks, which is nothing but the implicit price of risk.

Our empirical strategy assumes a tractable functional form for the utility function in equation (13). This yields an expression for the MRS equation that involves only observable data, unknown constant β and risk aversion parameter *c*, and implicit prices that are estimated from the first stage regression.

Let us assume a constant relative risk aversion utility function. It represents a specification of *U* with desirable properties that yield an estimable version of equation (13). This function in general equals: $U = a + bW^c$, where *a* and *b* are arbitrary constants and the constant *c* gives an index of worker's aversion to risk. Let $a = -1/c$ and $b = 1/c$. Then the utility function becomes: $U = (W^c-1)/c$. Therefore, the marginal utility $U' = W^{c-1}$ and $U/U' = (1/c)\,[W-W^{1-c}]$. Substituting this term in equation (13), we get:

$$\frac{\partial W(p)}{\partial p_j} = \frac{1}{c}[W - W^{1-c}]\left[\frac{1}{1-p_i} + \frac{\beta}{1-\beta(1-p_i)}\right] \tag{14}$$

Multiplying through equation (14) by cW^{c-1} and dividing by the term in brackets (and using the fact that $\partial W^c = cW^{c-1}\partial W$) yields:

$$W_i^c = 1 + [(1-p) - \beta(1-p)^2]\frac{\partial W^c}{\partial p_j} \quad (14a)$$

Evaluating equation (14a) as c approaches 0 yields the specification corresponding to the logarithmic utility function:

$$\mathrm{Ln}\, W_i = 1 + [(1-p) - \beta(1-p)^2]\frac{\partial\, \mathrm{Ln}\, W}{\partial p_j} \quad (14b)$$

Adding the vector X_2 of unobserved variables that capture individual differences in tastes and unobservable taste shifters, ε_2 and treat $1-p = (1-p)$ in equation (14b) yields:

$$\mathrm{Ln}\, W_i = (1-p)(1-\beta)\frac{\partial\, \mathrm{Ln}\, W}{\partial p_j} + \sum \gamma_k X_{2k} + \varepsilon_2 \quad (15)$$

In equation (15), the unobserved variable ($\partial W_i/\partial p_i$), which represents the implicit price for job risk can be computed from a first stage regression of wages on job risks and other control variables, X_1. This is the same as equation (6).

Thus, the empirical strategy consists of estimating the parameters of equation (6), computing the implicit prices from these estimates and using this variable as an explanatory variable in estimating equation (15). As the implicit prices and the term $1-p$ are endogenous, the TSLS method is used to estimate equation (15). The regional dummies and their interactions with risk variables in equation (6) are used as instruments.

Data and Variables

This study utilizes the data collected by means of a questionnaire study (survey) conducted in 1990. The multi-stage random sampling technique was adopted to draw the sample observations. First, Madras (later renamed as Chennai) district of Tamil Nadu, a state in southern India was chosen as the study area. In the second stage, the blue-collar male employees in manufacturing industries were considered since they alone faced employment-related death risks in the study area from 1987 to 1990. Then, these workers were stratified into 17 groups using their industrial codes at the 2-digit National Industrial Classification (NIC) level. Fixing 1 per cent from each stratum, the total sample size was fixed at 522. Then, 522 workers were drawn randomly for the interview. A maximum sample of four workers from each randomly selected factory was drawn.

The collected data set consists of information on workers' personal as well as enterprise's characteristics, including the worker's subjective risk assessment of whether his employment exposes him to dangerous or unhealthy conditions (DANGER). This binary variable takes a value of one if he feels that his job involves risks.

The source of data pertaining to job risk is the Administrative Report of the Chief Inspector of Factories, Madras. For the administrative purpose, Chennai district is divided into four divisions/regions (Shanmugam, 1996/7).[10] Our sample workers are distributed in all four regions. The administrative report of each division provides the data pertaining to the total number of male workers and the number of death and injury accidental cases among them on an annual basis at the 2-digit NIC level. For each division and for each type of industry, the probability of fatal risk per 100,000 workers is computed as:

> Probability of fatal risk per worker in *i*th Industry = (Number of fatal death in industry *i* in given year *t*/number of workers in *i*th industry in year t)*100,000.

[10] The first division consists of Mannady, Royapuram, Washermanpet, Basin Bridge and Mint areas. The second division covers Mount, Arumbakkam and Chindadiripet areas. In the third division, Adyar, Triplicane, Saidapet, Vadapalani and Kodampauk areas are covered. Areas like Guindy, Meenampakkam and Tiruvanmiyur come under the fourth division. For more details, see Shanmugam (1993).

These job risks may vary substantially over the years and can be particularly high when there is a major catastrophe resulting in multiple deaths. Therefore, the average probabilities of fatal risk per 100,000 workers (*p*) over the years 1987–90 were computed and matched to the sample workers, using their industrial codes and job location.[11] It is noticed that there are 522 workers in our sample, and we have data (variables) for these workers in our data-set collected through the sample survey. Then, we add risk variable computed previouslyfor each worker in the sample.

A well-known problem with the use of industry-level data to measure individual level of risks is that workers in the sample industry may face different risks in different occupations. Therefore, in order to introduce individual job-specific variations in the risk levels, we allow the fatal risk variable to interact with DANGER variable, which is a binary choice variable explained earlier. For workers who expressed that their jobs were not exposing any dangerous or unhealthy conditions, the probability of fatal risk will be zero even though it may be greater than zero for the industry in which they work. Information on the worker's age and sex and remaining life data from life expectancy tables (for males in Chennai district) are used to calculate the remaining life of sample workers (*T*). Mortality tables from Census of India are used to calculate the death risk of males in Chennai district. The final data set is a cross-sectional data for 522 workers. This is used to estimate the discount rates in all three alternative models. The means and standard deviations of the major study variables are provided in Table 2.3.

[11] For more details of distribution of fatal risk, see Shanmugam (1997). It is noted that the fatal risk data pertain only to the job-related accidents and not to other occupational causes. However, in order to control for other job attributes, the non-pecuniary variables such as job security, decisional-making and irregular job hours are included in the wage equation analysis.

Table 2.3:
Descriptive statistics of the study variables

Variables	*Mean (S.D.)*	*Variables*	*Mean (S.D.)*
Age in completed years	34.142 (6.687)	Supervisor status (yes=1, no=0)	0.2701 (0.444)
Life years lost (in years)	25.058 (6.687)	Job security indicator (yes=1, no=0)	0.6226 (0.485)
After tax hourly wage rate (in ₹)[a]	5.3026 (2.248)	Decision-making (Yes=1, No=0)	0.4617 (0.499)
Job-related fatal risk per 100,000 workers	10.441 (9.257)	Irregular job hours (yes=1, no=0)	0.4080 (0.491)
Indicator for high school education	0.2625 (0.440)	Job tenure (in months)	128.458 (73.671)
Indicator for higher secondary education	0.3985 (0.490)	Estimated wage-risk trade-off ($\partial W_i/\partial p_i$)	0.1035 (0.082)
Indicator for college education	0.0766 (0.266)	Indicator for region 1	0.1303 (0.337)
Job experience (in years)	13.952 (7.035)	Indicator for region 2	0.433 (0.496)
Indicator for backward community	0.6456 (0.478)	Indicator for region 3	0.2989 (0.458)
Indicator for union status	0.5249 (0.499)	Indicator for region 4	0.1379 (0.345)
Firm size	90.964 (273.66)	Indicator for own house	0.4348 (0.496)
Indicator for private job	0.8697 (0.3369)	Hazard perception (yes=1, no=0): DANGER	0.9000 (0.300)

Source: Estimated as explained in the text.
Notes: The mean value of (fatal risk × Danger) variable is 9.7304; [a] computed by assuming 2000 annual hours worked; Sample size—522.

Empirical Results

Discounted Expected Life Years Model Results

Column (1) of Table 2.4 presents the NLS estimation results of wage equation (2). The dependent variable is the natural logarithm of hourly wages after taxes. Signs and magnitudes of the parameters

Table 2.4:
Non-linear least square estimates of log wage equation

Variables	Coefficient (1)	t Value (1)	Coefficient (2)	t Value (2)
Region 1 × Job risk	–	–	0.0572	5.222
Region 1 × Job risk^2	–	–	–0.0013	–2.859
Region 2 × Job risk	–	–	0.0161	2.268
Region 2 × Job risk^2	–	–	0.00015	0.474
Region 3 × Job risk	–	–	0.0461	5.759
Region 3 × Job risk^2	–	–	–0.0009	–2.585
Region 4 × Job risk	–	–	0.0333	1.755
Region 4 × Job risk^2	–	–	–0.00026	–0.259
Expected life year lost	0.0022	2.952	–	–
Implicit discount rate–*r*	**0.0766**	2.032	–	–
Job tenure	0.0038	17.233	0.0035	16.204
Indicator for high school education	0.3276	9.154	0.3183	9.080
Indicator for higher secondary education	0.3758	10.820	0.393	11.385
Indicator for college education	0.5884	9.898	0.5832	9.809
Backward community (yes = 1, no = 0)	0.2446	8.779	0.2389	8.592
Union status (yes = 1, no = 0)	0.2238	7.115	0.2161	6.476
Supervisory status (yes = 1, no = 0)	0.0907	2.095	0.0548	1.317
Decision-making (yes = 1, no = 0)	0.1700	2.095	0.1971	5.262
Job security (yes = 1, no = 0)	0.1997	6.531	0.1985	6.403
Irregular work hours (yes = 1, no = 0)	–	–	0.1037	3.509
R-squared (adjusted R^2)	0.4152 (0.4037)		0.4517 (0.4342)	

Source: Estimated as explained in the text.

of almost all variables are largely as expected. Educational dummies are positive and are statistically significant at 1 per cent level. Wages increases with job tenure. The union differential is approximately 25 per cent.[12] Backward community workers tend to earn more, indicating that they are more productive in blue-collar risky

[12] This is computed using the formula: $e^{\beta}-1$, where β is the estimated coefficient of union status variable.

occupations. Supervisors and workers who make on-the-job decision also earn more.

Workers in the job providing good security receive somewhat more, which is unexpected. However, the higher wages of employees with job security is quite consistent with a greater security associated with upper blue-collar positions. Thus, this variable may be capturing the relative ranking of the worker's job rather than any particular job attribute that is not appropriately compensated.

The estimated *r* is 7.66 per cent. As it is statistically significant at 5 per cent level, we can reject both extreme alternative hypotheses that workers exhibit a zero discount rate or an infinite rate (i.e., workers are myopic) when making their job selections. As expected, the estimated effect of ELYL is positive and statistically significant at 1 per cent level. The implicit value per additional expected year of life is ₹1.04 million. Using the conversion rate provided by the Reserve Bank of India of US$1 = ₹18.07 in 1990, this amount equals US$0.58 million. Using the discounted number of life years as the denominator in the calculation yields the average value of year of life of ₹2.334 (US$0.129) million. This represents the average WTP for an additional year of life in present value term.

Since the value of life extension depends on *r*, additional life years increase in value for a decline in *r*. The employees in the sample with 25 years of life remaining (*T*) who value an extra year approximately at ₹0.35 (US$0.019) million when *r* is 7.6 per cent will value his marginal year of life at over ₹0.67 (US$0.37) million if *r* is 5 per cent. An old worker with five years of life remaining will value an extra year approximately at ₹1.6 (US$0.09) million if *r* = 7.6 per cent and ₹1.8 (US$0.1) million if *r* = 5 per cent.

Life Cycle Model Results

Column 2 of Table 2.4 presents the NLS estimation results of wage equation (6). Signs and magnitudes of the coefficients of almost all control variables are more or less similar to what is indicated in column 1 of Table 2.4. The results of primary interest are the estimated effects of the region–job risk interaction variables as they are used to compute the implicit prices. In terms of total effects, they perform well. The linear risk effect is positive and statistically significant at 5 per cent level in all regions, except in the fourth region where it is significant only at 10 per cent level. The region–risk squared term is negative and significant in regions 1 and 3, indicating that wage-risk locus is concave. However, this term is not significant in regions 2 and 4.

Evaluating the coefficients of risk variables at the mean wage level and job risk level and multiplying the resulting value by 2,000 hours to annualize the figure and by 100,000 to reflect the scale of the risk variable would yield a trade-off of ₹33.81(US$0.99) million per statistical life in region 1. The life values estimated for regions 2, 3 and 4 are ₹20.01 (US$1.107) million, ₹30.3 (US$1.677) million and ₹29.9 (US$1.654) million, respectively. The average value of life for the sample worker is approximately equal to ₹26.32 (US$1.456) million. Thus, a significant compensation for job risk is observed in all regions.

Column 1 in Table 2.5 displays the TSLS estimation results of implicit price equation (7). The dependent variable ($\partial W/\partial p$) is derived from results in column 2 of Table 2.4. Dummy indicators for education levels do not play a significant role in determining the implicit price variable. The union status variable has a positive and significant impact. Dummy indicators for backward community, own house and private job influence the MRS variable positively, but their impacts are statistically significant only at 10 per cent level.

The result of primary interest is the estimated effect of the longevity variable. As expected, its effect is negative and statistically significant at 1 per cent level, providing a strong support for the LC model of inter-temporal choice. The estimated real discount rate is approximately equal to 2.72 per cent.

Equation (7) is essentially a linear demand curve for longevity, where the implicit price of longevity is a declining function of the quantity demanded. Using a WTP approach, we can calculate the value of longevity by summing the area under this demand curve (see Moore and Viscusi, 1990; Shanmugam, 2011 for details).

Table 2.5:
Two-stage least square estimates of implicit price equation

Variables	Dependent Variable: $\partial Wi/\partial p$ (1)	Dependent Variable: Log Wage (2)
Constant	0.1458 (8.543)	0.9093 (25.299)
Life years lost ($-r^*$)	–0.0028 (5.301)	–
Discount rate (r)	***2.72***	–
Implicit price x (1–p) (1–β)	–	0.0915 (7.529)
Implied discount rate (r)	–	*10.07*
Indicator for high school education	–0.0041 (0.440)	0.0400 (1.180)
Indicator for higher secondary education	0.0025 (0.298)	0.1855 (5.886)
Indicator for college education	–0.0058 (0.421)	0.2697 (5.018)
Job tenure	–	0.0025 (12.644)
Backward community (yes = 1, no = 0)	0.0130 (1.872)	0.0559 (2.143)
Union status (yes = 1, no = 0)	0.0209 (3.032)	0.2019 (7.489)
Indicator for private job	0.0170 (1.712)	–
Indicator for own house	0.0111 (1.648)	–0.0579 (2.306)
Supervisory status (yes = 1, no = 0)	–	0.1217 (3.359)
Decision-making (yes = 1, no = 0)	–	0.0956 (2.953)
Job security (yes = 1, no = 0)	-	0.0486 (1.783)
Irregular work hours (yes = 1, no = 0)	-	0.0000 (0.690)
R^2 [Adjusted R^2]	0.1127 [0.0989]	0.5752 [0.5660]

Source: Estimated as explained in the text.
Note: Absolute t values are in parentheses.

Using the coefficients in column 1 of Table 2.5 and the average values of the explanatory variables given in Table 2.3, the implicit price when $T = 0$ (i.e., $\partial W/\partial p(0)$) equals 0.1842 and when $t = 25$ equals 0.1141. These values can be substituted in the formula for computing WTP for longevity: $[V(T) = T_0(\partial W/\partial p(T_0)) + (1/2)\,T_0(\partial W/\partial p(0) - (\partial W/\partial p(T_0))]$ to get the amount that a worker is willing to sacrifice, which is approximately ₹3.73 in hourly wages for a risk exposure of 25 additional years of life. In terms of annual premium, the same worker would accept annual compensation with a present value of approximately ₹7,450 for putting 25 years of longevity at risk. The worker with a risk exposure of one additional year of life would accept annual compensation with a present value of approximately ₹300. This WTP is fairly substantial as it constitutes about 2.8 per cent of annual earnings.

Markov Decision Model Results

As stated earlier, the empirical strategy of this approach involves the computation of implicit prices from the market wage equation estimations (shown in column 2 of Table 2.4) and uses this computed price variable as a regressor in the wage equation (15). Column 2 of Table 2.5 shows the TSLS estimation results of wage equation (15).

Other control variables perform as expected. Education dummies have positive impact on log wages. Job tenure is positively related with wages. Dummy indicators for backward community, union status, supervisory status, decision-making and job security have positive coefficients. Except job security indicators, all others are statistically significant at 5 per cent level. The job security parameter is significant only at 10 per cent level. The effect of own house is negative and significant at 5 per cent level. Dummy indicator for irregular works is insignificant.

The variable of interest is the implicit price. It is noted that the implicit price is allowed to interact with one minus mortality risk value p. The parameter of this variable provides an estimate of $(1-\beta)$, which equals $r/(1+r)$. As the estimated value of $(1-\beta)$ is 0.0915, the implied discount rate (i.e., the average worker's real discount rate) is 10.07 per cent.

Summary and Policy Implications

In this chapter, an attempt has been made to estimate the implicit discount rate that the Indian workers themselves place on intertemporal health risk, using three alternative models, namely the

DELY model, LC model and MD model. The implicit discount rates estimated from these models are 7.66 per cent, 2.72 per cent and 10.07 per cent, respectively. As explained earlier (and in footnote 3), these three models are equally plausible and no single model is dominant in terms of its theoretical and empirical properties even though they provide different values of discount rate.

The most notable result from these exercises is that the Indian workers discount future life years at a real rate of 2.7 to 10.1 per cent. That is, the discount rate is not a single number but it ranges between 2.7 and 10.1 per cent. The bank interest rate on fixed deposits given by private people in India was 12 per cent in 1990. However, the interest rate that India has to pay on external loans (i.e., the average interest rate on debt to private creditors such as the World Bank) was only 8 per cent in the same year. The estimated rates are closer to these two rates. Moreover, the estimated rate falls in 2–17 per cent range and it is consistent with earlier revealed preference studies from developed nations and an earlier labour market study (Shanmugam, 2006) from India.

Thus, the results of the study provide no empirical support for utilizing a separate rate of discount for health benefits of environment/development policies in developing countries like India. Both national and international agencies evaluating health benefits may use the same discount rate used for other benefits. This is the main policy implication emerged from this study.

In addition, the results of the study indicate that workers in the sample is willing to accept an annual compensation with a present value of ₹7,450 for putting 25 years of longevity at risk and ₹300 for putting one additional year at risk. This constitutes about 2.8 per cent of annual income of an average worker. The estimated implicit value of one's future life is about ₹26 million in 1990. When we convert our estimates in 1990 US dollars, we arrive at the value of US$1.45 million. Viscusi (1993) and Viscusi and Aldy (2003) listed almost all existing studies on life values and found that the range of value per statistical life (in 1990 dollars) was US$0.6–16.2 million in the United States, Britain, Canada, Australia and Japan. The estimated value of life of our study is lower than the values from developed nations. However, our value is closer to the estimated values from developing nations such as Taiwan (ranging from US $0.135 to 0.589 million in 1990 dollars). We hope our estimates can aid policymakers, international agencies and researchers in evaluating health projects in India and other developing countries. They can also be used to carry out comparisons with values obtained for developed nations.

References

Atmadja, S. 2008. 'Discount Rate Estimation and the Role of Time Preference in Rural Household Behavior: Disease Prevention in India and Forest Management in the US', *PhD Dissertation, Dept. of Forestry and Env. Resources, North Carolina State University.*

Bohm-Bawerk, E.V. 1884. *Positive Theory of Capital.* New York: Steedard.

Boscolo, M., Vincent, J.R., and Panayotou, T. 1998.'Discounting Costs and Benefits in Carbon Sequestration Projects', Environment Discussion Paper No. 41, International Environment Program, Harvard Institute for International Development.

Chapman, G.B. 1996. 'Temporal Discounting and Utility for Health and Money', *Journal of Experimental Psychology: Learning, Memory and Cognition*, 22(3): 771–91.

Clain, W.R. 1992. *The Economics of Global Warming.* Institute for International Economics, Washington DC.

Dillingham, A.E. 1985. 'The Influence of Risk Variable Definition on Value of Life Estimates', *Economic Inquiry*, 24: 277–94.

Cousineau, J.-M., Lacroix, R., and Girard, A.M. 1992.'Occupational Hazard and Wage Compensating Differentials', *Review of Economics and Statistics*, pp. 166–69.

Dreyfus, M. and Viscusi, W.K. 1995. 'Rate of Time Preference and Consumer Valuations of Automobile Safety and Fuel Efficiency', *Journal of Law Economics*, 38: 79–103.

Frederick, S., Loewenstein, G. and Ted O'Donoghue. 2002. 'Time Discounting and Time Preference: A Critical Review', *Journal of Economic Literature*, 40(2): 351–401.

Ganiats, T., Richard, G., Carson, T., Hamm, R.M., Cantor, S.B., Sumner, W., Spann, S.J., Hagen, M. and Miller, C. 2000. 'Health Status and Preferences: Population-based Time Preferences for Future Health Outcome', *Medical Decision Making: An International Journal*, 20: 263–70.

Garen, J.E. 1988. 'Compensating Wage Differentials and Endogeneity of Job Riskiness', *The Review of Economics and Statistics*, 70(1): 9–16.

Gately, D. 1980. 'Individual Discount Rates and the Purchase and Utilization of Energy-using Durables: Comment'. *Bell Journal of Economics*, 11(1): 373–74.

Hausman, J. 1979. 'Individual Discount rates and the Purchase and Utilization of Energy-using Durables', *Bell Journal of Economics*, 10(1): 33–54.

Herzog, H.W. and Schlottmann, A.M. 1990.'Valuing Risk in the Workplace: Market Price, Willingness to Pay and the Optimal Provision of Safety', *The Review of Economics and Statistics*, 72(3): 463–70.

Johannesson, M. and Johansson, P. 1997. 'Quality of Life and WTP for an Increased Life Expectancy at an Advanced Age', *Journal of Public Economics*, 65: 219–28.

Kniesner, T.J. and Leeth, J.D. 1991. 'Compensating Wage Differentials for Fatal Injury Risks in Australia, Japan and United States', *Journal of Risk and Uncertainty*, 4(1): 75–90.
Leigh, P.J. and Folsom, R.N. 1984. 'Estimates of Value of Accident Avoidnace at the Job Dependent on the Concavity of the Equalizing Difference Curve', *Quarterly Review of Economics and Business*, 24(1): 56–66.
Liu, J.T., Hammitt, J.K., and Liu, L.L. 1997. 'Estimated Hedonic Wage Function and Value of Life in a Developing Country', *Economics Letters*, 57: 353–58.
Loewenstein, G. 1987. 'Anticipation and the Valuation of Delayed Consumption', *Economic Journal*, 97: 666–84.
Krutilla, J.V. and Fisher, A.C. 1975. *The Economics of Natural Environments: Studies in the Valuation of Commodity and Amenity Resources.*, Washington, DC: Resources for the Future.
Kula, E. 2004. 'Estimation of a Social Rate of Interest for India', *Journal of Agricultural Economics*, 55(1): 91–99.
Marglin, S.A. 1967. *Public Investment Criteria*. London: Allen & Unwin.
Marin, A. and Psacharopoulos, G. 1982. 'The Reward for Risk in the Labor Market: Evidence from the United Kingdom and a Reconciliation with Other Studeis', *Journal of Political Economy*, 90(4): 827–53.
Markandya, A. and Pearce, D.W. 1988. 'Environmental Considerations and the Choice of the Discount Rate in Developing Countries', Environment Department Working Paper 3, World Bank, Washington, DC.
———. 1991. 'Development, the Environment and the Social Rate of Discount', *The World Bank Observer*, 6: 137–52.
Moore, M.J. and Viscusi, W.K. 1988. 'The Quantity-Adjusted Value of Life', *Economic Inquiry*, 26: 369–88.
———. 1990. 'Discounting Environmental Health Risks: New Evidence and Policy Implications', *Journal of Environmental Economics and Management*, 18: 381–401.
Ramsey, F.P. 1928. 'A Mathematical Theory of Saving', *Economic Journal*, 38: 543–59.
Shanmugam, K.R. 1993. 'An Econometric Study on the Compensation Differentials for Job Risks in India', Unpublished PhD thesis awarded by Madras University in January 1995.
———. 1996/97. 'The Value of Life: Estimates from Indian Labour Market', *Indian Economic Journal*, 44(4): 105–14.
———. 1997. 'Compensating Wage Differentials for Work Related Fatal and Injury Accidents', *The Indian Journal of Labor Economics*, 40: 251–62.
———. 2001. 'Self Selection Bias in the Estimates of Compensating Differentials for Job Risks in India', *Journal of Risk and Uncertainty*, 22: 263–75.
———. 2006. 'Rate of Time Preference and the Quantity Adjusted Value of Life in India', *Environment and Development Economics*, 11: 569–83.
———. 2011. 'Discount Rate for Health Benefits and the Value of Life in India', MSE Working Paper No. 60/2011.
Sharma, R.A., McGregor, M.J., and Blyth, J.F. 1991. 'The Social Discount Rate for Land use Projects in India', *Journal of Agricultural Economics*, 42: 86–92.
Storz, R. 1956. 'Myopia and Inconsistency in Dynamic Utility Maximization', *Review of Economic Studies*, 23: 165–80.
Thaler, R. and Rosen, S. 1976. 'The Value of Saving a Life: Evidence from the Market', in N.E. Terlecky (ed.), *Household Production and Consumption* (pp. 265–98). NBER, New York.

Van der Pol, M.M. and Cairns, J.A. 1999. 'Individual Time Preferences for Own Health: Application of a Dichotomous Choice Question with Follow Up', *Applied Economics Letters*, 6: 649–54.

———. 2001. 'Estimating Time Preferences for Health Using Discrete Choice Experiments', *Social Science Medicine*, 52: 1459–70.

Viscusi, W.K. 1979. *Employment Hazards: An Investigation of Market Performance*. Cambridge: Harvard University Press.

———. 1981. 'Occupational Safety and Health Regulation: Its Impact on Policy Alternatives', in J.Crecine (ed.), *Research in Public Policy Analysis and Management* (pp. 281–99). Greenwich, Conn: JAI Press.

———. 1993. 'The Value of Risks to Life and Health', *Journal of Economic Literature*, 31(4): 1912–46.

Viscusi, W.K. and Aldy, J.E. 2003.'The Value of a Statistical Life: A Critical Review of Market Estimates Throughout the World', *The Journal of Risk and Uncertainty*, 27: 5–76.

Viscusi, W.K. and Moore, M.J. 1989. 'Rate of Time Preference and Valuations of the Duration of Life', *The Journal of Public Economics*, 38: 297–317.

Von Thunen, J.H. 1826. *Isolated State* (English edition edited by P. Hall). Pergamon Press: London. (Name of German Edition: 'Der Isolierte Staat' in Beziehung auf Landwirtschaft und Nationalokonomic, Hamburg, Perths.)

3

Low Carbon Goods and Services: International Cooperation on Technological Innovation, Transfer and Funding Needs

Kaliappa Kalirajan, Anbumozhi Venkatachalam** and Thanh Nguyen****

The Setting

Greenhouse gas (GHG) emissions reduction is a global public good (GPG). As production of this pubic good is determined by the decisions of consumers and producers around the world, appropriate policies are needed for mitigation at local, national and global levels. Effective regional and international cooperation is central to improve the green growth and low-carbon societies at the individual national, regional and global levels. Regional and international cooperation can be a 'win–win' situation for the concerned countries to distribute their pooled resources fruitfully for the regional and international development without hurting national development, as these are not mutually exclusive. For example, in the case of energy generation, it is efficient and fruitful to collaborate with countries in the region rather than each country restricting itself to forming an autarchic energy policy.

*Crawford School of Public Policy, Australian National University, Canberra, Australia.
**Economic Research Institute for ASEAN and East Asia, Jakarta, Indonesia.
***Rector, Hanoi University of Natural Resources and Environment, Hanoi, Vietnam.

Collaboration with the neighbours will strengthen the domestic energy reserves and improve energy security through diversification of resources. In order to promote research and development in low-carbon goods and services (LCGS), it is necessary to cooperate internationally to maintain proper intellectual property rights (IPRs) regime at national levels. However, they need to fulfil certain minimum conditions. To mention a few, countries need a package of public and private investments in technological innovations, diffusions, financing, regional cooperation through trade, investment, aid and new institutions and governance systems. It is in this context, this chapter concentrates its discussion on the importance of international cooperation on technological innovation, transfer and funding for the LCGS.

The following section discusses the dominant forms of technological innovation and transfer concerning LCGS with a special reference to intellectual property rights (IPRs) regime. The next section examines the extent of funding needs for green growth under different international and regional sources. The final section brings out the policy conclusions for promoting technological innovation and transfer of LCGS through cooperation across countries.

LCGS Technological Innovation and Transfer

Though output growth results from inputs growth and technological progress, it is the latter source that can be sustained in the long run. The existing production network in Asia gives the impression that growth can be maintained by changing the allocation of human and physical resources across more productive sectors and countries. However, in the long run, it is technological innovations that facilitate the productive sectors and countries to retain their growth potentials. The evidence-based research across countries indicates that there is a substantial technological and innovation gap for Asian economies in developing and adopting clean low-carbon technologies (Anbumozhi, 2008) that facilitate the transformation to a low-carbon economy. In this context, Bowen and

Kattumuri (2012: 4) highlight the importance of technological progress in LCGS by saying, 'The transition to green growth can facilitate a broader transition to greater reliance on innovation as a source of sustainable economic growth'. Thus, research and development (R&D) is a crucial component of technological innovation. However, investment in R&D by countries across the globe is not encouraging. Except China and India, most developing countries in Asia spend little on R&D on low-carbon technologies and have a chronic shortage of competent managers with skills needed to develop and apply low-carbon technologies. Instead, these countries are highly dependent on the importation and transfer of technologies and skills developed in developed countries. It is recognized that the transfer of new technologies and skills facilitates the build-up of an indigenous technological capacity that enables long-term adaptation of technologies and future innovations. But most developing economies lack even the minimum capacity and skilled workforce to utilize advanced foreign technologies. The Republic of Korea (ROK) stands out as the number one country in the world in terms of encouraging businesses to engage in R&D activities by providing direct and indirect government funding to them in 2007 (Anbumozhi, 2010).

Improving the global architecture is crucial to implement actions for promoting LCGS. Developed countries such as the G8 economies should take the leading role in urging other countries to agree on the shape of a post-Kyoto deal by demonstrating the developed economies' commitment to building a low-carbon society. It is important that the major emerging economies like China, India, Brazil and South Africa are given an equal seat at the negotiations. The clout of the biggest markets certainly will drive innovation for LCGS around the world with enthusiasm. The need to focus on growth, employment generation and poverty reduction in the developing world means that required cuts in emissions will be contingent on striking a balance between GHG emissions reduction and other development goals (Planning Commission, 2011; Sankar, 2010). Thus, the importance of instituting the post-Kyoto regime based on common but differentiated responsibilities soon cannot be overemphasized. For example, it is important to engage countries like China, India and Indonesia in building consensus on their national targets in a progressive manner (Kawai, 2008). The international community should also reach an agreement not only to extend the clean development mechanism (CDM) beyond 2012 to include the reforms, but also to increase the coverage of sectors and countries. The most likely global policy platform for promoting such an urgent international action to facilitate technological innovation and transfer in LCGS is the G20 forum.

Innovation and dissemination of low-carbon technologies at large scale are needed to promote its use globally. This means that a large-scale investment in low-carbon systems over the coming decades is needed. The International Energy Agency (IEA, 2009) estimated that a worldwide investment of $20 trillion is required by 2030. Of this, more than half will be required for developing Asia alone. Bilateral and multilateral aid agencies, which possess sufficient resources and technical expertise, are well placed to help countries with financial difficulties to develop low-carbon systems. It is necessary for the multilateral organizations to coordinate with governments, the donor community, the capital market and the private sector to mobilize the resources and technical expertise. Donor countries, in conjunction with the private sector, need to invest in long-term carbon bonds issued by the international financial institutions. The Asian Development Bank (ADB)-supported trust funds under its integrated Carbon Market Initiative (CMI) are a good example of helping needy countries to promote green growth (Table 3.1). The objective of the CMI facilities is to encourage additional investments in clean energy projects by upfront financing, technical and market support. It provides finance to carbon projects at the most critical stage: project preparation and implementation (ADB, 2006). Innovative financial mechanisms, such as the Asia Pacific Carbon Funds (APCF), are intended to target programmes and projects as grants or concessional loans to facilitate the transfer and diffusion of low-carbon technologies. These types of business models are needed to enhance technological innovation and dissemination of LCGS.

Table 3.1:
Key funding mechanism of the Asian Development Bank for environmentally related projects

Climate Change Fund (CCF)	The CCF was established in 2008 to provide grant funding for climate-related projects, research and development, to assess causes and consequences. Funding is provided for projects that lead to the reduction of GHG emissions or adaptation to climate change.
Clean Energy Financing Partnership Facility (CEFPF)	The CEFPF was established in 2007 and provides grant funding to member countries in the region for improving energy security and transitioning to low-carbon economies, through cost-effective investments in technologies and practices. In addition to the funds allocated to CEFPF by the ADB, the fund receives contributions from countries such as Australia, Japan and Norway.
Asia Pacific Carbon Fund (APCF)	The APCF was established in 2007 as part of the ADB's Carbon Market Initiative (CMI). The APCF provides financial assistance for clean energy projects. The APCF receives funding commitments from several European countries such as Belgium, Finland, Luxembourg, Portugal, Spain, Sweden and Switzerland.
Future Carbon Fund (FCF)	The FCF was established in 2008 and provides funding for projects that will generate carbon credits for GHG reductions after 2012, to improve energy efficiency and renewable energy.
Water Financing Partnership Facility (WFPF)	The WFPF provides financial resources and technical support for water services and river basin water management.
Poverty and Environment Fund (PEF)	The PEF is multi-donor trust fund, administered by ADB that promotes mainstreaming of environmental considerations into broader development strategies, programmes and projects.

Source: Sharan (2008).

Intellectual Property Rights Regime

The IPR regime is crucial for developing technological innovation with respect to LCGS by developing countries from the basic research and development done in developed countries. At times, it may be necessary to combine different technologies innovated in different countries, which may pose problems due to the existence of different IPR regimes in those countries. These problems may inhibit or slow down technological innovation and adaptation by developing countries. In this context, a possible solution is regional cooperation in harmonizing the IPR regime across countries in the region. United Nations Economic and Social Commission for Asia and the Pacific (UN-ESCAP) through its Renewable Energy Cooperation Mechanism for Asia and the Pacific has been helping developing countries to overcome IPR issues with respect to energy.

Concerning the smooth transfer of technology, an important factor is how closely the national IPR regime is integrated with the global IPR regime. In this context, experiences of two major emerging economies in Asia, China and India, are worth noting. After the accession to WTO, China's IPR policies reflect China's willingness to accept higher degrees of interdependence. China has strived to conform to Trade-Related Aspects of Intellectual Property Rights (TRIPS) and has managed its enforcement issues with a number of practical administrative and judicial policies to assure foreign investors and a growing number of local IPR holders of the security of their IP. The global IPR regime has helped to influence a new agenda for China, which is to pursue a knowledge-based economy as a development goal. How effectively the central government is in enforcing IPR policy at every level of government is an important benchmark for China's success in integrating its national IPR regime with the global IPR regime.

Signing the TRIPS Agreement in 1994 triggered significant changes in the IPR-related legal framework of India (Planning Commission, 2009). Since then, several legislative and institutional adjustments have been made to protect IPR (Sankar, 2009). Although India has made significant strides towards harmonization of domestic IPR laws with the international system, there are several issues afflicting the IPR regime in India.

Drawing on the experiences of China and India with respect to IPR regimes, some of the key areas that need attention to facilitate the smooth transfer of technology can be identified as follows:

(a) Strengthening institutional mechanisms for protection of IPR—Regulatory, legal and administrative through assigning a high priority towards completion of required legislative provisions to harmonize IPR regime with international laws.

(b) Strengthening public–private R&D interface by adopting mechanisms such as an 'innovation bill' to enhance public R&D base wherein public researchers, research organizations and universities would be incentivized for commercialization of their innovation.
(c) Enhancing IPR literacy by disseminating IPR-related information to all relevant stakeholders.

The issue of IPR has been often considered as a constraint for international cooperation on green technology and acts as a barrier to share the technical know-how. Nevertheless, there have been success stories across the regions that suggest that joint ventures between collaborators provide a solution to the IPR issue (Table 3.2).

Extent of Funding Needs for Green Growth

One of the major constraints discouraging developing countries from reducing GHG emissions is the need to finance climate-change policies, and this factor has a bearing on regional and international cooperation. Since the 1992 Earth Summit in Rio de Janeiro, parties to the United Nations Framework Convention on Climate Change (UNFCCC) have been developing strategies, policies and measures for financing GHG emissions reduction. IEA (2009) estimated that to achieve a 50 per cent reduction in carbon emissions globally by 2030, an additional investment of US$7,585 billion would be needed. Half of this funding is expected to come from industrialized countries, while individual countries will be required to fund the remaining (see Figure 3.1).

Financial investment in clean energy in developing countries was estimated at US$36.6 billion in 2008, representing an increase of 27 per cent over the last year with China (US$15.6 billion) and India (US$3.7 billion) leading the way in Asia (UNEP, 2009). Existing estimates for funding of climate change and adaptation vary due to differences in the methodology used, the countries included,

Table 3.2:
IPR regimes and low-carbon industry policies in selected Asian countries

Type of Economy Based on Carbon Intensiveness	*Trade in Low-carbon Goods and Services*	*Foreign Direct Investment (FDI)*	*Trade in Knowledge (licensing)*	*Intellectual Property Rights (IPR)*	*Low-carbon Industrial Policies*
Domestic policies					
Low-carbon intensive—Bangladesh, Laos, Cambodia, Sri Lanka, Nepal	Liberal access	Non-discriminatory investment promotion	Improve information flows about public domain and mature technologies	Basic protection and minimum standards only	Basic education; improve infrastructure; reduce entry barriers
Low–medium carbon intensive—Indonesia, Thailand, Vietnam	Liberal access	Non-discriminatory investment promotion	Improve information; limited incentives for licensing	Wider scope of IPR protection; employ flexibilities	R&D support policies; improve infrastructure; reduce entry barriers
High–carbon intensive—China and India	Liberal access	Upstream supplier support programmes	Improve information; limited incentives for licensing	Apply full TRIPS	R&D support policies; improve infrastructure; reduce entry barriers
Developed-country policies towards emerging Asia					
Low-carbon intensive—Bangladesh, Laos, Cambodia, Sri Lanka, Nepal	Subsidize public-good-type imports; free trade	Incentives for outward flows exceeding those for FDI	Subsidize transfer of public domain and mature technologies	Forbearance in disputes; differential pricing for exports of IPR products; competition policy assistance	Support for general LC technology policies; public and public–private research facilities
Low–medium-carbon intensive—Indonesia, Thailand, Vietnam	Free trade; no controls	Incentives equal to those granted for own disadvantaged regions	Assistance in establishing joint venture partnerships; matching grants	Differential pricing of public-good type IPR protected goods; competition policy assistance	Support for general LC technology policies; fiscal incentives for R&D performed in DCs
High carbon intensive—China and India	Free trade; no controls	Incentives equal to those granted for own disadvantaged regions	Assistance in establishment of joint venture partnerships; matching	Differential pricing of public-good type IPR protected goods; competition policy assistance	Support for general LC technology policies; fiscal incentives for R&D

Source: Kalirajan (2011).

Figure 3.1:
Additional investment needed for emission reduction by 2030

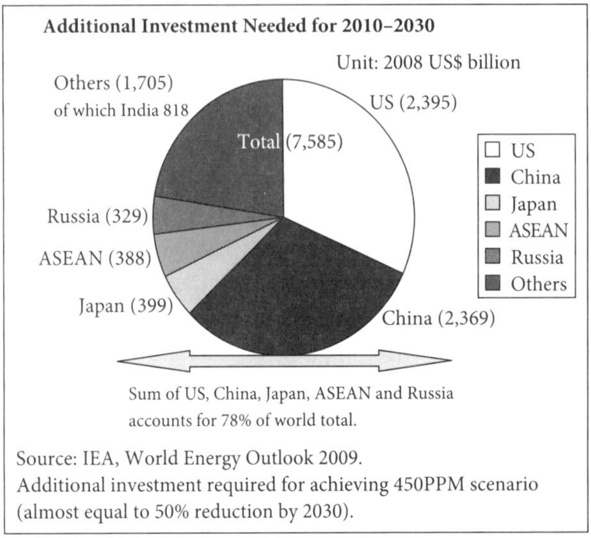

Source: Kalirajan (2011).

the types of gas emissions covered and the scenarios used. However, all estimates point to a need for huge investment, which developing countries are unable to meet with own resources. Generally, funding for climate change initiatives can be expected to come from developed countries, multilateral financial institutions, government funds and private financial institutions. The multilateral funding agencies include The World Bank, regional development banks such as the ADB and the United Nations agencies.

Major Sources of International Funding for Green Growth

The first attempt to support developing countries to mitigate emissions was the CDM that was defined in Article 12 of the Kyoto Protocol. The CDM is widely acknowledged as an important market-based mechanism for achieving the goal of a low-carbon economy in developing countries. The CDM was designed to help developed countries too to meet a part of their emission reduction targets and to assist them in achieving sustainable development. The projects of the CDM provided certified emission reduction (CER) credits, which could be traded or sold, by participants in the projects. The projects provide other benefits to the participating countries, such as encouraging new investment, the exchange of climate-friendly technologies, the improvement of livelihoods and skills, job creation and increased economic activity.

A review (UNFCCC, 2011) conducted on CDM-assisted projects showed mixed results. The reviewers found that CDM projects were making a contribution to sustainable development over and above the mitigation of GHG emissions in their host countries. The sustainable development benefits include increased employment rates, the reduction of noise and pollution, and the protection of the natural resources. The reviewers noted that investment flows under the CDM has been encouraging. However, the transfer of technologies between countries was found to be slow and modest. By mid-July 2011, there were over 3,200 projects underway that were worth US$140 billion. About 70 per cent of these projects were overwhelmingly in India and China together (Figure 3.2). A key

Figure 3.2:
Geographical distribution of CDM projects across the globe, 2012

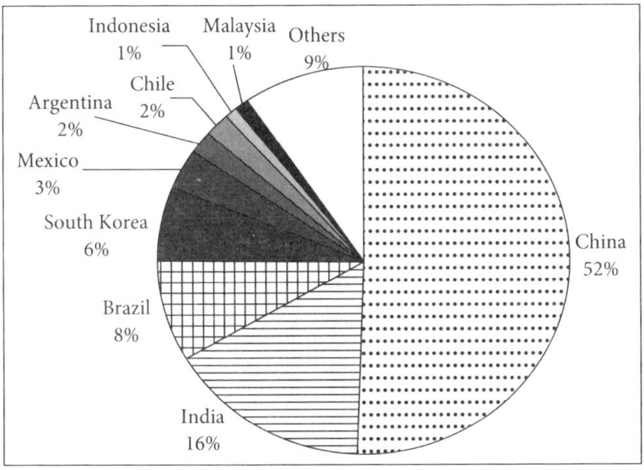

Source: UNFCCC (2012).

fund, dedicated to adaptation to climate change, is the Adaptation Fund (AF). The AF is financed through a 2 per cent levy on revenue generated by the CDM and through voluntary contributions, and it is estimated that it will be worth US$80 million to $1 billion per annum by 2012.

But the current system has many limitations. Firstly, most of the expected CER credits earned by 2012, when the Kyoto protocol expired, had been mainly from large scale projects, such as grid connected renewable energy systems, and methane capturing. The difficulty of applying CDM to projects in the transport sector and the energy conservation sector is an impediment, which limits the wider use of the mechanism. Secondly, the issue is that the growing investment uncertainty over the future of CDM and the global carbon market after 2012. This uncertainty has arisen from the lack of an international consensus to date on the post-Kyoto regime. Finally, the satisfaction of strict 'additional' criteria of the mechanism by the UN-CDM board has been one of the major obstacles in developing viable projects. To many, the CDM is a win–win solution for all countries as it provides developed countries with low-cost abatement opportunities and a way for engaging emerging and developing economies in mitigation efforts by providing them with funding for low-carbon technologies. CDM can achieve its potential gains, if the previously-cited limitations are eliminated.

Unfortunately, countries like Japan are not participating in the second commitment period of Kyoto Protocol, which started in 2013, and thus not allowed to trade emission credits internationally. The implication is that the balance between demand and supply of credits is severely affected and the carbon price is falling drastically. The result could be a large decline in the future expected number of CDM projects approved and CERs earned.

Nevertheless, Japan proposed a new approach called Joint Crediting Mechanism (JCM)/Bilateral Offset Credit Mechanism (BOCM). In order to contribute to global actions for emission reductions and removals by sinks, JCM/BOCM provides opportunities for developed countries to meet their emission reduction targets by flexibly and quickly. These opportunities of the developed countries are expected to meet the needs of national circumstances of developing countries to facilitate the diffusion of low-carbon technologies, products, systems, service, infrastructures and to making the measurement, reporting and verification (MRV) of those reduction effects effectively. Despite potential benefits and simplicity, issues relating to the MRV accounting rules, implications to carbon markets and overall integrity to UNFCCC process warrant further considerations of the scheme for global recognition.

At the 2000 Cancun Climate Change Conference in Mexico, it was agreed to establish a new Green Climate Fund to support climate change action in developing countries. A Transitional Committee was created in 2011 to design the new funding mechanism. The Cancun Agreements were built on the climate change financing framework set by the Copenhagen Accord, which was released in 2009. The Accord recognized the commitment undertaken by developed countries to provide new and additional resources for developing countries, to a level approaching US$30 billion, for the 'fast-start' period of 2010–12. To ensure transparency, developed countries were to provide annual reports to the UNFCCC on their progress in delivering 'fast-start' funds. As the financial mechanism of the UNFCCC, the GEF provides policy, finance, capacity and technology support to developing countries in their efforts to reduce GHG emissions. The GEF had approximately $250 million per annum in grants that were available for mitigation during 2006–10.

The World Bank and the United Nations have established carbon funds to support climate change projects. There are 13 different carbon funds, which assist climate change projects, increase private-sector investor confidence and provide capacity building for climate change. The major carbon funds are the Forest Carbon Partnership Facility (FCPF) and Community Development Carbon Fund (CDCF) that assist developing countries in managing carbon emissions in their domestic economies. The FCPF assists developing countries in reducing emissions from deforestation and forest degradation, while the CDCF supports developing nations in adapting to climate change.

While the carbon funds provide assistance for mitigation of climate change and adaptation, there is also international funding available specifically for adaptation in developing countries. The main vehicle for such funding is the UNFCCC, which has four funds relevant to adaptation. These funds are: The Least Developed Countries Fund, established to help developing countries prepare and implement their National Adaptation Programmes of Action, The Special Climate Change Fund, which supports a number of climate change activities such as mitigation and technology transfer, but with special focus on adaptation; Trust Fund's Strategic Priority for Adaptation, which supports piloting of 'operational' approaches to adaptation; AF, which was established under the Kyoto Protocol (International Energy Agency (IEA, 2009).

Official Development Assistance

Developed countries, especially those in the OECD, traditionally provide bilateral aid in the form of grants, loans and technical cooperation for the promotion of economic development and welfare of developing countries (Hongo, 2010). Official Development Assistance (ODA) financial flows comprise contributions of donor government agencies, to developing countries and to multilateral institutions. Between 1998 and 2000, ODA accounted for nearly 92 per cent of financial flows to the less developed countries for development initiatives (van Aalst and Agrawala, 2005). Specifically, the ODA is assisting developing countries to achieve their Millennium Development Goals, through the commitment of the OECD countries to allocate 0.7 per cent of their gross domestic product by 2015. The funds addressing climate change are not part of this commitment (Kalirajan et al., 2010). As the OECD countries are presently facing budgetary constraints, they may not be expected to contribute more for climate change efforts in developing countries over and above what has been committed as ODA (OECD, 2005).

Major Sources of Regional Funding for Green Growth in Asia

The Asian Development Bank (ADB) is a regional development bank that aims to assist member countries in Asia and the Pacific to reduce poverty and improve the quality of life for the people in the region. The Asia and Pacific region has one-third of the world's poorest people. Six hundred million people in the region live on $1 a day or less. The ADB's funding methods include loans, equity investments, guarantees, grants and technical assistance. Funding for climate change and adaptation is provided by the ADB through different projects. A number of funding mechanisms have been devised as shown in Table 3.1.

In 2005, ADB launched its Energy Efficiency Initiative with the aim of expanding the Bank's clean energy programme, enhancing the capacity for the Bank's operations departments to develop clean energy projects and establishing new and innovative financing instruments for clean energy investments. The initiative set the annual clean energy investment target at $1 billion. In 2008, Developing Member Countries of the ADB surpassed the target by $690 million in 2008 (see Figure 3.3). This was an important

Figure 3.3:
ADB's clean energy targets

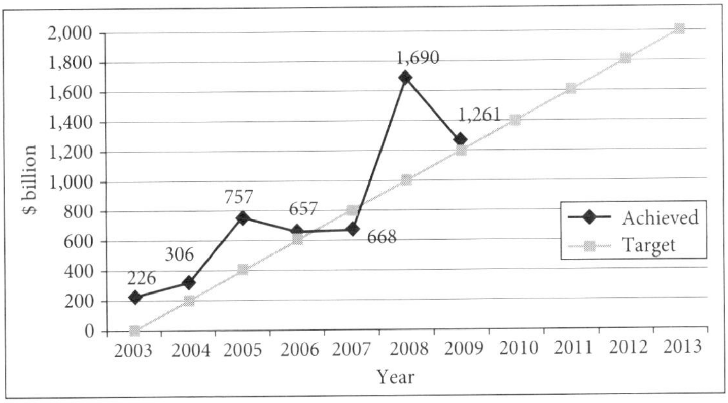

Source: Lockhart (2011).

achievement as this happened in the middle of the Global Financial Crisis, where most people are expected to be using cheap energy based on fossil fuels to be common (Peters et al., 2011).

Private Sector Participation

Private sector participation is extremely important as the magnitude of the investment necessary to manage climate change is huge, and the public sector and international sources alone cannot meet the challenge. However, a problem associated with green finance is that private funds are generally hesitant to provide their money to support green growth. However, if the participation of firms in green industries can generate sufficient profit for them, then private finance institutions become more eager to supply funding to those green firms. Prior to investment decisions being made, it is important to raise awareness of climate change and emission reductions among the community at large, and establish a system of information collection and performance monitoring.

Research has shown that public/private financial partnerships are crucial in financing green growth. Governments could act as facilitators and could monitor green growth and financing. Governments could also play a large part in creating an enabling environment, providing direction for green growth and improving the investment climate for private sector investment.

The involvement of the private sector is crucial for energy-efficient technological innovation and transfer. In this context, Japan's approach of providing ODA and funding for official collaboration with the private sector is a good model for other developed countries to follow. A market mechanism with private sector participation seems to be more effective and cost-effective in addressing climate change in many countries in Asia and the Pacific. Private financing to green industries comes from bank loans and capital market investment.

Private sector financing makes up the bulk of funding for climate change initiatives at the global level (Hongo, 2011). For example, according to UNFCCC estimates, in response to climate change, private sector investments contributed up to 86 per cent of the global investments and financial flows. However, private financing for climate change and adaptation in the Asia and the Pacific region has yet to be developed. This apparent lack of funding from the private sector, and the inability of many governments to provide their own funding, makes it necessary to explore specialized private financing mechanisms for the Asian region. Currently, the ADB is playing a regional financing role in partnership with donor countries in the region, such as Japan, ROK, China, Australia and New Zealand. The ADB also provides bilateral assistance to countries in the region.

Unfortunately, several reports highlight the lack of coordination between aid agencies and governments in tackling climate change. For example, there is lack of coordination between the aid agencies in Nepal regarding the work on the Tsho Rolpa project, where the most dangerous glacial lakes in Nepal are being lowered through drainage (Kim, 2011). Also, the lack of domestic capacity to respond to the needs of the aid agencies is cited as another reason for not accounting for climate change activities in government policy strategies (Gagnon-Lebrun and Agrawala, 2006). This raises the issue of training and capacity-building of people in developing countries to support climate change-related activities.

A Successful Global Public–Private Partnership (PPP) Project in India

A successful PPP towards climate change improvement is the partnership between World Renewal Spiritual Trust (WRST), which is a registered charity trust with headquarters in Mumbai and branches all over India, and the Government of India under the 'One India' programme. The WRST's major objective is to promote the use of alternative energies through carrying out research and demonstration of renewable energy systems. In order to pursue its aims, the WRST works in close association with the Prajapita Brahma

Kumaris Ishwariya Vishwa Vidyalaya (BKIVV), which is a premier spiritual university in India.

> After detailed evaluation of various solar technologies, WRST selected to make use of the in-house developed 60 m^2 Scheffler parabolic dish in order to set up a solar thermal power plant near its Shantivan Campus in Abu Road, Rajasthan. For this project, WRST has teamed up with Fraunhofer Institute (ISE) and enjoys the support of Wolfgang Scheffler. WRST is in close liaison with various solar R&D institutions and manufacturers and has initiated all necessary steps for completion of this project. The thermal solar power plant will be the first of its kind in the world in dish technology in direct steam generation mode, with full thermal storage for 16 hrs continuous operations for base load. The budget for the project is Rupees 66 crores excluding the cost of land. The WRST request for funding with the Indian Central Ministry of New and Renewable Energy Sources (MNRE) has been approved. The German Ministry for Environment, Nature Conservation and Nuclear Safety (BMU) has also agreed to support this project. (http://www.wrst.in/)

This is a good example of how the private sector could be engaged in a strategic way in a grand coalition scenario involving private, national and international government organizations (Kalirajan, 2011: 22–23).

Green Finance as a Facilitator

Green finance refers to the financial support for green growth, the advancement of the financial industry through the development of new financial products and the improvement of risk management techniques. While the participation of the corporate sector is vital in expanding the initiatives for a green economy, companies have a role to play in raising consumer awareness on improvement of the environment, through financing and introducing green products and services. An example is ROK's 'Low-Carbon Green Growth Basic Measure', which focuses on the:

> formation of financial resources and capital support for a green economy and green industry; development of new financial products to support

> low-carbon green growth; revitalization of private investment to facilitate low-carbon green growth; strengthening of the public notice system on the green management information of companies; expansion of financial support for green companies; establishment of a carbon market, where the rights to emit greenhouse gas or results of greenhouse gas reduction and absorption are traded; and revitalization of business. (Kim, 2011)

As discussed by Hongo (2011), the Asian carbon market is fragmented and unification of the market under a grand regional coalition scenario can improve financing support for green growth and can increase the pace of green growth in the region.

Another strategy to be considered by developing countries is to use, where feasible, their own resources to fund green growth, or to seek assistance from other countries within the region. Some Asian countries, such as China and those of ASEAN, while spending large amounts of funds for green growth, have the capacity also to provide funding for the needy countries in the region (Kalirajan, 2011). It is to be noted that China and Japan are the second and third largest economies, respectively, in the world and six out of the eight countries, with the largest foreign currency reserves are in Asia, as reported in the *Global Finance* December 2011 issue.

Government's Expanded Role in Green Finance

Green industry is strategically important in most countries, and has become a new growth engine for sustainable development in developing economies. There are several ways that governments can finance green growth. An important way is for governments to assist green technologies and green industries by using subsidies and tax incentives. Fiscal policy, therefore, is an important tool for greening the economy and a fiscal expansion could effectively raise the demand for environmental goods and services (Anbumozhi, 2010). In other words, appropriately designed fiscal policies are a prerequisite to increase private investment and to influence the composition of aggregate demand.

Governments need to encourage private institutions, including the capital market, to participate in green finance. As most green industries are in the early stages of development and need long-term investments to achieve outcomes, there is the difficulty that these investments are considered to be of high risk. To make efficient financing possible through banks and capital markets, governments must offer incentives and prepare policy solutions to deal with potential obstacles in the financing process. Most banks still have serious limitations on providing green finance. Efficient and consistent policies are necessary for banks to develop their capacity to provide green finance. There has been some increase in support for green industries in the capital market. Environmental information provided by firms will help and protect investors in stock markets and lead to further development. Governments around the globe are now taking serious steps to involve private financing into green growth by first creating Green Investment Bank with their capital. Few examples are given in the following paragraphs.

The Netherlands Green Fund Scheme

Currently, many banks seem to need incentives from governments to participate in green finance. The Netherlands Green Fund Scheme is an example of government support for bank financing to green growth. Under the Green Fund Scheme, funds to green projects are provided at low cost by taking full advantage of banks' financial intermediary functions. The programme consists of three parts: green projects, green institutions and tax incentives. Green banks are certified by the government, and the majority of major Netherlands banks are designated as green banks. The banks assess projects seeking funding. Projects that are assessed to be sufficiently 'green' under such projects are awarded a green certificate, which qualify for low-interest loans.

Green banks can issue bonds or accept deposits at rates below the market rate to finance green projects. Investors and depositors are compensated with tax. Green banks should put at least

70 per cent of that money into certified green projects. As they can fully utilize the remaining 30 per cent, financed at low cost, they have incentives to participate actively in the Green Fund Scheme. This scheme is designed for money inflow to green projects, with the cost of tax reduction. The Netherlands government scales up inflow under this scheme because it directs more private financial resources to green projects. Without those tax benefits, those funds would go elsewhere.

Green Bank in UK

Though the idea of establishing a Green Investment Bank in UK was initiated by the Labour government in 2010, only recently, the UK Conservative government has firmly announced its intention of creating a Green Investment Bank with £1 billion from taxpayers and up to £2 billion from sales of government assets with the objective of investing in green projects such as the development of LCGS. The Green Bank investment is expected to encourage more private sector investment in LCGS. The Chancellor is confident that the bank can generate £15 billion of green investment from the private sector. The bank is expected to start its operation by 2012 (Harvey, 2011).

Green Bank Proposal in the USA

Governments can build a policy bank that will be directly involved in green finance instead of indirectly supporting private banks. The green bank proposal in the USA is another example like the proposed Green Bank in the UK. The proposed Green Bank would be an independent, tax-exempt, wholly owned corporation of the USA. It was expected that the Green Bank Act of 2009 would provide the Green Bank with an initial capital of US$10 billion through the issuance of Green Bonds by the USA Department of Treasury, with a maximum authorized limit of $50 billion in Green Bonds outstanding at any one time. Unfortunately, the proposal did not materialize due to the controversial energy legislation. Nevertheless, recently, the Green Bank proposal and a competing form of financing institution, the Clean Energy Development Authority is being put forward by both the Republicans and Democrats as a source for employment generation (Thurston, 2011). When the UK Green Bank becomes operational in 2012, it would have a positive impact on US Congress to give green signal for the US Green Bank.

Policy Conclusions

GHG emissions reduction is a GPG. As there is no global government and the UNFCC has recognized differential responsibilities of countries due to differences in their cumulative contributions to GHG emissions, it is necessary to reach collective and binding decisions on the stabilization target and on the time trajectory of emission reductions at the global level. Therefore, effective intra-regional and inter-regional co-operation is crucial to promote and sustain low-carbon green growth across countries. The focus of this chapter is on international cooperation in LCGS technological innovation, transfer and availability of funding. Regional and international cooperation, not only through ODA, but through other means of communications and cooperation such as joint ventures are important in creating the enabling conditions for green growth and sustainable development. Nevertheless, ODA should be used for green growth not at the cost of activities aimed at poverty reduction.

Both development of new technologies and distribution of proven technologies are the twin engines to bring about a low-carbon society. International and regional cooperation is necessary for innovation, technology development and distribution. There is a need for instituting regional incubation centres for horizontal technology development. Though there is no need to create new centres, it is necessary to harmonize the mindset of the existing regional institutions towards promoting low-carbon growth. Already proven technologies should be transferred to developing countries at concessional rates from the private sector for which the private sector needs to be compensated for the difference between the commercial rate and the concessional rate. In order to implement this process, an important priority is to create specialized regional funds to address key region-specific climate change mitigation needs. Financing at the regional level does not necessarily mean that new structures and institutions be created at the sub-regional level. It will be possible to reform existing financial institutions such as the ADB with a clear focus on regional interests and circumstances.

Development of capacity is needed, particularly in the banking sector, because staff attached to banks and capital markets need to have professional knowledge about SRI investment, carbon trading and carbon tax. Also, capacity building is needed to contribute to R&D in LCGS, to improve the attitudes of consumers, producers and policymakers towards green growth. In this context, what is needed is a virtual university/research institute/secretariat involving selected top university/research institutions in the region to improve capacity building and understanding of green growth across countries in the region. Established regional institutions like ESCAP and ADBI need to play the coordinating role for effective functioning of the proposed regional virtual university/research institute/secretariat.

Many Asian and Pacific countries do not have developed capital markets, therefore financing through capital markets for green industries is limited. Various innovative financial products and services, from private institutions, can be useful in the development in capital markets. In order to motivate strong private sector involvement in low-carbon growth, it is necessary to support the establishment of new and innovative regional private financing mechanisms especially for risk transfer and insurance instruments. For this to occur, regional R&D efforts are necessary through the proposed regional virtual university/research institute/secretariat, and these require regional funding with liberal assistance from countries enjoying large foreign reserves within Asia.

As weak outcomes from the Copenhagen and Cancun meetings over two years made many countries hesitate to pursue strong green growth policy. Nevertheless, the foregoing analysis indicates that green growth issues cannot be handled by any single country effectively, but require considerable cooperation across countries in the region and beyond.

> Developing countries, must bargain for steep GHG emissions reductions by developed countries i.e. 40 percent by 2030 and 80 percent by 2050, compared with the 1990 levels. This commitment will enlarge the sizes of the CDM market and cap and trade systems in developed countries which would raise the carbon price and provide larger financial transfers to developing countries. This commitment would also stimulate RD&D on climate-friendly technologies. The developing countries must also bargain for larger financial transfers and easier access to climate-friendly technologies to developing countries to enable them to switch to low carbon growth path. As tackling climate change also yields co-benefits like improvement in well-being of poor, access to improved sanitation *via* treatment of solid wastes, and access to cleaner energy *via* shift from biomass to commercial energy, and as they have become GPGs by global public choice, they must seek financial support for meeting these Millennium Development Goals. (Sankar, 2009: 62)

References

ADB. 2006. *Carbon Market Initiative: The Asia Pacific Carbon Fund.* Manila, Asian Development Bank.

Anbumozhi, V. 2008. 'Businesses and Environment in India—An Overview in Corporate Environmental Management—Striving Perspectives from Asia', *IGES Kansai Centre Research Report*, Kobe, 21–60.

———. 2010. *Mainstreaming Climate Change Adaptation into Developmental Planning: Opportunities and Challenges for the Asia Pacific.* Tokyo: Asian Development Bank Institute ADBI (mimeo).

Bowen, A. and Kattumuri, R. 2012 'The Transition to Green Growth—Opportunities and Missed Chances', Background Paper presented to the ADB/ADBI Flagship Study Climate Change and Green Asia, Muliya Hotel, Jakarta, 19–20 January.

Gagnon-Lebrun, F. and Agrawala, S. 2006. *Progress on Adaption to Climate Change in Developing Countries: An Analysis of Broad Trends.* Paris: Organization for Economic Co-operation and Development (OECD).

Harvey, F. 2011. 'Budget 2011: Osborne's Green Bank Attacked from All Sides', *The Guardian*, 23 March, available at http://www.guardian.co.uk/environment/2011/mar/23/budget-2011-george-osborne-green-bank (accessed on 16 April 2012).

Hongo, T. 2010. 'Role of Finance for the Low Carbon Economy: Public Private Financial Partnership', Paper presented in the 'Financing Low-Carbon Infrastructure UNEP FI Korea Summit' 16–17 June at the Grand Sheraton Hotel (Walker Hill), Seoul, Republic of Korea.

———. 2011. 'Private Finance for Green Growth', Background Paper presented to the Climate Change & Green Asia: ADBI Study, Asian Development Bank Institute (28 February–1 March), Tokyo, Japan.

International Energy Institute (IEA). 2009. *World Energy Outlook, 2010*. Paris: IEA/OECD.

Kalirajan, K. 2011. 'Regional Cooperation Towards Green Asia: Trade and Investment', ADBI Working Paper No. 350, Asian Development Bank Institute, Tokyo.

Kalirajan, K., Anbumozhi, V., and Singh, K. 2010. 'Measuring the Environmental Impacts of Changing Trade Patterns on the Poor', ADBI Working Paper No. 239, Asian Development Bank Institute, Tokyo.

Kawai, M. 2008. 'Japan–China Cooperation for Achieving Carbon Neutral Society', Economists for Peace and Security Japan, Tokyo.

Kim, J. 2001. 'Public Role in Financing a Low-carbon Economy in Asia', Background Paper presented to the Climate Change & Green Asia: ADBI Study, Asian Development Bank Institute (28 February–1 March), Tokyo, Japan.

Lockhart, R. 2011. 'Low-carbon Technology & Finance', *Climate Change and Green Asia Inception Workshop*, ADBI, Tokyo Japan, 28 February–1 March.

Organization for Economic Co-operation and Development (OECD). 2005. 'Environmental Fiscal Policy Reform for Poverty Reduction', DAC Reference Document, OECD, Paris.

Peters, G.P., Marland, G., Le Quere, C., Boden, T', Candell, J.G. and Raucph, M.R. 2011. 'Rapid Growth in CO_2 Emissions after the 2008—2009 Global Financial Crisis' Opinion & Comment *Nature and Climate Change*, online publication www.nature..com/natureclimate change (accessed on 23 December 2011).

Planning Commission. 2009. *Annual Report 2009–2010*. Planning Commission, Government of India, New Delhi.

———. 2011. 'Low Carbon Strategies for Inclusive Growth: An Interim Report', Planning Commission, Government of India, New Delhi.

Sharan, D. 2008. 'Financing Climate Change Mitigation and Adaptation Role of Regional Financing Arrangements', *ADB Sustainable Development Working Paper Series*. Asian Development Bank Institute, Tokyo.

Sankar, U. 2009. 'Policy Instruments for Achieving Low Carbon and High Economic Growth in India'. Paper presented at the Roundtable on Fiscal and Non-Fiscal Instruments for Sustainable Development of India at the National Institute of Public Finance and Policy, New Delhi, 16 December.

———. 2010. 'India's Low Carbon Inclusive Growth Strategy', Working Paper 56/2010, Madras School of Economics, Chennai.

Thurston, C.W. 2011. 'Time for a Green Bank?', Financial and Legal Affairs, *PV Magazine*, 10: 1–2.

United Nations Environment Program (UNEP). 2009. *Global Trends in Sustainable Energy Investment 2009 Report, Analysis of Trends and Issuers in the Financing Renewable Energy and Energy Efficiency*. Nairobi: UNEP.

United Nations Framework Convention on Climate Change (UNFCCC). 2011. *Benefits of the Clean Development Mechanism*. Bonn: UNFCCC.

———. 2012. *Benefits of the Clean Development Mechanism 2012*, United Nations Framework Convention on Climate Change, United Nations Climate Change Secretariat, Germany.

Van Aalst, M. and Agrawala, S. 2005. 'Analysis of Donor-supported Activities and National Plans', in S. Agrawala (ed.), *Bridge Over Troubled Waters: Linking Climate Change and Development* (pp. 61–84). Paris: OECD.

4

Carbon Intensity and Labour Intensity in India

Brinda Viswanathan and Ishwarya Balasubramanian***

Introduction

Many developing countries face high unemployment rates, under-employment rates, or low wage employment and several other forms of vulnerable employment, which are associated with high poverty rates (ILO, 2009a). They also face severe environmental problems in terms of resource degradation and depletion affecting their livelihoods. Climate change impacts are shown to have a further adverse impact on the lives of poor living in these countries (UNDP, 2008). Though the challenges of providing stable and productive employment remain the key policy goals towards poverty reduction in all developing countries, there is no doubt that concerns of sustainable development are forcing these countries to look for alternative frameworks of development that are hitherto unknown. Options for industrialization and urbanization along the well-treaded pathways that were followed by the currently developed countries seem to no longer exist; both due to limited resources at disposal and also the international pressure to reduce greenhouse gas (GHG) pollution. Countries like India and China,

*Associate Professor, Madras School of Economics, Chennai.
**Research Scholar, IGIDR Mumbai.

owing to their high economic growth rates and large populations, are increasingly contributing to the overall green-house gas emissions. Nevertheless, this economic growth has given ample scope for employment generation and poverty reduction, and even small improvements in the living standards makes a dent in the number of absolute poor in these regions.

Given this backdrop, economic growth has to take place allowing for inclusive growth which is also environmentally sustainable; that is, both intra- and inter-generational equity needs to be addressed effectively. However, diverting funds for investments in reducing carbon dependency alone as is being done by developed countries would come in conflict with achieving other goals of development. Especially, there is a wide belief that reducing carbon intensity may have adverse impacts on employment. Clearly, the policy framework, institutional arrangement, investment strategies and technological regimes are all gearing up towards reducing carbon dependency of the economy so as to green the economy while also attempting to increase the adaptive capacity of the economy which would not only lead to improving employment and living standards but also to avoid harsher impacts of climate change.[1]

Few years back, countries like India put in place missions that would lead to low-carbon, high-growth economy, that is, reducing GHG emissions without affecting the economic activities. But thanks to the intervention from several quarters, most importantly from UNEP, there has been a turnaround rather recently to address social dimensions while addressing the goal of sustainable development. What is, however, not yet clearly spelt out in these documents are which sectors will be focused upon on a higher priority that could lead to employment generation and can improve productivity while also reduce carbon emission.

This study discusses the opportunities that some sectors of the economy have in terms of its high growth potential in generating

[1] Ministry of Environment and Forest initiated a Dialogue on Green Economy and Inclusive Growth in October 2011 prior to the Rio+20 summit (http://envfor.nic.in/modules/others/?f=dmd). For a more recent study on this aspect, see Kumar et al. (2012).

employment and value addition and simultaneously improving the environmental quality possibly at a lower cost.

Objective and Scope

The focus of this study is on the intersection of environment and employment concerns. If employment and environment policies have common elements, aligning them would reduce costs and welfare losses. There are several instances in developed countries where green investments undertaken to mitigate climate change have led to the creation of gainful employment known as 'low-carbon' jobs. Developing countries like India need not mimic the West in creating 'low-carbon' jobs (jobs that are created as a result of greening activities) and instead focus on creating more jobs for the growing workforce, which might have opportunities to be green. In other words, developing countries need to create decent employment that could address environment problems *also*. This is in contrast to developed countries where low-carbon jobs are created *in the process of* undertaking mitigation activities.

A second aspect of employment creation that poses a challenge in developing countries is that these could be under harsher working conditions including weak forms of labour contract. The tenuous arrangements in the labour market leave them exposed to (relative) poverty though abject (absolute) poverty may be reduced. Hence, we argue that creation of employment in labour-intensive sectors that is *clean* both from the perspective of working conditions and environmental quality should ideally qualify as *green* jobs in the context of developing countries like India. Country-level experiences show that countries with similar level of economic growth differ in employment intensity due to variations in how the production process takes place. There are also instances when employment intensity could be high but output growth could be very modest leading to low labour productivity growth thereby increasing the working poor (Kapsos, 2005). Thus employment intensity improves if there is both a higher share of employed in the total output and also a higher share of wages in the total output.[2]

In this context, the objective of this study is to assess the empirical evidence for India on the linkages between carbon intensity and labour intensity at the regional and sectoral levels. Employment intensity is defined as the employed workforce to total value added as measured by the domestic product while labour intensity is defined as the share of total wages in the value added. Carbon intensity is taken as the share of CO_2 equivalent emissions generated during the process of producing the goods and services. In this context, this study tries to assess the scope for intersection of employment and environment policies. Another way to look at this would be to understand if there is a positive relationship between employment creation and carbon reduction, which could be exploited for green and inclusive growth.

Carbon Intensity

Before the 2009 COP summit in Copenhagen, the then environment minister of India announced at the Indian Parliament the decision to cut India's carbon intensity by 20–25 per cent below 2005 levels by 2020.[3] Since then an 'unheard' term, 'carbon intensity'—CO_2 equivalent of emissions per unit of gross domestic product (GDP)—has become the buzzword in India's approach towards environmental concerns. In the following sections, we take a look at definitions of carbon intensity and labour intensity prevailing in the literature and the evidence so far on the linkages between the two.

Carbon intensity is widely talked about, most often synonymously with emissions intensity because of the over-riding contribution of energy-related CO_2 emissions in total GHG emissions.

[2] There may be some sub-sectors of economic activity where there could be a trade-off between wage growth and employment growth but for overall for the country as whole employment and productivity should grow.

[3] See http://www.thehindu.com/news/national/jairam-ramesh-2025-pc-carbon-emission-intensity-cut-by-2020/article59592.ece (accessed September 2015).

Emissions (carbon) intensity is defined as emissions (CO_2 emissions) per unit of GDP. Figure 4.1a shows that for the world as a whole, carbon intensity has been rather stable, with OECD countries showing a decline from its lower values while non-OECD countries show a marginal increase since 1980, there is a decline in the decade of 1990s and it has been stable since then. Segregating across broad regions of the world (Figure 4.1b), Middle East and Asia–Oceania regions have increased the carbon intensity from their already high levels while North America and Europe show a decline though Europe has always been lower than North America. Taking the end points of the periods, Africa and Central and South America have been stable with the latter now ranked above North America though they had initially been below this region.

Focussing on the BRIC nations (Figure 4.1c), we note that all these nations except Brazil have carbon intensity values above the world's average. China and Russia show decline in carbon intensity recently while India and South Africa show an increase in the mid-1990s but have gone back to their old levels in the 2000s. Finally, we take a look at a few selected states of India (Figure 4.1d) for changes in carbon intensity. The data on CO_2 emissions are obtained from Ghoshal and Bhattacharyya (2008) and the state GDP estimates are at 1980–81 prices obtained from the Central Statistical Organisation, Government of India. The data on carbon emissions are available only up to 2,000 so the emission intensity is also estimated up to that time period. As it can be noted, the units of measurement are different for Indian states so that values of carbon intensity cannot be directly compared with country-level data. States of India have different rates of GDP growth and also the share of different sectors vary across regions and also their changes. For example, Punjab is among the states of India with largest share of agricultural GDP while Gujarat has high share of industry and Tamil Nadu has high share of services. States like Uttar Pradesh and West Bengal are among the populous states and Gujarat is among the fastest growing states of India. Though at the all-India level, the carbon intensity has more or less remained stable during this period, Gujarat and to some extent West Bengal show a decline while it increases substantially for Uttar Pradesh.

Figure 4.1:
Carbon intensity across world regions, countries and states of India

4.1a: World, OECD and Non-OECD

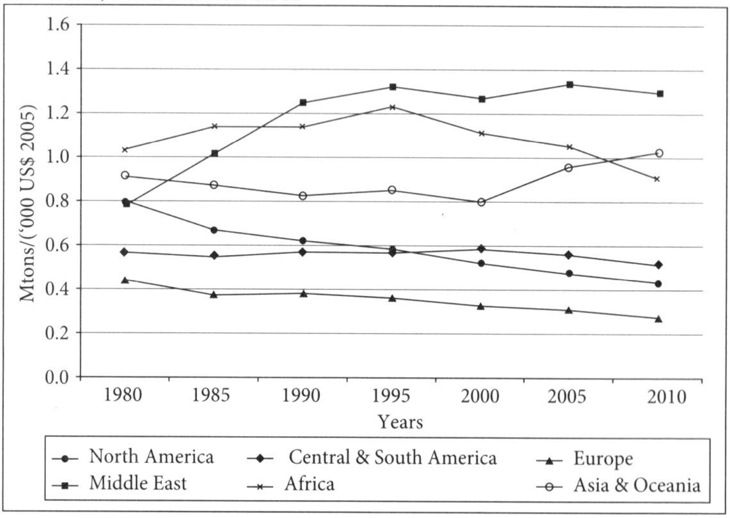

4.1b: Regions of the World

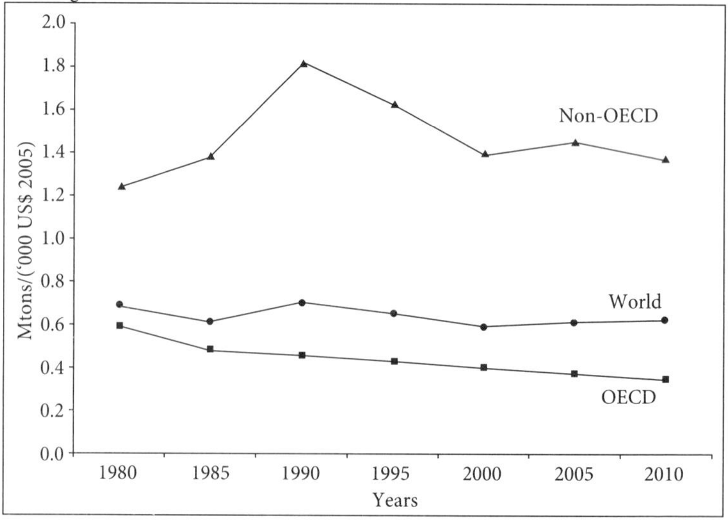

4.1c: BRICS Nations and World as a Whole

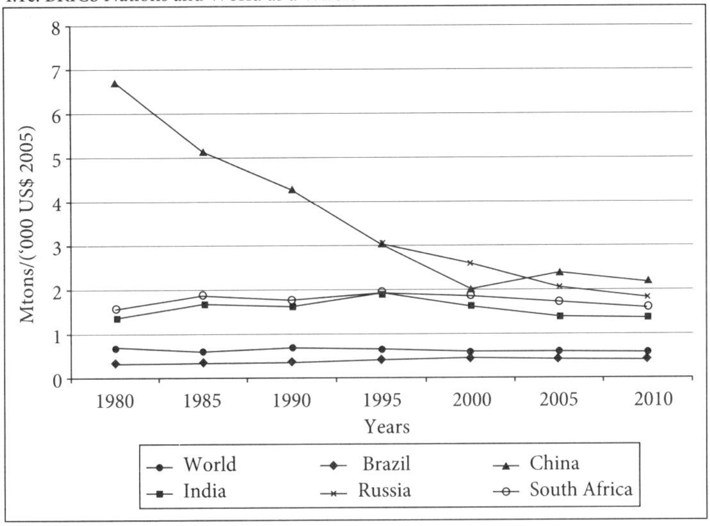

4.1d: Select States of India and All-India

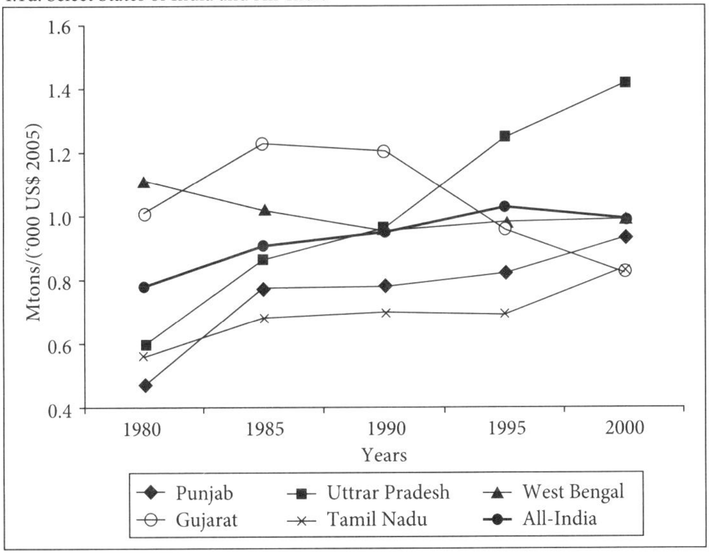

Sources: For country-level data, carbon intensity estimates are directly from EIA. For state-level estimates in India, carbon intensity ratios are authors' own calculations based on carbon emissions from Ghoshal and Bhattacharyya (2008) and State Domestic Product estimates are at 1980–81 constant prices.

A more detailed analysis of carbon intensity across Indian states is available in Giri (2010). However, more research studies have to be carried out to appropriately estimate the carbon emissions across sectors for each of the states to assess the changes and variations in carbon intensity. For instance, the carbon emissions in Ghoshal and Bhattacharya (2008) are estimated on the basis of the production activities in that region. Though this may be appropriate for economic activities in many sectors but exceptions are important to consider. In economic activities like electricity production, the consumption may take place in other states purchased from the producing state and therefore the emission estimates should be adjusted to account for this.

Though estimating emissions at regionally disaggregated levels within countries for global pollutants like carbon emissions may be considered problematic, it is nevertheless useful to monitor greener economic growth at the regional and sectoral level. Presence of such an information base would enable framing policies for production and consumption pathways that would realign to reduce the rate of growth of carbon intensity. This would have lower carbon emissions than the conventional process of growth. More importantly, this framework does not seem to emphasize on sustainable development that aligns itself to the goals of (i) ecological conservation focusing on inter-generational equity and (ii) social justice focusing on intra-generational equity. Recently with the notion of green economy being brought in limelight since UNEP's report on wide-ranging sectors of the economy, productive employment generation in both developed and developing countries as well as poverty reduction and improving living standards have drawn the attention of the policymakers in India (UNEP, 2011).

Employment/Labour Intensity

Employment intensity is the ratio of employed to the total output or value added (GDP) where the employed would be the number of working population in a particular sector. Another approach to measure employment intensity would be to capture it through employment elasticity, that is, for a relative change in GDP what would be the relative change in the number employed (Kapsos, 2005; Rangarajan, 2006; Rangarajan et al., 2007; Sundaram, 2007). In comparison to this, labour intensity is defined as the proportion of labour input measured in the total input cost required to produce the goods and services. However, there may be practical difficulties of measuring inputs, which will have different units and the common practice is to convert them in monetary unit.

In this sense, labour intensity would also capture the productivity aspect of this important input. In these studies, labour is measured commonly in terms of the wages and salaries (rent that accrues to them) while the ratio that measures labour intensity has varying numeraires (denominator) like value added, or total output in that sector, sales or investment and others. Rajan and Subramanian (2005) and Kochhar et al. (2006) identify the most labour-intensive industries on the basis of the average (across countries) of the share of labour compensation to value added in each industry. They further define a measure of concentration of labour-intensive industries for each country as the ratio of the total value added by above-median labour-intensity industries to the total value added by below-median labour-intensity industries. Loayza and Raddatz (2009) use labour intensity at a sectoral level where they define it as the difference between labour share in total employment and its share in total output. Narayanan and Sahu (2010) use ratio of wages and salaries to sales to measure labour intensity across different firms in the paper and pulp industry of India. An exception to this definition of labour intensity is Gokarn and Gulati (2006) who use number of workers per crore rupees of invested capital as a measure of labour intensity.

Employment intensity faces a greater risk of not taking into consideration the productivity aspect while labour intensity can more often capture both the number employed as well as the remuneration that accrues to the workers. To highlight the differentiation between the two, both the agricultural sector and health sector are labour-intensive while agriculture sector is more employment-intensive but with lower labour productivity.

Thus, highly employment intense sectors may be low on productivity while highly labour-intensive sectors could be employment intense as well as have a higher labour productivity. The success of East Asian countries was largely due to increased employment in manufacturing sector with higher wages compared to the earnings in the agricultural sector.

To understand the variations in employment elasticity across different sectors in India, we use the information provided by the Task Force on Employment by the Planning Commission in the decades of 1970s, 1980s and 1990s in Table 4.1.

Table 4.1:
Sectoral employment elasticity in India

		Estimated Elasticities		
S. No.	*Sector*	*1977–78 to 1983*	*1983 to 1993–94*	*1993–94 to 1999–2000*
1.	Agriculture	0.45	0.50	0.00
2.	Mining and quarrying	0.80	0.69	0.00
3.	Manufacturing	0.67	0.33	0.26
4.	Electricity	0.73	0.52	0.00
5.	Construction	1.00	1.00	1.00
6.	Wholesale and retail trade	0.78	0.63	0.55
7.	Transport, storage and construction	1.00	0.49	0.69
8.	Finance, real estate and business services	1.00	0.92	0.73
9.	Community, social and personal services	0.83	0.50	0.07
All sectors		0.53	0.41	0.15

Source: Report of Task Force on Employment Opportunities, Planning Commission, GOI (2001: 46).

Table 4.1 shows the employment elasticities of various sectors during three time periods. If employment elasticity is low, it could be good or bad depending on whether productivity has increased or employment has saturated. It can be seen that the employment elasticity of agriculture, mining and electricity is zero implying that there is no more potential for employment in these sectors.[4]

[4] With programmes like NREGS that create assets in rural areas to improve productivity, there is scope for changing this. NREGS in this sense creates green jobs.

However, the employment elasticity of construction and service sectors such as transport and finance are high and hence has significant employment potential. Sectors such as buildings and transport have significant potential in the direction of a low-carbon economy. For a low-carbon inclusive growth, the sectors that have a high employment potential and a high mitigation potential should be targeted for immediate results.

Using ASI data and the definitions of labour intensity as defined previously (ratio of wages to GVA, number of workers per rupee crore of invested capital), labour-intensive industries were identified as those that had a labour intensity above the median (for the year 2001–02) as per both or either one definition. There has been a declining trend in labour intensity over the years (from 1973–74 to 2003–04) though the rate of decline has been different across the sectors. This declining trend in labour intensity has been observed for both labour-intensive industries and capital-intensive industries as shown in Figures 4.2a and 4.2b.

Linking Carbon Intensity with Labour Intensity

The effect of a shift to a less carbon-intensive growth on employment is complex and hence is not very clear. ILO estimates that about 38 per cent of workers in the world are employed in high carbon-intensive sectors, which are about 600 million workers (ILO, 2009b). These are the section of workers who will be affected in the process of transition to a low-carbon economy in terms of job losses or having to acquire different skills in order to adjust to a transformed job. The employment effect varies in the short, medium and long term. As Fankhauser et al. (2008) argue a move to low-carbon sectors in the short run will lead to some displaced jobs in the high-carbon sectors and some additional and transformed jobs in the low-carbon sectors, but there will be net job creation as these sectors tend to be labour-intensive at least until efficiency gains are fully exploited. In the medium term, the effect is more difficult to assess as the change in production patterns alters the

Figure 4.2a:
Trend in labour intensity in labour-intensive industries

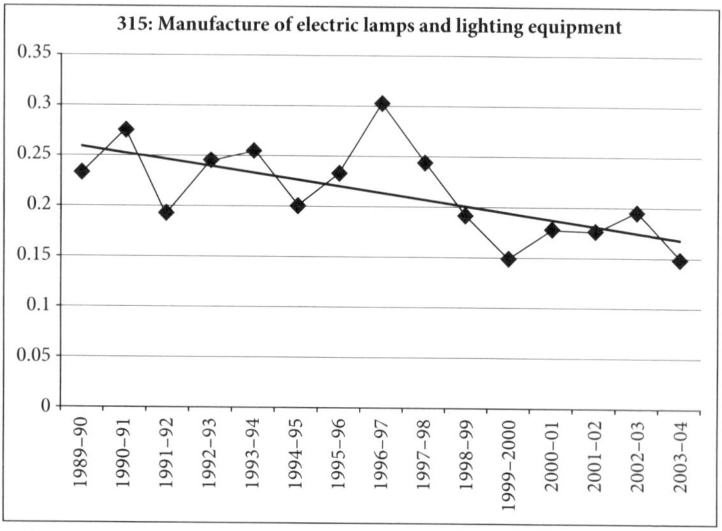

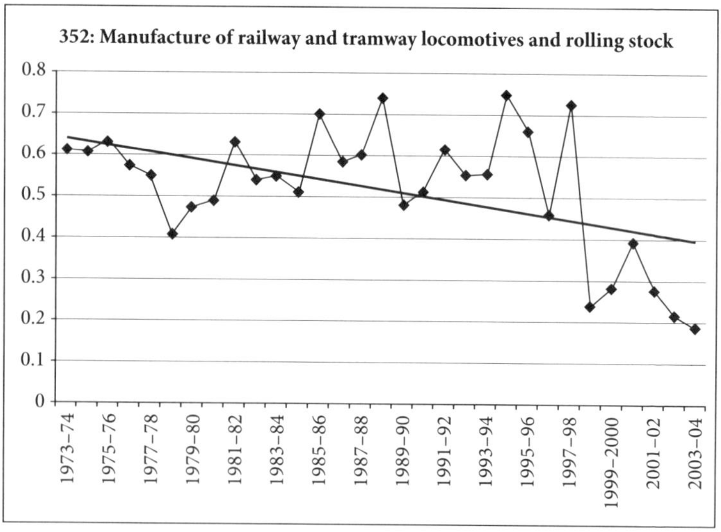

Figure 4.2b:
Trend in labour intensity in capital-intensive industries

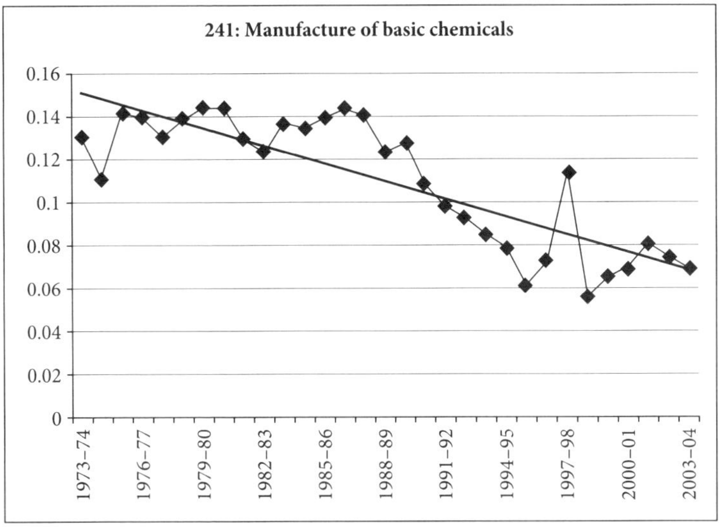

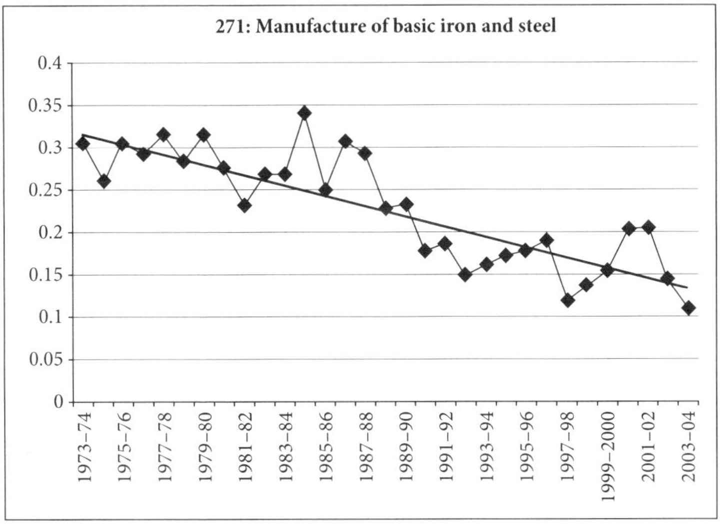

Source: Authors' calculations based on data from Annual Survey of Industries (various years).

entire value chain. It is claimed that the long run effect will be a change in structural pattern in favour of a low-carbon economy, which is generally associated with growth, innovation and huge employment gains.

The reverse linkage: the effect of higher employment intensity on carbon intensity is also not widely discussed in the literature. An employment-intensive economy is likely to have low-carbon intensity mainly because it would use less of other inputs, most important among these would be capital and energy and hence less carbon dependent. Nonetheless, there seems to have been no systematic effort to support this claim or otherwise. Among the few studies that focus on limited sectors (48 industrial sectors) and few (32) countries Douglas and Nishioka (2009) show inverse U-shaped relationship between capital intensity (as measured by the ratio of capital to labour) and emissions intensity for the year 2000. The intention of their study was not to focus on labour or employment intensity but whether production technique or specialization matters in explaining international differences in emission intensity. In a more recent study based on Indian manufacturing industries, Sahu and Narayanan (2013) find that firms that are more labour-intensive have lower CO_2 intensity (after controlling for energy intensity and capital intensity). However, the magnitude of the impact is only marginally higher than that of firms that are capital-intensive.

Until recently even efforts by UNEP were largely focused towards creation of green jobs but the recession in the developed world and in its impact on some parts of the developing world directed the focus towards green jobs that are productive and provide long-term stability. This paved the way for developing countries like India to take a look at the double benefits even though they were not affected that severely by the global recession but for whom vulnerable employment, poverty and environmental degradation are important aspects of the growth story. There exists ample scope for intersection of environment and employment policies provided adequate regulatory measures and management practices are aimed at increasing labour intensity alongside a decline in carbon intensity. Figure 4.3 shows how low-carbon

Figure 4.3:
Pathway to a low-carbon economy with higher labour intensity

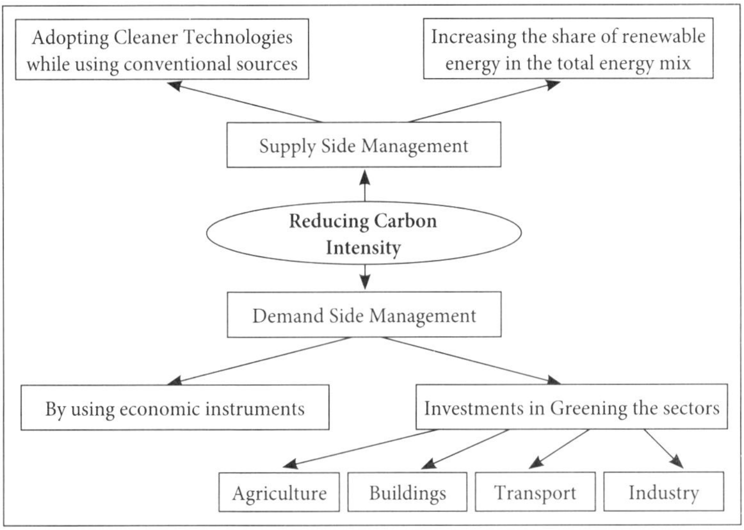

Source: Authors' own framework.

growth in both demand side and supply side managements have to be considered for a low carbon growth. The supply side aspect deals with cleaner inputs primarily in the form of right energy mix while technologies to achieve this are also a key to this transformation. The demand side management involves economic instruments that will induce or keep in place practices and use of products that have lower carbon content.

In order to assess the relationship between labour intensity and carbon intensity, we use data from UNIDO's statistical country briefs to measure labour intensity across countries[5] while carbon intensity (defined as CO_2 emissions per unit of GDP) across countries is available from WRI/CAIT database. Figure 4.4 shows that

[5] We used share of wages in value added for the manufacturing sector as a measure of labour intensity across countries. Data availability on wages across countries adjusted to PPP has been rather difficult. Also as focussing on manufacturing sector is useful as that sector is usually the driving force for development as was observed in the case of East Asian growth, it can employ large numbers of people and with adequate domestic and foreign demand for such goods, the wages accruing to workers is also good.

Figure 4.4:
Labour intensity and carbon intensity

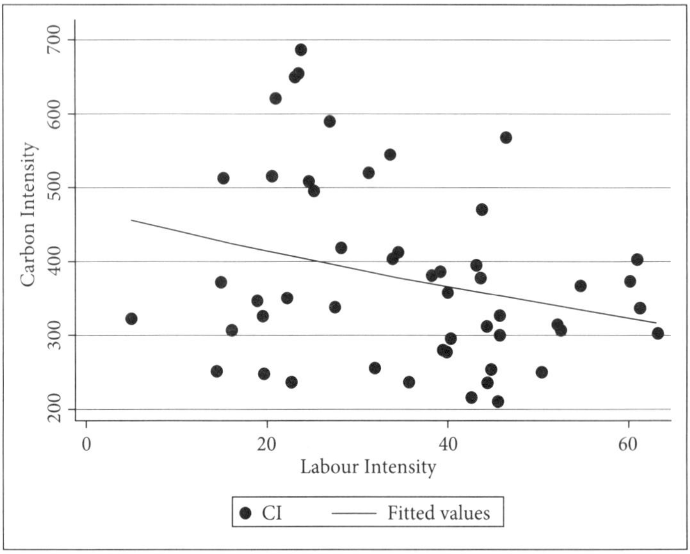

Source: Authors' calculations based on data from UNIDO and WRI (CAIT, 2009).

there is a negative relationship between carbon intensity and labour intensity across countries.

For the Indian context, labour intensity is estimated as number of people employed per unit of GDP for a panel of 19 states and three years—1993–94, 1999–2000 and 2005–06 (NSS 50th round, 55th round and 62nd round, respectively). The reports provide data on state-wise distribution of usually employed persons (in principal as well as subsidiary status) per 1000 persons under four categories: rural male, rural female, urban male and urban female. This is the work force participation rate (WFPR). A state-wise estimate of the number of employed is obtained by multiplying WFPR by the respective state's population. Data for population for the years 1993 and 1999 are obtained by interpolating population between the two census years 1991 and 2001. For the year 2005, projected population given by the census as on 1 March 2006 is used. NSS reports provide state-wise per 1,000 distribution usually employed by broad industry division. This ratio is multiplied by the estimated number of employed to get an estimate of industry-wise employment for each state. State-wise and sector-wise GDP for all the years are taken from EPW statistics. GDP is measured at constant 1993–94 prices. Labour intensity is estimated based on the NSSO data, and the data on emissions intensity is from Ghoshal and Bhattacharyya (2008). We observe the pattern of the relationship between these two variables as shown in Figure 4.5.

Figure 4.5:
Emissions intensity and labour intensity, states of India

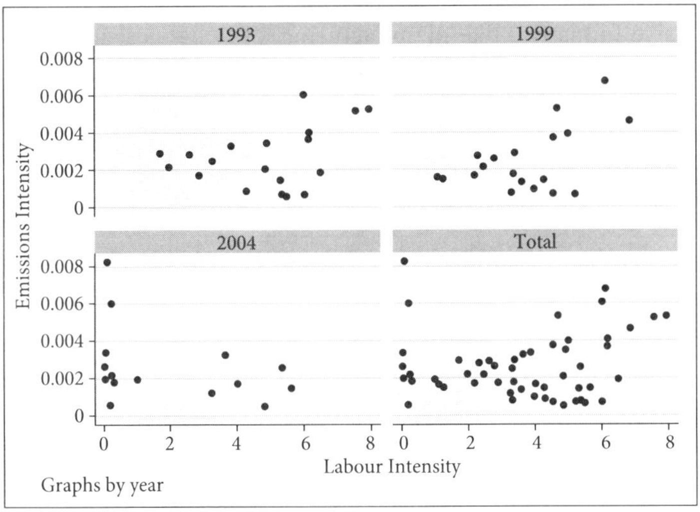

Source: Author's calculations based on data from NSSO (various years) and Ghoshal and Bhattacharyya (2008).

The relationship between emissions intensity and labour intensity is not very strong but there are measurement problems and one should consider this somewhat indicative. For the years 1993 and 1999, there is a non-linear relationship where for medium levels of labour intensity, the carbon intensity is also low. For fairly large levels of labour intensity, emissions intensity is rather high compared to that at lower levels of labour intensity. The picture for the combined years (if considered appropriate to do so) shows that there is some potential at the middle levels of labour intensity to reduce emissions intensity. At very high levels of emissions intensity are states like Bihar and Madhya Pradesh due to the presence of thermal based electricity generation, but being states with high poverty levels, the wage rates are lower and hence the labour intensity is also very low. As mentioned earlier, the emissions have to be adjusted to the electricity consuming states rather than the electricity producing states.

Focussing only on sectors that are energy-intensive, we note that the relationship is somewhat non-linear (for the combined years) as shown in Figure 4.6a. Using the data from select emission-intensive industries like manufacturing and chemical industries based on the data from Annual Survey of industries (Figure 4.6b),

Figure 4.6:
Emissions intensity for the industrial sector

Figure 4.6a: Secondary Sector (using NSSO data for labour intensity)[6]

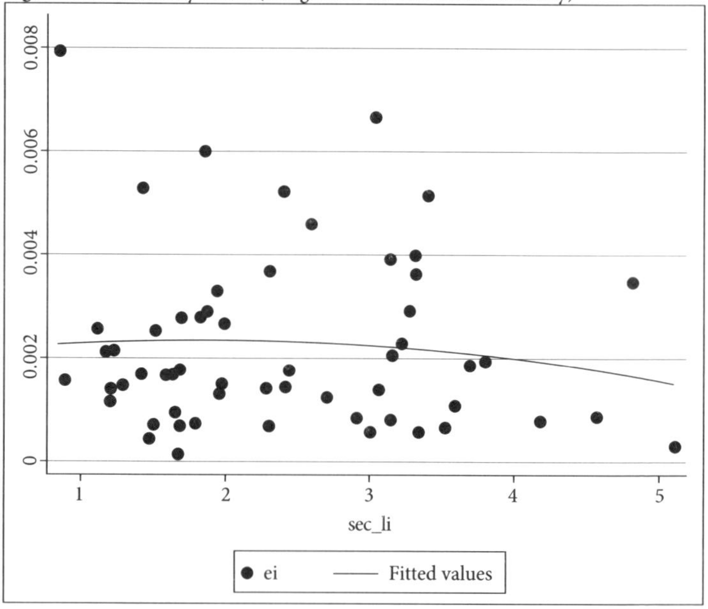

[6] Figure 4.6a uses the NSSO data for labour intensity across states for the years, 1993, 1999–2000 and 2004–05. Figure 4.6b uses the estimates for labour intensity based on industrial Sector data from Annual Survey of Industries across states.

Figure 4.6b: Industrial Sector (Using ASI data for labour intensity)

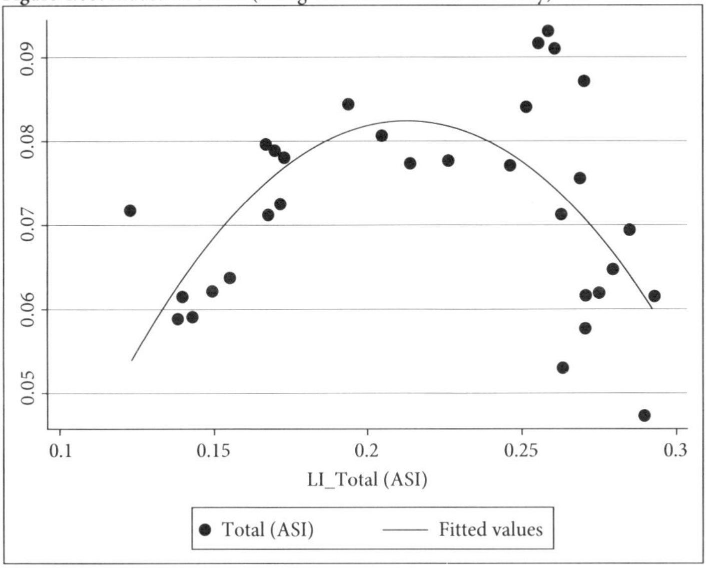

the relationship is explicitly inverted U shaped with states in the middle level of labour intensity showing far higher levels of emissions intensity.

Thus, the overall picture that emerges from this is very mixed. The data issues both in assessing labour intensity and emissions intensity abounds. This study shows results that are indicative of the kind of relationship that one can expect between carbon intensity and labour intensity.

Conclusions

The study has made an attempt to gather empirical evidence on the relationship between emissions intensity and employment and/or labour intensity for India. This study has shown that there is inadequate information to generate the required data at the regional (states) level or at the sectoral (across different economic activities) level. The challenges for measuring employment intensity arise from large informal sector in urban areas as well as the presence of underemployment. Further measuring labour intensity from the NSSO data has a major lacuna as income from self-employment is not available and hence a large segment of the employed are not accounted for. Annual survey of industries provides data on wages across industries but there is no measure of quality of labour force that is an indication of variation in skill levels across industries or across firms within industries and hence poses a limitation to assessing changes in labour intensity across time and its variations across states.

As discussed earlier, measures of carbon intensity have to be improved so that a better comparison across states and over time is possible. There has been very limited effort by the government in this direction. One hopes that this study has been able to highlight this aspect and stresses the fact that a high-quality information base is essential to state's role in policy intervention and regulation. To have a low-carbon growth that is inclusive, focusing both on sustainable development in the long run and reducing regional inequality and poverty in the short run, a minimum requirement is a good database.

With the onset of economic reforms in India, one had anticipated that there would be more flexibility in hiring labour and hence there would be a large employment generation. Recent studies show that there has been no job creation in labour-intensive manufacturing industries (Das and Kalita, 2009; Sen and Das, 2014). On the other hand, India has also seen services-led growth, which is known for being less energy-intensive and hence carbon-intensive. However, the services sector that grew at a faster rate generated employment mainly for the skilled and thereby the less skilled seemed to have not benefitted at all (Ramaswamy and Agarwal, 2012). As Bhandari and Heshmati (2005) highlight that loosening of labour market regulations seems to have positively influenced job creation only to a limited extent and that also reduced economic security in terms of labour contracts. In this sense, the step forward for India is more challenging to balance the two features of creating more and secure employment and address the concerns of local and global environmental pollution that the labour-intensive industries like manufacturing pose compared to the services sector.

In this sense, India has to develop its strategy of 'Make in India'[7] with the goal of sustainable development in the true sense of taking care of the needs of current as well as future generations. Green investments in developed countries that have been undertaken to mitigate climate change have led to the creation of gainful employment dubbed as 'low-carbon' jobs. Developing countries like India do not need to mimic the West in creating 'low-carbon' jobs (jobs that are created as a result of greening activities); rather, the need of the hour is to create more jobs for the growing workforce, which might have opportunities to be green. In other words, developing countries need to create green jobs that address environment problems in contrast to developed countries where low-carbon jobs are created when addressing the environment. Against this background, there is interest now in the intersection of environment and employment policies. The new strategy of 'Make in India' though focuses on the manufacturing industry but there seems to be less attention to green investment for a secure future. The measures taken to achieve more employment, if designed carefully, could also reduce the carbon footprint of the country and build the resilience of the economy to climate-related shocks.

References

Bhandari, A.K. and Heshmati, A. 2005. 'Labour Use and Its Adjustment in Manufacturing Industries', MTT Discussion Paper, 4, Finland.

Climate Analysis Indicators Tool Version 7.0 (CAIT). 2009. *World Resources Institute*. Washington, DC, http://cait.wri.org/historical (accessed 10 February 2012).

Das, K.D. and Kalita, G. 2009. 'Do Labour Intensive Industries Generate Employment? Evidence from firm Level Survey in India', Working Paper No. 237, ICRIER, New Delhi.

Douglas, S. and Nishioka, S. 2012. 'International Differences in Emissions Intensity and Emissions Content of Global Trade', *Journal of Development Economics*, 99(2): 415–27.

Fankhauser, S., Sehlleier, F., and Stern, N. 2008. 'Climate Change, Innovation and Jobs', *Climate Policy*, 8: 421–429.

[7] http://www.narendramodi.in/pm-launches-make-in-india-global-initiative/ (accessed September 2015).

Ghoshal, T. and Bhattacharyya, R. 2008. 'State Level Carbon Dioxide Emissions of India: 1980–2000', *Contemporary Issues and Ideas in Social Sciences*, 4(1). http://journal.ciiss.net/index.php/ciiss/article/viewFile/60/54 (accessed on 11 March 2013).

Giri, N. 2010. '*Variation In Carbon Intensity Across States Of India: An Empirical Assessment*', Unpublished master's thesis, Madras School of Economics, Chennai.

GOI. 2001. *Report of Task Force on Employment Opportunities*. New Delhi: Planning Commission, Government of India.

Gokarn, S. and Gulati, G. 2006. *India: Country Growth Analysis*. Asian Development Bank Monograph. Available at http://www2.adb.org/Documents/Assessments/Economic/IND/Economic-Assessment.pdf (accessed on 15 June 2010).

International Labour Organisation (ILO). 2009a. *Global Employment Trends Reports 2009*. Available at http://www.ilo.org/wcmsp5/groups/public/---dgreports/---dcomm/documents/publication/wcms_101461.pdf (accessed 14 March 2012).

ILO and International Institute for Labour Studies. 2009b. 'Green Policies and Jobs: A Double Dividend?' *World of Work Report 2009: The Global Jobs Crisis and Beyond*, International Labour Organisation, Geneva.

Kapsos, S. 2005. 'The Employment Intensity of Growth: Trends and Macroeconomic Determinants', *ILO Employment Strategy Paper 2005/12*, Available at http://www.ilo.org/wcmsp5/groups/public/---ed_emp/---emp_elm/documents/publication/wcms_143163.pdf (accessed on 22 March 2012).

Kochhar, K., Kumar, U., Raghuram, R., Subramanian, A., and Tokatlidis, I. 2006. 'India's Pattern of Development: What Happened, What Follows?', IMF Working Paper WP/06/22, International Monetary Fund, Washington D.C.

Kumar, K.S.K., Sengupta, R., Saleth, M., Ashok, K.R., and Balasubramanian, R. 2012. 'Green Economy—Indian Perspective', *MSE Monograph 23/2012*, Madras School of Economics, Chennai.

Loayza, N.V. and Raddatz, C. 2010. 'The Composition of Growth Matters for Poverty Alleviation', *Journal of Development Economics*, 93(1): 137–51.

Narayanan, K. and Sahu, S.K. 2010. 'Labour and Energy Intensity: A Study of Pulp & Paper Industries in India', Paper presented at the Joint Annual International Conference of IASSI & Knowledge Forum on 'Science, Technology and Economy: Human Capital and Development', IIT Bombay.

Sahu, S.K. and Narayanan, K. 2013. 'Carbon Dioxide Emissions from Indian Manufacturing Industries: Role of Energy and Technology Intensity', MSE Working Paper No. 82/2013, Madras School of Economics Chennai.

Rajan, R.G. and Subramanian, A. 2005. 'What Undermines Aid's Impact on Growth?', IMF Working Paper WP/05/126, International Monetary Fund, Washington D.C.

Ramaswamy, K.V. and Agarwal, T. 2012. 'Services-led Growth, Employment Job Quality: A Study of Manufacturing and Services Sector in India', Working Paper-2002-007, IGIDR, Mumbai.

Rangarajan, C. 2006. *Employment and Growth*. Madras School of Economics, Monograph 2/2006.

Rangarajan, C., Iyer, P. and Kaul, S. 2007. 'Revisiting Employment and Growth', *ICRA Bulletin: Money and Finance*. Available at http://eac.gov.in/aboutus/chspe/art_revisit.pdf (accessed on 5 January 2012).

Sen, K. and Das, D.K. 2014. 'Where Have the Workers Gone? The Puzzle of Declining Labour Intensity in Organised Indian Manufacturing', DEPP Working Paper No. 36, IDPM, University of Manchester, Manchester, UK.

Sundaram, K. 2007. 'Employment and Poverty in India: 2000-2005', Working Paper 155, Centre for Development Economics, Delhi School of Economics, Delhi.

UNDP. 2008. 'Human Development Report, 2007/8: Fighting Climate Change—Human Solidarity in a Divided World', United Nations Development Programme, New York.

UNEP. 2011. 'Green Economy Report: Towards a Green Economy: Pathways to Sustainable Development and Poverty Eradication', United Nations Environment Programme, Geneva.

World Resources Institute. 2009. 'Climate Analysis Indicators Tool Version 7.0 (CAIT)'. *World Resources Institute*, Washington, D.C.

5

Natural Solutions to Environmental Issues: The Case of the Textile Sector

*Badri Narayanan G.**

Introduction: Background and Motivation

Environmental hazards associated with industrial activities have been predominant for the past few centuries all over the world. Before the advent of the industrial revolution, such hazards were almost unheard of. Most products were made from organic and natural inputs, causing little or no pollution. Today, pollution has become so rampant that the health of millions of people is at risk due to polluted water, air and land. Several modern techniques to control pollution have often resulted in process improvements, but quite a few of them are costly and some of them even cause new unanticipated problems.[1] Therefore, it is high time that industrialists and academicians alike consider natural solutions from the ancient and medieval world, in order to reduce pollution in a cost-effective way. The textile sector is a suitable example in this regard, since it had evolved and matured thousands of years ago, but has been facing pollution issues in countries like India today.

*Research Economist, Center for Global Trade Analysis, Purdue University, USA. E-mail: badri@purdue.edu

[1] For example, the process of effluent treatment does address the problem of toxicity in water, but it results in accumulation of sludge, which can cause land degradation.

Historically, natural dyes were used to colour clothing or other textiles, and by the mid-1800s chemists began producing synthetic substitutes for them. By the early part of this century only a small percentage of textile dyes were extracted from plants. Lately, there has been an increasing interest in natural dyes, as the public has become aware of ecological and environmental problems related to the use of synthetic dyes. The use of natural dyes cuts down significantly on the amount of toxic effluent resulting from the synthetic dye process.

Natural dyes generally require a mordant, which are metallic salts of aluminium, iron, chromium, copper and others, used for ensuring the reasonable fastness of the colour to sunlight and washing. Customers who have become accustomed to the dazzling colours and fastness of synthetic dyes are hard to convince, as only a few of the natural dyes have good all-round fastness. Most of the natural dyes produce comparatively dull shades. But there are chemicals and methods available now, which can enhance the colour and fastness of the natural dyes. This raises the question of whether the natural dyes reduce emissions or not, since some additional inorganic chemicals are required for them.

The objectives of this study are to analyse the environmental emissions that could be reduced by the introduction of natural dyes in the Indian textile Industry. Also by the year 2020 under various scenarios, to prioritize the dyes for different fibres based on their emission levels, costs and fastness, and to propose some policy implications for emission reduction using the natural dyes in the Indian textile dyeing sector. In this study, the following sectors and dyes have been chosen for analysis of emissions.

Sectors: Natural fibres: Cotton, Wool and Silk
Synthetic fibres: Polyester and Nylon

Dyes: Natural dyes: Fenugreek, Golden Dock, Gallnut, Dolu, Gum Arabic, Indigo, Shellac, Kamala, Madder and Pomegranate
Synthetic dyes: Acid dyes, reactive dyes, sulphur dyes, azo dyes, disperse dyes and direct dyes

To verify the claim that natural dyes reduce pollution in textile-processing industries, a multi-scenario analysis of adaptation of natural dyes has been done for the period up to 2020, under different rates of adaptation to natural dyes in different sub-sectors. The overall results confirm that by 2020 natural dyes will cause significant reductions in the total dissolved solids (TDS). Based on the Analytical Hierarchical Programming (AHP) analysis to rank dyes, natural dyes were found to be better than other dyes in many cases, though there were quite a few cases in which synthetic dyes were better. Encouragement of research in the application of natural dyes, especially on synthetic fibres, implementation of better emission standards, and planning for adaptation of natural dyes at an optimal pace are the policy implications.

Literature Review

A wide range of literature is available in the context of various technological research and developments taking place in the field of natural dyes. But very few published papers are available in the area of emission analysis of the dyes as a whole. There has been no significant work done to compare emission levels due to natural dyes and those due to synthetic dyes.

Pophalia et al. (2003) analysed the emission levels of synthetic dyes in India to compare them with those resulting from the application of Collective Effluents Treatment Plant (CETP) technology in the dyeing houses. These data were useful in checking whether the theoretically calculated emission levels of different dyes lie within the practical range. The source of data for the dyeing procedures for different natural dyes was www.alpsind.com, which is noted throughout this chapter using their trademark name of Alps Industries, Ghaziabad. Many other websites cited in the reference list have been useful for the data regarding the dyeing procedures of synthetic dyes, production figures and the standards of emission levels.

Bechtold et al. (2003) discuss the various merits and demerits of natural dyes in the current industrial situations in a technical manner. Dheeraj et al. (2003) have tested the eco-friendliness of natural dyes using the values of effluent concentrations obtained from informal sector-dyers in Rajasthan. Agarwal et al. (2003) have analysed the compatibility of natural dyes to the modern dyeing houses. Holme (2003) have listed the recent developments in the textile dyes, in which some facts and figures about natural dyes sound significant. Rubeena et al. (2002) have analysed the bio-chemical features of the natural dye effluents such as toxicity and their bio-degradability. Patra et al. (2002) have studied the performance of some natural dyes on cotton fabrics in terms of fastness and depth. Teli et al. (2000) have given an overall account of natural dyes—their classification, technology and future prospects. Paul et al. (1996) have described the extraction and application of various natural dyes on different fibres.

Nousiainen (1997) has provided a detailed explanation of natural dyes. According to this author, environmental awareness is setting tough demands for textile dyeing technology, and at the same time keen competition in the world of fashion textiles requires quick responses, quality and low production costs. Demand is increasing for eco-textiles, certified with various official labels defining colour fastness and the maximum concentrations of toxic or harmful impurities. The standard methodologies that have been developed for certification are also ensuring the use of best available technology in production processes. Although natural dyes can serve as models, there is no way that the annual consumption of 0.5 million tonnes of textile dyes can be met by natural dyes.

According to Parham (1994), new technology in application of natural dyes allows a wide range of shades with good fastness properties, no salt use, elimination of heavy metals in processing, safe effluent and rational methods for sourcing raw materials with possible effects on the environment. Glover (1995) argues that synthetic dyes are more user- and environment-friendly than natural dyes. The arguments put forward are those related to the excessive use of supporting chemicals, possible over-intensification of agriculture and low quality of natural dyes.

Kharbade and Agrawal (1988) have described the identification of natural dyes in historic textiles from the mid-19th century. Seventy samples taken from museum textiles were compared with reference materials prepared in the lab as well as with major dye components of natural dyes. One yellow, two brown, one blue and two red natural dyes were identified in different primary and secondary coloured samples. It is also seen from the results that mixtures of two dyes have been used to obtain desired shades. Bahl and Gupta (1988) have developed a method for mordant dyeing of silk with cutch natural dyes in the presence of different mordants (alum, chrome, $CuSO_4$, $FeSO_4$) for a wide variety of colours. The dyed fabrics exhibited fair-to-good wash fastness and light fastness. Moses (2003) applied the waste grape skin for the application on protein textiles such as silk and wool in combination with other similar natural resources like pomegranate rind, orange rind and annatto seed. They have observed that the results such as colours obtained, fastness towards rubbing, light, heat and washing are very much convincing.

In the study by Auslander et al. (1977), naturally occurring dyes were discussed in the form of a monograph with screening studies on their stability. Duff et al. (1977a) have assessed wash fastness of natural dyes on wool by tests conducted under standard conditions. A number of dyes underwent marked changes in hue on washing that was due to the effect of small amounts of alkali in washing mixtures. In a study by Duff et al. (1977b), the colour changes accompanying light fading were followed visually and instrumentally and characterized in terms of light-fastness grades, grey-scale differences, colour differences in CIELAB colour space, and in Munsell colour coordinates. The light-fastness grades were similar to those previously reported for daylight exposures. The various methods of expressing colour change gave detailed and quantitative measures of the effects of light on the colour of natural dyes; this type of information could be of value in predicting the original colour of ancient textiles.

Kirtikar (1947) and Gulati (1949) have analysed the Indian indigenous natural dyes in terms of their eye appeal, colour value and fastness, and found them to be less valuable than the synthetic dyes. An interesting study by Furry (1945) has shown that the cotton fabrics dyed with natural dyes such as osage orange and quercitron showed excellent mildew resistance, which persisted even after six weeks of weathering.

From the literature, it emerges that the natural dyes are, in general, inferior to synthetic dyes in colour value or eye appeal and colour fastness. However, there has been significant progress in the research on enhancing the dyeing characteristics of the natural dyes for the past five decades, and today there are many natural dyes with colour value and fastness comparable to those of synthetic dyes. There is a debate among various technologists, researchers and scientists regarding the utility of natural dyes. While some of them claim that natural dyes can be widely used as 'better substitutes' for the synthetic dyes in terms of emissions and cost, others claim that the colour value is not as good in the case of natural dyes as in the synthetic dyes. A betterment of colour value of natural dyes would involve use of some chemicals, which in turn, would cause pollution again.

Some researchers have even expressed their doubts over the validity of the widely held idea that natural dyes essentially reduce the pollution levels. A relatively small number of scientists predict that substitution of the synthetic dyes with the natural dye would cause serious problems of environmental concern in terms of exploitation of agricultural land, deforestation, etc. Hence, to end with a meaningful decision, a balanced multi-scenario approach that considers all relevant aspects of natural dyes and synthetic dyes at a macro-level, for the entire sector in the country, with proper projections about the future, with different assumptions on the adaptation rates of natural dyes, is necessary.

Methodology

Steps Involved for the Multi-scenario Analysis

Step 1: The Indian production figures of dyed yarn and cloth made of cotton, silk, wool, polyester and nylon are projected for 2005,

2015, 2025 and 2030 based on the average annual growth rate calculated from the data available for the years 1985–99.

Step 2: The inorganic chemical composition or TDS of the effluents generated by dyeing different materials for different colours using natural and synthetic dyes is calculated using the procedure explained.

Step 3: The emission levels (kg of inorganic chemicals per kg production of the material) calculated previously are compared with the standards fixed by the Government of India.

Step 4: Different scenarios are constructed based on different rates of adaptation of the natural fibres and synthetic fibres sectors to the natural dyes.

Business as usual (BAU): 100 per cent of the dyes used for all the categories of materials are synthetic throughout the period of analysis, except for silk, in which 70 per cent are natural dyes. For the proposition that natural dyes reduce emissions to be true, BAU should cause maximum emissions.

Scenario 1 (optimistic): The shares of natural dyes and synthetic dyes for different years start at 20 per cent in 2005 and increase by 10 per cent points every five years, except for silk for which 70 per cent natural dyes is assumed for all periods. This scenario would be expected to cause least emissions if natural dyes were 'pollution-reducers'.

Scenario 2 (realistic): For cotton, wool and silk, the same percentage of dyes are maintained as in Scenario 1, while for synthetic fibres, the rates of 0 per cent for 2005 and a rise of 10 per cent points every five years, are assumed. Hence, this scenario is realistic given the lower applicability of natural dyes on natural fibres. To claim that natural dyes reduce pollution, Scenario 2 should give second least levels of emissions, since it has the second fastest adaptation rates for synthetic fibres and fastest rates for natural fibres.

Scenario 3 (pessimistic): In this scenario, the assumption is that natural dyes are not adapted to synthetic fibres throughout the period of analysis and that they are adapted to natural fibres at a pace at which they were assumed to be adapted to synthetic fibres in Scenario 2. Silk is assumed to use natural dyes at 70 per cent throughout the period. Though this scenario is termed as a pessimistic one, it should be noted that even this is not as pessimistic as BAU, in which the natural dyes were assumed to be totally absent in all sectors throughout the period of study. Hence, this scenario should give the second largest level of emissions.

Scenario 4 (no synthetic fibres with natural dyes): Natural dyes are adapted by the natural fibres at a pace defined in Scenario 1, while synthetic fibres do not adapt them at all. As the natural fibres adapt to natural dyes at a higher pace in this scenario than in Scenario 3, this scenario should cause less emissions than Scenario 3, that is, the third largest level of emissions.

Stcp 5: Bascd on thc cmission levels obtained under each scenario, different questions could be raised so as to suggest few policy implications.

Assumptions Involved in the Multi-scenario Analysis

The production of the materials grows at an average annual rate calculated from the data for the years 1985–99. For synthetic dyes, 40 per cent of the chemicals added in the recipe are retained in effluent. For both the synthetic and natural dyes, 10 per cent of the chemicals remain in the effluent after proper treatment in effluent treatment plant (ETP). For the natural dyes, 70 per cent of chemicals added in the recipe are retained in effluent. Light, medium and dark shades form equal proportions of the total materials dyed.

Silk is dyed with 50 per cent natural dyes now, and it may not go beyond 70 per cent in the future. The measure of emissions is GPL (grams of TDS per litre of effluent) of TDS (only inorganic material) and hence it does not include any organic material in the effluent. Hence, natural dyes are assumed to be non-polluting in nature as they are organic. The rates of adaptation have been designed based on the fact that many synthetic dyes are being banned (e.g., azo dyes) in the international market and many more are anticipated to be banned in the future.

The extent to which the sectors are expected to adapt the natural dyes is based on the expectation that other dyes will be banned but there is no concrete set of data available in this regard. Hence, we assume some reasonable adaptation rates, and the inclusion of different scenarios would serve the purpose of including all possible ranges of adaptation.

Steps Involved in the AHP-based Ranking of the Dyes

AHP is the Advanced Hierarchical Programming technique, which is used to prioritise among various options based on qualitative and/or quantitative criteria.

Step 1: The emission levels of different dyes for different shades in the case of different sectors are calculated in terms of GPL.
Step 2: For each shade, dye and sector, the values of GPL, cost and fastness index (average of light fastness, wash fastness and rubbing fastness) are listed.
Step 3: The reciprocals of GPL and cost, and the fastness index value are used for the AHP analysis. A matrix is formed for each dye-shade sector combination, whose rows are the different dyes and columns are 1/GPL, 1/cost and fastness index.
Step 4: Based on a survey conducted with industrialists, academicians and research students, the weights for each of the criteria are calculated and written in vector form. The matrix obtained in Step 3 is multiplied by this vector.
Step 5: The vector resulting from Step 4 is normalized and based on the values of this normalized vector, the dyes are ranked. The higher the value, the higher is the rank.

Assumptions Involved in the AHP-based Ranking of the Dyes

All criteria are quantitative, that is, possibilities of taking durability (rather than fastness) or pollution/health hazards (rather than emission level in GPL) as qualitative criteria are ruled out.

The three criteria considered here are assumed to be the only ones for the ranking of dyes used for a same type of shade. International prices are taken as the cost criteria.

Results

Emission Levels of Different Dyes

Table 5.1 shows that natural dyes are the most preferable for cotton, at least in the context of the environmental emissions for the light and dark shades. This is not so in the case for the medium shade since Golden Dock is a natural dye requiring many supporting chemicals and sulphur dye causes less TDS in all cases.

Table 5.1:
Ranking of dyes for cotton based on emission

Rank	*Light Shade*	*Medium Shade*	*Dark Shade*
1	Fenugreek	Sulphur	Gallnut
2	Sulphur	Sahara	Sulphur
3	Direct	Acid	Reactive

Source: Author's results and calculations.

Table 5.2 indicates that natural dyes cause less emission than the synthetic dyes in the case of wool. For silk, as seen in Table 5.3, natural dyes are least polluting and the difference in GPLs of TDS for natural and other dyes is significant. Table 5.4 shows the fact that for polyester, natural dyes are more polluting than the synthetic disperse dyes. This is to be taken as evidence in favour of the proposition that dyeing of natural dyes, on synthetic fibres, is so complicated and cumbersome a process that it would necessitate the addition of quite a few supporting chemicals, due to which the pollution caused by natural dyes turns out to be higher than that caused by the corresponding synthetic dyes.

Table 5.2:
Ranking of dyes for wool based on emission

Rank	*Light Shade*	*Medium Shade*	*Dark Shade*
1	Dolu	Sahara	Gum Arabic
2	Acid	Acid	Acid

Source: Author's results and calculations.

Table 5.3:
Ranking of dyes for silk based on emission

Rank	*Light Shade*	*Medium Shade*	*Dark Shade*
1	Pomegranate	Madder	Shellac
2	Azo	Azo	Azo
3	Reactive	Reactive	Reactive

Source: Author's results and calculations.

Table 5.4:
Ranking of dyes for polyester based on emission

Rank	*Light Shade*	*Medium Shade*	*Dark Shade*
1	Disperse	Disperse	Disperse
2	Kamala	Indigo	Shellac

Source: Author's results and calculations.

In the case of nylon, unlike polyester, the natural dyes are again less polluting than synthetic dyes because of the fact that nylon requires so high a concentration of the synthetic dyes and its supporting chemicals for its dyeing, that even the natural dyes, despite causing a higher level of pollution than in other sectors, cause a lower level of pollution than the synthetic dyes.

LEAP Results of the Scenario Analysis

Long-range energy alternatives planning (LEAP) is a software package used to calculate the pollution levels and energy consumption levels of any system based on its various branches and for different years in the future for different scenarios. In our case, we do not include any analysis on energy consumption in this context, but focus on environmental aspects alone. This is a major deviation from routine uses of LEAP. The system may consist of different sectors, each of which may, in turn, be composed of sub-sectors. Each sub-sector would have different end uses and each of which would make use of different pollution-causing elements. In this study, the sectors are the different fibres, the sub-sectors are the different shades and the end use is the 'type of dye'. The last level in this hierarchy tree is the name of the particular dye, for which the emission level is fed as input in GPL. This exercise is repeated for each of the scenarios mentioned earlier with proper feeding of the data regarding the adaptation rates for the different years. The data of production in each sector, with its share in each level, are also fed into LEAP.

The average annual growth rates as illustrated in Table 5.5 were calculated using MS-Excel, based on the data available for the years 1985–99. A glance at the rates and figures would confirm that polyester would dominate the textile industry, comprising more than 90 per cent of the total production in 2020. This, in turn, would imply that polyester sector, in addition to being one with high pollution intensity, is going to be the major contributor to the pollution because of its size effect. This observation, when linked with another note made in the previous section, that the technology of application of natural dyes on polyester is not very advanced, would

Table 5.5:
Production of dyed fabrics and yarns in the sectors (in billion kilograms)

Sector	*1990*	*Growth Rate (%)*	*2005*	*2010*	*2015*	*2020*
Cotton	1.306	5.51	2.92	3.818	4.992	6.528
Wool	0.024	4.55	0.047	0.058	0.073	0.091
Silk	0.02	11.33	0.1	0.171	0.293	0.5
Polyester	0.21	22.06	4.177	11.316	30.659	83.065
Nylon	0.021	0.33	0.022	0.022	0.023	0.023

Source: Author's results and calculations.

imply that a concrete policy to encourage the technical research in this area is essential for a significant emission reduction.

Based on Table 5.6, many inferences can be made, such as the following:

1. Maximum possible reductions in the emission of TDS by the penetration of natural dyes (at the most optimistic pace) = *E*(BAU)–*E*(Scenario 1) = 4.96167 billion kg. *E*(X) is the emission levels in scenario X, as seen in Table 5.6.
2. Emission reductions by promotion of natural dyes for both synthetic and natural fibres at equal pace (rather than depriving synthetic fibres of natural dyes) = *E*(Scenario 4)–*E*(Scenario 1) = 3.56296 billion kg (a reduction in GPL of 1.98).
3. Emission reduction if natural dyes are adapted to synthetic fibres to some extent and to natural fibres to a much greater extent = *E*(BAU)–*E*(Scenario 2) = 3.1802 billion kg.

Table 5.6:
Overall results (LEAP) of emissions of TDS under different scenarios

Scenario		*2005*	*2010*	*2015*	*2020*
	Total (billion kg)	0.64	1.56	4.05	10.86
BAU	GPG	0.0881	0.1014	0.1124	0.1204
	GPL	4.4041	5.0699	5.6188	6.0195
	Total (billion kg)	0.5195	1.1215	2.5444	5.8983
Scenario 1	GPG	0.0715	0.0729	0.0706	0.0654
	GPL	3.5745	3.6447	3.5299	3.2693
	Total (billion kg)	0.64	1.55	4.02	10.81
Scenario 2	GPG	0.0881	0.1008	0.1115	0.1198
	GPL	4.4041	5.0374	5.5771	5.9918
	Total (billion kg)	0.5916	1.3161	3.0708	7.6798
Scenario 3	GPG	0.0814	0.0856	0.0852	0.0851
	GPL	4.0713	4.2773	4.2602	4.2568
	Total (billion kg)	0.5916	1.4134	3.5971	9.4613
Scenario 4	GPG	0.0814	0.0919	0.0998	0.1049
	GPL	4.0713	4.5935	4.9905	5.2442

Source: Author's results and calculations.

4. Emission reduction if natural dyes are not at all adapted to synthetic fibres and to natural fibres to some extent, as compared to the BAU = *E*(BAU)–*E*(Scenario 4) = 1.3987 billion kg.
5. With relatively realistic assumptions, emission reduction as compared to BAU is 3.1802 billion kg. Hence, the natural dyes cause a clear drastic reduction in emissions of TDS.
6. Emission reductions in the case of equally fast promotion measures of natural dyes for both natural and synthetic dyes, compared to:

   (a) BAU: 4.96167 billion kg (45.69 per cent reduction)
   (b) Scenario 3: 4.9117 billion kg (45.44 per cent reduction)
   (c) Scenario 2: 1.782 billion kg (23.2 per cent reduction)
   (d) Scenario 4: 3.56296 billion kg (37.66 per cent reduction)

7. Even in terms of grams of TDS emitted per gram of dyed material (GPG) and grams per litre of TDS in the effluent (GPL), the reductions are significant. As compared to the different scenarios, the final reduction in GPL by the year 2020 if Scenario 1 is implemented are as follows:

   (a) BAU: 2.75 GPL (45.69 per cent reduction)
   (b) Scenario 3: 2.72 GPL (45.44 per cent reduction)
   (c) Scenario 2: 0.987 GPL (23.2 per cent reduction)
   (d) Scenario 4: 1.98 GPL (37.66 per cent reduction)

The basic purpose of the previous inferences is to quantify the benefits of adapting to natural dyes in terms of TDS and percentage. More importantly, this exercise aims at precisely disaggregating the consequences of adaptation in different sectors at different rates, which is solved by the definition of scenarios. For example, the reductions by not adapting to natural dyes only in synthetic fibre sectors compared to those by uniformly adapting to all sectors would be as shown in inference 2.

As seen in the Table 5.7, the cotton sector has least emissions in three scenarios—Scenario 1, Scenario 2 and Scenario 4. This is

Table 5.7:
Emission of TDS in cotton dyeing sector

Scenario	*Years →*	*2005*	*2010*	*2015*	*2020*
BAU	Total emissions in million kg	135.32	176.94	231.37	302.53
	GPG	0.046342	0.046344	0.046348	0.046343
	GPL	2.317123	2.317182	2.317408	2.317172
Scenario 1	Total emissions in million kg	119.17	145.27	176.14	212.26
	GPG	0.040812	0.038049	0.035284	0.032515
	GPL	2.040582	1.902436	1.764223	1.625766
Scenario 2	Total emissions in million kg	135.32	166.38	203.75	257.4
	GPG	0.046342	0.043578	0.040815	0.03943
	GPL	2.317123	2.178889	2.040765	1.971507
Scenario 3	Total emissions in million kg	119.17	145.27	176.14	212.26
	GPG	0.040812	0.038049	0.035284	0.032515
	GPL	2.040582	1.902436	1.764223	1.625766
Scenario 4	Total emissions in million kg	119.17	145.27	176.14	212.26
	GPG	0.040812	0.038049	0.035284	0.032515
	GPL	2.040582	1.902436	1.764223	1.625766

Source: Author's results and calculations.

because of the fact that the adaptation rates for this sector have not changed in these scenarios. The emission reductions are about 30 per cent by the adaptation of natural dyes, that is, from 302.53 million kg or 2.317 GPL in BAU to 212.26 million kg or 1.626 GPL in these scenarios. Even in Scenario 3, the reductions are almost 20 per cent, that is, from 302.53 million kg or 2.317 GPL in BAU to 257.4 million kg or 1.972 GPL in Scenario 3. This implies that, by 2020, the cotton sector would reduce its emissions by 20 per cent under pessimistic rates of adaptation of natural dyes and 30 per cent under normal rates of adaptation.

As seen in Table 5.8, the wool sector has least emissions in three scenarios—Scenario 1, Scenario 2 and Scenario 4. This is because of

Table 5.8:
Emission of TDS in wool dyeing sector

Scenario	*Years* →	*2005*	*2010*	*2015*	*2020*
BAU	Total emissions in 1,000 kg	2,045.73	2,556.68	3,195.24	3,993.3
	GPG	0.043526	0.044081	0.04377	0.043882
	GPL	2.176309	2.204034	2.188521	2.194121
Scenario 1	Total emissions in 1,000 kg	1,793.52	2,084.71	2,409.66	2,767.11
	GPG	0.03816	0.035943	0.033009	0.030408
	GPL	1.908	1.797164	1.650452	1.52039
Scenario 2	Total emissions in 1,000 kg	2,045.73	2,400.69	2,805.34	3,384.18
	GPG	0.043526	0.041391	0.08429	0.037189
	GPL	2.176309	2.06956	1.921466	1.85944
Scenario 3	Total emissions in 1,000 kg	1,793.52	2,084.71	2,409.66	2,767.11
	GPG	0.03816	0.035943	0.033009	0.030408
	GPL	1.908	1.797164	1.650452	1.52039
Scenario 4	Total emissions in 1,000 kg	1,793.52	2,084.71	2,409.66	2,767.11
	GPG	0.03816	0.035943	0.033009	0.030408
	GPL	1.908	1.797164	1.650452	1.52039

Source: Author's results and calculations.

the fact that the adaptation rates for this sector have not changed in these scenarios. Just similar to the cotton sector, by 2020, the wool sector would also reduce its emissions by 20 per cent under pessimistic rates of adaptation of natural dyes and 30 per cent under normal rates of adaptation.

In the case of the silk dyeing sector, as seen in Table 5.9, there is no change in emission level because of the fact that the assumptions on the adaptation rates of natural dyes for the silk sector are the same for all scenarios.

As seen in Table 5.10, the polyester sector has least emissions in Scenario 1. The emission reductions are about 45 per cent by the adaptation of natural dyes, that is, from 10.53 billion kg or

Table 5.9:
Emission of TDS in silk dyeing sector

Scenario	*Years →*	*2005*	*2010*	*2015*	*2020*
BAU	Total emissions in million kg	0.42	5.86	10.01	17.13
	GPG	0.0342	0.034269	0.034164	0.03426
	GPL	0.4275	0.428363	0.427048	0.42825
Scenario 1	Total emissions in million kg	3.42	5.86	10.01	17.13
	GPG	0.0342	0.034269	0.034164	0.03426
	GPL	0.4275	0.428363	0.427048	0.42825
Scenario 2	Total emissions in million kg	3.42	5.86	10.01	17.13
	GPG	0.0342	0.034269	0.034164	0.03426
	GPL	0.4275	0.428363	0.427048	0.42825
Scenario 3	Total emissions in million kg	3.42	5.86	10.01	17.13
	GPG	0.0342	0.034269	0.034164	0.03426
	GPL	0.4275	0.428363	0.427048	0.42825
Scenario 4	Total emissions in million kg	3.42	5.86	10.01	17.13
	GPG	0.0342	0.034269	0.034164	0.03426
	GPL	0.4275	0.428363	0.427048	0.42825

Source: Author's results and calculations.

6.338 GPL in BAU to 5.66 billion kg or 3.41 GPL in Scenario 1. Even in Scenario 2, the reductions are almost 30 per cent, that is, from 10.53 billion kg or 6.338 GPL in BAU to 7.44 billion kg or 4.478 GPL in Scenario 2. This implies that, by 2020, the polyester sector would reduce its emissions by 30 per cent under modest (as in Scenario 2) rates of adaptation of natural dyes and 45 per cent under Scenario 1 rates of adaptation. This indicates the significance of development of technology of applying the natural dyes on the polyester sector, arising out of the huge potential of emission reductions in this sector.

Table 5.11 shows that a maximum of 42 per cent reduction of TDS is possible by 2020 in the case of nylon, since the difference

Table 5.10:
Emission of TDS in polyester dyeing sector

Scenario	*Years →*	*2005*	*2010*	*2015*	*2020*
	Total emissions in billion kg	0.5	1.37	3.8	10.53
BAU	GPG	0.1197	0.121068	0.123944	0.126768
	GPL	5.985157	6.053376	6.197201	6.33841
	Total emissions in billion kg	0.39224	0.96568	2.35347	5.66411
Scenario 1	GPG	0.093905	0.085338	0.076763	0.068189
	GPL	4.695236	4.266879	3.838139	3.409444
	Total emissions in billion kg	0.5	1.37	3.8	10.53
Scenario 2	GPG	0.119703	0.121068	0.123944	0.126768
	GPL	5.985157	6.053376	6.197201	6.33841
	Total emissions in billion kg	0.46387	1.15975	2.87927	7.44484
Scenario 3	GPG	0.06896	0.07743	0.08021	0.0896
	GPL	4.1423	4.2467	4.3465	4.478
	Total emissions in billion kg	0.5	1.37	3.8	10.53
Scenario 4	GPG	0.119703	0.121068	0.123944	0.126768
	GPL	5.985157	6.053376	6.197201	6.33841

Source: Author's results and calculations.

between the emissions of BAU and OPTI scenarios is (3562.27–2074.55) million kg or (7.744–4.51) GPL. Considering Scenario 2, the possible reduction is 21 per cent. Thus the potential to reduce the emissions in the Nylon sector by adapting the natural dyes is high (21–42 per cent).

A striking observation from Table 5.12 of standards of TDS concentration and emission levels in different sectors is that in most of the scenarios of almost all sectors, the emission levels are too high to be within the standards. Only in the case of silk, in which the natural dyes are most predominant, the standards are satisfied. In the cotton and wool sectors, the emission levels are relatively lower than others because of their better adaptability to

Table 5.11:
Emission of TDS in nylon dyeing sector

Scenario	*Years →*	*2005*	*2010*	*2015*	*2020*
	Total emissions in 1,000 kg	3,390.51	3,446.82	3,504.07	3,562.27
BAU	GPG	0.15411	0.1567	0.1524	0.1549
	GPL	7.7057	7.8337	7.6175	7.7441
	Total emissions in 1,000 kg	2,824.11	2,583.12	2,333.34	2,074.55
Scenario 1	GPG	0.1284	0.1174	0.1015	0.0902
	GPL	6.4184	5.8707	5.0725	4.5099
	Total emissions in 1,000 kg	3,390.51	3,446.82	3,504.07	3,562.27
Scenario 2	GPG	0.15411	0.1567	0.1523	0.1549
	GPL	7.7057	7.8337	7.6175	7.7441
	Total emissions in 1,000 kg	3,390.51	3,158.92	2,918.7	2,818.41
Scenario 3	GPG	0.15411	0.1436	0.1269	0.1225
	GPL	7.7057	7.1794	6.345	6.127
	Total emissions in 1,000 kg	3,390.51	3,446.82	3,504.07	3,562.27
Scenario 4	GPG	0.1541	0.1567	0.1524	0.1549
	GPL	7.7057	7.8337	7.6175	7.7441

Source: Author's results and calculations.

Table 5.12:
Indian standards of TDS concentration in effluents

STDS:	*Inland Surface Water*		*Public Sewers*		*Land for Irrigation*		*Marine Coastal Areas*	
M:L	1:20	1:80	1:20	1:80	1:20	1:80	1:20	1:80
GPG	0.0113	0.0452	0.0279	0.1116	0.0137	0.0548	0.0133	0.0532
GPL	0.5652		1.3952		0.6854		0.6654	

Source: Author's results and calculations.

natural dyes. Polyester and nylon cause the highest GPL emissions of TDS, because of their non-compatibility with natural dyes, being synthetic fibres.

Most significantly, cotton and wool sectors can be, on an average, developed as the sectors with emission levels conforming to the standards under the optimistic scenario (Scenario 1). All these observations, in addition to the previous inferences from the overall and sector-wise results, lead us to conclude that natural dyes not only reduce the emissions significantly, but also to an extent that at least the natural fibre sectors can conform to the Indian standards for the effluents. As for the synthetic fibres, it would depend on the technological developments that could improve the compatibility of natural dyes with them.

Ranking of the Dyes Based on AHP

For the different sectors, the dyes have been ranked based on three criteria for each shade—cost, colour fastness and emission level (Table 5.14). The international prices and fastness indices of various dyes have been tabulated in Table 5.13.

A comparison of Table 5.15 with Table 5.1 would highlight the fact that the inclusion of cost and fastness as the criteria for ranking the dyes, in addition to the emission levels, has changed the order of ranking. The natural dye has moved to second and third place, respectively, for dark and medium shades. This may be due to the fact that the cost of Golden Dock and gallnut is not low enough to compensate their low fastness value.

Table 5.16, when compared to Table 5.2, shows that only Golden Dock natural dye has been rejected for the first place due to its low fastness, relatively high cost and not low enough emissions. The other natural dyes have retained their first place despite the inclusion of the new criteria.

A comparative glance of the Tables 5.17 and 5.3 would again support the proposition that natural dyes are better than synthetic dyes even when cost and fastness are included as criteria, but for the fact that Madder natural dye has become least preferred after the inclusion of these criteria. An important note to be made here is that, though azo dye causes low emission of TDS, the content of this effluent is highly toxic and hence azo dye has been banned widely. In this case, a measure of toxicity such as LC_{50} should have

Table 5.13:
Costs and fastness indices of different dyes

S. No.	Dye	Cost (US$/Lb)	Fastness Index
1.	Acid dye	25	5
2.	Azo dye	20	5
3.	Direct dye	20	5
4.	Disperse dye	26	5
5.	Reactive dye	30	5
6.	Sulphur dye	19	5
7.	AmberM	43	4
8.	Kamala	8.25	3
9.	Gum Arabic	18	4
10.	Fenugreek	43	4
11.	Dolu	27.5	4
12.	Madder	25	4
13.	Indigo	28	4
14.	Pomegranate	19	4
15.	Shellac	14	4
16.	Sahara	14	3

Source: Author's results and calculations.

Table 5.14:
Ranking of the dyes for cotton

Rank	Light Shade	Medium Shade	Dark Shade
1	Fenugreek	Sulphur	Sulphur
2	Sulphur	Acid	AmberM
3	Direct	Sahara	Reactive

Source: Author's results and calculations.

Table 5.15:
Ranking of dyes for wool

Rank	Light Shade	Medium Shade	Dark Shade
1	Dolu	Acid	Gum Arabic
2	Acid	Sahara	Acid

Source: Author's results and calculations.

Table 5.16:
Ranking of dyes for silk

Rank	*Light Shade*	*Medium Shade*	*Dark Shade*
1	Pomegranate	Azo	Shellac
2	Azo	Reactive	Azo
3	Reactive	Madder	Reactive

Source: Author's results and calculations.

Table 5.17:
Ranking of dyes for polyester

Rank	*Light Shade*	*Medium Shade*	*Dark Shade*
1	Disperse	Disperse	Shellac
2	Kamala	Indigo	Disperse

Source: Author's results and calculations.

Table 5.18:
Ranking of dyes for nylon

Rank	*Light Shade*	*Medium Shade*	*Dark Shade*
1	Dolu	Disperse	Gum Arabic
2	Disperse	Sahara	Disperse

Source: Author's results and calculations.

been included in the analysis. However, this would matter much only in the case of azo dyes and since the objective is more towards checking for the feasibility of natural dyes, it can be safely concluded that, for the medium shade, Madder natural dye is clearly not the preferable one, and is inferior at least to the reactive dye.

In the case of polyester, the natural dye Shellac has become a better dye than disperse dye with the inclusion of additional criteria, because of its sufficiently low cost and/or sufficiently high fastness and/or sufficiently low emission. For light and medium shades, natural dyes retain their last rank (Table 5.18). This reiterates the importance of encouragement of innovations in the area of application of natural dyes to synthetic fibres, especially, polyester.

As in most other cases, the natural dye Golden Dock has been found to be less preferred to synthetic dyes with the inclusion of other criteria for nylon. For light and medium shades, natural dyes still dominate the first place.

Conclusion

Adaptation to natural dyes would cause a significant reduction of 20–50 per cent in the emission of TDS by the year 2020 depending on the rate of adaptation. A reasonably fast (OPTI scenario) adaptation would bring the emission levels for the natural fibres (cotton, wool and silk) well within the Indian standards. For reducing the emissions within the standard limits in the case of synthetic fibres (polyester and silk), a combination of fast adaptation and encouragement of research in the application of natural dyes on the synthetic fibres are required.

Polyester, being the single major polluting sector, requires maximum attention in this context, in terms of research as well as adaptation policy. An individual analysis of the dyes for each sector-shade pair shows that natural dyes cause significantly lower emissions in all cases except a very few, for example, polyester, which is due to not-so-developed technology. The fact that the ranking of the dyes, after the inclusion of the criteria of cost and fastness, has changed in some cases and unchanged in quite a few, reiterates the overall feasibility of natural dyes. Other than the natural dye Sahara, most other natural dyes have been able retain their ranks even after including these criteria.

A well-designed policy should be framed for the promotion of natural dyes in particular and reduction of emissions in the textile dyeing sector in general. This should include features that would encourage the research in the application of natural dyes on the synthetic fibres and improvement of the colouring properties of the natural dyes. A meticulous action plan comprising rates of adaptation to the natural dyes should be framed. A set of rules and regulations should be designed for the dyeing factories throughout the country for the adaptation of natural dyes. The natural dyes, which are found to be outstanding based on different criteria, as analysed in this study, should be chosen and promoted commercially.

If, as found in this study, the natural dyes are not feasible for certain applications, then synthetic dyes that are less polluting or are better than others as per the ranking, should be promoted in such cases. Techno-economic feasibility analysis of natural dyes would prove useful in tracking the practical issues involved in the adaptation of natural dyes and hence should be encouraged. The standards of emissions in the effluents should be fixed in a scientifically reasonable manner and implemented strictly. One way of promoting natural dyes could be a systematic setting of the emission standards in such a way that the adaptation of natural dyes would be mandatory to achieve such standards.

In short, we come up with the following policy conclusions:

1. Promotion of natural dyes can reduce pollution due to the textile industry substantially. The current policy dilemma due to the failure of ETPs and collective ETPs could be addressed well by this approach.
2. Given that natural dyes are not so compatible with synthetic fibres, policymakers could incentivize and promote research efforts in this area.
3. Stringent implementation of standards in water quality of rivers near the textile processing plants could be in effect a policy of promoting natural dyes.
4. Techno-economic feasibility studies indicate that natural dyes are both less polluting and cost-effective. Such analysis needs to be done on case-by-case basis.
5. If natural dyes are just not feasible, for example, due to the lack of fastness, policies should have some flexibility, but promote less polluting synthetic dyes.

Several extensions of this study could be undertaken in the future. An AHP analysis could be done by including other criteria such as quality of the colour, durability, health hazards and collecting the opinion of experts from different areas. A cost-benefit analysis of natural dyes could be done by including various factors such as savings in ETP costs, cost differences of dyes and environmental costs. Environmental costs of natural dyes, due to over-intensification of the land for their cultivation, could be analysed.

Organic dyes, which are currently under development and are claimed to be eco-friendly and better in quality and fastness than natural dyes, could be compared with natural dyes in terms of costs, emissions, etc. Inclusion of a measure of toxicity of the effluent, such as LC_{50}, could be done so that the toxicity of some natural dyes would also be internalized in the analysis. The extension of this analysis to some more sectors, dyes and scenarios based on different assumptions on the production could be done.

References

Agarwal, K.K. 2003. 'Problems and Prospects of Using Natural Dyes in an Industrial Enterprise', *Colourage*, 50(6): 37–40.

Auslander, D.E., Goldberg, M., Hill, J.A. and Weiss, A.L. 1977. 'Naturally occurring colorants, a stability evaluation', *Drug & Cosmetic Industry*, 121(5): 36, 38, 40, 105, 114.

Bahl, D. and Gupta, K.C. 1988. 'Development of Dyeing Process of Silk with Natural Dye-cutch', *Colourage*, 35(22): 22–24.

Bechtold, T., Turcanu A., Ganglberger E. and Geissler S. 2003. 'Natural Dyes in Modern Textile Dyehouses—How to Combine Experiences of Two Centuries to Meet the Demands of the Future?', *Journal of Cleaner Production*, 11(6): 499–509.

Dheeraj, T., Priyanka, T., and Monika, M. 2003. 'Eco-friendliness of Natural Dyes', *Colourage*, 50(7): 35–36, 38, 40–42, 44.

Duff, D.G., Sinclair, R.S. and Stirling, D. 1977a. 'The Fastness to Washing of Some Natural Dyestuffs on Wool', *Studies in Conservation*, 22(4): 170–76.

———. 1977b. 'Light-induced Color Changes of Natural Dyes', *Studies in Conservation*, 22(4): 161–69.

Furry, M.S. 1945. 'Some Natural Dyes Give Long Life to Cotton Fabric', *Rayon Textile Monthly* 26, 603–05.

Glover, B. 1995. 'Are Natural Colorants Good for your Health? Are Synthetic Ones Better?', *Textile Chemist and Colorist*, 27(4): 17–20.

Gulati, A.N. 1949. 'Natural Indian Dyes and the Art of their Application', *Indian Textile Journal*, 60: 223–29.

Holme, I.A. 2003. 'Recent Developments in Colorants for Textile Applications', *Colourage Annual*, 50(4): 81–106.

Kharbade, B.V. and Agrawal, O.P. 1988. 'Analysis of Natural Dyes in Indian Historic Textiles', *Studies in Conservation*, 33(1): 1–8.

Kirtikar, D.B. 1947. 'Indigenous Indian Dyes', *Indian Textile Journal*, 58(2): 137, 159–60.

Moses, J.J. and Ravi, N. 2003. 'Application of Grape Skin Powder Extract on Protein Textile Fabrics', *Man-Made Textiles in India*, 46(8): 295–300.

Nousiainen, P. 1997. 'Modern Textile Dyeing Takes Note of the Environment', *Kemia-Kemi*, 24(5): 376–80.

Parham, R.J. 1994. Elimination of Production and Environmental Problems in Cellulose Dyeing: Neutral Dyeing Reactives, Bifunctional Reactives, and Natural Dyes, Book of Papers—International Conference & Exhibition, AATCC (1994), 398–403.

Patra, A.K., Sareen, A. and Vohra, D. 2002. 'Performance Studies of Some Natural Dyes on Cotton', *Man-Made Textiles in India*, 45(8): 319–23.

Paul, R., Jayesh, M. and Naik, S.R. 1996. 'Natural Dyes: Classification, Extraction and Fastness Properties', *Textile Dyer & Printer*, 29(22): 16–24.

Pophalia, G.R., Kaula, S.N. and Mathur, S. 2003. 'Influence of Hydraulic Chock Loads and TDS on the Performance of Large-scale CETPs Treating Textile Effluents in India', *Water Research*, 37(3): 353–61.

Rubeena, S., Sharma, R.C. and Pandey, G.P. 2002. 'Biochemical Analysis of Natural Dyes: An Empirical Study', *Research Journal of Chemistry and Environment*, 6(4): 67–72.

Teli, M.D., Paul, R. and Pardeshi, P.D. 2000. 'Natural Dyes: Classification, Chemistry and Extraction Methods Part-I: Chemical Classes, Extraction Methods and Future Prospects', *Colourage*, 47(12): 43–48.

List of Websites

www.alpsind. com
www.emich.edu/textiles/PDFs/wfacid/hot.pdf
www.metricchemical.com/tmetagenas.pdf
www.chinadyestuff.com
www.aurorasilk.com/info/naturaldyes_faq.shtml
www.swicofil.com/setilawidnaucationic.html

6

Are Fiscal Subsidies Harmful for the Environment?

Sacchidananda Mukherjee and Debashis Chakraborty***

Introduction

The World Commission on Environment and Development (1987) defined sustainable development as, 'development that meets the needs of the present without compromising the ability of future generations to meet their own needs' (UN, 1987). The principle has been reiterated in all the subsequent major policy forums to discuss environmental concerns. For instance, the Earth Summit at Rio de Janeiro (1992) declared that:

- To achieve sustainable development and a higher quality of life for all people, States should reduce and eliminate unsustainable patterns of production and consumption and promote appropriate demographic policies. (Principle 8)
- States should effectively cooperate to discourage or prevent the relocation and transfer to other States of any activities and substances that cause severe environmental degradation or are found to be harmful to human health. (Principle 14) (IISD, undated)

*Associate Professor, National Institute of Public Finance and Policy (NIPFP), New Delhi, India. E-mail: sachs.mse@gmail.com

**Assistant Professor, Indian Institute of Foreign Trade (IIFT), New Delhi, India. E-mail: debchakra@gmail.com

The principles in essence indicated the need to curb unwanted subsidies, which might lead to environmental degradation (e.g., deforestation and generation of higher pollution load). Along similar lines, the Copenhagen Accord (2009) stressed the need to reduce emissions from deforestation and forest degradation (UNFCCC, 2009). Similar concerns in the era of globalization have been reiterated by UNCSD (2012) in their declaration at the Rio+20 Conference released on 19 June 2012, 'We remain focused on achieving progress in addressing a set of important issues, such as, inter alia, trade-distorting subsidies and trade in environmental goods and services'. However, government support and subsidies in several resource-intensive sectors, namely primary sector (including mining and quarrying activities), transport, energy, water and others is still rampant with enormous environmental ramifications (van Beers et al., 2004).

The tradition of providing subsidies by national governments for supporting domestic business vis-à-vis their foreign counterparts is in practice for a long time (Giuliani et al., 2011). One of the major motivations behind provision of the subsidies often originates from the infant industry argument as proposed by the international trade literature (Chang, 2001). Subsidies can either be provided to the domestic players for boosting domestic production (domestic subsidy) or for promoting exports (export subsidy) or both. The subsidies extended to the local players by the government can either be direct transfer of financial resources (per unit production subsidy) or indirect support (e.g., in terms of income foregone by offering tax concessions). The support can also be extended through concessional credit lines, monopoly rights or lax environmental standard (i.e., 'race-to-the-bottom' phenomenon), and others, among other means (Kelly, 2009). The existing trade literature has noted the adverse impact of the subsidies on trade flows on several occasions, which could manifest itself in terms of export dumping and price crash (Anderson et al., 2006; OXFAM, undated).

Existence of subsidies per se does not necessarily lead to adverse environmental consequences. For instance, carefully crafted subsidy policies can contribute significantly for ensuring environmental protection in an economy (e.g., subsidies for promoting organic farming or other forms of environment-friendly agriculture, technology upgrade support to industry for securing lower emissions). Nevertheless, the adverse environmental implications of subsidies are well documented in existing literature (Mukherjee and Chakraborty, 2014, 2015a). In addition, subsidies generally encourage overuse of dirty inputs and enable the environmentally inefficient producers to continue in the market (Barde and Honkatukia, 2004). Conversely, reduction of subsidies enhances environmental sustainability by lowering pollution-causing capital accumulation, shifting of capital and labour to less pollution-intensive firms, and enhancing the output of more productive firms (Bajona and Kelly, 2012).

The realization on the long-term adverse implications of subsidies on trade front has motivated inclusion of the Agreement on 'Subsidies and Countervailing Measures' (ASCM) under the wings of WTO since its inception in 1995. The WTO discussion aims at classifying the subsidies under two broad categories, namely actionable (i.e., subsidies that are trade-distorting) and non-actionable (i.e., subsidies with minimal impact on trade). At present, the WTO member countries are discussing the need to contain the subsidies being provided by the member countries.

In addition to the more obvious trade-distorting effects, the domestic or export subsidies are potentially associated with overproduction and the consequent irreversible environmental damage. Notably, the subsidies being provided in the area of agricultural sector and other resource-intensive sectors deserve special mention in this regard. Overproduction in both these sectors, aided by subsidies, may have serious adverse implications for the environment apart from their trade consequences. In addition, subsidies provided to the manufacturing sector, especially through fuel subsidies may lead to air pollution and emissions of greenhouse gases (GHGs) (i.e., through higher volume of fossil fuel burning) and ultimately to environmental disasters and loss of biodiversity.

The less than desired pace of subsidy reforms across countries and the growing concerns over climate change, as reflected through GHG emissions, calls for a deeper analysis to identify whether there exists any linkage between the two. In this context, the current analysis intends to explore the statistical relationship between devolution of budgetary subsidies and transfers and per capita carbon dioxide (CO_2) emissions for 134 countries over 1990–2010. The current analysis is restricted only to the per capita CO_2 emission as an indicator of climate change owing to limited availability of long-time series data on other GHGs for a large number of countries.

The present analysis intends to contribute to the existing pool of literature on subsidy–climate change nexus. A large body of studies in the theoretical as well as empirical literature have adopted general equilibrium framework, data envelopment analysis modelling technique and others to analyse the impacts of subsidy on environment and climate change (Bajona and Kelly, 2012; Heutel and Kelly, 2013; Managi, 2010; Yagi and Managi, 2011). However, empirically explaining the relationship between government budgetary subsidies and per capita CO_2 emissions in a cross-country panel data framework is a relatively less researched area. The current chapter bridges this gap by testing the statistical relationship between the two series. In addition, the present analysis particularly contributes to the literature by attempting to understand the influences of various government subsidy reporting standards on CO_2 emission patterns.

The chapter is arranged along the following lines. First, a brief discussion of the subsidies being provided to the agricultural, fishery and the manufacturing sectors of select countries and their potential implications on environment are noted. A cross-country empirical analysis is conducted next for understanding the influence of subsidies on per capita CO_2 emission. A brief analysis on subsidies provided to Indian players is conducted in the following. Finally, on the basis of the findings, a few policy conclusions are drawn.

Subsidies: Evidence from the Literature and the Implications

It has been observed that the global agricultural production and government support is marked by a fundamental difference between two set of countries. On the one hand, the developed countries characterized by capital-intensive production structure provides considerable subsidy to the local farmers in crops like rice, wheat, maize, corn, and dairy products, which are of considerable export interest of the developing countries (WTO, 2010, 2011a). The support provided by developed countries to their farmers covers both the field of input and output subsidies. On the other hand, the labour-intensive agricultural system in developing countries generally relies on input subsidies (Chand and Philip, 2001).

Looking at the implications of the difference between the two forms of subsidies, it is observed that the input subsidy (e.g., fuel, fertilizer and pesticide subsidy) can lead to lower per unit variable costs and hence motivates overproduction. Steenblik (1998) noted that input subsidies are more prone to input overuse and consequent biodiversity loss. Atici (2009) reports the link between fertilizer usage in OECD countries and their CO_2 emission levels. Similarly, the output linked production subsidy (e.g., price support linked with volume of agricultural output) motivates the producer to go beyond the level of economic production (UIC-CMDA, 2003). For instance, Robin et al. (2003) have reported water and soil pollution (Scherr, 2003); conversion of forests, rainforests and wetlands into cultivable lands (OECD, 2003) and diversion of water (Myers and Kent, 2001) resulting from intensive cropping across countries. In other words, both forms of support to the agricultural sector may bear adverse consequences for the environment.

Keeping generally the trade-related concerns in mind, a limit on the subsidy to be provided by the member countries within the WTO Agreement on Agriculture has been defined in the following manner. The subsidies are classified under three boxes: *Amber Box* (production-linked subsidies, which are most trade-distorting), *Blue Box* (subsidies linked with farm size, hard size, etc., rather than absolute level of production, with relatively smaller effect on trade) and *Green Box* (subsidies linked to R&D and other activities, which are either not trade-distorting or least trade-distorting). The developed countries are supposed to keep the value of their *Amber Box* measures within 5 per cent of the value of their agricultural production, while the corresponding figure for their developing counterparts is 10 per cent. However, it has been noticed that all support measures are not subject to discipline (Gulati and Narayanan, 2003). There have been certain reforms in EU and US agricultural policies over the years since the initiation of the Doha Round of WTO in 2001, but the actual level of reform is subject to question (Anderson et al., 2008). For instance, the level of actual EU Common Agricultural Policy (CAP) reform to decouple the subsidies from production (i.e., to convert into *Blue Box* measures) has been challenged by Oxfam (2005). Similarly, the reforms proposed by the Farm Bill 2008 in the US have been criticized by other WTO member countries (Morgan, 2010). Substantial environmental externalities in the US through the hidden subsidies have widely been reported in the literature (Myers and Kent, 2001).

Table 6.1 shows the five-year annual average Producer Support Estimate (PSE) in agriculture for a few selected countries, as reported by the OECD database. It is observed from the table that the average agricultural support in all the countries have not declined uniformly since the initiation of the Uruguay Round

Table 6.1:
Annual average producer support estimate in selected countries

(US$ billions)

Period	*Australia*	*Canada*	*EU*	*Japan*	*South Korea*	*US*
1986–90	1.42	5.87	95.39	47.92	14.76	35.83
1991–95	1.55	4.91	113.24	60.23	21.29	29.48
1996–2000	0.97	3.54	106.25	51.11	18.75	42.79
2001–05	0.92	5.23	108.77	45.50	17.84	42.28
2006–10	1.34	6.52	120.33	42.95	19.58	30.22
2011–13	1.18	7.11	111.84	59.96	21.20	31.86

Source: OECD Database.

discussions of General Agreements on Tariffs and Trade since 1986. On the contrary, the average subsidy level has increased in Australia, EU, Japan and South Korea in early nineties. Similarly, the average subsidy level has increased in case of US after inception of WTO in 1995. In more recent period, the economic recession since 2009 has caused an increase in trade protectionism (Chaisse et al., 2011) and in particular, agricultural subsidies have also increased in several countries. The slow progress of the Doha Round makes the possibility of a speedy resolution on the reform of agricultural subsidies unlikely (Chakraborty and Khan, 2008), and the rise in PSE figures for Canada, Japan, South Korea and US during 2011–13 is a case in point. The downward rigidity in the level of agricultural subsidies in major developed countries (WTO, 2010, 2011a) as well as in several developing countries (Anderson and Martin, 2009) raises a consequent question on the environmental sustainability as well.

The evolving relative importance of output-based and input-based support measures for agriculture in OECD countries has been reported in Figures 6.1 and 6.2, respectively. Oskam and Meester (2006) have noted that output-based support is one of the major components of the aggregate agricultural support measures. It is observed from Figure 6.1 that the proportional importance of output-based support in case of Australia, EU and US has declined considerably over the years. This indicates that several *Amber Box* subsidies in the EU are getting converted into *Blue Box* categories (Atici, 2009). On the other hand, these measures are still quite large in case of Canada and Japan. Conversely, the proportional importance of the input-based subsidy programmes is on the rise in Australia and the US (Figure 6.2). However, Canada and Japan are yet to switch their attention on these latter measures.

The environmental implications of subsidies, especially reflected through loss of biodiversity, are particularly evident in case of marine fisheries. Huge devolution of funds to domestic players can lead to fishing with over-capacity, which may in turn result in overexploitation of the fish stocks owing to increased fishing intensity (Porter, 2000; WWF, undated). One additional problem is that in presence of subsidies, the economic signals of overcapacity and

Figure 6.1:
PSE payments based on commodity output (%)

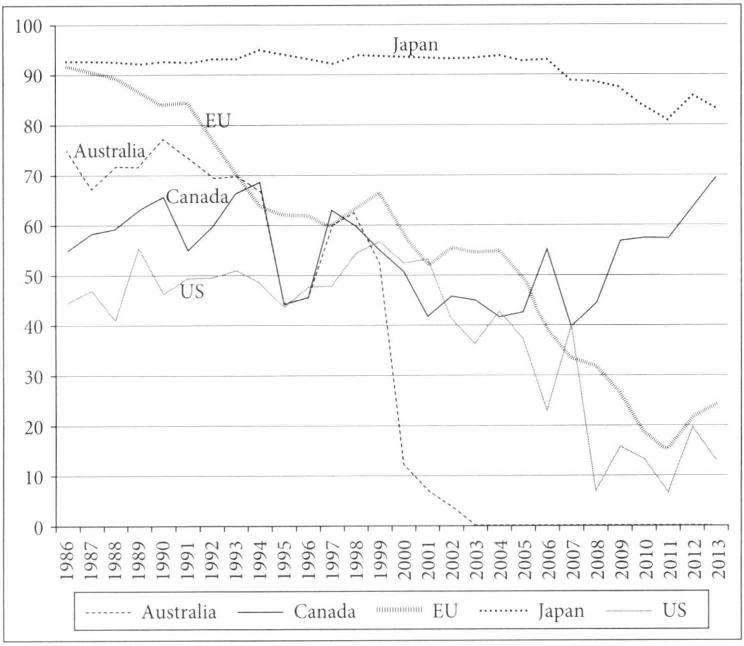

Source: Constructed from the OECD (undated) data.

overexploitation (e.g., reduced productivity, lower catches) might go unnoticed (Chakraborty and Kumar, 2010). Moreover, subsidies through price support measures may increase the number of players, and lead to resource overexploitation. WTO (1999) estimated the annual volume of trade-distorting fishing subsidies at around US$54 billion, and reported overcapitalization and over-fishing as a consequence. A decade later, persistence of the problem led WTO Director-General Pascal Lamy to caution that:

> [T]oday, we run the risk that over-fishing will so deplete fish stocks in our oceans that many species will disappear forever... . It is bad news for the world's 43.5 million full time fishers. Governments have contributed to this problem by providing nearly $16 billion annually in subsidies to the fisheries sector. This support keeps more boats on the water and fewer fish in the sea.... (WTO, 2009)

Figure 6.2:
PSE payments based on input use (%)

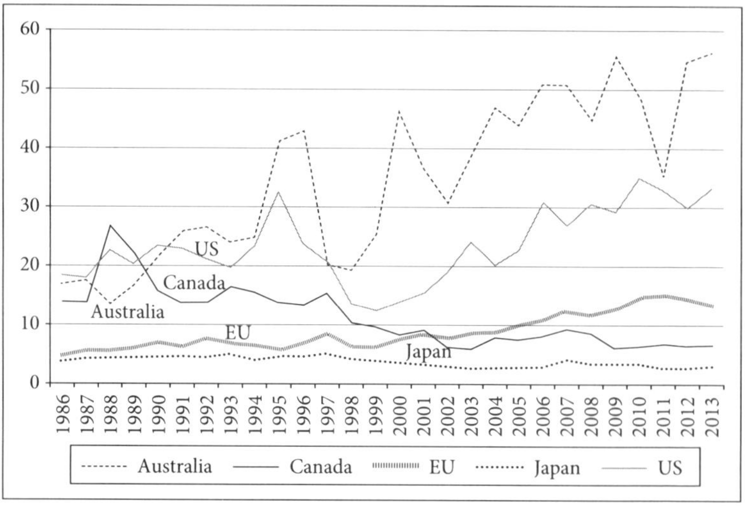

Source: Constructed from the OECD (undated) data.

The composition and implications of fisheries subsidies has been a widely researched area. It has been noted that fuel subsidies constitute a major part of the financial devolution to the fisheries sector (Sumaila and Pauly, 2006; Sumaila et al., 2008; Tyedmers et al., 2005). In addition, tax exemption schemes and interest subsidies are another major channel for helping domestic players (Sharp and Sumaila, 2009). The data on Government Financial Transfers (GFTs) to the fisheries sector as obtained from OECD Factbook (OECD, 2009) are reported in Table 6.2. It has been observed that during eighties and nineties, the developed countries dominated the list of fisheries subsidies providers. However, in the recent period, several developing countries (e.g., South Korea, Turkey) are also playing a key role in this regard. While in 1996 the total amount of fisheries subsidies provided in these countries stood at US$5,997.79 million, the figure has increased to US$6,726.67 million in 2006.

It is a matter of grave concern that the fisheries subsidies have not declined to any considerable extent in the recent period. The continuation of the fisheries subsidies and its adverse implications

Table 6.2:
Average annual government financial transfers to fishing sector

(US$ million)

S. No.	Country	1996–2000	2001–06
1.	United States	1,015.12	1,334.42
2.	Japan	2,743.74	2,299.43
3.	South Korea	350.14	559.87
4.	Canada	537.38	568.33
5.	Spain	330.28	357.93
6.	Norway	154.94	141.05
7.	Turkey	17.88	56.95
8.	Italy	168.15	158.18
9.	United Kingdom	98.34	92.36
10.	France	134.20	158.93
11.	Denmark	60.48	61.26
12.	Australia	53.63	80.23

Source: OECD (2009).

on trade and environment has forced the UNCSD (2012) declaration to put their faith on the ongoing WTO discussions for future reforms on this front:

> We reaffirm our commitment in the Johannesburg Plan of Implementation to eliminate subsidies that contribute to illegal, unreported and unregulated fishing and overcapacity, taking into account the importance of this sector to developing countries, and we reiterate our commitment to conclude multilateral disciplines on fisheries subsidies that will give effect to the WTO Doha Development Agenda and the Hong Kong Ministerial Declaration mandates to strengthen disciplines on subsidies in the fisheries sector, including through the prohibition of certain forms of fisheries subsidies that contribute to overcapacity and overfishing....

However, Chakraborty et al. (2011) and Chakraborty and Kumar (2010) have noted that fisheries subsidies data in several countries suffer from underreporting. In addition, the data reporting format varies from country to country and hence cross-country comparison of the harmful subsidies are not easily doable. As a result, the WTO negotiations regarding discipline on fisheries subsidies is not proceeding at the required pace. In addition, the underreporting of fisheries subsidies highlights the associated concerns on underestimation of their environmental implications and validity of the future projections.

In addition to resource overexploitation in own country due to devolution of fisheries subsidies, the same can occur in other countries as well (generally developing countries and least developed countries [LDCs]) through access rights transfers route (Scherr, 2003). Developing countries/LDCs may decide to sell their Exclusive Economic Zones access rights to foreign fleets for an agreed period of time in return for financial contributions, if domestic capacity is limited. For instance, UNEP (2004) has noted that during early nineties, the US vessels was paying almost one-third of the fishing rights access charge in the Pacific Island States vis-à-vis other vessels. The remainder cost of access was paid for by the US Government through a US$15 million grant to the host countries. The entry of developed country fleets in developing country/LDC waters in this manner might lead to over-fishing, which the access agreements may not completely take care of. For instance, the potential problems associated with resource overexploitation by EU vessels in Africa through the bilateral fisheries agreements has been reported in the literature (Kaczynski and Fluharty, 2002; Porter, 1997). Similar overexploitation from access right transfers has been observed in other regions as well (Mwikya, 2006; UNEP, 2003). DFID (undated) reported that in recent period EU is introducing a Vessel Monitoring System (VMS) Protocol for improving monitoring and compliance level in the newly formed Economic Partnership Agreements. However, while, on one hand, many LDCs do not yet have the technical capabilities for introducing the protocols, several small countries even with a VMS in place has to rely on foreign vessels to report their catches owing to lack of expertise and the required fleet network on the other. As a result, the potential threat on environment still remains considerable.

Like the case of agriculture, the WTO ASCM attempts to limit the extent of actionable subsidies to the *de minimis* level (within *ad valorem* 5 per cent) in case of manufacturing products. However, the use of subsidies in international trade and associated disputes are quite frequent (Chakraborty et al., 2011). For instance, extension of fuel subsidies to various manufacturing activities is considerably high in several countries, which significantly harm environmental sustainability. Estimation of the value of annual global energy subsidy is, however, a critical question due to under-reporting. It has been noted that annual global energy subsidy level is greater than US$300 billion (Victor, 2009). It is estimated that world emissions of CO_2 and GHGs can be reduced by 13 and 10 per cent, respectively, by 2050 with the removal of fossil fuels and electricity subsidies in 20 non-OECD countries (Burniaux et al., 2009). Although developed countries are among the major providers of energy subsidy, the developing countries are also coming up in recent period on this front. On one hand, Templet (2001) has reported presence of huge volume of energy, pollution and tax subsidies across US states. On the other, UNEP (2008) has noted that:

> ... the twenty largest non-OECD countries amount to around US$220 billion based on 2005 data, of which subsidies to fossil fuels account for around $170 billion ... Russia has the largest subsidies in dollar terms, amounting to about $40 billion, most of which go to natural gas... Iran's energy subsidies are almost as large, at an estimated $37 billion. Six other countries—China, Saudi Arabia, India, Indonesia, Ukraine and Egypt—each have subsidies in excess of $10 billion per year. (UNEP, 2008)

The continuation of the energy subsidies has forced UNCSD (2012) to note in the Rio+20 declarations that, 'Countries reaffirm the commitments they have made to phase out harmful and inefficient fossil fuel subsidies that encourage wasteful consumption and undermine sustainable development'. However, the negotiations on emission cut commitments by the countries from fossil fuel burning have hit a roadblock, which is an area of serious concern (EEPSPL, 2009). In particular, the use of various subsidy programmes in China towards the environmentally sensitive sectors has come to light repeatedly over the last decade. NCTO (undated) has reported that China is helping the textile producers through a number of export incentive programmes. Haley (2008) noted that the energy subsidies declined in China during 2002–03 after its entry into WTO in 2001 but has increased considerably in the subsequent period. Price et al. (2007) observed that more than US$52 billion has been spent in subsidies given to Chinese steel producers, which included preferential loan, credit, land-use discount and others. Chow (2007) has observed an interrelationship between use of energy from exhaustible resources in China and environmental degradation there.

Data and Empirical Model

The present analysis attempts to understand the role of subsidy provided by the General Government or Central Government (or Budgetary Central Government) on the overall environmental performance for a set of 134 countries through a cross-sectional time series analysis for the period over 1990–2010. In accordance with the availability of the latest data, 1990–2010 has been taken as the period of our analysis. The data series used for the current analysis has been obtained from various agencies, published by academic forums as well as international and multilateral agencies. A total of 134 countries, for which data on subsidy, per capita income and CO_2 emission are available consistently have been considered here for the analysis. The analysis deals with the direct subsidy, which is reported in government expenditure side of budget and reported in Government Finance Statistics (GFS) of IMF.[1] It is observed that GFS compiles the government subsidy figures for countries from different government sources as per their reporting practice. Three types of government reporting have been observed in the GFS data for which the required data on subsidy is available. First, the *general government* (GG) includes all the central government (CG) transfers plus budgetary expenses of all the Central Ministries/Departments and the same for the state governments (including provincial or regional) and local governments. The CG transfers, on the other hand, represent the consolidated transfers of the CG

[1] Available online at http://elibrary-data.imf.org/QueryBuilder.aspx?key=19784658&s=322 (accessed on 11 July 2014).

(including transfers of Central Ministries/departments). Finally, subsidies reported under *Budgetary Central Government* (BCG) covers, 'Any central government entity that is fully covered by the central government budget' (IMF, 2005). In addition, the GFS generally reports the budgetary statistics for countries adopting cash accounting method, but for several countries accrual (non-cash) accounting method has been reported. When data are available for a country for different level of government, preference is given to GG over CG and similarly CG over BCG.

The following panel data regression model is estimated here for 131 countries over 1990–2010 for analysing the effect of budgetary subsidies on per capita CO_2 emission:

$$\begin{aligned}\log(CO_{2it}) = \alpha &+ \beta_1 \log(SUB_{it}) + \beta_2 \log(SUB_{i(t-1)}) \\ &+ \beta_3 \log(PCGDP_{it}) + \beta_4 \log(PCGDP_{it})^2 \\ &+ \beta_5 \log(AGRIGDP_{it}) + \beta_6 \log(MFGGDP_{it}) \\ &+ \beta_7 \log(SERVGDP_{it}) + \beta_8 \log(URB_{it}) + C_{it} \\ &+ GOV_{it} + T_t + \varepsilon_{it} \qquad (1)\end{aligned}$$

where,

log or prefix	the logarithmic transformation of the variables
α	the constant term
βs	*coefficients*
CO_{2it}	per capita CO_2 emission (in tonne per annum) of country *i* for year *t*
SUB_{it}	budgetary subsidy (as percentage of GDP) provided by country *i* for year *t*
$SUB_{i(t-1)}$	budgetary subsidy (as percentage of GDP)provided by country *i* for year *t–1*
$PCGDP_{it}$	per capita GDP (current US$) of country *i* for year *t*
$AGRIGDP_{it}$	agriculture value added (expressed as percentage of GDP) of country *i* for year *t*
$MFGGDP_{it}$	manufacturing value added (expressed as percentage of GDP) of country *i* for year *t*

$SERVGDP_{it}$	services, and other value added (expressed as percentage of GDP) of country *i* for year *t*
URB_{it}	level of urbanization (urban population expressed as percentage of total population) in country *i* in year *t*
C_{it}	Cash dummy in country *i* in year *t* (takes the value of 1 if the country follows cash accounting method, and 0 if the country follows accrual accounting system)
GOV_{it}	government financing dummy in country *i* in year *t* (takes the value of 1 if the subsidy corresponds to GG, and 0 for BCG or CG)
$PCGNI_{it}$	per capita nominal gross national income (US$ at current prices and current exchange rates) of country *i* for year *t*
LIC	low income country (PCGNI: US$1,035 or less) dummy, which has a value of 1 for the corresponding countries and 0 otherwise
LMIC	lower-middle income country (PCGNI: US$1,035–4,085) dummy, which has a value of 1 for the corresponding countries and 0 otherwise
UMIC	upper-middle income country (PCGNI: US$4,085–12,615) dummy, which has a value of 1 for the corresponding countries and 0 otherwise
HIC	high income country (PCGNI: US $12,616 or more) dummy, which has a value of 1 for the corresponding countries and 0 otherwise
T_t	time dummies (i.e., T_1=1 for 2000 and 0 otherwise)
ε_{it}	disturbance term

The advantage of using the log-linear model in the current context is that the estimated coefficients can be interpreted as the elasticity between budgetary subsidy and per capita CO_2 emission and other variables.

The subsidies considered in the current analysis include only direct budgetary subsidies provided by general government, central government or budgetary central government of a country.[2] The indirect or implicit subsidies (i.e., income foregone in terms of tax rebate/exemptions, etc.) are not covered due to non-availability of consistent cross-country data on that front. The effect of subsidies is estimated by considering per capita annual emission of CO_2 (in metric tonne) as an indicator of climate change impact in a country. The per capita CO_2 data are obtained from World Development Indicators database (World Bank, 2013).

For the control variables, the data on per capita GDP, share of agriculture, manufacturing and services sectors in GDP and level of urbanization have been taken from World Development Indicators database. The dummy variables have been generated from the obtained data series as per the defined specifications.

The emerging trends in the major series considered in the regression analysis, namely budgetary subsidies, per capita CO_2 emissions, per capita GDP, share of the three sectors in GDP and level of urbanization and others are illustrated with their descriptive statistics summarized in Table 6.3 (for equal interval of five years). First, it is observed that while a fluctuating trend is being noticed for both the average budgetary subsidies expressed as percentage of GDP and per capita CO_2 emission, a rise has been noted in the former series. Similarly, average share of agriculture and manufacturing sectors has declined over the period, while the same for the services sector is showing a rising trend. A rise in level of urbanization has also been noticed.

Empirical Results

The panel data regression analysis has been undertaken with help of the STATA software (version 13.1). To understand the

[2] For detail discussion on IMF Database of subsidy for various level of governments and accounting methods (cash versus non-cash or accrual accounting), see Mukherjee and Chakraborty (2014).

Table 6.3:
Discrriptive statistics for the key variables included in the regression model for selected countries

	Average per Capita CO_2 Emission (in Tonne)	*Average Budgetary Subsidy (% of GDP)*	*Average per Capita GDP (current US$)*	*Average Share of Agriculture in GDP (%)*	*Average Share of Manufacturing in GDP (%)*	*Average Share of Services in GDP (%)*	*Urban Population (as % of Total Population)*
1990	3.96 ± 5.45	1.76 ± 2.32	5426 ± 8045	18.88 ± 14.82	17.23 ± 8.34	49.3 ± 13.66	51.5 ± 23.65
	(0.02 – 26.2)	(0.01 – 14.38)	(161 – 36337)	(0.62 – 61.55)	(2.93 – 39.17)	(15.9 – 81.04)	(6.27 – 99.76)
1995	4.67 ± 7.18	1.3 ± 1.16	6773 ± 10293	18.04 ± 16.09	16.25 ± 7.37	52.59 ± 14.69	53.03 ± 23.5
	(0.04 – 61.51)	(0.01 – 5.84)	(65 – 50593)	(0 – 81.82)	(2.31 – 39.06)	(12.91 – 85.3)	(7.21 – 100)
2000	4.72 ± 6.85	1.28 ± 1.1	7130 ± 10073	14.88 ± 14.3	15.13 ± 7.76	54.98 ± 15.44	54.34 ± 23.35
	(0.04 – 58.5)	(0 – 6.95)	(92 – 46453)	(0 – 76.07)	(1.44 – 38.67)	(3.35 – 87.54)	(8.25 – 100)
2005	5.04 ± 7.2	1.79 ± 1.7	10934 ± 15608	13.27 ± 13.23	14.65 ± 7.24	56.97 ± 15.21	55.85 ± 23.23
	(0.02 – 63.18)	(0 – 8.16)	(133 – 80925)	(0 – 67.01)	(2.01 – 38.93)	(2.96 – 91.26)	(9.38 – 100)
2010	5 ± 6.44	1.91 ± 2.04	13716 ± 18555	11.69 ± 12.01	13.44 ± 6.87	59.98 ± 14.23	57.45 ± 23.09
	(0.01 – 40.31)	(0 – 9.57)	(211 – 103574)	(0 – 57.3)	(0.87 – 35.62)	(20.79 – 92.84)	(10.64 – 100)

Source: Compiled by authors from various sources as mentioned in the text.
Notes: Figures in the parentheses show the range for the corresponding average value, figure after ± is the standard deviation.

working of the model for proposed relationship in equation (1),[3] Hausman specification test is first conducted. It is observed that the Chi-square test statistics of 313.19 (Prob.: 0.0000) is statistically significant. The Hausman test suggests the presence of an underlying fixed effect model. For detecting the presence of first order autocorrelation in the model, the Wooldridge test is then performed. The *F*-test statistics of 26.016 (Prob.: 0.0000) indicates the presence of first order autocorrelation. To check the existence of heteroskedasticity in the estimated model, the Breusch-Pagan/Cook-Weisberg test has been conducted. The Chi-square test statistics of 106.29 (Prob.: 0.0000) indicates the presence of heteroskedasticity. Estimated mean variance inflation factor (VIF) is 11.56, which results from the inclusion of both Log(PCGDP) and its square term in the model. For other variables, the values of VIF are within the tolerance limit of multi-collinearity. Based on these diagnostic tests, the present analysis adopts feasible general least square method with time-specific fixed effects. The estimated models make correction for the presence of heteroskedasticity and first order panel specific autocorrelation [PSAR(1)] within unbalanced panel data framework.

The estimation results for various specifications of equation (1) are summarized in Table 6.4, from which the following conclusions can be drawn. First and foremost, the estimation results strongly underline the adverse influence of government subsidies on per capita CO_2 emissions ($lpcco_2$) in the sample countries, as reflected from the positive and highly significant coefficients. The relationship is found to be robust for all the model specifications of the budgetary subsidies term, namely *lsub and lsub(-1)*. The empirical results in elasticity terms underline that with proportional increase in the budgetary subsidy level in a country, the rate of per capita emission of CO_2 also rises significantly. Interestingly, in models 3 and 4, the coefficient of *lsub(-1)* is found to be higher vis-à-vis the corresponding coefficients for *lsub*, which demonstrates the importance of the lagged effects of budgetary subsidies on per

[3] In equation (1), we drop $lsub_{i(t-1)}$ from the list of regressors to carry out diagnostic tests for selection of appropriate specification of the regression model.

Table 6.4:
Estimated results on the relationship between budgetary subsidy and CO_2 emissions

	Model 1		*Model 2*		*Model 3*		*Model 4*		*Model 5 LIC & LMIC*		*Model 6 UMIC & HIC*		*Model 7 Difference#*	
lsub	0.018	***	0.018	***	0.021	***	0.015	***	0.019	***	0.012	**	0.005	***
	(0.004)		(0.004)		(0.004)		(0.004)		(0.005)		(0.005)		(0.001)	
lsub(-1)					0.026	***	0.019	***						
					(0.004)		(0.004)							
lpcgdp	1.154	***	1.225	***	1.269	***	1.378	***	1.065	***	1.399	***	0.275	***
	(0.081)		(0.083)		(0.075)		(0.077)		(0.201)		(0.215)		(0.058)	
lpcgdp2	−0.042	***	−0.048	***	−0.051	***	−0.054	***	−0.037	***	−0.057	***	−0.006	*
	(0.005)		(0.005)		(0.004)		(0.004)		(0.014)		(0.011)		(0.003)	
lagrigdp	−0.137	***	−0.17	***	−0.252	***	−0.158	***	−0.151	***	−0.048	**	0.055	***
	(0.019)		(0.018)		(0.016)		(0.019)		(0.031)		(0.02)		(0.013)	
lmfggdp	0.200	***					0.208	***	0.295	***	0.151	***	0.089	***
	(0.021)						(0.021)		(0.022)		(0.025)		(0.019)	
lservgdp			−0.222	***	−0.291	***								
			(0.048)		(0.054)									

lurban	1.049	***	1.174	***	0.939	***	0.816	***	0.996	***	0.154	**	1.054	***
	(0.048)		(0.05)		(0.042)		(0.051)		(0.048)		(0.073)		(0.202)	
Cash	0.061	***	0.079	***	0.047	***	0.047	***	0.109	***	0.064	***	0.016	***
	(0.017)		(0.018)		(0.017)		(0.017)		(0.034)		(0.019)		(0.004)	
Gov	−0.027	*	−0.035	**	−0.038	**	−0.016		−0.104	***	−0.032	*	−0.003	
	(0.016)		(0.016)		(0.015)		(0.015)		(0.032)		(0.017)		(0.004)	
Constant	Omitted		Omitted		−8.284	***	−9.951	***	−10.195	***	Omitted		0.005	
					(0.311)		(0.326)		(0.664)				(0.009)	
Time Fixed Effect	Yes		Yes		Yes		Yes		Yes		Yes		Yes	
Number of observations	1661		1736		1549		1491		824		831		1472	
Number of groups	131		134		131		129		90		70		129	
Wald chi2	14855.66		12468.86		8516.87		7132.02		5420.11		15994.62		592.89	
Prob>chi2	0.000		0.000		0.000		0.000		0.000		0.000		0.000	

Source: Authors' estimation results.

Notes: #- first difference of all continuous variables.

Figures in the parentheses show the heteroskedasticity [*Panel(hetero)*] and Panel-Specific First Order Autocorrelation [*PSAR(1)*] corrected standard error of the estimated coefficient.

***, ** and * imply estimated coefficient is significant at 0.01, 0.05 and 0.10 level, respectively.

capita CO_2 emissions in the selected sample. Second, sign of the coefficients with respect to per capita income indicates that for one percentage point increase in *lpcgdp*, $lpcco_2$ emission generally increases by a higher proportion, barring the exception in model 7. Third, the higher order terms of income ($lpcgdp^2$) are associated with a negative sign in all the estimated models. Fourth, the contribution of manufacturing sector in GDP is found to be positively influencing per capita CO_2 emission, while the reverse is noted in case of primary (agriculture) and service sectors. In other words, growth in composition of manufacturing sector in an economy results in growth of CO_2 emissions, while the rise in primary and service sectors contribute in curbing the same. The PCGDP and economic composition results provide a strong support to the existence of the EKCH phenomenon. Fifthly, the *lurb* variable is found to be positive in most of the selected model specifications, signifying the negative repercussions of urbanization. Finally, the cash and government dummies are found to be significant, implying the importance of the underlying accounting method and level of government data reporting practices in influencing the subsidy–climate change nexus. The result indicates that adoption of accrual accounting across the countries is desirable.

Moreover, the estimated result of regression models could be specific to functional form. Therefore, to check the robustness of our estimated result, we have estimated model 7 where first differences of all continuous variables are taken. Neither the sign nor the significance level of key policy variables change in this model. In addition, by splicing the sample countries into two groups, namely LIC & LMIC and UMIC & HIC as per the relevant income definitions, the robustness of the proposed relationship has been checked through models 5 and 6. The coefficient of *lsub* is found to be positive in both models, but the coefficient for the lower income countries are found to be larger vis-à-vis the same for their higher income counterparts. The observation can be explained by the fact that provision of subsidies in the lower income countries may potentially lead to greater CO_2 emissions given the possibility of natural resource base erosion.

A couple of interesting conclusions on the influence of subsidies on CO_2 emissions can be drawn by summarizing the regression results. First, the coefficient of *lsub* for the lower and higher income countries is 0.019 and 0.012, respectively, signifying greater emission growth in the former group in response to percentage increase in budgetary devolutions. In addition, the coefficients of *lpcgdp* for the lower and higher income countries are 1.065 and 1.399, respectively. The observation indicates that per capita income growth in developed countries potentially leads to higher CO_2 emissions, vis-à-vis the corresponding figures for their lower income counterparts. The difference in CO_2 emissions pattern across the two income groups can be explained by existing higher level of output in the richer economies. However, growth in devolution of subsidies may harm the sustainability of the lower income countries more severely.

Secondly, the coefficients of *lmfggdp* for the lower and higher income countries are found to be 0.295 and 0.151, respectively. In other words, the growth in manufacturing sector output in lower income countries potentially leads to higher CO_2 emissions growth, vis-à-vis the corresponding figures for their higher income counterparts. The result underlines the evidence that the rise in manufacturing sector output, if not associated with adequate compliance mechanism, may add to sustainability challenges.

Finally, the negative coefficient of $lpcgdp^2$ both in lower as well as higher income countries indicates the decline in the per capita CO_2 emissions with further rise in income. The estimated results signify the presence of an EKCH type relationship with reference to emission of per capita CO_2. Nevertheless, the coefficient for lower income countries (–0.037) is found to be smaller than the corresponding figure for the higher income countries (–0.057), indicating a sharper fall in the latter set of economies. The notion of development difference receives further support from the difference in the magnitude of the coefficient for the *lurb* variable for the two set of countries. While the coefficient is found to be 0.154 for the higher income countries, the same for the lower income countries is 0.996. In other words, the growth in urban population and consequent deepening of economic activities leads to far greater per capita CO_2 emissions growth in lower income countries. The result underlines the existence of a rising demand for cleaner environment and better environmental governance in higher income economies.

Subsidies and Environment in India: The Scenario

The discussion so far has concentrated on the cross-country evidence on the relationship between subsidies and environmental sustainability. The findings underline the negative influence of the subsidies on the global environmental scenario in no uncertain terms. In this background, an analysis of the subsidies being provided in the Indian context and their potential environmental repercussions would not be inappropriate here. The focus of discussion under this section is restricted to subsidies that are detrimental to environment or having potential to affect resource use pattern which could results in depletion and degradation of natural resources. The term 'subsidies' in this context denotes combined (central as well as state governments) budgetary subsidies provided on account of fertilizer subsidy, irrigation subsidy (major, medium and minor), petroleum subsidies and subsidies to promote export of primary sector outputs.

It has already been noted that developing countries generally depend on provision of input subsidies for supporting their agricultural sector and India is no exception to this trend. In particular, the fertilizer subsidy being provided in the country deserves special mention. Like any input subsidy, fertilizer subsidy is associated with consequent negative environmental impacts. The subsidy reduces the cost of the fertilizers for the farmers, which in turn encourages them to over-use and in an unbalanced way the subsidized fertilizers in their fields during the cultivation process. While, on one hand, this may lead to reduced fertility of the soil, pollution of ground and surface water is likely to happen, on the other, in the long run (Mukherjee, 2010). Output subsidy is also provided in terms of minimum support price, which sets a higher price vis-à-vis the actual prices for meeting the requirements of Targeted Public Distribution System (TPDS) and other welfare schemes (WTO, 2011b). However, subsidy under this front is not substantial in recent period.

Shamrao (2011) has noted that the fertilizer subsidy policy regime of the country can be categorized under three phases. The first phase (1977–91), which coincided with the later part of green revolution phase, was important for food security concerns of the country. The government attempt to reform of the subsidies during the second phase (1991–2003) with growing fiscal concerns in mind was only moderately successful. The third phase (since 2003) is more geared towards ensuring efficiency in production. At present, the fertilizer policy of the country is biased towards urea, which is the only controlled fertilizer and sold at statutory notified uniform sale prices across all-India. The government support is currently being provided in the following manner. The decontrolled phosphatic and potassic fertilizers are sold across the country at uniform indicative maximum retail prices (MRPs). However, the statutorily notified sales price and indicative MRP is generally lower vis-à-vis the cost of production of the respective manufacturing units. The government bridges the difference between the cost of production and the selling price/MRP as subsidy/concession to manufacturers (Government of India, undated). Since the consumer prices of both indigenous and imported fertilizers are fixed uniformly, financial support is also given on imported urea and decontrolled phosphatic and potassic fertilizers. However, all these subsidies may lead to potentially adverse environmental degradation.

Figure 6.3 in the following attempts to explore the source-wise composition of fertilizer subsidy in the country. It is observed from the figure that after nineties the proportional importance of the subsidies on imported fertilizer declined, but the same has resurfaced again after 2004–05. Subsidies to indigenous fertilizers for a long period accounted for the highest proportion of the government support, but the scenario has undergone a change from 2008–09 onwards. Presently, subsidies to the manufacturers/agencies for sale of decontrolled fertilizers explain the highest proportion of the subsidies on this front. WTO (2011b) has noted that the objective

Figure 6.3:
Source-wise share in total fertilizer subsidy in India

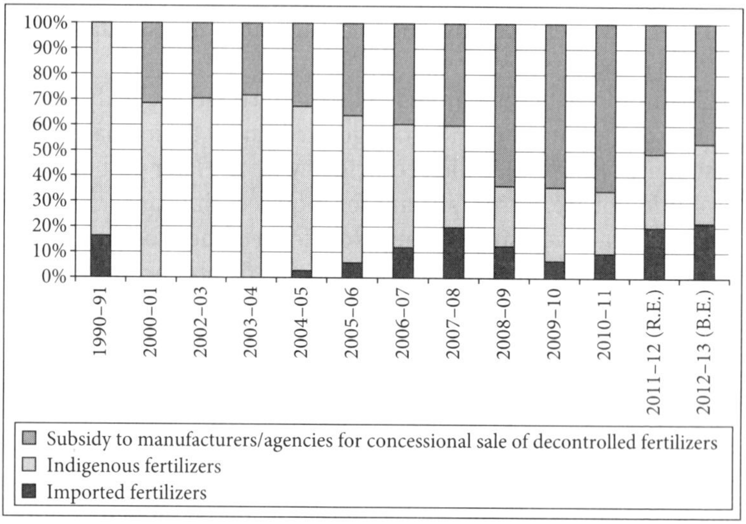

Source: Government of India (2013, 2011, 2010).

of India behind provision of the fertilizer subsidies is to '...keep the price of fertilizers under control, and to give producers a "reasonable" return on investment'.

Given the fact that a considerable part of the country is still heavily dependent on the monsoons for the cultivation, the role of the government in expansion of the irrigation network is obvious. However, indiscriminate expansion of the irrigation network may end up creating more problems than it originally intends to solve. Subsidy on the irrigation front constitutes both direct subsidy (government revenue and capital expenditure on major, medium and minor irrigation) and indirect subsidy on account of supplying free or partially free electricity in agriculture. Now, the practice of not pricing water and electricity on a volumetric basis gives pervasive signals to farmers who have no incentive to conserve water (either surface or ground water) and electricity. In the absence of institutional mechanism for fair and timely distribution of water under surface irrigation systems, farmers are compelled to invest on groundwater extraction infrastructure. Larger the reliability of water supply and fair distribution of water across all reaches of surface water distribution network, the lower will be the investment on groundwater extraction infrastructure. High cost of investment and low or negligible costs of operation (due to free or partially free electricity supply) make farmers' choice biased in favour of water-intensive crops (which also fetch higher return on investment) that results in indiscriminate extraction of groundwater. The water-intensive crops are by nature fertilizer- and pesticide-intensive, as a result of which large scale leaching of nitrates and pesticides into aquifers is reported from intensively cultivated areas of India (Mukherjee, 2012). Run-off of nutrients and pesticides also results in surface water eutrophication and large-scale endangering of agriculture ecosystem by wiping out agriculturally beneficial species like frogs/toad, earthworms, small fishes, snakes and others. The large-scale depletion of groundwater is also reported from various parts of intensively cultivated areas of India. It has been observed that failure of well and subsequent sunk costs often force farmers to fall in trap of indebtedness.

Among other subsidy measures, petroleum subsidy constitutes of payments made by the CG to oil marketing companies to compensate a part of their under-recoveries on account of sales of domestic LPG and kerosene below the desired price. In India, for the same set of petroleum products sale price does not reflect either international market price of crude oil or domestic cost of refining and marketing (Mukherjee and Rao, 2015). Unlike subsidy on domestic LPG and kerosene, administered pricing of diesel and petrol gives pervasive signals, which are detrimental to environment and natural resources (indiscriminate extraction of groundwater for agriculture and vehicular pollution). Subsidy on domestic LPG and kerosene is assumed to be beneficial to local environment as it reduces the dependence on biofuels (which is potential source of indoor air pollution) and could potentially protect local forest cover. However, in several instances it is observed that availability of subsidized LPG discourages adoption of household type biogas plants in areas where potential for adoption exists and for families who has the required herd size for adoption of family type biogas plant and could also potentially invest in terms of time and money for the plant (Mukherjee, 2008). Similarly, availability of subsidized kerosene through PDS facilitates farmers to use it (either directly or by mixing with diesel) as fuel for pump sets used to extract/draw water.

The composition of the agricultural subsidies being extended to the Indian players and its proportional importance is summarized in Table 6.5. The first column shows the monetary value of the subsidy under a particular category while the figure in the parentheses indicates the percentage share of the same in the GDP figures reported at factor cost. The agricultural subsidies in the country can be classified under three broad categories: fertilizer subsidy, energy subsidy and irrigation subsidy. In addition, presence of certain product-specific subsidies (e.g., tea, coffee, jute) can be noted. It is observed from the table that the proportional importance of the fertilizer subsidies has fluctuated over the last decade. The percentage share of the energy subsidies and irrigation subsidies is, however, almost unchanged over this period. On the whole, the percentage share of the agricultural subsidies has increased from 1.4 per cent in 2000–01 to 2.0 per cent in 2008–09.

The environmental implications of agricultural subsidy remain a major area of concern. Overuse of fertilizers in the post-Green revolution period has led to higher per acre yields, but is also associated with its environmental challenges (Kushwaha, 2008; Shamrao, 2011; Mukherjee, 2010). In India among all the forms of agricultural subsidies, fertilizer and petroleum subsidies are considered to be environmentally most harmful subsidies. In particular, fertilizer subsidy is biased in favour of nitrogenous fertilizers, which has resulted in unbalanced and over-application of nitrogen on farmland, with far-reaching long-run consequences (Mukherjee, 2010). Sidhu (2002) has reported alarming degradation of soil quality in Punjab resulting from excessive use of chemical fertilizers and near mono-cultural cropping pattern. Moreover, the subsidies on electricity front also exert significant negative influence on the environment. Sidhu (2002) has reported that in Punjab more than nine lakh tube wells are recipients of electricity free of cost, which caused substantial overuse of the facilities. As a result, underground water in the agricultural belts of the state is depleting at an alarming

Table 6.5:
Agricultural subsidies in India

(₹ crore)

Year	Fertilizer Subsidy (Central Budget)	Petroleum Subsidy[#]	Combined Revenue and Capital Expenditure of the Centre and the States			Subsidy to Tea and Coffee Plantations	Subsidy to Jute Corporation of India	Subsidy to Marine Products to Export Development Authority	Subsidy on Agricultural Products to Export Development Authority	Total Agricultural Subsidy	GDP at Factor Cost (Current Prices)
			Major and Medium Irrigation	Minor Irrigation	Total Irrigation						
(1)	(2)	(3)	(4)	(5)	(6)=(4)+(5)	(7)	(8)	(9)	(10)	(11)*	(12)
1990–91	4,400 (0.8)	–	3,278	1,482	4,760 (0.9)	–	8	–	–	9,168 (1.7)	5,31,814
2000–01	13,811 (0.7)	–	12,071	2,889	14,960 (0.7)	10	–	20	33	28,834 (1.4)	20,00,743
2001–02	12,596 (0.6)	–	11,822	3,103	14,925 (0.7)	30	–	30	30	27,611 (1.3)	21,75,260
2002–03	11,015 (0.5)	5,225 (0.2)	14,250	2,998	17,247 (0.7)	64	30	40	22	33,643 (1.4)	23,43,864
2003–04	11,847 (0.5)	6,292 (0.2)	17,175	3,552	20,727 (0.8)	26	30	41	30	38,993 (1.5)	26,25,819
2004–05	15,879 (0.5)	2,956 (0.1)	13,854	4,743	18,597 (0.6)	104	30	44	30	37,640 (1.3)	29,71,464
2005–06	18,460 (0.5)	2,683 (0.1)	24,864	5,345	30,209 (0.9)	40	30	54	43	51,519 (1.5)	33,90,503
2006–07	26,222 (0.7)	2,699 (0.1)	30,003	8,470	38,472 (1)	57	28	50	61	67,589 (1.7)	39,53,276
2007–08	32,490 (0.7)	2,820 (0.1)	30,793	6,695	37,488 (0.8)	36	30	84	63	73,011 (1.6)	45,82,086
2008–09	76,603 (1.4)	2,852 (0.1)	32,684	7,634	40,319 (0.8)	73	37	95	63	1,20,042 (2.3)	53,03,567

(Table 6.5 Contd)

(Table 6.5 Contd)

Year	Fertilizer Subsidy (Central Budget)	Petroleum Subsidy#	Combined Revenue and Capital Expenditure of the Centre and the States: Major and Medium Irrigation	Minor Irrigation	Total Irrigation	Subsidy to Tea and Coffee Plantations	Subsidy to Jute Corporation of India	Subsidy to Marine Products to Export Development Authority	Subsidy on Agricultural Products to Export Development Authority	Total Agricultural Subsidy	GDP at Factor Cost (Current Prices)
(1)	(2)	(3)	(4)	(5)	(6)=(4)+(5)	(7)	(8)	(9)	(10)	(11)*	(12)
2009–10	61,264 (1)	14,951 (0.2)	34,606	10,094	44,700 (0.7)	72	37	90	89	1,21,203 (2.0)	61,08,903
2010–11	62,301 (0.9)	38,371 (0.5)	34,670	12,126	46,797 (0.6)	61	30	90	100	1,47,750 (2.0)	72,48,860
2011-12 (R.E.)	67,199 (0.8)	68,481 (0.8)	37,260	16,416	53,675 (0.6)	161	55	110	125	1,89,806 (2.3)	83,91,691
2012-13 (B.E.)	60,974 (0.6)	43,580 (0.5)	47,171	19,007	66,178 (0.7)	145	55	110	125	1,71,167 (1.8)	94,72,291

Source: Government of India (2013, 2011, 2010).

Notes: Figure in the parentheses shows the percentage of GDP at Factor Cost (at current prices).

– Not entire petroleum subsidy is attributable to agriculture sector; however, apportionment based on agricultural consumption of subsidized petroleum products is difficult due unavailability of data.

R.E., revised estimate; B.E., budget estimate.

* – (11)=(2)+(3)+(6)+(7)+(8)+(9)+(10).

rate of 23 cm per annum. Pandey and Srivastava (2001) have reported that subsidies on all forms of irrigation (major, medium and minor), and command area development as well as fertilizers, pesticides and chemicals bear serious environmental repercussions. The possibility of pollution through shrimp culture has also been mentioned in the literature (Bhatta, 2012).

Agricultural subsidies in India are subject to various political economic forces (Birner et al., 2011) and their budgetary devolutions may not always be a strict function of the environmental parameters. Therefore, predicting the future path of agricultural subsidies in India would be a difficult exercise. The saving grace is that, a number of recent measures unilaterally undertaken for improving the environment have also contained the adverse impact of the government support policies.[4] For instance, the 45-day monsoon ban on mechanized fishing in Tamil Nadu deserves mention (Francis, 2012). On the other hand, the international pressure-led environmental reforms in the Indian context are also not uncommon. The April 2011 Stockholm Convention discussions, where India agreed to ban the insecticide endosulfan over 11 years, only after it was isolated at the negotiating forum could be mentioned in this regard (Haq et al., 2011). On the non-agricultural front, reduction in certain subsidies has been noted as well. HT (2011) has noted that the export incentives being provided to some 1,100-odd product groups under Duty Entitlement Pass Book scheme is presently being phased out. Sen (2012) reported that on the face of the protest from the EU, US, Japan and Turkey, India is currently removing textile export subsidy gradually, which were being provided under various channels, including export promotion capital goods scheme, focus market, focus product scheme and others. On the other hand, certain recent government support measures play a crucial role in containing environmental pollution in the manufacturing sector. For instance, environmental impacts of textile bleaching and dyeing industries are well documented in India (Appasamy

[4] For example, central government provides assistance to state governments for setting up soil testing laboratories for issuing Soil Health Cards to farmers (source: http://pib.gov.in/newsite/efeatures.aspx?relid=108692, accessed on 31 March 2015).

and Nelliyat, 2000; Mukherjee and Nelliyat, 2007). Similar concerns have been noted on the pollution load of the leather firms as well (Chakraborty and Chakraborty, 2007; Sankar, 2006). The provision of central and state government subsidies for creation of common effluent treatment plants (CETPs) has contributed positively in this regard (Chakraborty and Banerjee, 2009).

Future Concerns

The adverse effect of global warming is a widely discussed area in the recent period and the need to reduce carbon emissions and other harmful pollutants is increasingly being felt by the countries. Overexploitation of resources and overproduction, aided by subsidies on various fronts including energy subsidy and various types of production subsidies (input and output subsidies) is, however, a serious threat against achieving that goal. In addition, a major challenge for the countries would be to bridge the conflict between 'the needs of the present' and the 'future generations', before reaching the path of sustainable development. As the discussions under the current analysis indicates, often the countries operate from a selfish standpoint, and in order to provide an edge to the local producers vis-à-vis foreign players, adopt an active policy of subsidization with less considerations for the environmental concerns. The driving motivation behind the support measures may vary from country to country from the domestic infant-industry protection argument to explicit export subsidization schemes for displacing foreign competitors. In addition, indirect support measures for the local producers could be extended through the prevalence of relatively lax environmental standards in a country, which would provide lower variable cost for them (i.e., lower pollution abatement expenses). The empirical evidence on 'Pollution Haven Hypothesis' provides instances of this type of indirect support (Chakraborty, 2012; Cole et al., 2008; He, 2006; Merican et al., 2007; Wagner and Timmins, 2009).

Several UN-led international forums have attempted to contain the adverse impacts of the subsidization programmes through multilateral negotiations. Among the leading UNEP/UNFCCC discussion forums which directly or indirectly focus on the reduction of subsidies, Rio Declaration, Kyoto Protocol, Johannesburg Plan of Implementation, Copenhagen Accord and others deserve special mention (Mukherjee and Chakraborty, 2015b; UN, undated). The recently concluded Rio+20 discussions have also explicitly dealt with the adverse environmental implications of the subsidies, and concluded by encouraging the WTO member countries to, '…redouble their efforts to achieve an ambitious, balanced and development-oriented conclusion to the Doha Development Agenda' (UNCSD, 2012). However, the actual progress on this front so far has been limited. For instance, Lassa (2006) notes the reasons behind weaker outcome of the discussions under Kyoto Protocol.

Besides the limitations faced by the UN bodies, the progress under the WTO Doha Development Agenda Negotiations has also given fewer reasons to cheer. As per the WTO commitments, the member countries are expected to reduce their actionable agricultural subsidies (Shah, 2012). In line with this principle, the Doha Declaration (2001) underlined the need to phase out the trade-distorting agricultural support measures as well as all forms of export subsidies (WTO, 2001). However, the developed countries have always been guarded during the negotiations, resulting to the stalemate at the Doha Round (Chakraborty and Khan, 2008; Chakraborty and Singh, 2006). A speedy resolution of the disagreements among countries and the conclusion of the Doha Round is not expected very soon. However, the delay in conclusion of trade deal implies continuation of the agricultural subsidies. The experience of the cotton subsidies in the US is a case in point (Baffes, 2011).

The discussions and empirical analysis undertaken in the current study clearly indicate that despite the efforts of reducing subsidies through the WTO framework on one hand and the UN forums on the other, limited success has been observed till date. The positive relationship observed between subsidies and per capita CO_2

emission is a worrying trend in this background. The failure to contain provision of subsidies through timely conclusion of the Doha Round negotiations and the discussions under the aegis of the UN forums are therefore posing a serious threat to the global climate change related concerns.

In India, the literature on environmental impacts of subsidies is sparse and till recently government initiatives have been restricted to only process modification of channelizing the subsidies rather than on containing the subsidy bill to the exchequer. Large-scale leakage and diversions of subsidy are the main critiques of the present system rather than on environmental impacts of these subsidies. However, Government of India (2012) has recently announced to contain subsidy to less than 2 per cent of GDP to control burgeoning fiscal deficit and several other measures are in the offing. Containing the subsidy on fertilizer and fuel and ensuring leakage-proof delivery system could be environmentally benign in the long run as well.

The chapter has restricted the discussion on subsidies, which are environmentally detrimental and have serious consequences on resource use pattern. However, there are also subsidies, which are specific to induce environmental compliance. For example, in the Indian context, the capital subsidy provided to construct CETP (50 per cent subsidy on project capital costs—25 per cent each by central and concerned state government (CPCB, 2005)) and provision for 100 per cent depreciation benefits for investment on air pollution, water pollution and solid waste control equipments, are expected to minimize the environmental impacts caused by industrial operations. A suitable design of subsidy scheme for both capital investment and operation and maintenance could potentially encourage informal sectors to take measures for pollution abatement. There is a need for exploring similar 'green' support measures in other countries as well through systematic development of an exhaustive database.

References

Appasamy, P.P. and Nelliyat, P. 2000. 'Economic Assessment of Environmental Damage: A Case Study of Industrial Water Pollution in Tiruppur', Environmental Economics Research Committee (EERC) Working Paper Series: IPP-1. Available at http://coe.mse.ac.in/eercrep/fullrep/ipp/IPP_FR_Paul_Appasamy.pdf (last accessed on 27 June 2012).

Anderson, K., Kurzweil, M., Martin, W., Sandri, D. and Valenzuela, E. 2008. 'Measuring Distortions to Agricultural Incentives, Revisited', World Bank Policy Research Working Paper No. 4612, Washington, DC.

Anderson, K. and Martin, W. (eds) 2009. *Distortions to Agricultural Incentives in Asia*. Washington, DC: World Bank.

Anderson, K., Martin, W. and Valenzuela, E. 2006. 'The Relative Importance of Global Agricultural Subsidies and Market Access', *World Trade Review*, 5(3): 357–76.

Atici, C. 2009. 'Pollution without Subsidy? What is the Environmental Performance Index Overlooking?', *Ecological Economics*, 68(7): 1903–07.

Baffes, J. 2011. 'Cotton Subsidies, the WTO, and the Cotton Problem', World Bank Policy Research Working Paper No. 5663, Washington, D.C.

Bajona, C. and Kelly, D. 2012. 'Trade and the Environment with Pre-Existing Subsidies: A Dynamic General Equilibrium Analysis', *Journal of Environmental Economics and Management*, 64(2): 253–78.

Barde, J.-P. and Honkatukia, O. 2004. 'Environmentally Harmful Subsidies', in T. Tietenberg and H. Folmer (eds), *The International Yearbook of Environmental and Resource Economics 2004/2005* (pp. 254–88). Northampton, MA: Edward Elgar.

Bhatta, R. 2012. 'Economics of Sustainable Shrimp Aquaculture in India', in S. Mukherjee and D. Chakraborty (eds), *Environmental Scenario in India: Successes and Predicaments* (pp. 45–64). London: Routledge.

Birner, R., Gupta, S. and Sharma, N. 2011. 'The Political Economy of Agricultural Policy Reform in India: Fertilizers and Electricity for Irrigation', Research Monograph, International Food Policy Research Institute, Washington, D.C.

Burniaux, J.-M., Chanteau, J., Dellink, R., Duval, R. and Jamet, S. 2009. 'The Economics of Climate Change Mitigation: How to Build the Necessary Global Action in a Cost-effective Manner', OECD Economics Department Working Papers, No. 701, OECD Publishing, Paris.

Chaisse, J., Chakraborty, D. and Nag, B. 2011. 'The Three-pronged Strategy of India's Preferential Trade Policy—A Contribution to the Study of Modern Economic Treaties', *Connecticut Journal of International Law*, 26(2): 415–55.

Chakraborty, D. 2012. 'Is India Turning into a Pollution Haven? Evidences from Trade and Investment Patterns', in S. Mukherjee and D. Chakraborty (eds), *Environmental Scenario in India: Successes and Predicaments* (pp. 243–66). UK: Routledge.

Chakraborty, D. and Banerjee, K. 2009. 'Environment-related Trade Barriers: An Analysis of Indian Leather Sector', *GALT Update*, 3(2): 12–17.

Chakraborty, D. and Khan, U.K. 2008. *The WTO Deadlocked: Understanding the Dynamics of International Trade*. New Delhi: SAGE Publications.

Chakraborty, D., Chaisse, J., and Kumar, A. 2011. 'Doha Round Negotiations on Subsidy and Countervailing Measures: Potential Implications on Trade Flows in Fishery Sector', *Asian Journal of WTO & International Health Law and Policy*, 6(1): 201–34.

Chakraborty, D. and Kumar, A. 2010. 'Implications of Fishery Sector Subsidies: A Review of Issues in light of WTO Negotiations', Centre for WTO Studies Discussion Paper No. 7, IIFT, 2010.

Chakraborty, P. and Chakraborty, D. 2007. 'Environmental Regulations and Indian Leather Industry', *Economic and Political Weekly*, 42(19): 1669–71.

Chakraborty, D. and Singh, Y. 2006. 'Agricultural Subsidy: The Major Hurdle to Free Trade', in D. Sengupta, D. Chakraborty, and P. Banerji (eds), *Beyond the Transition Phase of the WTO: An Indian Perspective on the Emerging Issues* (pp. 75–108). New Delhi: Academic Foundation.

Chand, R. and Philip, L.M. 2001. 'Subsidies and Support in World Agriculture: Is WTO Providing Level Playing Field?', Policy Brief No. 14, National Centre for Agricultural Economics and Policy Research, New Delhi.

Chang, H.-J. 2001. 'Infant Industry Promotion in Historical Perspective—A Rope to Hang Oneself or a Ladder to Climb With?', presented at the Conference, 'Development Theory at the Threshold of the Twenty-first Century', 28–29 August 2001, ECLAC, Santiago, Chile.

Chow, Gregory C. 2007. 'China's Energy and Environmental Problems and Policies', CEPS Working Paper No. 152, Princeton University, New Jersey.

Cole, Matthew A., Robert J.R. Elliott, and Jing Zhang. 2008. 'Growth, Foreign Direct Investment and the Environment: Evidence from Chinese Cities'. Available at www.ceauk.org.uk/2008-conference-papers/Cole-Elliott-Zhang.doc (last accessed on 19 June 2012).

Department for International Development (DFID). Undated. 'Fisheries and Access Agreements', Policy Brief No. 6, Marine Resources Assessment Group (MRAG) Ltd., DFID, London.

Ethical Energy-Petrochem Strategies Pvt. Ltd. (EEPSPL). 2009. 'Strategy For Post 2012 Kyoto Protocol Agreement'. Available at http://unfccc.int/resource/docs/2009/smsn/ngo/169.pdf (accessed on 19 June 2012).

Francis, I. 2012. 'Impact of the Monsoon Trawling Ban on Marine Fisheries in Tamil Nadu', in S. Mukherjee and D. Chakraborty (eds), *Environmental Scenario in India: Successes and Predicaments* (pp. 65–81). London: Routledge.

Giuliani, E., Morrison, A. and Rabellotti, R. (eds) 2011. *Innovation and Technological Catch-Up: The Changing Geography of Wine Production*. Edward Elgar publications.

Government of India. 2010. 'Indian Public Finance Statistics 2009–10', Department of Economic Affairs, Ministry of Finance, Government of India, New Delhi.

———. 2011. 'Indian Public Finance Statistics 2010–11', Department of Economic Affairs, Ministry of Finance, Government of India, New Delhi.

———. 2012. 'Union Budget 2012–13', Ministry of Finance, Government of India, New Delhi.

———. 2013. 'Indian Public Finance Statistics 2012–13', Department of Economic Affairs, Ministry of Finance, Government of India, New Delhi.

Government of India. Undated. 'Fertilizer Policy', Department of Fertilizers, Ministry of Chemicals and Fertilizers, Government of India, New Delhi. Available at http://fert.nic.in/page/fertilizer-policy (accessed on 2 July 2012).

Gulati, A. and Narayanan, S. 2003. *Subsidy Syndrome in Indian Agriculture*. London: Oxford University Press.

Haley, U.C.V. 2008. 'Shedding Light on Energy Subsidies in China: An Analysis of China's Steel Industry from 2000 to 2007', Alliance for American Manufacturing. Available at http://www.americanmanufacturing.org/wordpress/wp-content/uploads/2008/01/energy-subsidies-in-china-jan-8-08.pdf (last accessed on 19 June 2012).

Haq, Z., Chauhan, C. and Choudhury, G. 2011. 'India has 11 years to Ban Endosulfan', *Hindustan Times*, 29 April, New Delhi.

He, J. 2006. 'Pollution Haven Hypothesis and Environmental Impacts of Foreign Direct Investment: The Case of Industrial Emission of Sulfur Dioxide (SO_2) in Chinese Provinces', *Ecological Economics*, 60(1): 228–45.

Heutel, G. and Kelly, D.L. 2013. 'Incidence and Environmental Effects of Distortionary Subsidies', NBER Working Paper No. 18924, Cambridge, MA.

Hindustan Times (HT). 2011. '1100 Items to be Hit as Export Incentives Cut', 17 September, New Delhi.

International Institute for Sustainable Development (IISD) (undated), 'Complete Text of Rio Declaration'. Available at http://www.iisd.org/rio+5/agenda/declaration.htm (accessed on 19 June 2012).

IMF. 2005. 'Government Finance Statistics Manual 2001—Companion Material: Instructions for Compiling the Institutional Table'. Available at http://www.imf.org/external/pubs/ft/gfs/manual/intbin.pdf (accessed on 29 November 2013).

Kaczynski, W.K. and Fluharty, D.L. 2002. 'Balancing Socio-Economic Interests of West Africa with the European Union's Fisheries Policy: Who Benefits from Fisheries Agreements?', *Marine Policy*, 26(2): 75–93.

Kelly, D. 2009. 'Subsidies to Industry and the Environment', NBER Working Paper No. 14999, Cambridge, MA.

Kushwaha, N. 2008. 'Agriculture in India: Land Use and Sustainability', *International Journal of Rural Studies*, 15(1): 1–10.

Lassa, J. 2006. 'Kyoto Protocol Dilemma: Better to Have a Weak Agreement Than No Agreement at All?', Indosasters Working Paper 4, University of Bonn, Germany.

Managi, S. 2010. 'Productivity Measures and Effects from Subsidies and Trade: An Empirical Analysis for Japan's Forestry', *Applied Economics*, 42(30): 3871–83.

Merican, Y., Yusop, Z., Zaleha Mohd. Noor, and Law Siong Hook. 2007. 'Foreign Direct Investment and the Pollution in Five ASEAN Nations', *International Journal of Economics and Management*, 1(2): 245–61.

Morgan, D. 2010. 'The Farm Bill and Beyond', Economic Policy Paper Series, German Marshall Fund of the United States, Washington, D.C.

Mukherjee, S. 2008. 'Economics of Agricultural Nonpoint Source Water Pollution: A Case Study of Groundwater Nitrate Pollution in the Lower Bhavani River Basin, Tamilnadu', Unpublished PhD Thesis, Madras School of Economics and University of Madras, Chennai.

Mukherjee, S. 2010. 'Nutrient-Based Fertiliser Subsidy: Will Farmers Adopt Agricultural Best Management Practices?', *Economic and Political Weekly*, 45(49): 62–72.

Mukherjee, S. 2012. 'Issues and Options to Control Agricultural Nonpoint Source Pollution: A Case Study from India', in S. Mukherjee and D. Chakraborty (eds), *Environmental Scenario in India: Successes and Predicaments* (pp. 21–44). UK: Routledge.

Mukherjee, S. and Chakraborty, D. 2014. 'Relationship between Fiscal Subsidies and CO_2 Emissions: Evidence from Cross-Country Empirical Estimates', *Economics Research International*, 2014(2014), Article ID 346139.

Mukherjee, S. and Chakraborty, D. 2015a. 'Relationship between Fiscal Subsidies and CO_2 Emissions: Evidence from Cross-Country Empirical Estimates', in S. Dinda (ed.),

Handbook of Research on Climate Change Impact on Health and Environmental Sustainability. USA: IGI Global.

Mukherjee, S. and Chakraborty, D. 2015b. 'Editors' Introduction: Environmental Challenges in the Times of Economic Growth—An Asian Odyssey', in S. Mukherjee and D. Chakraborty (eds), *Environmental Challenges and Governance: Diverse perspectives from Asia* (pp. 1–29). UK: Routledge.

Mukherjee, S. and Rao, R. Kavita. 2015. 'Policy Options for Including Petroleum, Natural Gas and Electricity in the Goods and Services Tax', *Economic and Political Weekly*, 50(9): 98–107.

Mukherjee, S. and Nelliyat, P. 2007. 'Groundwater Pollution and Emerging Environmental Challenges of Industrial Effluent Irrigation in Mettupalayam Taluk, Tamilnadu', Discussion Paper No. 4, Comprehensive Assessment ofWater Management in Agriculture, IWMI, Colombo, Sri Lanka.

Mwikya, Mbithi S. 2006. 'Fisheries Access Agreements: Trade and Development Issues', International Trade and Sustainable Development Series Issue Paper No. 2, ICTSD: Geneva.

Myers, N. and Kent, J. 2001. *Perverse Subsidies: How Tax Dollars Can Undercut the Environment and the Economy*. Washington, D.C.: Island Press.

National Council of Textile Organizations (NCTO). Undated. 'Government of China Industry Subsidies: Applicable to Textile Industry'. Available at www.ncto.org/Newsroom/chinesesubsidies.pdf (accessed on 19 June 2012).

Organization for Economic Co-Operation and Development (OECD). 2003. *Perverse Incentives and Biodiversity Loss*. Paris: OECD.

———. 2009. *OECD Fact Book 2009: Economic, Environmental and Social Statistics*. Paris: OECD.

———. Undated. 'OECD Producer and Consumer Support Estimates Database'. Available at http://www.oecd.org/document/59/0,3746,en_2649_33797_39551355_1_1_1_1,00.html (accessed on 19 June 2012).

Oskam, Arie J. and Meester, G. 2006. 'How Useful is the PSE in Determining Agricultural Support?', *Food Policy*, 31(2): 123–41.

OXFAM. 2005. 'A Little Blue Lie: Harmful Subsidies Need to be Reduced, not Redefined', OXFAM Briefing Note, London.

———. Undated. 'Cultivating Poverty: The Impact of US Cotton Subsidies on Africa', OXFAM Briefing Paper No. 30. Available at http://stats.oecd.org/Index.aspx?DataSetCode=MON20113_5 (accessed on 19 June 2012).

Pandey, R. and Srivastava, D.K. 2001. 'Subsidies and Environment: With Special Reference to Agriculture in India', Environmental Economics Research Committee (EERC) Working Paper Series: NIP-6. Available at http://coe.mse.ac.in/eercrep/fullrep/nip/NIP_FR_RitaPandey.pdf (accessed on 27 June 2012).

Porter, G. 1997. 'The Euro-African Fishing Agreements: Subsidizing Over-fishing in African Waters', Background Paper for UNEP/WWF Workshop, Washington, D.C.

———. 2000. 'Fisheries Subsidies and Overfishing: Towards a Structured Discussion', United Nations Environment Programme, Geneva.

Price, A.H., Brightbill, T.C., Weld, C.B. and Nance, D.S. 2007. 'Money for Metal: A detailed examination of Chinese Government Subsidies to its Steel Industry', Canada Border Services Agency, Available at http://www.cbsa-asfc.gc.ca/sima-lmsi/i-e/ad1389/ad1389-i10-attachment-piecejointe-vol4-tab16-1.pdf (last accessed on 19 June 2012).

Robin, S., Wolcott, R. and Quintela, Carlos E. 2003. 'Perverse Subsidies and the Implications for Biodiversity: A Review of Recent Findings and the Status of Policy Reforms', Presented at 5th World Parks Congress: Sustainable Finance Stream, Durban, South Africa.

Sankar, U. 2006. 'Trade Liberalisation and Environmental Protection: Responses of the Leather Industry in Brazil, China and India', *Economic and Political Weekly*, 41(24): 2470–77.

Scherr, S. 2003. 'Securing Protected Areas and Ecosystem Services in the Face of Global Change', Working Group 1, Understanding Global Change: Socioeconomic Factors, World Resources Institute, Washington, D.C.

Sen, A. 2012. 'India to Remove Textile Subsidy Gradually', *Economic Times*, 14 May, New Delhi.

Shah, A. 2012. 'Agriculture and Environment in India: Policy Implications in the Context of North-South Trade', in S. Mukherjee and D. Chakraborty (eds), *Environmental Scenario in India: Successes and Predicaments* (pp. 219–42). London: Routledge.

Shamrao, T.S. 2011. 'A Study of Fertilizer Policy in India', *International Journal of Agriculture Sciences*, 3(3): 145–49.

Sharp, R. and Sumaila, Ussif R. 2009. 'Quantification of U.S. Marine Fisheries Subsidies', *North American Journal of Fisheries Management*, 29(1): 18–32.

Sidhu, H.S. 2002. 'Crisis in Agrarian Economy in Punjab: Some Urgent Steps', *Economic and Political Weekly*, 37(30): 3132–38.

Steenblik, R. 1998. 'Previous Multilateral Efforts to Discipline Subsidies to Natural Resource based Industries', OECD, Paris.

Sumaila, Ussif R. and Pauly, D. (eds) 2006. 'Catching More Bait: A Bottom-up Re-estimation of Global Fisheries Subsidies', 14 (6), Fisheries Centre Research Reports, 2nd Version, Vancouver: University of British Columbia.

Sumaila, U.R., Teh, L., Watson, R., Tyedmers, P. and Pauly, D. 2008. 'Fuel Price Increase, Subsidies, Overcapacity, and Resource Sustainability', *ICES Journal of Marine Science*, 65(6): 832–40.

Templet, Paul H. 2001. 'Defending the Public Domain: Pollution, Subsidies and Poverty', Working Paper No. 12, University of Massachusetts, Amherst, Massachusetts.

Tyedmers, P., Watson, R. and Pauly, D. 2005. 'Fuelling global fishing fleets', *Ambio*, 34: 59–62.

United Nations (UN). 1987. 'World Commission on Environment and Development'. Available at http://www.un-documents.net/wced-ocf.htm (accessed on 25 June 2012).

———. Undated. 'Johannesburg Plan of Implementation'. Available at http://www.un.org/esa/sustdev/documents/WSSD_POI_PD/English/POIChapter4.htm (last accessed on 27 June 2012).

United Nations Conference on Sustainable Development (UNCSD). 2012. 'Rio+ 20: The Future We Want'. Available at http://www.uncsd2012.org/content/documents/727The%20Future%20We%20Want%2019%20June%201230pm.pdf (accessed on 26 June 2012).

United Nations Environment Programme (UNEP). 2003. 'Fisheries Subsidies and Marine Resource Management: Lessons learned from Studies in Argentina and Senegal', UNEP, Nairobi.

———. 2004. 'Analyzing the Resource Impact of Fisheries Subsidies: A Matrix Approach', Economics and Trade Branch, UNEP, Geneva.

United Nations Environment Programme (UNEP). 2008. 'Reforming Energy Subsidies Opportunities to Contribute to the Climate Change Agenda', Division of Technology, Industry and Economics, UNEP, Geneva.

United Nations Framework Convention on Climate Change (UNFCCC). 2009. 'Copenhagen Accord'. Available at http://unfccc.int/resource/docs/2009/cop15/eng/11a01.pdf (accessed on 18 June 2012).

Unisféra International Centre and Centro Mexicano de Derecho Ambiental (UIC-CMDA). 2003. 'The Economic and Environmental Impacts of Agricultural Subsidies: A Look at Mexico and Other OECD Countries', Report prepared on behalf of Instituto Nacional de Ecologia (INE), Mexico.

van Beers, Cees, Jeroen C.J.M. van den Bergh, André de Moor, and Frans Oosterhuis. 2004. 'Determining the Environmental Effects of Indirect Subsidies', Discussion Paper No. 3, Tinbergen Institute, Amsterdam.

Victor, D. 2009. *The Politics of Fossil Fuel Subsidies*. Manitoba: Global Subsidy Initiative and International Institute of Sustainable Development.

Wagner, Ulrich J. and Timmins, C. 2009. 'Agglomeration Effects in Foreign Direct Investment and the Pollution Haven Hypothesis', *Environmental and Resource Economics*, 43(2): 231–56.

World Bank. 2013. World Development Indicators. Available at http://databank.worldbank.org/databank/download/WDIandGDF_excel.zip (accessed on 22 March 2013).

World Trade Organization (WTO). 1999. 'Trade and Environment', WTO Special Study No. 4, Geneva.

———. 2001. 'Official Text of Doha Ministerial Declaration'. Available at http://www.wto.org/english/thewto_e/minist_e/min01_e/mindecl_e.htm (accessed on 28 June 2012).

———. 2009. 'Lamy Urges Doha Deal for Sustainable Fishing'. Available at http://www.wto.org/english/news_e/sppl_e/sppl129_e.htm (accessed on 18 June 2014).

———. 2010. *Trade Policy Review—United States*. Geneva.

———. 2011a. *Trade Policy Review—European Union*. Geneva.

———. 2011b. *Trade Policy Review—India*. Geneva.

World Wide Fund for Nature (WWF). Undated. 'Underwriting Overfishing', WWF Briefing Note. Available at http://www.worldwildlife.org/what/globalmarkets/fishing/WWFBinaryitem8633.pdf (accessed on 18 June 2012).

Yagi, M. and Managi, S. 2011. 'Catch Limits, Capacity Utilization and Cost Reduction in Japanese Fishery Management', *Agricultural Economics*, 42(5): 577–92.

7

Climate Change Burden Sharing: A Reappraisal of the Equity Debate

Anubhab Pattanayak and K.S. Kavi Kumar

Introduction

Climate change is one of the most complex global challenges faced by the human race. It is a threat to the current and future economic development of many countries and finds an important place in the contemporary geopolitical discussions. The climate negotiations reckon that higher atmospheric concentration of greenhouse gases (GHGs) caused by anthropogenic activities could lead to rise in the earth's average surface temperature (Solomon et al., 2007). With the broad objective to protect the global climate system, these negotiations advocate GHG mitigation strategies, that is, the reduction or control of anthropogenic GHG emissions in the atmosphere. It is widely recognized that this would help stabilize the concentration of GHGs in the atmosphere, thereby limiting the climate change and its adverse consequences.

While the economic rationale for GHG emission reduction is similar to that behind the reduction of local environmental pollution, certain inherent characteristics of climate change make the phenomenon and its mitigation an unprecedented challenge. First, like open access resources there are no property rights assigned to the atmosphere. Therefore, no costs are incurred to occupy additional space in the atmosphere leading to unrestricted use of the atmospheric space. Second, the uniformly mixed nature of GHGs makes their mitigation independent of location. This gives rise to the problem of 'free riding'. Third, the long life span of the GHGs in the atmosphere and the resulting impacts accruing over a long period of time makes the phenomenon of climate change a daunting intergenerational issue, which is also surrounded by large uncertainties.

Since there are significant costs associated with any serious emission reduction agreement, historically almost all countries have shown strong reluctance to undertake emission reduction commitments and even greater reluctance to implement them. Finding a way to equitably distribute the costs between countries is a major hurdle in the climate negotiations. International negotiations therefore confront the problem of 'burden sharing' in the context of climate change mitigation. Ringius et al. (2000) define burden sharing as the way in which countries benefiting from a public good (here, climate change mitigation) agree to share the cost of providing that good.

In the purview of GHG abatement, the issue of burden sharing translates to the question of which countries should be asked to reduce emissions and by how much they must reduce their GHG emissions. Underlying the question, there are concerns over which countries should be held responsible and how to account for their responsibilities for the given problem. Further, there is no clear answer pertaining to the intergenerational distribution of emission reductions. Any attempt to answer such a cobweb of complex questions surrounding the phenomenon has led to the so-called '(Climate) Equity Debate', which underlies the burden sharing problem of climate change mitigation. The equity debate arose primarily because of the clashing interest of countries in the north (broadly the developed countries) and in the south (broadly the developing countries), and a lack of appropriate methodology to address the north–south divide (Sagar, 2000). Though the present-day climate negotiations do not take place strictly across the north–south divide, their divergent demands and perspectives have contributed significantly towards the slow progress of climate negotiations.

Numerous attempts have already been made in the literature to address the problem of burden sharing. This includes viewpoints (Muller, 2002; Parikh, 1994; Parikh et al., 1997; Rose, 1998), formulations and policy prescriptions based purely on equity principles (Gupta and Bhandari, 1999; Grubler and Nakićenović, 1994; Jacoby et al., 2008; Mattoo and Subramanian, 2010; Parikh and Parikh, 2009; Rose, 1990), frameworks based on single and multiple criteria (Ringius et al., 1998, 2000; Sagar, 2000), approaches based on welfare analysis and so on (Rose et al., 1998). The literature recognizes existence of differences in a wide range of national characteristics. These include, but not limited to, their (country's) *ability* to bear the burden (cost) of mitigating climate change, their *current and historical responsibilities* in contributing to the problem, and also their *vulnerabilities* to climate change (Parikh, 1994). Therefore, a multi-criteria-based approach that captures more of the differences in national characteristics is preferred compared to the single-criteria-based formulations and could be more promising for successful negotiations (Cazorla and Toman, 2000; Sagar, 2000). Therefore, any burden sharing rule must account for these multitudes of disparities between countries in order to be treated fair and to yield an equitable allocation of the burden. The principle of 'common but differentiated responsibility' advocated in the United Nations Framework Convention on Climate Change (UNFCCC, 1992) acknowledges the same in the context of climate change mitigation.

Some of the proposed approaches briefly reckon the differences existing between countries in their 'vulnerability' to climate change. Nevertheless, attempts to incorporate the vulnerability aspect into any of the burden sharing framework have been rather rare (Kverndokk and Rose, 2008). Since countries in general cannot avoid the impacts imposed by the climate change, the high-vulnerable countries would have to allocate more resources to ameliorate the climate change impacts compared to the low-vulnerable countries. To compensate for the external damages imposed by the climate change, one may argue that the high-vulnerable countries may be given higher GHG emission entitlements to keep their overall costs (i.e., sum of mitigation and adaptation costs) due to climate change at fair levels.

Although the proposed frameworks in the literature incorporate several equity principles, they do not always explicitly analyse the welfare implications of various burden sharing rules. It is necessary to ascertain whether the *positive* distribution(s) obtained using a framework confirms to the *normative* principles advocated by any general theory of welfare. Therefore, welfare analysis must become the foundation of any analysis of burden allocation and implied policy prescriptions.

The present study incorporates vulnerability to climate change into a burden sharing framework that accounts for country-wise differences in attributes like population, current and historic GHG emissions, and capabilities to bear the mitigation burden. The chapter argues that such augmented burden sharing framework would ensure a 'fair' distribution of emission rights that is in accordance with the principles of distributive justice.

The rest of the chapter is organized as follows: the second section gives the background of the equity debate underlying the problem of burden sharing and reviews the various burden sharing approaches and the proposed rules. The third section of the paper discusses the methodology and the underlying data requirements for the study. The results of the proposed framework and their welfare implications are presented in the fourth section of the chapter. The final section provides the concluding remarks.

Literature Review

Article 3 of the Framework Convention on Climate Change mandates that the parties (group of developed and developing countries) should act 'on the basis of equity and in accordance with their common but differentiated responsibilities and respective capabilities'. The catchphrase 'Common but Differentiated Responsibility' has become the touchstone of the international climate-equity debate and serves as a guiding principle for an equitable burden distribution (Cazorla and Toman, 2000). The principle advocates burden differentiation on the basis of variations in national circumstances (attributes) like economic status. As the principle requires, poor countries should therefore reduce emissions to a lesser extent than their rich counterparts. Similarly, the principle calls forth special consideration for countries that are vulnerable to the impacts of climate change.

The Kyoto Protocol adopted in 1997 at the third Conference of Parties (COP-3) to the UNFCCC in Kyoto, reiterates the Convention's guiding principle. The protocol, which came into effect in 2005, ensures binding commitments for industrialized (called Annex I) countries to reduce their emissions in 2008–12 period by approximately 5 per cent compared to their 1990 levels. Although a historic international attempt, the protocol is widely considered to be a failure as the Annex I countries were unable to meet their Kyoto targets. Critics point out that the negotiation process which led the protocol to set the target emission reductions lacks transparency and is devoid of any logical or scientific framework (Claussen and Mcneilly, 2000; Sagar, 2000). Not only the 5 per cent emissions reduction target is a 'back-of-the-envelope' calculation, the annual targets assigned to different nations in the protocol are also *ad hoc*. Moreover, the targeted reductions are insufficient to stop the adverse impact of climate change from inflicting human activities. It fails to bring the developing countries (non-Annex I) countries 'onboard' to an abatement regime, and sticks to a medium-term emissions reductions and fails to provide a 'roadmap' for future emission reduction targets. Thus, devising a burden sharing rule, which overcomes the limitations of the protocol and is in line with the principles of the Convention, is pressing. Several burden sharing rules existing in the literature are discussed further.

Burden Sharing Literature

There are numerous discussions in the literature on the emission allocation issue. These include ethical perspectives on GHG allowances (Kverndokk and Rose, 2008; Parikh, 1994; Rose, 1998), fairness principles and proposals (Ringius et al., 2000), and analytical examinations of single- and multi-criteria-based allocation frameworks (Gupta and Bhandari, 1999; Grubler and Nakićenović, 1994; Mattoo and Subramanian, 2010; Ringius et al., 1998; Rose, 1990; Sagar, 2000). The recent literature ranges from economic approaches with specific arguments of 'rent seeking' or 'rights to the atmosphere' (Parikh and Parikh, 2009) to approaches that could be politically feasible (Frankel, 2008). Renewed interest in principles of ability to pay, future development opportunities and invoking some adjustment costs (Jacoby et al., 2008; Mattoo and Subramanian, 2010) is also found in the literature.

The very pervasive role of fossil fuels in economic development and in aggravating climate change problem holds the key to sharing the responsibility of mitigation burden. Some approaches therefore attempt to address specifically the much controversial responsibility dimension under the equity debate. These studies trace back the underlying anthropogenic causes to the individual level by studying the national income distribution (across individuals) (Chakravarty et al., 2009) or more particularly distribution of consumption (Davis and Caldeira, 2010). Individuals whose unsustainable consumption results in the climate change problem and have the capability are asked to share the mitigation burden, irrespective of where they live.

Summarizing the literature, Mattoo and Subramanian (2010) present an analytical framework to discuss the existing contributions to the literature on equity in climate change. The authors analyse the consequences of different approaches to equity in terms of allocation of future emission rights in climate change mitigation policy. The framework attempts to project potential emission allocation scenarios using four equity-based approaches, namely equal per capita, historic responsibility, ability to pay and future development opportunities. The equal per capita emissions, historic responsibility and ability to pay are shown to benefit large and poor countries allocating substantial share of future emission rights. Allocation based on future development opportunities is most appealing for developing countries, as the burden sharing or emission abatement cost falls entirely on industrial countries. However, the country-based adjustment costs tend to favour the large current emitters, suggesting status quo emission allocations.

Compared to approaches based on a single equity principle or criteria, such as the one discussed previously, multi-criteria-based framework could prove to be more promising for successful negotiation over the long term (Cazorla and Toman, 2000). One such multi-criteria-based allocation framework is proposed by Sagar (2000), which overcomes several shortcomings of the single-criteria-based allocation. Population, per capita income and per capita cumulative emissions are the attributes taken into the analysis to decide upon an equitable allocation of emission rights. The approach of the study is suitable for decoupling the allocation issue from that of determination of a long-term stabilization target of GHG concentration in the atmosphere. The novelty of the approach lies in its ability to identify the prominent differences in several characteristics between the developed and developing countries, and also making apparent the not so obvious differences within each of these groups. For many of its clear advantages, this chapter adheres to the basic framework proposed by Sagar (2000). However, as mentioned earlier, the chapter takes departure from the basic framework by including the aspect of vulnerability to climate change into the framework. In order to incorporate climate change impact into its framework, this chapter reflects on the literature discussed further.

Climate Change Impact Literature

It has long been recognized that developing countries are more vulnerable to climate change as compared to their developed counterparts (Schelling, 1992). This has been attributed to their endowed geography and climate, lower adaptive capacity and higher dependence on climate-sensitive sectors such as agriculture (Mendelsohn et al., 2006; Tol et al., 2004). Most developing countries are low latitude countries having, on an average, hotter climate to start with than majority of developed countries. Such natural endowment effect would lead to higher impact of climate change for developing countries compared to their high latitude counterparts (Mendelsohn, 2009). Dell et al. (2009) empirically establish this fact by showing that higher temperature is associated with greater losses not only in the level of GDP but also in growth rate of GDP for developing countries as compared to the developed nations. Further, the level of technological advancement of a country plays an important role in determining its climate sensitivity and the future of climate change impact (McKinsey and Evenson, 1998). Thus, the susceptibility to climate change of a developing country compared to that of a developed country could be significantly different (Mendelsohn et al., 2001).

Several studies estimating the market impacts of climate change (e.g., Mendelsohn et al., 2000; Tol et al, 2004; Mendelsohn et al., 2006; Cline, 2007) confirm that developing countries in general stand to lose more from the effects of global warming than the industrialized countries. Such skewed distribution of climate change impacts across countries suggests a large equity problem, which could be addressed through a compensation programme (Mendelsohn and Williams, 2004). The design of an equitable burden sharing framework, with focus on the worst victims of climate change therefore necessitates the incorporation of such climate change impact estimates into it (Parikh, 1994). This chapter recognizes that developing countries with their primary dependence on climate-sensitive sectors like agriculture are the most vulnerable ones. That is, the adverse effects of climate change on the developing countries would be adequately reflected in the agriculture sector, although the country-level aggregate impacts are no way limited to this sector alone.

Cline (2007) estimates the market impacts of climate change on agriculture by the end of this century for 69 countries. Using preferred estimates which take the average of the market estimates based on the Ricardian rent model and the crop model, Cline (2007) reports the country-specific market value of the impacts of climate change on agriculture by the final three decades (2070–99) of the century. The present study utilizes these climate change impact estimates in its analysis on allocating GHG mitigation burden across the countries.

Methodology and Data

As mentioned previously, the present study explores a multi-criteria-based burden sharing framework. The framework determines the emission allocations for the *initial* year T based on the population (Pop) and per capita GDP ($pcGDP_{PPP}$) in the base year, the per capita cumulative historical responsibility (pcCR) until the year T–1, and climate change impacts (M).

The multi-criteria allocation can be specified as:

$$F_i = \frac{\text{Pop}_i * f(\text{pcGDP}_{\text{PPP}_i}) * h\,(M_i) \,/\, f(\text{pcCR}_i)}{\sum_{i=1}^{n} [\text{Pop}_i * f(\text{pcGDP}_{\text{PPP}_i}) * h\,(M_i) \,/\, f(\text{pcCR}_i)]} \quad (1)$$

where F_i is the fraction of the global emissions allocated to country i, and f, g and h are functions of the $pcGDP_{PPP}$, pcCR and climate change impact (M), respectively. Exploring the burden sharing rule through variations in functional forms of the indicators taken into analysis, the study obtains four allocation *schemes* which, along with their underlying principles, are presented in Table 7.1. The allocation could be on the basis of either egalitarian principle, or reducing adjustment costs, or accounting for historic responsibilities, or all three. The allocation schemes are categorized into burden sharing schemes *with* and *without* climate change impacts depending on whether the framework's schemes incorporate impacts of climate change into the analysis or not. Burden sharing 'without impacts' schemes form the *base* against which the burden sharing 'with impacts' schemes can be compared. burden sharing framework with impacts schemes use two indices of relative impacts of climate change across countries, namely impacts per unit of agricultural GDP and impacts per capita.

Knowing the emission budget over a period of time in future for the world, the country-specific fraction of emission entitlements assessed with the help of equation (1) and the schemes described in Table 7.1 can be used to estimate the emission entitlement for each country. Recognizing that there exist significant differences not only between the developed and developing countries, but also within each of such broad country-groups, the study adopts a detailed country classification based on the four criteria (*viz.*, per capita income, per capita cumulative historical emission, total population and climate change impacts) used in the burden sharing framework and two classes (*viz.*, high and low) corresponding to each criteria. Although such classification is an abstraction from reality—where one could conceive of more than two classes (e.g., high, moderate and low per criteria)—in essence it captures a *modus operandi* to which the burden sharing framework could potentially adhere. Thus, by adhering to this approach, questions like how much emission rights should go to a country that is a rich-polluter with low population and faces low climate change impact

Table 7.1:
Burden-sharing schemes and underlying principles

Framework	*Scheme*	*Allocation*	*Underlying Principles*
Burden Sharing Framework Without Impacts (BSWOI)	(1)	$\frac{Pop_i * pcGDP_i}{pcCR_i}$	Egalitarian, adjustment cost, historic responsibilities
	(2)	$\frac{Pop_i * \log(pcGDP_i)}{\log(pcCR_i)}$	Egalitarian, adjustment cost, historic responsibilities
Burden Sharing Framework With Impacts (BSWI)	(3)	$\frac{Pop_i * pcGDP_i}{pcCR_i} * \left(1 + \frac{M_i}{agGDP_i}\right)$	Egalitarian, adjustment cost, historic responsibilities, victim compensation (based on impact per-unit of agricultural GDP)
	(4)	$\frac{Pop_i * pcGDP_i}{pcCR_i} * \left(1 + \frac{M_i}{Pop_i}\right)$	Egalitarian, adjustment cost, historic responsibilities, victim compensation (based on impact per-capita)

Source: Adapted from Sagar (2000).

Notes: In schemes 1, 3 and 4, the denominator was set at 1 for the countries where pcCR < 1. In scheme 2 for which log (pcCR) becomes infinitesimally small when pcCR approaches 1, the denominator was log (pcCR) for CR > 10; (1 + log (pcCR))/2 for 10 > pcCR >1; 0.5 for pcCR < 1.

as compared to a poor-low emitting-highly populous-high climate change impact-bearing country can be fairly answered.

A total number of 69 countries, for which climate change impact estimates are available, are taken into consideration for the analysis.[1] Grouping these 69 countries as per the above multiple-criteria-based classification results in 12 possible country-groups, which are presented in Table 7.2. Thus, the study attempts to analyse the distributions (of emission rights) resulting from several schemes of the framework presented in Table 7.1 across the 12 country-groups, given in Table 7.2.

Data Sources

Data pertaining to population, purchasing power parity adjusted GDP for 69 countries for 2004, which is considered as the *initial* year, are obtained from the *Human Development Report: 2007/08* (HDR 2007–08). The country-wise data on current (2010) emissions are taken from the Carbon Dioxide Information Analysis Center (CDIAC), Oak Ridge National Laboratory (USA). Few countries for which the above indicators were not available from the HDR 2007–08 are obtained from the World Economic Outlook Data, 2007, International Monetary Fund and World Resources Institute.

Estimating the cumulative emissions (pcCR) is complex and a difficult exercise, which requires estimates of national emissions of various GHGs, and their lifetime in the atmosphere. However, in view of the surrounding uncertainty in the calculations of life time of gases (other than CO_2), it is inappropriate to use estimates of the other gases into the analysis. To avoid such uncertain information, the paper carries out pcCR calculations on the basis of only CO_2 emissions (in *carbon equivalent* from fossil-fuel burning, cement manufacture and gas flaring). Moreover, from the study's

[1] The 69 countries analysed account for nearly 92 per cent of total world current (2010) emissions.

Table 7.2:
Classifications of countries using different criteria

Country-groups	*No. of Countries*	*Interpretation (Income-Emission-Population-Impact)*	*Includes*
Poor country-groups			
L L H L	5	Low Pc GDP–Low Pc CE–High Pop–Low Impact	China, Indonesia, Brazil, Nigeria
L L L L	13	Low Pc GDP–Low Pc CE–Low Pop–Low Impact	Vietnam, Philippines, African Countries
L H L L	4	Low Pc GDP–High Pc CE–Low Pop–Low Impact	Ukraine, Romania, Kazakhstan, Uzbekistan
L H L H	1	Low Pc GDP–High Pc CE–Low Pop–High Impact	Venezuela
L L L H	21	Low Pc GDP–Low Pc CE–Low Pop–High Impact	Iran, Thailand, Turkey, Syria, Morocco, Zimbabwe, Sri Lanka
L L H H	2	Low Pc GDP –Low Pc CE–High Pop–High Impact	India, Pakistan
Rich Country-groups			
H H H L	3	High Pc GDP–High Pc CE–High Pop–Low Impact	USA, Russia, Japan
H H L L	8	High Pc GDP–High Pc CE–Low Pop–Low Impact	Germany, U.K., France, Poland, Belgium, Canada
H L L L	2	High Pc GDP–Low Pc CE–Low Pop–Low Impact	Argentina, Portugal
H L L H	2	High Pc GDP–Low Pc CE–Low Pop–High Impact	Malaysia, Chile
H L H H	1	High Pc GDP–Low Pc CE–High Pop–High Impact	Mexico
H H L H	7	High Pc GDP–High Pc CE–Low Pop–High Impact	Italy, South Africa, Spain, Australia, Saudi Arabia, Netherlands, Greece

Source: Prepared by authors.

Notes:
1. Pc - per capita; CE - cumulative emission; Pop - population; 69 countries average (mean) of Pc GDP - Pc Cumulative Emission and Population determine the threshold to classify as 'high' or 'low'. However, in view of the skewed distribution of GDP and climate change impact across countries, the median value of impact-to-GDP ratio for 69 countries is appropriately taken as the threshold.
2. First letter of a country group corresponds to 'per capita income'. Country groups with the first alphabet as '*H*' refer to groups with *high* per capita income, and referred together as a 'Rich' group. Similarly, groups with '*L*' as the first alphabet stand for groups with *low* per capita income, and named as 'Poor' group.

standpoint, which embarks on a cross-country burden sharing framework, it becomes all the more necessary to incorporate the current and historical emissions data for CO_2 that are easily available relative to data on other GHGs.

Year-wise historical emissions data for 1950–2004 period for all 165 countries have been calculated by *CDIAC*. The analysis requires the year-wise CO_2 emissions data to be summed up over all years up to 2004 for each country to get an estimate of the cumulative emissions or the CR. Country-wise historical emission data pose the challenge of apportioning the emissions between countries which come to exist after the partition of a former political territory.

For instance, emission data for former USSR that faced partition in 1992 were available from 1950 up to 1991 and data for the post-partition entities, including present Russia and 14 other countries,[2] were available for years 1992–2004. To calculate the cumulative emissions of 1950–91 for each of the 15 countries the proportion (share) of emissions in 1992 by each 15 countries was applied to USSR's total cumulative emissions of 1950–91. These cumulative emissions (1950–91) estimated for 15 countries are then added to the respective country's cumulative emissions for the period 1992–2004 to get the cumulative emission figures from 1950 to 2004.

The framework's impact analysis takes into account climate change impact as an additional factor over and above the other factors included in the without impacts framework. The study uses the market impacts of climate change on agriculture. Agriculture being one of the highly climate-sensitive sectors there is sufficient justification for its inclusion in the analysis. Cline (2007) provides a rigorous and comprehensive assessment of aggregate agricultural impact due to climate change on 69 countries for 2080s (2070–99). Climate change impact has been incorporated into the framework in two different ways namely climate change impact as a

[2] Armenia, Azerbaijan, Belarus, Estonia, Georgia, Kazakhstan, Kyrgyzstan, Latvia, Lithuania, Republic of Moldova, Tajikistan, Turkmenistan, Ukraine and Uzbekistan were all part of the USSR prior to 1992.

proportion to agricultural GDP and per capita climate change impact (Table 7.1). In order to compute the former, data on agricultural value added to GDP are obtained from World Development Indicators of the World Bank database.

Results

In line with the proposed methodology, the results are first discussed for the multi-criteria framework without incorporating climate change impact and thereafter for the framework with climate change impact.

Allocation of Emission Rights: Without Climate Change Impacts

Schemes 1 and 2 together constitute the base (reference) schemes. Both schemes are based on the egalitarian principle, reducing adjustment costs, and accounting for historic responsibilities, and analysed across 12 country-groups consisting of 69 countries. Difference between these two schemes is mainly in terms of their construction: all the variables are in level terms in scheme 1 and they are in logarithmic terms in scheme 2.[3] The results for both schemes are presented in Figure 7.1.

Emission rights distribution based on scheme 1 (and scheme 2) suggests that nearly 87 per cent (85 per cent) of the total emission should be allocated to the poor country-groups.

Within the poor groups, maximum share goes to groups that are characterized by high population and have contributed little to the built-up of the GHGs in the atmosphere (e.g., *LLHL* and *LLHH*). Poor country-groups with low per-capita cumulative emissions and

[3] Using a logarithmic specification compresses the variations across nations. Thus, such specification facilitates better comparability between countries.

with low population get the next highest shares of emission rights under scheme 1 or scheme 2. The rich country-groups get significantly lower shares (below 15 per cent) than the poor country-groups with relatively lower variation across the sub-groups. The allocation of emission rights across the groups of countries is almost similar across both the schemes. Scheme 2 provides relatively more emission rights to the rich country-groups compared to scheme 1 and thus leads to a more uniform distribution of emission rights across countries.

Figure 7.1 also compares the distribution of emission rights estimated using schemes 1 and 2 with that observed presently. The comparison suggests that significant *net* transfers (nearly 45 per cent) of emission rights would be needed from the rich country-groups to their poor counterparts if the world were to move from the current emission regime to the regime suggested by scheme 1 or 2. Poor country-groups with low historic contribution to GHG emissions are primary beneficiaries of such transfers.

Figure 7.1:
Multi-criteria burden sharing: Base scenario

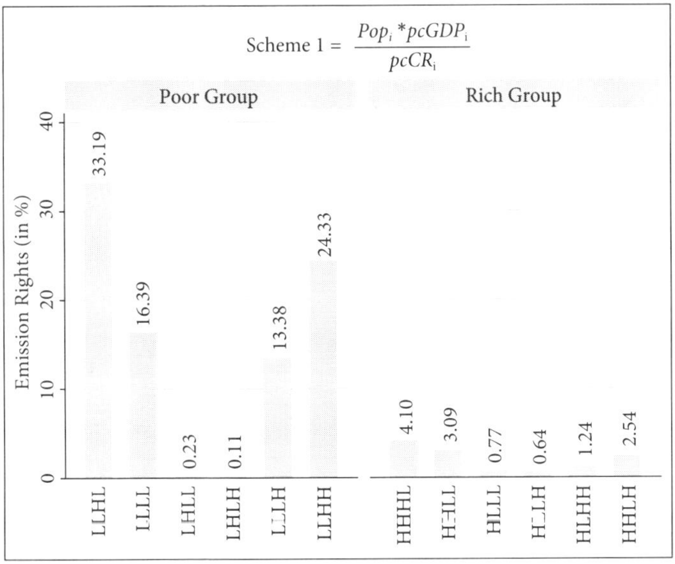

(Figure 7.1 Contd)

(Figure 7.1 Contd)

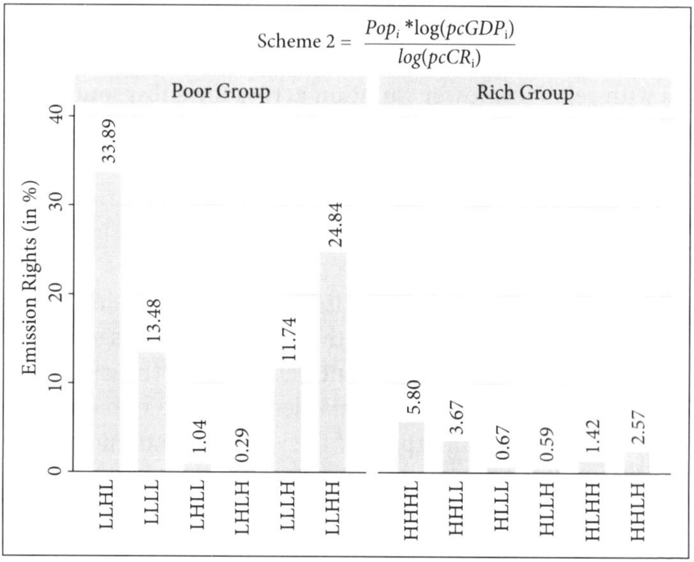

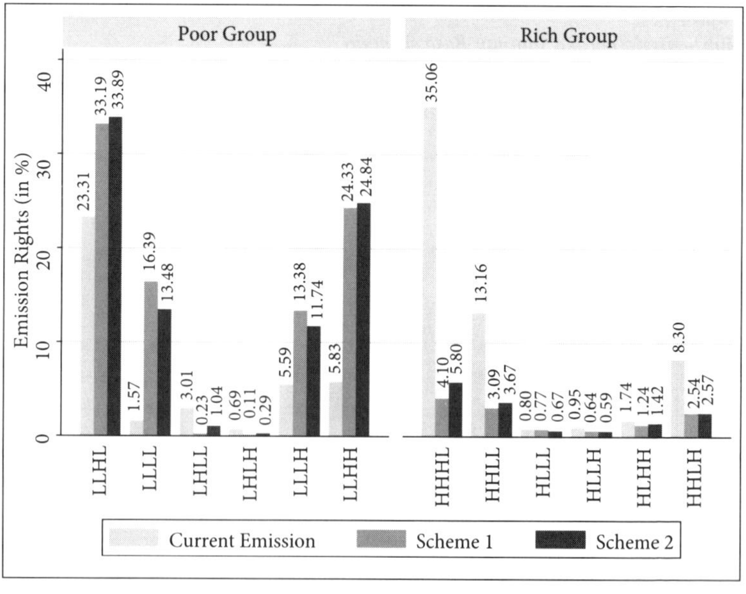

Source: Based on authors' calculations.

Allocation of Emission Rights: With Climate Change Impacts

The schemes proposed in 3 and 4 incorporate climate change impacts into the burden sharing framework. Thus, these schemes include the principle of victim compensation. While scheme 3 uses 'impacts per unit of GDP' as a proxy for climate change impacts, scheme 4 incorporates climate change impacts through 'impacts per capita' index. Figure 7.2 compares the distribution of emission rights thus obtained with the base scheme and also with the current emission distribution.

Few key points emerge from the results presented in Figure 7.2:

(a) Incorporation of climate change impacts has significant impact on the distribution of emission rights across country-groups.

Figure 7.2:
Comparison of burden sharing with and without climate change impacts

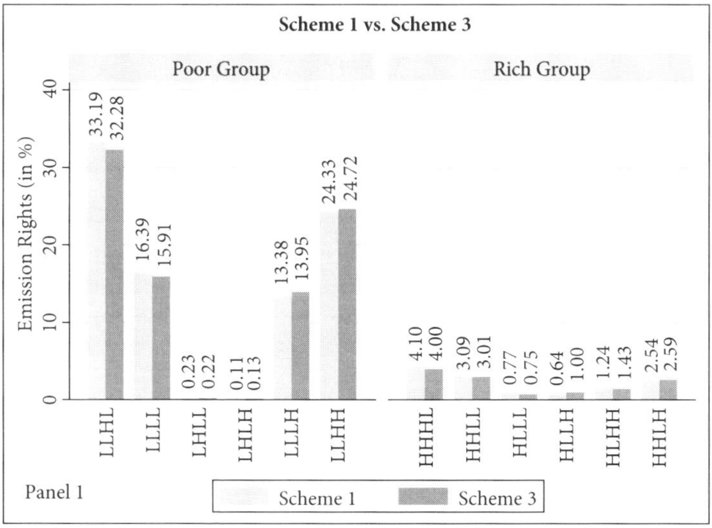

(Figure 7.2 Contd)

(Figure 7.2 Contd)

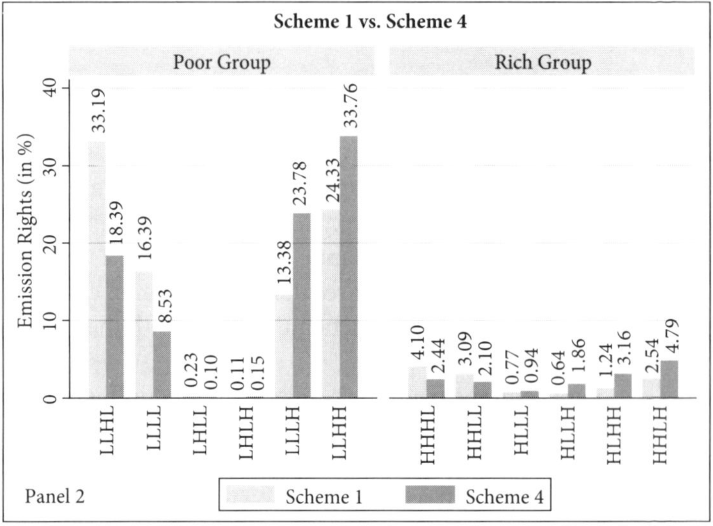

Panel 2

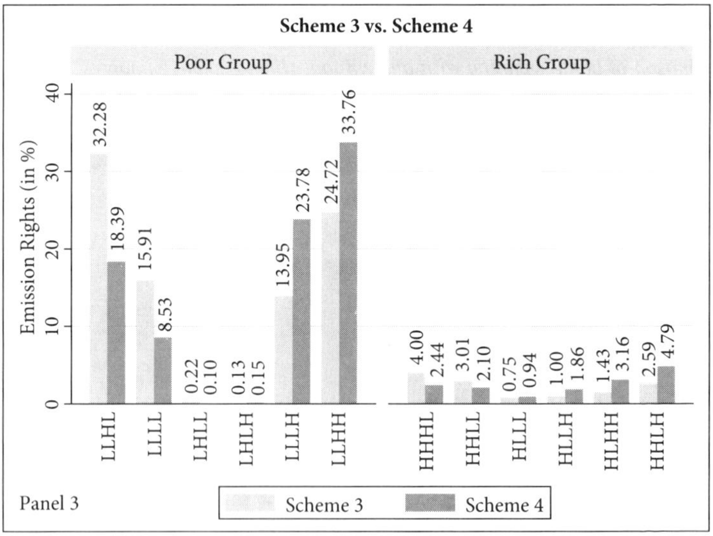

Panel 3

(Figure 7.2 Contd)

(Figure 7.2 Contd)

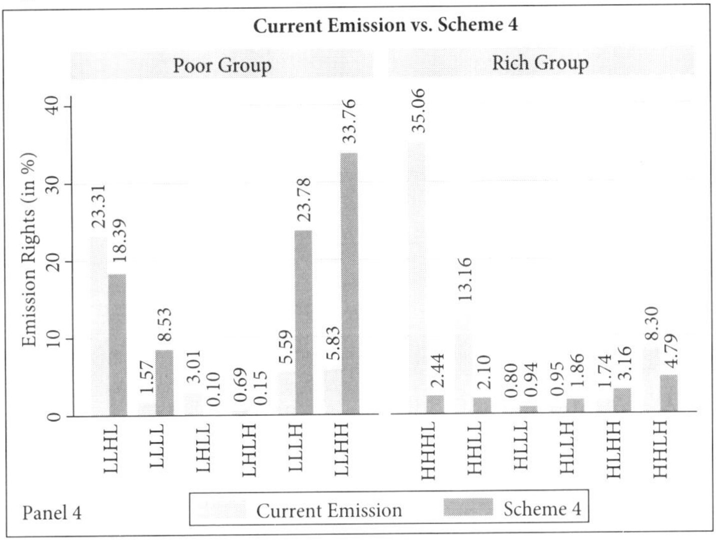

Source: Based on authors' calculations.

(b) Consideration of climate change impacts leads to re-distribution of emission rights within both the rich and poor country-groups. The re-distribution is more pronounced under scheme 4 compared to scheme 3.

(c) Inclusion of climate change impacts (on a per capita basis) in the framework clearly favours the vulnerable country-groups. In essence, the 'with impacts' framework seeks to compensate the vulnerable by allowing them to bear less burden of mitigation, that is, by allocating maximum rights.

Welfare Implications

It is important to understand the welfare implications of the proposed emission allocation framework. The intra-generational distribution of emission rights resembles the distribution of wealth.

Inequitable distribution of emission rights can lead to unequal distribution of wealth. In the development economics literature wealth inequalities between two groups of individuals, rich and poor, are addressed through redistribution (transfer) of income from one group to the other. Such redistribution can also be conceived to reduce the existing inequality in the distribution of emission rights. Redistribution of emission rights (or wealth) changes the status quo welfare for both country-groups under comparison, affecting the inequality in their welfare.

Several normative principles advocated in the literature address *inequity* in the distribution of wealth, and welfare. These principles suggest ways in which equality in the level of welfare between individuals (or groups of individuals) can be achieved by means of income redistribution (transfers). More precisely, such transfers advocate *greater* income to compensate individuals who are less well off relative to their peers.

For example, the 'Difference' or 'Maxi–min' principle of Rawls (1971) gives absolute priority to the *worst-off* and prescribes compensation to maximize their welfare. However, transfer of the entire income of the better-offs may not fully compensate the worst-off. Such loophole leading to a 'corner solution' makes it less applicable in practice (Sen, 1973).

The Weak Equity Axiom (WEA) advocated by Sen (1973) is another principle of distributive justice to address inequality in the level of welfare between two individuals. The WEA has much weaker requirements compared to the Rawlsian principle and overcomes several of its key limitations. The WEA posits that corrective measures to reduce welfare inequality can be achieved through income transfers between individuals. It is argued that two individuals having the same level of income but different needs will have different welfare levels: person with *higher* needs will have *lower* welfare level than the person with lower needs. To balance welfare between the two individuals, the WEA *recommends* allocating a *higher* income to the person having a lower level of welfare, that is, the one having *higher* needs.

In line with the arguments of the WEA discussed previously, this chapter in the climate change mitigation context assesses the equitability of the outcomes (emission rights distributions) emanating from different burden sharing schemes. Consider two countries *i* and *j*, both having the same level of income but the country *i* facing lower climate change impacts than *j*. Therefore, country *i* will have higher welfare than country *j*. Hence, the WEA would advocate higher emission rights allocated to country *j* with higher impacts and lower welfare relative to the rights allocated to country *i*.

In order to understand whether a burden sharing scheme is equitable in its distribution of emission rights, comparison across burden sharing schemes for the country-groups is necessary. To assess the equitability of the framework outcomes by relating it to the WEA, schemes may be compared across broader country clusters than the more disaggregated level of 12 country-groups discussed so far. One such comparison is presented in Figure 7.3. Aggregating the 12 country-groups based on economic status and climate change impacts results in four broad groups, namely poor countries facing high and low impacts, and rich countries facing high and low impacts. Heterogeneity in each of the four groups

Figure 7.3:
Welfare analysis of burden-sharing schemes

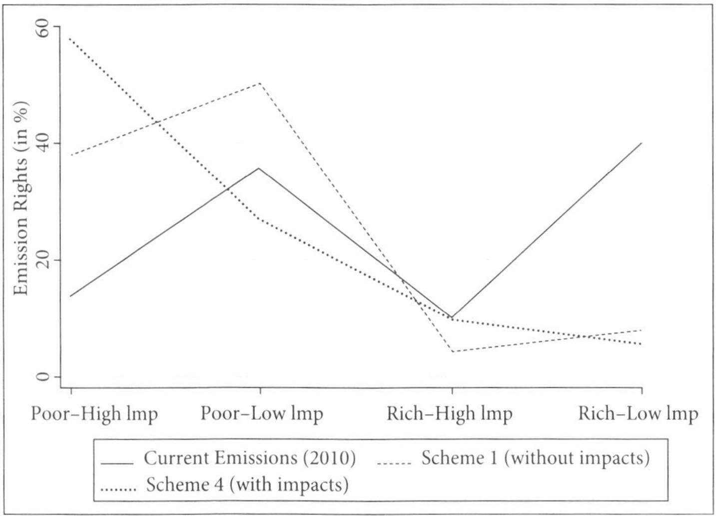

Source: Based on authors' calculations.

attributable to population and cumulative emissions criteria in the framework is getting enveloped by the broader classification based on the above two criteria that take precedence.

Figure 7.3 compares the allocation of emission rights across the broad country-groups under 'current emission' scheme, 'scheme 1' without incorporating the climate change impacts, and 'scheme 4' that incorporates climate change impacts into the burden sharing framework. The 'base' scheme (i.e., 'scheme 1') pivots the current emissions distribution between the rich and poor groups of countries as a whole. But, within the poor (and the rich) group of countries, this scheme allocates more rights to groups expected to face less climate change impacts. This seems at odds with the WEA which would reverse the allocation. Emission distribution resulting from scheme 4 using per capita climate change impacts conforms to the WEA: maximum rights are allocated to the poor with high impacts and vice versa. Compared to the current emissions, these schemes result in significant redistribution. This results in *direct* transfers of rights from the 'Rich–Low impacts' group to 'Poor–High impacts' group, holding the allocation for the 'Poor–Low impacts' and the 'Rich–High impacts' groups almost close to current emissions levels.

Conclusions

This study examines the issue of burden sharing in the context of GHG emission mitigation. The study argues that in addition to the often discussed criteria like population, historical emissions and income, the burden sharing framework could include country-specific climate change impacts in the allocation scheme to arrive at a more equitable regime. The study's analysis shows that taking cross-country climate change impacts along with other factors into a burden sharing framework significantly increases the emission allocation going to poor country-groups, which are little responsible for the problem, and have large population and least capability to bear the brunt of climate change impacts in the future. Moreover the study demonstrates that such framework also results in distribution of emission rights that is in accordance with the principles of distributive justice. Hence, the proposed framework can yield an equitable distribution of the cost of mitigating climate change across countries. It is also notable that the framework based on per capita climate change impact could ensure more equitable distribution of emissions compared to that based on impact per GDP. This is in line with the long-standing arguments that favour use of population-based criteria for allocating climate change mitigation costs. From the developing country perspective, the study results suggest that there should be continued emphasis on an emissions–allocation framework based on 'rights to the atmosphere'. This is particularly important in the context of increasing demands for more active GHG emission reduction from the developing countries.

References

Cazorla, M. and Toman, M. 2000. 'International Equity and Climate Change Policy', Climate Issue Briefs No. 27. Resources for the Future, Washington, D.C.

Chakravarty, S., Chikkatur, A., de Coninck, H., Pacala, S., Socolow, R., and Tavoni, M. 2009. 'Sharing Global CO_2 Emission Reductions Among One Billion High Emitters', *Proceedings of National Academy of Sciences*, 106(29): 11884–88.

Claussen, E. and Mcneilly, L. 2000. 'Equity and Global Climate Change: The Complex Elements of Global Fairness', *Policy Report prepared by the Pew Centre on Global Climate Change*, United Kingdom.

Cline, W.R. 2007. *Global Warming and Agriculture: Impact Estimates by Country*. Washington, D.C.: Centre for Global Development and the Peterson Institute for International Economics.

Davis, S.J. and Caldeira, K. 2010. 'Consumption-based accounting of CO2 emissions', *Proceedings of National Academy of Sciences*, 107(12): 5687–92.

Dell, M., Jones, B.F. and Olken, B.A., 2009. 'Temperature and Income: Reconciling new cross-sectional and Panel Estimates', *American Economic Review: Papers and Proceedings*, 99(2): 198–204.

Frankel, J. 2008. 'An Elaborated Proposal for Global Climate Policy Architecture: Specific Formulas and Emission Targets for All Countries in All Decades', Discussion Paper 2008-08, Cambridge, Massachusetts Harvard Project on International Climate Agreements, October 2008.

Grubler, A. and Nakićenović, N. 1994. 'International Burden Sharing in Greenhouse Gas Reduction'. International Institute for Applied Systems Analysis Research Report No. RR–94–9.

Gupta, S. and Bhandari, P.M. 1999. 'An Effective Allocation Criterion for CO_2 Emissions', *Energy Policy*, 27: 727–36.

Jacoby, H.D., Babiker, M.H., Paltsev, S. and Reilly, J.M. 2008 '*Sharing the burden of GHG Reductions*', Harvard Kennedy Discussion Paper 08-09. Harvard University, Cambridge, MA.

Kverndokk, S. and Rose A. 2008. 'Equity and Justice in Global Warming Policy', *International Review of Environmental and Resource Economics*, 2(2): 135–76.

Kyoto Protocol. UNFCCC. 1997. Available at http://unfccc.int/kyoto_protocol/items/2830.php (accessed on 11 February 2013).

Mattoo, A. and Subramanian, A. 2010. 'Equity in Climate Change: An Analytical Review', Working Paper No. 5383, World Bank Policy Research.

McKinsey, J. and Evenson, R. 1998. 'Technology–climate Interactions: Was the Green Revolution in India Climate Friendly?', in A. Dinar, R. Mendelsohn, R. Evenson, J. Parikh, A. Sanghi, K. Kumar, J. McKinsey and S. Lonergan (eds), 'Measuring the Impact of Climate Change on Indian Agriculture', World Bank Technical Paper No. 402, Washington, D.C.

Mendelsohn, R. 2009. 'The Impact of Climate Change on Agriculture in Developing Countries', *Journal of Natural Resources and Policy Research*, 1(1): 5–19.

Mendelsohn, R., Dinar, A. and Sanghi, A. 2001. 'The Effect of Development on the Climate Sensitivity of Agriculture', *Environment and Development Economics*, 6(1): 85–101.

Mendelsohn, R., Dinar, A. and Williams, L. 2006. 'The Distributional Impact of Climate Change on Rich and Poor Countries', *Environment and Development Economics*, 11(2): 159–78.

Mendelsohn, R., Wendy M., Schlesinger, M.E. and Andronova, N.G. 2000. 'Country-specific Market Impacts of Climate Change', *Climatic Change*, 45(3): 553–69.

Mendelsohn, R. and Williams, L., 2004. 'Comparing Forecasts of the Global Impacts of Climate Change', *Mitigation and Adaptation Strategies for Global Change*, 9(4): 315–33.

Muller, B. 2002 *Equity in Climate Change: The Great Divide*. Oxford: Oxford Institute for Energy Studies, UK.

Parikh, J. 1994. 'North-South Issues for Climate Change', *Economic and Political Weekly*, 29(45/46): 2940–43.

Parikh, J., Babu, P.G. and Kavi Kumar, K.S. 1997. 'Climate Change, North-South Cooperation and Collective Decision Making Post-Rio', *Journal of International Development*, 9(3): 403–13.

Parikh, J. and Parikh, K.S. 2009. 'Climate Change: A Parking Place Model for A Just Global Compact'. http://policydialogue.org/files/events/Parikh_-_Parking_Place_Model.pdf (accessed 2 September 2015).

Rawls, J. 1971. *A Theory of Justice*. Cambridge, MA: Harvard University Press.

Ringius, L., Torvanger, A. and Underdal, A. 1998. 'Can Multi-criteria Rules Fairly Distribute Climate Burdens? OECD Results from Three Burden Sharing Rules', *Energy Policy*, 26(10): 777–93.

Ringius, L., Torvanger, A. and Underdal, A. 2000. 'Burden Differentiation: Fairness Principles and Proposals. Joint CICERO-ECN project on sharing the burden of greenhouse gas reduction among countries', CICERO Working Paper No. 1999: 13, Centre for International Climate and Environmental Research, Oslo.

Rose, A. 1998. 'Global Warming Policy: Who Decides What Is Fair?', *Energy Policy*, 26(1): 1–3.

———. 1990. 'Reducing Conflict in Global Warming Policy: The Potential of Equity as a Unifying Principle', *Energy Policy*, 18(10): 927–35.

Rose, A., Stevens, B., Edmonds, J. and Wise, M. 1998. 'International Equity and Differentiation in Global Warming Policy: An Application to Tradable Emission Permits', *Environmental and Resource Economics*, 12: 25–51.
Sagar, A. 2000. 'Wealth, Responsibility, and Equity: Exploring an Allocation Framework for Global GHG Emissions', *Climatic Change*, 45: 511–27.
Schelling, T.C. 1992. 'Some Economics of Global Warming', *American Economic Review*, 82(1): 1–14.
Sen, A.K. 1973. *On Economic Inequality*. Delhi: Oxford University Press.
Solomon, S., Qin, D., Manning, M., Chen, Z., Marquis, M., Averyt, K.B., Tignor, M. and Miller, H.L. (eds), 2007. *Climate Change 2007: The Physical Science Basis*. Contribution of Working Group I to the Fourth Assessment Report of the Intergovernmental Panel on Climate Change (p. 996). Cambridge, United Kingdom and New York: Cambridge University Press.
Tol, R.S J., Downing, T.E., Kuik, O.J. and Smith, J.B. 2004. 'Distributional Aspects of Climate Change Impacts', *Global Environmental Change*, 14: 259–72.
United Nations Framework Convention on Climate Change (UNFCCC). 1992. Article 3. Available at http://unfccc.int/essential_background/convention/background/items/1355.php (accessed on 14 April 2011).

8

Economic Value of Water Using Hedonic Price Method

Haripriya Gundimeda and Vinish Kathuria**#*

Introduction

The main objectives of this chapter are two-fold: (i) to estimate the willingness to pay (WTP) for avoiding water shortages and (ii) for the households facing no water scarcity, improving the quality of water. The objectives are carried out using hedonic price (HP) technique in a metropolitan city of India. The motivation for doing this study comes from Wipenny (1994) who stated: 'Water is becoming one of the largest, and certainly the most universal of the problems facing mankind as the earth moves into the 21st century'.

*Professor, Department of Humanities and Social Sciences, Indian Institute of Technology Bombay, Powai, Mumbai. E-mail: haripriya.gundimeda@iitb.ac.in

**Professor, Shailesh J Mehta School of Management, Indian Institute of Technology Bombay, Powai, Mumbai. E-mail: vinish@iitb.ac.in

#Acknowledgements: This chapter forms part of a project awarded by South Asian Network of Economic Initiatives (SANEI). We are extremely thankful to SANEI for the funds and other support. Earlier versions of the chapter have been presented in a seminar at Institute of Behavioral Sciences, University of Colorado, Boulder on 9 October 2006 and at the 14th Annual Conference of the European Association of Environmental and Resource Economists held at Bremen, Germany during 24–26 June 2005 and 3rd International Conference on Model and Methods in Economics held at Indian Statistical Institute, Kolkata, during 8–11 December 2004. We are extremely thankful to the seminar and conference participants for very useful comments. The chapter benefited from the comments from Chris Goemans and Nick Flores. Usual disclaimers nevertheless apply.

Water scarcity can affect the rich and poor countries alike. In poorer countries, it breeds sickness, hampers development, deepens inequalities and undermines the survival of the entire society. In developed countries water scarcity curtails economic growth and results in poor quality of life. The problem of the availability of water can be viewed from at least three perspectives. First, the resource is clearly a limited one. Second, the demand for water is increasing due to economic and demographic growth. Third, the forecasted demand for water availability and quality cannot be relied upon because of several other environmental variables. Managing water scarcity effectively and fairly is thus one of the great imperatives of governance today. One of the impediments to manage water scarcity is non-existence of market mechanism for water and subsequent lack of proper valuation.

Recognizing the need for non-market valuation of environmental resources, economists have over the years developed several techniques to value them. Methods commonly used to value such resources include (i) the hedonic technique pioneered by Griliches (1971) and formalized by Rosen (1974); and (ii) the travel cost-valuation methods first proposed by Hotelling (1931), and subsequently developed by Clawson (1959) and Clawson and Knetsch (1966). Some authors have used the contingent valuation method (CVM) to estimate the WTP for water (Anand and Perman, 1999; Reddy, 1999).

The hedonic technique utilizes the fact that the quantity and quality of an attribute in question in a particular zone may affect the preferences of the households to reside in that area or not. These preferences get translated in property and rental prices (Boyle and Kiel, 2001). The case of coastal regions in India and elsewhere are an interesting illustration of this phenomenon. In coastal regions, the location of a parcel of land with respect to its proximity to the sea, defines the quality of groundwater supplies accessible to the residents of the parcel. Mining the ground water beyond a particular threshold would lead to instability of the interface between the saltwater and freshwater, resulting in saltwater replacing the freshwater. Thus, proximity of a land parcel to the sea can be a proxy for the existence and extent of saltwater intrusion in the parcel's groundwater supplies (Kounduri, 2004). As groundwater sources are contaminated, if other sources of drinking water are not readily available, new wells must be drilled, or the residents in that parcel of land have to buy water for their needs, which imply an additional cost and inconvenience to the residents. The salinity in groundwater supplies can influence household's preferences to reside in that area or not. Under the situation, the structure of land rents and prices (or house rents and prices) will reflect these preferences. Hence, by using data on land rent or land value for different properties, the contribution made by water quality and quantity to the value of (WTP for) the traded good, that is, land or house can be identified. This identifies an implicit or shadow price for the fresh water availability and quality, which in turn can be interpreted as an estimate of the *in situ* scarcity value of the marginal unit of the environmental resource. This study contributes to the literature as it is one of its kinds that values water scarcity. So far most studies have either valued air pollution or noise pollution or view from a property and so on, but not water scarcity. A 2004 survey paper by Chau et al. compiling a list of 85 studies carried out since 1967 for different environmental attributes does not have a single study pertaining to water scarcity.

Under this backdrop, the main objective of this chapter is to analyse the influence of water scarcity on house rents in Chennai, India using HP method and thus get an estimate of WTP by the people to improve the water supply situation in the city. Chennai, the capital city of Tamil Nadu and one of the four major metropolitan cities of India, is located in the south and in particular makes a very interesting case as it has the dubious distinction of the metropolitan city without a perennial source of fresh water with only 78 litres per capita per day (lpcd) during normal years of rainfall. However, during drought years availability is as low as 32 lpcd. Several times the lake levels from which Chennai draws water have reached below the 500 million cubic feet (mcft) and on several occasions the lakes have even dried up.[1] There is

[1] Figure A 8.1 in Appendix 8.1 gives the summer water level in different lakes of Chennai since 1950.

considerable variation in the availability of water across different sections of the people and also in different pockets of the city. According to a study undertaken in 1993 by the Centre for Environmental Planning and Technology, Ahmedabad, while the average gross availability of water in Chennai was 69 lpcd, it was 8 lpcd in the slums.

The acute water shortage has forced many households in Chennai to use two or more sources of water. In terms of institutional arrangements, four distinct systems of water supply can be found: (i) supply of water by the Chennai Metropolitan Water Supply and Sewerage Board—for Chennai city and few adjoining urban centres (called as Metro water); (ii) some extent of municipality supply—in the case of the nine adjoining urban areas within Madras Urban Agglomeration, referred to as nine Towns; (iii) self-provision by many households and industries—by digging shallow wells or deep tube wells; and (iv) private market—(a) bulk supply by means of tanker trucks of 12,000 litres capacity and (b) retail distribution of 'mineral or treated water' in jerry cans of 10, 12 and 25 litres capacity. Groundwater, the city's major source of water, is mainly drawn from the well fields along the coast, south of Chennai. The well-fields yield 148 million litres per day (mld) and the southern aquifer supplies 10 mld. However, groundwater extraction is reaching its limits. This groundwater scarcity has an important qualitative dimension that further limits the supply of usable water. Due to the variability in water supplies (quantity and quality) in several pockets, our proposition is that in Chennai market values can differ quite significantly depending on whether water is scanty or abundant and also depending on whether groundwater is saline or sweet.

The remainder of the chapter is organized as follows: the next section reviews the relevant literature. The theoretical model is explained in the section 'The Theoretical Hedonic Price Model'. Section 'Data and Variables' explains how the data are collected and the variables are constructed. This is followed by empirical estimation in section 'Empirical Estimation for Hedonic Price Function'. The aggregate WTP for improved water availability and quality is computed in section 'Aggregate Willingness to Pay for Improved Water Supply and Quality' and final section concludes the chapter.

Literature Review

The HP technique has primarily been used to examine the effect of air quality on residential prices (see Smith and Huang, 1995 and Chau et al., 2004 for a review of literature). The technique has also been used in other settings to estimate the value of different attributes. For instance, Spalatro and Provencher (2001), Legget and Bockstael (2000), Michael et al. (1996), Steinnes (1992), Young (1984), Epp and Al-Ani (1979) and David (1968) among others have used the HP technique to estimate the value of water resources such as lakes and reservoirs on nearby property values.

David (1968) studied the variation in land value to water quality in 60 artificial lakes in Wisconsin, US, using tax data from 1952, 1957 and 1962. The study finds that while property on more polluted lakes was less valuable than property adjacent to cleaner lakes, the influence of pollution on land values was not more significant than most other variables. Epp and Al-Ani (1979) utilized data from public records and telephone interviews for rural, non-farm communities in Pennsylvania, US, from 1969 to 1976 to estimate two different equations. The first equation used the actual pollution levels (pH) and the interaction between pH and percentage change in population for the years 1960–70. The second equation used the perceived water quality (based on survey responses) and the interaction of perceived water quality with percentage change in population. Results showed that water quality, measured both in terms of pH and owner's perceptions do have a significant effect on property values. A one-point increase in pH was found to result in a 5.9 per cent increase in the mean sales value of residential properties. Young (1984) estimated two equations—one with measure of water quality (=1 if adjacent to bay and 0 otherwise) and another with a rating of water quality (ranging from 1 to 10 from the lowest to the highest) to study the effects of perceived water quality on homes in the vicinity of St. Albans Bay on Lake Champain in Vermont. Along the bay, a malfunctioning municipal waste treatment plant was located causing pollution problems. The study found that location of a house near the bay reduced the property values by an average of 20 per cent.

Steinnes (1992) estimated three equations using appraisal data on leased plots along 53 Minnesota lakes to estimate the impact of water quality on land value. The authors included land value instead of sales price because water quality does not affect structure values. The study found that water clarity had significantly affected the property values. Mendelsohn et al. (1992) applied a panel data approach in their estimation of a hedonic model to examine the impacts of New Bedford, Massachusetts harbour for the years 1969–88. The use of panel data allowed them to control for variables that do not change over time. As explanatory variables they included per capita income, interest rates and whether renovations had been undertaken between sales. The pollution variables included a dummy variable for whether the sale occurred before or after the pollution event and interactions between the year and two dummy variables to indicate homes whose surrounding water quality was affected by Poly chlorinated biphenyls (PCBs) pollution. The study found that properties that were affected by the PCB pollution fell in value by $7,000–$10,000. Michael et al. (1996) in a study of 34 Maine lakes, examined property records for sales occurring between 1 January 1990 and 1 June 1994. For the various areas of the state, the authors found that a one-meter improvement in lake clarity would result in changes in average property prices ranging anywhere from $11 to $200 per foot frontage. Legget and Bockstael (2000) examined house sales in Anne Arundel County, Maryland, US, along the Western shore of the Chesapeake Bay. In addition to a pollution variable that measured median faecal coliform concentration at the site of the nearest monitoring station for sales occurring between July 1993 and August 1997, variables that measured distance from the various sources of pollution were also included in the regressions. The inclusion of various sources of pollution was primarily to reduce potential omitted variable bias. They concluded that the faecal coliform counts have a significant negative effect on property values. Results showed that a change of 100 faecal coliform count/100 mL resulted in a change in property prices of around 1.5 per cent.

Some other studies have also applied the hedonic property price method to estimate the value of reservoir level changes (Khairi-Cherti and Hite, 1990), river views (Kulshreshtha and Gillies, 1993) and restoration of urban streams (Streiner and Loomis, 1995). Other applications include evaluating the relation between land prices and surface and ground water access (both in quality and quantity) (see Kounduri and Pashardes, 2003 for literature).

Studies in India

For India, no study exists using the hedonic technique to value water scarcity though other methods have been employed to estimate the value. Anand and Perman (1999) has used multiple choice CVM to quantify the value of improvement in water supply in Madras. The study is based on a 1996 survey of households in the city. Another study by Reddy (1999) estimated households' willingness and ability to pay for water using the CVM for a water-scarce district in western Rajasthan. Another study by Roy et al. (2004) uses actual behaviour of 240 households in 92 wards of Kolkata in the form of defensive/averting expenditure incurred and computes their WTP for improved water quality. As can be seen, the first two studies are based on hypothetical WTP rather than using data from actual behaviour, whereas the third one uses actual behaviour but is concerned with water quality and not water scarcity. This scarcity value is captured in the present study through HP method.

The Theoretical Hedonic Price Model

Rosen (1974) was the first to formalize the theory underlying the market for heterogeneous goods. In the Rosen framework, the price of any unit of a quality-differentiated good is a function of the levels of the characteristics embodied in that good. For example, a housing unit comprising a bundle of different characteristics commands a price in the market (Rosen, 1974). Various bundles and their associated prices reveal the implicit prices of characteristics, known as HP. These prices are determined empirically from regressions of prices on characteristics. If the HP function is accurately estimated, then the slope of the function with respect to a characteristic, such as ambient environmental quality, evaluated at the individual's optimal choice, represents that individual's marginal WTP for that characteristic.

To apply this technique to the housing market requires the identification of the set of structural and locational characteristics, which describe a house and which may influence its selling price. Let $Q = (Z_1, Z_2, Z_3, \ldots, Z_4)$, Z_j representing the jth characteristic of that house, which is a vector of housing characteristics.

The household decision is characterized by the following utility function:

$$U = U(Z, X) \tag{1}$$

where Z is the housing commodity described by Q, X is a vector of composite goods. The utility function is constrained by the following budget constraint (assuming that x is a numeraire good):

$$I = x + P(Z) \tag{2}$$

where I equals household monetary income and $P(Z)$ is the price of housing. The consumer determines his optimal choice by solving the equation

$$\frac{\partial P}{\partial Z_i} = \frac{\partial U / \partial z_i}{\partial U / \partial x} \tag{3}$$

Equation (3) states that the marginal price of attribute z_i equals marginal WTP or the marginal rate of substitution between attribute z_i and x. The marginal WTP function on the right hand side is also referred to as the inverse demand function for attribute z_i.

The procedure discussed earlier involves specification of the form of the housing price function and econometric estimation of its parameters. Marginal prices for a housing attribute are then determined by taking the derivative of the HP function with respect to the attribute in question. WTP can be measured through the estimated hedonic slope. However, to analyse the exact impact on welfare, the inverse demand function has to be estimated, which forms the second stage. Once the HP function is estimated, the implicit marginal price of the environmental good of interest (water scarcity and water quality in this study) is estimated for each observation. Using these implicit price estimates, the implicit inverse demand function for the environmental good (implicit price as a function of the environmental good and socioeconomic features of the individuals) is estimated. The estimates of the second stage are then used to obtain the consumer surplus (calculating the area under the demand curve between the observed level of water scarcity and the new levels using integration).

Consistent HP estimation involves addressing three important issues: functional form, identification and market segmentation. The identification issue is addressed by carrying out the analysis in two stages with the second stage using implicit rent as obtained from HP. The issue of functional form is discussed later in empirical estimation section, whereas the market segmentation issue is addressed by carrying out the study for only those areas where residents can participate in an active rental market. It is to be noted that the city of Chennai can be geographically divided into northern and southern parts. The north of Chennai, which is more traditional and older, has a different residential profile and socioeconomic characteristics of the residents than the newer southern part. In other words, residents of north Chennai do not take part in the rental or housing market of the southern part. Keeping this division in mind, the analysis has been carried out only for residents in the southern part, which thus takes care of the market segmentation issue.

Data and Variables

In specifying the HP function the first concern is the choice of the dependent variable, that is, a choice has to be made between land values and house values. In reality, since the environmental amenities of interest are location-specific, the land values can reflect the price of that attribute. Most of the hedonic studies have used the actual values of house sales, but in this study we use the rental values. The choice of rental values rather than the house sales is dictated due to the active rental market in Chennai, where rents differ due to availability and quality of water. Box A8.1 in Appendix 8.1 gives an illustration of this active rental market in the case of one locality in Chennai.

The selection of explanatory variables for a HP function is another issue that must be meaningfully addressed. Since the objective of the hedonic analysis is to determine the effect of one amenity (here water availability and quality) on property values, other things being equal, the key issue is the control for structural, neighbourhood and other environmental attributes. The concern is the likelihood of multi-collinearity among housing characteristics. This raises the troublesome question of the trade-off between increasing bias through the variable of concern and increasing the variance or imprecision of coefficient estimates when collinear variables are included.

As indicated, the variables included in the analysis can be divided into three categories: structural, neighbourhood and environmental. Area of the house, type of dwelling (flat, independent house, chawl, etc.), number of rooms and bathrooms, presence of garage and others, are the structure-specific characteristics. The environmental characteristics considered include the kind of locality (clean, type of roads, air pollution, water availability (frequency of water supply during summer), type of water available (whether sweet or salty) and others. Neighbourhood characteristics include distance to the nearest market or centre, distance from railway station, airport, schools and other prominent centres. Environmental amenities include proximity to beach, park, and others. While estimating the HP method, all these attributes need to be controlled.

Data Collection

Regarding the procedure for obtaining the data, most of the hedonic studies, we are aware, have used data from the census of population and housing. The census asks each owner to estimate the value of his or her property and also gathers data on structural characteristics, as well as socio-economic data of occupants. In this chapter we could not use the census data because of two reasons: (i) in India, the stated house price/values are mostly undervalued; (ii) the non-availability of relevant housing and environmental characteristics of the house. Alternatively, we could have used the property tax data. But this is also inflicted with the same problems, as property tax is computed on some notional value fixed by the government, not the actual market value. To overcome these problems, we have relied on primary survey to collect information about the house and household.

With respect to the main variables of interest, that is, water scarcity, we are aware that even in the same street in an area, the availability of water can differ. However, the availability issue was circumvented using a broader definition, where if the household has any source in its premise, is considered to have no water scarcity. With respect to quality, the perception of the household has been used. Ideally, we could have tested the water samples from different households, given the scope and budget of the study, we could not do this.

For the primary survey, first localities in south Chennai were selected such that they fall within a radial distance of 10 km from either of the two city centres—T-Nagar or Adyar. After selection of localities, through random sampling a primary survey of 1,750 households was carried out to obtain information about house characteristics and households' socio-economic conditions.[2]

[2] The questionnaire canvassed can be obtained from the authors on request.

To check if the WTP estimates are affected by seasonality, the survey was carried out in two phases. The first phase covering 1,100 households was from 1 June to 20 September 2003 and the second phase involving 650 households was from March 2004 to 26 June 2004. To carry out the survey, field investigators were employed, who were mainly university students taking or had taken basic courses in environmental economics.

Of these 1,750 households, 367 questions had to be discarded for the following reasons: (i) missing information; (ii) respondents not willing to divulge income and other details; (iii) the owners had no idea about expected rent or the respondent had no idea about the area of the house and (iv) respondent staying in slum clearance or housing board provided by the government where the rents are not determined by market forces. For instance, in some of the housing board houses, the rent was merely ₹25[3] per month for a two-room apartment. The cleaning of data, thus left a sample of 1,383 completed questionnaires, of which 950 (i.e., 68.5 per cent) were from phase 1 and 433 (i.e., 31.5 per cent) from phase 2. Table 8.1 gives the definition of different variables used in the HP equation and their expected sign. Table 8.2 gives the mean statistics of different variables.

The expected sign for most of the variables like area, rooms, garage and others is self-explanatory. However, for some structural characteristics and other variables like ownership, household size and others, relation with the rent paid (or expected rent) is not very obvious. For example, for owned houses, the expected rent may be biased upwards or downwards depending upon owners' perception of the house, knowledge about the housing market and other traits linked to personality.[4] Similarly, whether a household having larger members will be willing to pay higher rent or vice versa, is difficult to construe.

[3] US$1 = ₹45 (approx.) in 2004.

[4] As mentioned, in order to remove owner-induced bias, the expected rent has been verified from real estate agents. Alternatively, one can carry out the analysis separately for the two categories of households to see if the bias still persists. The present study carries out the analysis for these two categories of households separately.

Table 8.1:
Variables and definitions of variables used in the hedonic price equation

S. No.	Variables (1)	Definitions (2)	Expected Sign (3)
1.	*Rent*	*Rent paid or expected rent* of the house in ₹*	
Structural Characteristics			
2.	*Area_sq ft*	Area of the house in square feet	+
3.	*Rooms*	No. of Rooms	+
4.	*Bathroom*	Number of bathrooms in the house (0 if the bathroom is shared or common)	+
5.	*Age_hse_yrs*	Age of the house in years	–
6.	*Hstyp*	Type of the house (1—bungalow, 2—independent house, 3—flat, 4—portion, 5—chawl and 6—hut)	–
7.	*Length of stay*	Length of stay in years	–
8.	*Garage*	Whether house has exclusive car-parking	+
9.	*Floor*	Floor	–
10.	*Ownership*	Own house or on rent (1—owned house; 0 otherwise)	?
Neighbourhood Characteristics			
11.	*Distance from city centre*	Distance of house from city centre in km	–
12.	*Qlty_localty*	Quality of the locality ranked from 1 to 4 (1—very clean, 2—clean, 3—not clean, 4—dirty)	–
13.	*Qlty_roads*	Quality of the roads in the locality ranked from 1 to 4 (1—if very wide, 2—wide, 3—narrow, 4—very narrow)	–
14.	*Location_noisy*	If the location is noisy ranked from 1 to 4 (1—very quiet, 2—quiet, 3—noisy, 4—very noisy)	–
15.	*Location scenic*	Location scenic (1 for yes and 0 otherwise)	+
16.	*Posh*	If the locality is posh (1 for posh, and 0 otherwise)	+
17.	*Bus_freq*	Frequency of buses ranked from 1 to 4 (1—very often, 2—often, 3—infrequent, 4—no buses)	–
18.	*Greenery*	Presence of greenery in the locality ranked from 1 to 3 (1—green, 2—somewhat green and 3—not green)	–

(Table 8.1 Contd)

(Table 8.1 Contd)

S. No.	Variables (1)	Definitions (2)	Expected Sign (3)
19.	*Env_ disamenities*	Environmental disamenities like water logging, solid waste etc. (1—yes, 0—no)	–
Environmental Characteristics			
20.	*Water_quality*	Perception of respondents about ground water quality ranked in increasing order (1—good, 4—very bad).	–
21.	*Water_scarcity*	Water fetching (0—if at home; 1—outside).	–
22.	*Air_qlty_ problem*	Perception of respondents about air quality ranked in increasing order (1—good, 4—very bad)	–
Socio-economic Characteristics			
23.	*Education*	No. of years of education	+
24.	*Profession*	In increasing order (0—not working/ low income, 1—salaried and 2—business/ self-employed)	+
25.	*Hhd_members*	Total members in the house	?
26.	*Hhd_income*	Total household income in increasing order (1—less than ₹10,000 to 6—₹45,000 and above)	+

Source: Authors' own analysis.
Note: *For the owned houses, we verified the expected rent from the real estate agent.

Table 8.2:
Summary statistics of various variables used in the hedonic price equation (N = 1383)

S. No.	Variable	Mean	S. D.	Min	Max
1.	Rent	2959.64	2521.91	150	30000
Structural Characteristics					
2.	Area_sqft	684.07	456.99	100	5000
3.	Rooms	4.43	1.82	1	12
4.	Bathroom	1.46	0.81	0	5
5.	Age_hse_yrs	18.22	12.82	1	125
6.	Hstyp	3.04	1.21	1 = bungalow	6 = hut
7.	Length of stay	14.34	12.91	.05	125
8.	Garage	0.24	0.43	0	1

(Table 8.2 Contd)

(Table 8.2 Contd)

S. No.	*Variable*	*Mean*	*S. D.*	*Min*	*Max*
9.	Floor	0.22	0.59	0	4
10.	Ownership	0.69	0.46	0	1
Neighbourhood Characteristics					
11.	Distance from city centre	4.14	2.53	.5	12.75
12.	Qlty_localty	2.52	0.64	1 = very clean	4 = dirty
13.	Qlty_roads	2.46	0.59	1 = very wide	4 = very narrow
14.	Location_noisy	2.43	0.60	1 = very quiet	4 = very noisy
15.	Location scenic	2.37	0.53	1 = very good	3 = no view
16.	Posh	0.21	0.40	0	1
17.	Bus_freq	1.33	0.50	1 = very frequent	3 = not frequent
18.	Greenery	2.42	0.58	1 = very green	3 = not green
19.	Env_disamenities	0.20	0.40	0	1
Environmental Characteristics					
20.	G_Water_quality#	2.16	0.73	1 = not salty	4 = contaminated
21.	Water_scarcity	0.64	0.48	0	1
22.	Air_qlty_problem	2.19	0.74	1 = very serious	4 = no problem
Socio-economic Characteristics					
23.	Education	11.08	5.55	0	20
24.	Profession	0.36	0.66	0 = not working	2 = business
25.	Hhd_members	4.31	1.64	1	21
26.	Hhd_income	1.79	0.97	1 (<10K)	6 (>45K)

Source: Primary Survey.
Note: #G_Water_quality (Ground water quality) is only for those households which are dependent on ground water (N = 723).

Empirical Estimation for Hedonic Price Function

Since the exact functional form of the HP function is unknown, we have used a Box-Cox transformation. The use of the Box-Cox transformation enables the functional form to be dictated by the transformation parameters, which are estimated in the regression.

The advantage of Box-Cox model is that it searches over alternative functional forms, thereby minimizing the specification error.

The general form of Box-Cox model is:

$$p(z)^{(\theta)} = \eta_0 + \sum_{ii=}^{k} \eta_i z_{\ i}^{\lambda} + 0.5 \sum_i \sum_j \gamma_{ij} z_i^{(\lambda)} z_j^{\lambda} \qquad (4)$$

where $P(z)^{(\theta)} = [(P(z))^{(\theta)} - 1)]/\theta$ and $z^{(\lambda)} = ((z^{\lambda}) - 1)/\lambda$. With varying choices of the triplet {θ, λ, γ}, several functional forms emerge. The following are the forms that emerge for different values of {θ, λ, γ}.

1. $\theta = 1, \lambda = 1, \gamma_{ij} = 0$: Linear
2. $\theta = 0, \lambda = 1, \gamma_{ij} = 0$: Semi-log
3. $\theta = 0, \lambda = 0, \gamma_{ij} = 0$: Log-log
4. $\theta = 1, \lambda = 1$: Quadratic
5. $\gamma_{ij} = 0$: Box-Cox linear
6. $\{\theta, \lambda, \gamma\}$ unrestricted : Box-Cox quadratic.

The purpose of the transformation is to have compliance, with greater degree of assumption, with three common assumptions of the regression model. These assumptions are: (i) there is an additive error term; (ii) the additive error has a constant variance and (iii) the error distribution is symmetric and possibly nearly normal (Kim and Hill, 1993: 307).

Thus, the Box-Cox transformation is applied to the data so as to allow variation in the functional form of the dependent variable and the independent variables. It needs to be mentioned that to carry out transformation, the variable should be strictly positive. Thus, dummy variables like 'Garage', 'Ownership' and others cannot be transformed. In order to shed some light on the estimation errors that may occur if a particular functional form is forced on the data, results for two most frequently used functional forms—linear and semi-logarithmic—are also presented. Table 8.3 gives the estimated HP equation for linear and semi-logarithmic models and after Box-Cox transformation.

Table 8.3:
Estimated coefficients for various functional forms of hedonic price equation (dependent variable: linear, semi-log and box-cox transformation of monthly rent) (N = 1383)

		Linear		*Semi-Log*		*Box-Cox*	
S. No.	*Variable (1)*	*Coefficient (2)*	*T-ratios (3)*	*Coefficient (4)*	*T-ratios (5)*	*Coefficient (6)*	*χ^2 Statistics (7)*
Structural Characteristics							
1.	Area_sqft	1.50*	10.58	0.0003*	7.53	0.569*	147.35
2.	Rooms	208.36*	5.49	0.112*	10.80	0.468*	70.97
3.	Hstyp	101.08*	2.14	−0.075*	−5.78	−0.092	2.43
4.	Length of stay	−8.72*	−2.11	−0.005*	−4.74	−0.072*	15.16
5.	Garage$	1050.85*	7.72	0.306*	8.21	0.386*	59.57
6.	Floor$	190.97*	2.24	0.081*	3.49	0.064*	4.11
7.	Ownership$	220.54*	1.88	0.080*	2.50	0.078*	2.86
Neighbourhood Characteristics							
8.	Distance city	−99.51*	−5.01	−0.014*	−2.66	−0.107*	16.14
9.	Qlty locality	−25.93	−0.23	−0.110*	−3.51	−0.362*	13.84
10.	Qlty roads	−511.22*	−4.84	−0.231*	−8.00	−0.804*	73.82
11.	Location_noisy	−176.07*	−1.82	−0.099*	−3.75	−0.276*	11.09

12.	Posh$	954.05*	6.75	0.223*	5.76	0.295*	30.84
13.	Greenery	–533.98*	–4.64	–0.069*	–2.19	–0.139	2.48
Environmental Characteristics							
14.	Air_quality	–161.94	–1.53	–0.008	–0.27	0.061	2.41
15.	Water_scarcity$	–585.05*	–5.67	–0.182*	–6.43	–0.276*	52.86
16.	Constant	4124.82*	9.68	8.526*	73.12	6.716	
17.	λ	1		1		–0.0156	
18.	θ	1		0		0.043	
19.	Loglikehood					–11434.56	
20.	Adj. R^2	0.557		0.687			
21.	LR χ^2					1734.92	
22.	Sigma					0.608	

Source: Authors' own analysis.

Note: $ indicates the variable has not been transformed, as it is not strictly positive—a necessary condition for transformation. *indicates significance at minimum 10 per cent level. LR, likelihood ratio.

The table indicates that the results obtained from linear model, semi-log model and Box-Cox transformed variables are entirely different. Examining the likelihood ratios (LRs), Box-Cox clearly rejects the linear and semi-log model.[5] The estimated theta value is 0.043 and the lambda value is –0.0156. The *t*-test indicates that both are statistically different from –1, 0 and 1. This implies that the semi-log, double-log and the linear specifications are inappropriate. Thus, we need to transform the variables according to the value of λ and θ and use the ordinary least squares on the transformed variables.

Table 8.4 gives the estimation results for different Box-Cox transformations. The model fits best when both dependent and independent variables are transformed. The discussion of results is given only for this model (i.e., coefficients given in column 6). Rows 1 to 7 give the sign and significance levels of various structural variables used in the HP estimation. Baring one (Hstyp) all the structural variables are significantly different from zero and have the expected sign. The rent (or expected rent) appears to be rising with area of the house (Area_sqft), number of rooms (Rooms),[6] presence of garage (Garage). However, the type of the house does not seem to have a significant impact on the rent, although it carries the right sign. The Ownership variable is found to be positive and statistically significant. This could be because for the owned-house, it is the expected rent and not the actual rent and since the owners are not in the rental market, they may have over-reported the expected rent.[7] Similarly, the longer a person stays in a house (Length_stay), lesser is the rent paid. This is quite likely, as the rents become sticky with the existing tenant and may not see upward revision every now and then.

[5] Using chi-squared LRs for the linear and semi-log models nested in the Box-Cox model, the LR statistic is $2*(LR_{linear}-LR_{Box\text{-}Cox})$, which is compared with the critical chi-squared value (Halstead et al., 1997: 763).

[6] Number of rooms in a house (Rooms) is found to be highly correlated with number of bedrooms (Bedrooms) and bathrooms (Bathrooms); hence the model has been run with Rooms only (for correlation between different variables, see Table A8.1 in Appendix 8.1). The results, though not reported, remain same even with Bedrooms and Bathrooms instead of Rooms.

[7] Despite doing a cross-verification with the real estate agent, we feel, such upward bias may be still existing.

Table 8.4:
Estimated hedonic price equation for different box-cox transformations (dependent variable: monthly rent) (N = 1383)

		Dependent Variable Transformed		*Independent Variable Transformed*		*Both Dependent and Independent Variables Transformed*	
S. No.	*Variable* (1)	*Coefficient* (2)	χ^2 *Statistics* (3)	*Coefficient* (4)	χ^2 *Statistics* (5)	*Coefficient* (6)	χ^2 *Statistics* (7)
Structural Characteristics							
1.	Area_sqft	0.001*	60.91	13.55*	116.64	0.569*	147.35
2.	Rooms	0.200*	109.20	274.59*	19.59	0.468*	70.97
3.	Hstyp	–0.118*	24.23	198.46*	8.01	–0.092	2.43
4.	Length of stay	–0.009*	19.97	–18.67*	3.33	–0.072*	15.16
5.	Garage$	0.572*	70.40	1015.42*	55.14	0.386*	59.57
6.	Floor$	0.144*	11.75	161.79*	3.58	0.064*	4.11
7.	Ownership$	0.145*	6.28	200.48*	2.75	0.078*	2.86
Neighbourhood Characteristics							
8.	Distance city	–0.029*	8.90	–162.33*	27.14	–0.107*	16.14
9.	Qlty locality	–0.191*	11.34	–51.00	0.12	–0.362*	13.84
10.	Qlty roads	–0.417*	62.78	–670.29*	23.33	–0.804*	73.82

(Table 8.4 Contd)

(Table 8.4 Contd)

S. No.	*Variable (1)*	*Dependent Variable Transformed*		*Independent Variable Transformed*		*Both Dependent and Independent Variables Transformed*	
		Coefficient (2)	*χ^2 Statistics (3)*	*Coefficient (4)*	*χ^2 Statistics (5)*	*Coefficient (6)*	*χ^2 Statistics (7)*
11.	Location_noisy	−0.174*	13.25	−200.24	2.49	−0.276*	11.09
12.	Posh$	0.429*	37.12	944.29*	44.05	0.295*	30.84
13.	Greenery	−0.142*	6.24	−655.99*	20.11	−0.139	2.48
Environmental Characteristics							
14.	Air_quality	−0.027	0.26	−117.10	1.22	0.061	2.41
15.	Water_scarcity$	−0.332*	42.05	−599.93*	33.95	−0.276*	52.86
16.	Constant	12.046		2517.44		6.716	
17.	λ			0.692		0.0244	
18.	θ	0.078				0.0500	
19.	Loglikehood	-11490.55		-12219.16		-11702.191	
20.	LR χ^2	1622.93		1150.9		1782.88	
21.	Sigma	0.827		1662.89		0.6527	

Source: Authors' own analysis.
Note: Same as Table 8.3.

Rows 8–13 give the sign and significance of various neighbourhood variables. The quality of roads (row 10) and the locality (row 9) have a significantly positive impact on the rental values. Similarly, houses in the posh areas (row 12) carry higher rents. An area with less noise (also a reflection of the fact that the house will be little away from the main road) fetches more rent vis-à-vis noisy houses or the houses closer to the main road.[8] Lastly, the more the house is distant from the city centre (row 8), the lesser the rent it is going to fetch. Though noisy location (Location_noisy) is an environmental attribute of the area, it needs to be kept in mind that over time people have tendencies to adapt their behaviour accordingly. Alternatively, these attributes are under-represented in their choice and usually given less preference unless the situation is acute (such as residence by the side of an airport or railway station).

The availability and quality of water is mainly localized. The availability of water to a household has been captured in the present study by asking how the water is being fetched—whether the household has 24 hours metro water or assured metro water supply at some fixed time during a day or there is a borewell at home. If the house is using either of the sources, this implies water is available. If the household depends on any other mode of fetching water implies scarcity of water. However, quality ascertainment requires testing the water samples for different parameters. As stated earlier, we relied on the perception of the people about the quality. Moreover, quality has relevance only when water is available. Thus, the study first checks the relationship with availability and then for those households having no scarcity of water, the impact of (perception) quality is tested.

Row 15 indicates the availability environmental attribute of the study. Water scarcity is found to be directly influencing the rental price of a house. A house where water is scarce (be it ground or metro water) is fetching significantly less rent. Row 14 giving the impact of air quality on rent indicates that a house having better

[8] Good frequency of public transport (Bus_freq) can also have a direct impact on the rental value of a house. But as most of the surveyed people stated that the bus frequency in their locality is not infrequent, the variable has not been included in the analysis.

air quality would fetch less rent, though the impact is not statistically significant. There are two possibilities of this perverse result: it is quite likely that in the present study, other neighbourhood characteristics like Posh, Qlty_localty, Qlty_roads and others may have taken care of air quality influence. Alternatively, the study uses only perceptions and not actual concentration of pollutants. Since these 21 locations of the present study have only two air monitoring stations, actual air quality parameters cannot be used. Table 8.5, however, gives the results for both the models—with and without using air quality as an attribute. The results hardly change and air quality perception is found to have no statistically significant impact on the rent.

As mentioned, only when the water is available to meet the needs, efforts can be made to bring it to the desired quality. To test this conjecture, the sample is divided into two parts—households having scarcity of water and households having no scarcity of water. The analysis thus becomes nested as it tests the impact of quality depending upon whether the water is available in plenty. Table 8.6 gives the results of the Box-Cox transformation for the nested HP equation.

Columns 2 and 3 report results when air quality variable is included, whereas columns 4 and 5 report results with the exclusion of air quality variable. The variable sign and significance is same in both the models except that air quality improvement in an area fetches less rent. This implies that residents place emphasis on the air quality, only if they are assured of water in Chennai. Area, number of rooms, garage, posh locality, quality of roads and locality, and greenery fetches more rent. On the other hand, House type, length of stay and other variables have no impact on the rent.

Row 16 gives the results of impact of water quality on rents. The sign and significance of the coefficient validates our conjecture that people place more value on water availability and then worry about water quality. In regions where water is available in plenty, the rents do not have a statistical significant relationship with the water quality (column 2). This implies people are willing to pay more for areas that have some water, irrespective of the quality.

Table 8.5:
Estimated hedonic price equation for box-cox transformation (impact of water scarcity on rent with or without air quality) (dependent variable: monthly rent) (N = 1383)

		Impact on Water Scarcity with Air Quality Variable		*Impact on Water Scarcity without Air Quality Variable*	
S. No.	*Variable (1)*	*Coefficient (2)*	*χ^2 Statistics (3)*	*Coefficient (4)*	*χ^2 Statistics (5)*
Structural Characteristics					
1.	Area_sqft	0.57*	147.35	0.51*	144.95
2.	Rooms	0.47*	70.97	0.47*	71.88
3.	Hstyp	-0.09	2.43	-0.10*	2.93
4.	Length of stay	-0.07*	15.16	-0.07*	15.66
5.	Garage$	0.39*	59.57	0.39*	58.50
6.	Floor$	0.06*	4.11	0.06*	3.99
7.	Ownership$	0.08*	2.86	0.08*	2.77
Neighbourhood Characteristics					
8.	Distance city	-0.11*	16.14	-0.11*	16.82
9.	Qlty locality	-0.36*	13.84	-0.36*	13.32
10.	Qlty roads	-0.80*	73.82	-0.83*	77.36
11.	Location_noisy	-0.28*	11.09	-0.29*	11.97
12.	Posh$	0.29*	30.84	0.31*	33.59
13.	Greenery	-0.14	2.48	-0.13	2.21
Environmental Characteristics					
14.	Air_quality	0.06	2.41		
15.	Water_scarcity	-0.28*	52.86	-0.29*	54.81
16.	Constant	6.72		7.12	
17.	λ	-0.016		0.006	
18.	θ	0.043		0.047	
19.	Loglikehood	-11434.56		-11435.76	
20.	LR χ^2	1734.92		1732.51	
21.	Sigma	0.61		0.63	

Source: Authors' own analysis.
Note: Same as Table 8.3.

Table 8.6:
Estimated nested hedonic price equation for box-cox transformation (impact of water quality on rent without scarcity) (dependent variable: monthly rent) (N = 342)

S. No.	*Variable (1)*	*Coefficient (2)*	*χ^2 Statistics (3)*	*Coefficient (4)*	*χ^2 Statistics (5)*
Structural Characteristics					
1.	Area_sqft	6.21*	44.59	5.54*	42.23
2.	Rooms	1.38*	18.99	1.43*	19.62
3.	Hstyp	0.13	0.20	0.086	0.08
4.	Length of stay	-0.02	0.06	-0.006	0.006
5.	Garage$	0.79*	21.17	0.79*	19.27
6.	Floor$	0.02	0.042	0.013	0.017
7.	Ownership$	-0.35*	3.73	-0.39*	4.35
Neighbourhood Characteristics					
8.	Distance city	0.04	0.08	-0.06	0.17
9.	Qlty locality	-0.94*	5.7	-0.93*	5.17
10.	Qlty roads	-1.19*	8.99	-1.16*	7.94
11.	Location_noisy	0.28	0.71	0.26	0.57
12.	Posh$	0.38*	4.15	0.57*	9.38
13.	Greenery	-0.84*	6.76	-0.89*	7.02
Environmental Characteristics					
14.	Air_quality$	0.41*	6.16		
15.	Water_quality	0.15	0.66	0.10	0.28
16.	Constant	-5.69		-3.79	
17.	λ	-0.25		-0.23	
18.	θ	0.13		0.14	
19.	Loglikehood	-2986.96		-2990.04	
20.	LR χ^2	376.46		370.31	
21.	Sigma	1.217		1.28	

Source: Authors' own analysis.
Note: Same as Table 8.3.

However, their preference of water quality changes once they are assured of water. The only possible explanation for this perverse result is that people may be valuing the availability of water more than the quality.[9]

As mentioned, the owned houses are not in the rental market, hence may have some bias for implied rent. Thus, to see the impact of this bias, the analysis is carried out separately for two groups of households—owned and rented. Table 8.7 reports the results. From the table (row 13), it can be seen that the effect is more pronounced for households staying in rented houses. A household living in a rented house values scarcity (coefficient value = –0.76) nearly thrice than the household owning the house (coefficient value = –0.27). Even other structural and neighbourhood variables such as distance to city centre (Distance city), Greenery or the floor on which the house is located hve a differential impact.

Aggregate Willingness to Pay for Improved Water Supply and Quality

The main interest in this study has been to estimate the value of the benefits of a programme that would bring about a non-marginal change in the availability (and quality) of the water. As stated in the third section, the marginal price function provides the WTP (or demand) function for different perception about the availability and quality. This is obtained as the absolute value of the derivative of hedonic property value function given the observed values of the variables rent and water scarcity/water quality. The household marginal WTP function for the improvement in water supply and quality is estimated by regressing the implicit marginal prices

[9] Another reason for the perverse result could be the way the variable has been constructed. This study considers the perception of the people rather than the actual water quality. In fact, many of the households though are using only metro water, have stated that the water is salty, which only reflects perception and not the true assessment. Under the circumstances, quality results need to be viewed with some caution.

Table 8.7:
Estimated hedonic price equation for box-cox transformation (impact of ownership on rent) (dependent variable: monthly rent)

		Rented Houses		*Owned Houses*	
S. No.	*Variable (1)*	*Coefficient (2)*	*χ^2 Statistics (3)*	*Coefficient (4)*	*χ^2 Statistics (5)*
Structural Characteristics					
1.	Area_sqft	0.54*	109.52	0.64*	70.20
2.	Rooms	0.78*	28.08	0.50*	46.50
3.	Hstyp	0.07	0.19	-0.11	2.07
4.	Length of stay	-0.16*	14.36	-0.03	0.99
5.	Garage$	0.99*	24.58	0.36*	38.35
6.	Floor$	0.14	1.56	0.08*	4.27
Neighbourhood Characteristics					
7.	Distance city	0.01	0.025	-0.16*	21.67
8.	Qlty locality	-0.98*	9.15	-0.32*	7.51
9.	Qlty roads	-0.71*	6.99	-1.10*	83.41
10.	Location_noisy	-0.11	0.19	-0.40*	14.11
11.	Posh$	0.71*	9.78	0.27*	20.98
12.	Greenery	0.83*	8.14	-0.29*	7.27
Environmental Characteristics					
13.	Water_scarcity	-0.76*	35.27	-0.27*	32.65
14.	Constant	8.46		7.12	
15.	λ	0.18		-0.065	
16.	θ	0.16		0.039	
17.	Loglikehood	-3371.62		-8015.21	
18.	LR χ^2	642.05		1103.24	
19.	Sigma	1.17		0.61	
20.	*N*	431		952	

Source: Authors' own analysis.

Notes: Same as Table 8.4. As mentioned in the text, the models do not include Air Quality as an explanatory variable. Though the model was run with Air Quality as an explanatory variable—results varied depending upon whether the house is owned or rented. For an owned house, the relation was as per prediction, but for rented houses it was perverse.

on income, education and other socio-economic variables (refer Table 8.2 for definition of these variables) and the water scarcity and/or quality parameter.

The implicit marginal price for unit change in the water quality will be:

$\partial Y_1/\partial X_{water\_quality} = (\beta_{water\_quality})X^{\lambda-1}{}_{water\_quality}/Y_1^{\theta-1}$. Since the variable 'water scarcity' is used as a dummy, it has not been transformed in the analysis. The marginal impact price for the variable is $\partial Y_1/\partial X_{water\_scarcity} = (\beta_{water\_scarcity})/Y_1^{\theta-1}$.

Table 8.8 gives the estimated WTP for improved availability and quality of water for households having available water. Columns 2 and 3 give results for water scarcity, whereas columns 4 and 5 give

Table 8.8:
Estimated willingness to pay equation for improved availability and quality (dependent variable = implicit price)

		Availability		*Quality for Available Water*	
S. No.	*Variables (1)*	*Coefficient (2)*	*χ^2 Statistics (3)*	*Coefficient (4)*	*χ^2 Statistics (5)*
1.	Education$	0.08*	225.22	0.13*	46.93
2.	Profession$	-0.031	0.89	0.04	0.13
3.	Monthly_hhd_income	1.37*	358.04	1.94*	62.55
4.	Household Size	-0.42*	16.37	-1.45*	12.52
5.	Water_scarcity$	-0.28*	34.18		
6.	Water_quality			-5.61*	292.98
7.	Constant	6.88		9.76	
8.	λ	-0.41		-0.64	
9.	θ	0.07		0.251	
10.	Loglikehood	-9,605.41		-1763.28	
11.	LR χ^2	797.33		3,60.98	
12.	Sigma	0.91		1.5	
13.	*N*	1383		342	

Source: Authors' own analysis.
Note: Same as Table 8.4.

results for water availability for those households having no scarcity. As expected, the WTP for improved availability and quality of water for a household increases with their monthly income and education level. Profession, however, does not affect the marginal WTP, in statistical terms. However, increased household size has a negative effect on the WTP. One reason could be that with more members, they can be engaged in fetching water even from a public tap.

The variables for water availability and/or scarcity indicates that with the change in the existing situation from fetching water through different means to a better situation of piped water supply directly in homes, there is an increase in WTP. For a household that is facing acute water shortage, his/her WTP increases by ₹1,064 (≈US$25) if the water scarcity changes from scarcity to availability stage. Since quality is relevant for only those households which have no scarcity, the WTP for improved quality does not rise by the same amount. A household which is receiving contaminated water is willing to pay an amount equal to ₹53.40 (≈US$1.3) to get almost clean water.

As we are interested in aggregate WTP for improved water availability and quality for the whole Chennai city, the individual WTP needs to be converted to aggregate WTP. The Census 2001 indicates that the number of households in Chennai is nearly 850,000. Thus, the aggregate consumer surplus for the entire population of Chennai is around ₹904 million per month (≈US$21 million) and ₹45.39 million (≈US$1.1 million), respectively. The estimates though quite high, are still lower bound for many reasons. First of all, the estimates do not consider the opportunity cost of collecting water supply.[10] Second, given the short-term nature of the study, the survey was carried out mainly in south Chennai. The areas in the north of Chennai though are facing equally acute water shortage, but the water quality may be worse than that of in the south. This is because most of the large industrial units, many of them are polluting in nature, are in north Chennai.

[10] For many households having larger family size, the social cost of fetching water may not be very high. In fact, avenue may be used for more socializing.

The next step is comparing this aggregate consumer surplus with that of costs incurred for providing safe water supply to population of Chennai. Table 8.9 gives a rough estimate of these costs. Given the investment needed in different projects to supply water to the Chennai city, the aggregate consumer surplus as calculated is much lower. The discrepancy between costs and benefits is due to following reasons. The cost of supplying water to Chennai also includes cost of supplying water to industries located in Chennai and to adjacent and distant urbanized areas falling under Chennai. This study, however, has attempted to find value only for domestic use.

Conclusions

The main objectives of this chapter were two-fold: (i) to estimate the WTP for avoiding water shortages, and (ii) for the households facing no water scarcity, improving the quality of water for residents of Chennai, India. The choice of Chennai for the study is governed by the fact that it does not have a perennial source of fresh water and often faces scarcity problem. This study has estimated the aggregate WTP for improving the water supply and quality situation in Chennai from the present state of water fetching from an (uncertain) public source to getting water directly through piped water supply through a HP model of house rents using a primary survey of 1383 households spread over 21 locations. All the issues considered vital for the estimation of HP function—functional form, identification, market segmentation—have been accounted for in the study. The estimated coefficients in the hedonic model all have the expected signs and almost all of them are significant at the 95 per cent level.

The study finds that the impact of improvement in water scarcity situation on rental values is of considerable magnitude. The aggregate WTP for an increase in water supply situation from the existing state of fetching water through different sources (like ground water, private tankers, metro tanker, public taps, etc.) to getting water through piped water and improved water quality in their houses

Table 8.9:
Costs of different projects implemented and in implementation

	Scheme	*Implement*	*Cost (in ₹ million)*	*Cost (in million US$)*	*Area Covered*	*Year of Completion*
1.	Veeranam project (Chennai Water Supply Augmentation Project I)	1968[i]	7,200[ii]	167.4	Chennai	2004
2.	Chennai Water Supply Augmentation Project II		1,100	25.58	To construct check dams across Palar and Kosastalayar rivers and improve storage capacity of Rettai Eri, Ambattur, and Korattur lakes	2004
3.	Telugu Ganga Project (TGP)	27April 1983	6,370–increased to 24,700[iii]	148.14 increased to 574.4	To irrigate 5.75 lakh acres in Andhra Pradesh. To supply 15 TMC of water to Chennai city	2005
4.	Second Chennai Water Supply Project (WB assisted)	1995	7,790[iv]	181.16	Project aims at improving water supply distribution system in Chennai city	2005
5.	Water Supply Improvement Schemes	2003–04	2,680	62.32	Benefit a population of about 26 lakhs	
6.	Chennai city river conservation project[v]	2001	7,201.5	167.47	Adyar, Buckingham canal, Coovum, Otteri Nullah, Captain Cotton Canal and Mambalam Drain waterways	2005
7.	Sea water desalination plant	2003–04	15,000	348.83		2006
8.	Third Chennai Project (proposed)		7,500	174.42		2006

Source: Different websites and www.chennaimetrowater.com and Metrowater (2003)

Notes: Despite visit to the Chennai Metropolitan Water Board, we could not get information on the revenues generated from different schemes. (i) In April 2003, chief minister announced in the State Assembly that the project would be completed by June; (ii) the project was revised and the cost was estimated at ₹16,380 million. To prevent rain water running off into the sea, construction of check dams, reservoirs, tanks, etc., is proposed to store surplus water in Kortalaiyar, Coovum, Adayar and Palar rivers; (iii) first figure is at 1983–84 prices, whereas second figure is based on the review of the project in 1997; (iv) The funding of the project is 17.25 per cent from Chennai Metrowater Board's internal generation, 17.25 per cent from T.N. Govt. as grant and the balance 65.5 per cent is funded by the World Bank (≅US$86 million); (v) Diversion and treatment of sewage and providing additional 264 mld (million litres a day) capacity sewage treatment plants at Perungudi (54 mld), Koyambedu (60), Nesapakkam (40) and Kodungaiyur (110).

was estimated at approximately ₹904 million (US$21.12 million) and ₹45.39 million (US$1.05 million), respectively. This value provides a useful estimate of the order of magnitude of the benefits resulting from initiating new water projects. The estimated order of magnitude clearly suggests that there is room for implementing more water supply projects in Chennai that could have positive welfare effects on the population.

Appendix 8.1

Figure A8.1:
Summer water levels in different lakes in Chennai since 1950 (April to August)

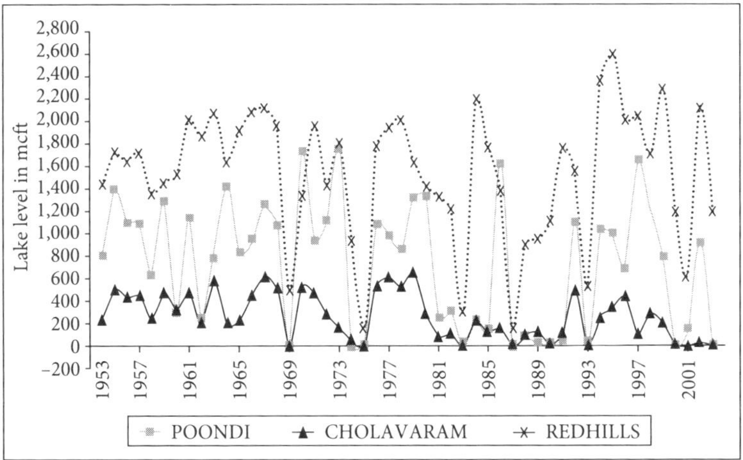

Box A8.1:
Active rental market in Chennai: An illustration

Three advertisements depicting different status of water in one single area

- Thiruvanmiyur, nr Sacred Heart College, 650 sqft, grd flr, 1 B/R, granite flrg, 24 hrs sweet water, small family pref, ₹4,000, Anbalagan, Mb: 944175519
- Thiruvanmiyur, Radhakrishna ngr, independent, 1,300 sqft, 1 flr, 3 B/R, carpark, 24 hrs water, ₹7,000/pm, Natrajan, Mb: 32150928
- Thiruvanmiyur, behind post office, 400 sqft, 1 flr, B/R, ₹2,000, Rajagopalan, Ph: 24929581. Ch-41.

Source: Free Ads, Chennai, 11–14 July 2004.

Table A8.1:
Correlation between different variables

	Rent (in ₹)	*Area (in sq ft)*	*Rooms*	*No. of Bathrooms*	*Bedroom*	*Age of the House (in years)*	*House Type*	*Length of Stay (in years)*	*Distance to City Centre (in km)*	*Quality of Locality*	*Location Noisy*	*Location Scenic*	*Good Water*	*Garage*	*Floor*	*Water Scarcity*	*Ownership*	*Posh*
Rent (in ₹)	1																	
Area (in sq ft)	0.59	1																
Rooms	0.55	0.65	1															
No. of bathrooms	0.55	0.59	0.75	1														
Bedroom	0.56	0.63	0.79	0.82	1													
Age of the house (in years)	−0.009	0.09	−0.03	−0.07	−0.03	1												
House type	−0.21	−0.36	−0.44	−0.39	−0.44	0.01	1											

Length of stay (in years)	−0.02	0.12	0.03	−0.01	0.01	0.73	−0.05	1										
Distance to city centre (in Kms)	0.13	0.22	0.20	0.27	0.26	0.01	−0.14	−0.01	1									
Quality of locality	−0.37	−0.27	−0.42	−0.42	−0.41	0.12	0.31	0.14	−0.15	1								
Location noisy	−0.34	−0.27	−0.41	−0.41	−0.39	0.13	0.32	0.13	−0.21	0.48	1							
Location scenic	−0.36	−0.28	−0.35	−0.41	−0.40	0.07	0.27	0.13	−0.21	0.49	0.46	1						
Good water	−0.26	−0.31	−0.30	−0.42	−0.44	−0.03	0.18	−0.03	−0.04	0.20	0.27	0.26	1					
Garage	0.55	0.47	0.43	0.38	0.39	0.01	−0.05	−0.03	0.15	−0.26	−0.21	−0.25	−0.21	1				
Floor	0.23	0.13	0.12	0.17	0.14	−0.09	0.21	−0.15	0.10	−0.09	−0.05	−0.16	−0.12	0.30	1			
Water scarcity	−0.20	−0.03	0.02	0.11	0.10	−0.05	−0.12	0.006	−0.008	0.06	−0.02	−0.008	0.08	−0.21	−0.12	1		
Ownership	0.19	0.28	0.32	0.33	0.32	0.17	−0.23	0.42	0.10	−0.11	−0.13	−0.13	−0.19	0.09	−0.007	0.09	1	
Posh	0.50	0.39	0.38	0.39	0.36	0.08	−0.09	0.02	0.24	−0.30	−0.24	−0.29	−0.34	0.45	0.18	−0.30	0.12	1

References

Anand, P.B. and Perman, R. 1999. 'Preferences, Inequity and Entitlements: Some Issues from a CVM Study of Water Supply in Madras, India', *Journal of International Development*, 11(1): 27–46.

Boyle, M.A. and Kiel, K.A. 2001. 'A Survey of House Price Hedonic Studies of the Impact of Environmental Externalities', *Journal of Real Estate Literature*, 9(2): 117–44.

Chau, K.W., Yiu, C.Y., Wong, S.K. and Lai, L.W. 2004. 'Hedonic Price Modelling of Environmental Attributes: A Review of the Literature and a Hong Kong Case Study', *Welfare Economics and Sustainable Development—Vol II, Encyclopedia of Life Support System*, UNESCO. Available at http://www.eolss.net/sample-chapters/c13/E1-21-05-04.pdf

Clawson, M. and Knetsch, J. 1966. *Economics of Outdoor Recreation*, Baltimore, MD: Johns Hopkins University Press.

Clawson, M. 1959. 'Methods of Measuring the Demand for and Value of Outdoor Recreation', REF Reprint No. 10, Washington, DC, Resources for the Future.

David, E.L. 1968. 'Lakeshore Property Values: A Guide to Public Investment in Recreation', *Water Resources Research*, 4(4): 697–707

Epp, D. and Al-Ani, K.S. 1979. 'The Effect of Water Quality on Rural Non Farm Residential Property Values', *American Journal of Agricultural Economics*, 61(3): 529–34.

Griliches, Z. 1971. *Price Indexes and Quality Change*. Cambridge, MA: Harvard University Press.

Halstead, J.M., Bouvier, R.A., and Hansen, B.E. 1997. 'On the Issue of Functional Form Choice in Hedonic Price Functions: Further Evidence', *Environmental Management*, 21(5): 759–65.

Hotelling, H. 1931. 'The Economics of Exhaustible Resources', *Journal of Political Economy*, 39(1): 1937–75.

Khatri-Chetri, J.B. and Hite, J.C. 1990. 'Impact of Reservoir Levels on the Market Value of Lakeshore Properties', *Rivers*, 1(2): 138–47.

Kim, M. and Hill, R.C. 1993. 'The Box-Cox Transformation of Variables in Regression', *Empirical Economics*,18(2): 307–19.

Kounduri, P. 2004. 'Current Issues in the Economics of Groundwater Resource Management', *Journal of Economic Surveys*, 18(5): 703–40.

Kounduri, P. and Pashardes, P. 2003. 'Hedonic Price Analysis and Selectivity Bias', *Environmental and Resource Economics*, 26(1): 45–56.

Kulshreshtha, S.N. and Gillies, J.A. 1993. 'Economic Evaluation of Aesthetic Amenities: A Case Study of River View', *Water Resources Bulletin*, 29(2): 257–66.

Legget, C.G. and Bockstael, N.E. 2000 'Evidence of the Effects of Water Quality on Residential Land Prices', *Journal of Environmental Economics and Management*, 39(2): 121–44.

Mendelsohn, R., Hellerstein, D., Huguenm, M., Unsworth, R. and Brazee, R. 1992. 'Measuring Hazardous Waste Damages with Panel Models', *Journal of Environmental Economics and Management*, 22(3): 259–71.

Michael, H., Boyle, K. and Bouchard, R. 1996. 'Water Quality Affects Property Prices: A Case Study of Selected Maine Lakes', *Maine Agricultural and Forest Experiment Station Miscellaneous Report*, 398, Feb, University of Maine.

Metrowater 2003. 'Chennai Metrowater: A Profile', Chennai Metropolitan Water Supply and Sewerage Board, Government of Tamil Nadu, Chennai.

Reddy, R.V. 1999. 'Quenching the Thirst: The Cost of Water in Fragile Environment', *Development and Change*, 30(1): 79–113.

Rosen S. 1974. 'Hedonic Prices and Implicit Markets: Product Differentiation in Pure Competition', *Journal of Political Economy*, 82(1): 34–55.

Roy, J., S. Chattopadhyay, Mukherjee, S., Kanjilal, M., Samajpati, S. and Roy, S. 2004. 'An Economic Analysis of Demand for Water Quality: Case of Kolkata', *Economic and Political Weekly*, 39(2): 186–92.

Smith, V.K. and Huang, J.C. 1995. 'Can Markets Value Air Quality? A Meta-Analysis of Hedonic Property Value Models', *Journal of Political Economy*, 103(1): 209–27.

Spalatro, F. and Provencher, B. 2001. 'An Analysis of Minimum Frontage Zoning to Preserve Lakefront Amenities', *Land Economics*, 77(4): 469–81.

Steinnes, D.N. 1992. 'Measuring the Economic Value of Water Quality', *Annals of Regional Science*, 26: 171–76.

Streiner, C. and Loomis, J. 1995. *Estimating the Benefits of the Urban Stream Restoration Program*. Fort Collins, Colorado: Department of Agricultural and Resource Economics, Colorado State University.

Wipenny, J. 1994 *Water as an Economic Resource*. London: Routledge.

Young, C.E. 1984. 'Perceived Water Quality and the Values of Seasonal Homes', *Water Resources Bulletin*, American Water Association, 20(2): 163–68.

9

Assessing On-farm Conservation and Farmer's Willingness to Participate: A Case Study of Minor Millet

Sukanya Das, Prabhakaran T. Raghu and E.D. Israel Oliver King

Introduction

Underutilized plant species can be characterized by the fact that they are locally abundant but globally rare, that scientific information and knowledge about them is scant, and that their current uses are limited relative to their economic potential (Gruere et al., 2009). Minor millets are a group of annual grasses found mainly in arid and semi-arid regions. They are cultivated on 29.1 million hectares (ha) in India, accounting for nearly 25 per cent of the total acreage under cereal crops. In India's dry lands, they play a significant role in meeting food and fodder requirements of farming communities. Three species of minor millets—finger millet (*Eleusine coracana*) foxtail millet (*Setaria italica*) and little millet (*Panicum sumatrense*)—are widely cultivated. These crops are often classified as 'minor or coarse grains' in agricultural statistics. 'Minor' refers not only to the smaller size of the grains, but also to their lesser importance in trade. The scientific knowledge about them is limited. Despite national efforts to collect minor millet germplasm from farmers, research to improve these crops has been negligible. Liberalization of the Indian seed sector in the 1990s favoured dry land cereals and legumes, with little impact on research and formal distribution channels for minor millets. Currently, the states of Andhra Pradesh, Karnataka and Tamil Nadu lead in crop improvement research on minor millets. However, the range of improved varieties is narrow. Private companies show little interest in developing new varieties, due to their lack of commercial importance and the limited scope for developing new hybrids.

In the Kolli Hills of Tamil Nadu, a genetically diverse pool of minor millet intra-specific landraces has been grown by the tribal farming communities for their own consumption. Despite a traditional consumption preference for minor millets by the local population, in recent years the area devoted to minor millets has declined considerably to the advantage of substitute crops such as tapioca (cassava), pineapple, pepper and coffee plantation, which are grown exclusively for market. In response to this development, the M.S. Swaminathan Research Foundation (MSSRF), a leading non-governmental organization based in Chennai, India, has led "Integrated 4c Approach for Conservation of Millet diversity' since 1996 in Kolli Hills. These programmes aim to promote the role of custodian farmers and community seed banks and to raise the market potential of minor millets through value addition and help the farming communities maintain their agro-biodiversity by providing economic incentives for its conservation (King, 2015; King et al., 2013, 2014, 2015; MSSRF, 2002).

Lack of attention from researchers, policymakers, donors, farmers and consumers is increasingly threatening the genetic diversity of minor millets. This is an irreversible loss to the humanity, particularly the poor who heavily depend on these crops for their food and nutritional security and income generation. In this context, the main objective of this study is to facilitate the conservation of agro-biodiversity, improved indigenous farmer livelihoods and policy through the development of innovative economic analytical methods and incentive mechanisms. This chapter investigates the farmer's decision for the conservation of minor millets at Kolli Hills. To this end, a non-market valuation method—the contingent valuation method (CVM) study—on minor millet conservation was undertaken in January–May 2010 covering 454 respondents from 50 villages. An open-ended questionnaire was applied to assess the potential willingness to accept (WTA) for payment on agro-biodiversity conservation services schemes to create incentives for the conservation of agro-biodiversity and improve indigenous farmer livelihoods.

Of the five small millet species, there are 20 landraces of four or five species under cultivation in our study area in Kolli Hills. There are seven landraces in little millet, six landraces in finger millet, five landraces in Italian millet, and one each landrace in proso millet and kodo millet. This chapter contributes to the literature in two ways. First, only a few previous applied economics studies have investigated the determinants of minor millets in India (Gruere et al., 2007a, 2007b, 2009; King et al., 2009). Second, this study adds to the growing literature that employs the stated preference method—CVM—to estimate farmer valuation of various components of agro-biodiversity (Ndjeunga and Nelson, 2005; Scarpa et al., 2003a, 2003b).

In the context of agricultural biodiversity, CVM has not been widely employed, though it has been applied extensively in valuing rare and endangered animal species such as pandas (Kontoleon and Swanson, 2003), habitats like the riparian forests and landscapes (Desaigues and Ami, 2001). It has been especially useful in *ex ante* and *ex post* assessment of conservation policy (Pearce and Moran, 2001). Some studies have undertaken the stated preference techniques to estimate the economic value of genetically modified crops like rice and maize (Birol et al., 2009; Horna et al., 2005).

The next section presents the background. The third section describes the study area, theoretical framework, data collection and the analysis. The fourth section reports and discusses the econometric results. In the final section, we draw conclusions and discuss policy implications.

Background

Cash Economy, Institutional Change and Local Seed Systems in Kolli Hills

The agro-biodiversity in Kolli Hills has been declining over the last three decades due to several factors such as expansion of commercial agriculture, market links, unsustainable use of forest resources and modification of the landscape, land alienation, land use changes and cultural erosion that resulted in shrinkage of area under cultivation of millets. The introduction of cash crops like tapioca, drudgery involved in the processing of millets, lack of market linkages for millets, expanding transport facilities, availability of food grain especially rice at reasonable cost through the public distribution system (PDS), rice consumption as a symbol of social status and mobility are also the key factors responsible for decline in cultivation and consumption of minor millets.

During the 1970s, the state sponsored a road-laying programme, which linked most settlements in the Kolli Hills with metalled roads (Kumar-Range, 2001). This change helped in the mobility of the people to other villages and towns in the plains and brought in its wake a band of merchants and contractors for the marketing links for agricultural produce. Since the 1980s, four market centres were developed in Kolli Hills that covered the entire hills setting the base for constant interaction of local people with outside merchants. Financial support like advance crop loan and transportation facilities for industrial cash crop such as tapioca produce was provided by merchants and contractors leading to large-scale expansion of tapioca cultivation in uplands and modification of rocky undulating terrains that were traditionally under mixed cropping and monoculture of millets. The move from subsistence agriculture to commercial agriculture led to the loss of not only food but also soil fertility due to continuous monoculture of tapioca. Figure 9.1 gives an overview of the cultural and agro-biodiversity impacts in Kolli Hills.

Figure 9.1:
Cultural transitions, agro biodiversity impacts in Kolli Hills

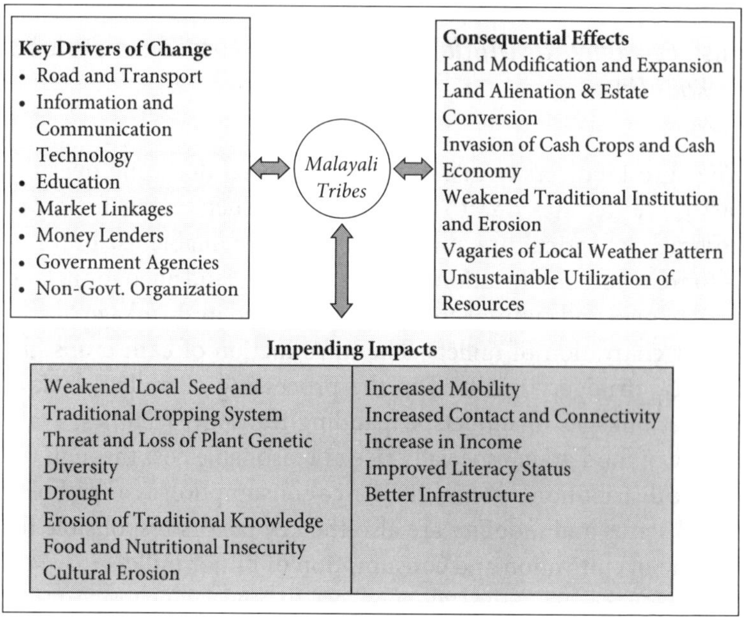

Source: Modified from King et al. (2009).

Since 1990s the interest towards commercial horticulture such as plantation of silver oak, pepper, coffee and cardamom has brought additional pressures on traditional agriculture. This change is evident from Tables 9.1 and 9.2 that convey that commercially oriented agricultural development is a key challenge to continue traditional agriculture particularly among younger generation.

The interest and attitude of the tribal community towards commercial horticulture such as plantation of silver oaks, pepper, coffee and cardamom have increased the pressure on traditional agriculture. Moreover, state policies related to crop loan, subsidies, favourable conditions for commercial agriculture, supply of food items like rice, wheat, maida, rava at reasonable cost through the PDS have shaped the minds of people to neglect minor millets. One of the important impacts on millet farming systems brought out

Table 9.1:
Trend in cultivation area of small millets, tapioca and pineapple (in ha) in Kolli hills

Year	*Small Millets*	*Finger Millets*	*Tapioca*	*Pineapple*
1970–71	1,799	N/A	0	40
1995–96	950	N/A	2,020	740
1996–97	967	N/A	5,000	900
1999–2000	645	841	6,255	323
2000–01	501	991	6,254	295
2001–02	651	756	5,891	616
2002–03	782	750	2,454	602
2003–04	101	509	6,221	610
2004–05	152	78	6,436	608
2005–06	184	81	7,170	604
2006–07	177	90	6,701	563
2007–08	160	86	6,332	543
2008–09	154	77	5,974	566
2009–10	146	68	5,675	565

Source: Modified Gruere et al. (2009).

Table 9.2:
Estate establishment trend in Kolli hills

Year	*No. of Estates*	*Area in Acres*	*Crop Introduction*
1970	1	2	Coffee, pepper
1980–89	8	225	Coffee, pepper, clove, orange, jackfruit, banana
1990–99	59	1,453.5	Coffee, pepper, clove, orange, jackfruit
2000–10	97	1,976.5	Coffee, pepper, clove, orange, jackfruit, banana, pine, cardamom, silver oak, tapioca

Source: Field observation (2010).

by these changes due to these multiple factors was the erosion of traditional agricultural practices like mixed cropping, crop rotation and relay cropping that has strong dependence on self-reliance local seeds systems.

Contingent Valuation Study on Farmer's Assessment of Minor Millets Conservation

Study Area

Kolli Hills is a mountainous area with a temperate climate located on the eastern border of the Namakkal district in Tamil Nadu, India. Forests occupy 44 per cent of the total area of 28,293 ha, while agricultural activities take place in 52 per cent of the area, leaving 4 per cent for other activities (Kumaran, 2004). More than 95 per cent of the estimated 50,000 inhabitants of Kolli Hills are tribals from the Malayali community (MSSRF, 2002). Kumaran (2004) classified the land-use for agriculture in Kolli Hills. Pradeep and Rajasekeran (2006) estimated that tapioca land represents about 75 per cent of the total dry lands. Irrigated land comprises less than 15 per cent of the cultivable area (MSSRF, 2002). More than 95 per cent of the inhabitants are tribal people belonging to the Malayali community. The population density is 119 per km^2.

Theoretical Framework

Following the study by Dupraz et al. (2003), the following theoretical framework was used. The behaviour of the farm household is formalized by the maximization of its utility. Initially in the absence of any proposed contract with the farmers, the budget constraint involved the off-farm incomes and the profit generated from the on-farm activities:

$$\begin{aligned} &\underset{c,m}{\mathrm{Max}}\, U(c,m) \\ &\text{Subject to } c \leq \Pi(p,m,Z)+v \\ &m \geq 0 \end{aligned} \tag{1}$$

where c is the household private consumption, expressed in monetary values and m is the millet conservation programme. The function is assumed to be increasing, concave and differentiable in c. The vector Z represents characteristics of the farm and household.

The profit function $\Pi(p, m, Z)$ is assumed to be convex. The p vector includes the prices of factors and products freely allocated. The v represents off-farm incomes that are assumed to be exogenous in model (1).

To define the household WTA compensation for participating in the millet conservation programme, we assume that the farm household is invited to increase its cultivation of millet by a fixed quantity such that: $\Delta m = m_1^s - m_0 \succ 0$.

Its WTA is classically formalized by the surplus variation (WTA^s). This WTA is derived from equation (2), which defines the expenditure function

$$e(p,m,Z,U_0) = \underset{c}{\mathrm{Min}}\{c - \Pi(p,m,Z); U(c,m) \geq 0\} \quad (2)$$

$$\mathrm{WTA} = e(p,m_1^s,Z,U_0) - e(p,m_0,Z,U_0) = e(p,m_1^s,Z,U_0) - e_0 \quad (3)$$

Equation (3) expresses the minimum payment that the household would accept in order to increase its production of minor millets from m_0 to m_1.

Data Collection

The study was carried out in five zones in Kolli Hills namely Devanur, Alathur, Thiruppuli, Gundani and Selur (five dotted regions in Figure 9.2). Out of 72 villages in the study site, about 69.4 per cent of villages were covered for the total survey. The sample size comprises random and non-random samples of 454 respondents. At least 50 per cent of the millet cultivators were targeted from each village. From the survey, we find that 69 per cent are millet cultivators and 31 per cent are non-millet cultivators.

In this study, we used CVM to find WTA to conserve millet cultivation in Kolli Hills. Since the property rights of minor millets and their outputs and functions reside with the farmers (Freeman, 2002), this proxy monetary attribute represents WTA compensation, that is, a benefit, rather than a cost measured by willingness to pay. This indirect measure is preferred over a direct monetary variable, because for most families, not much have been traded

Figure 9.2:
Map of Kolli hills showing the study area

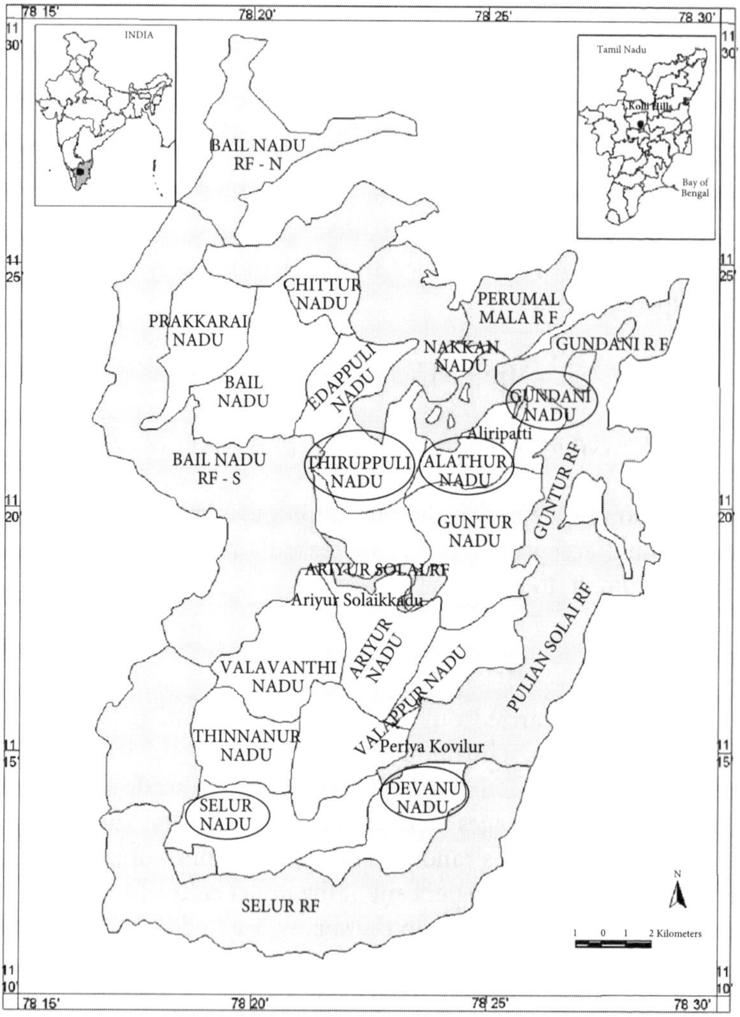

Source: Block Development Office, Kolli Hills.

as of yet and rather there is a shift to the other crops. Hence, the respondents were not likely to be familiar with a direct monetary measure of millets' output.

The finalizing of the WTA questionnaires stretched over three months after the pilot study. Pre-testing of questionnaire was done by selecting 10 respondents from farm households of the five selected zones and changes were made in the final version. It follows from the pilot survey that the enumerators needed to be clear while depicting the true scenario to the respondents. The list of most preferred varieties (MPV) and least preferred varieties (LPV) landraces of the five zones are given in Table 9.3.

Table 9.3:
Landraces of the MPV and LPV varieties of millets

Zone No.	*Zone Name*	*Most Preferred Varieties*	*Least Preferred Varieties*
1.	Devanur	Arisikaizhvaragu (FM), Sattaikaizhvaragu (FM) and Vellaperumsamai (LM)	Thirivaragu (KM)
2.	Alathur	Karunguliyankaizhvaragu (FM) and Karakaizhvaragu (FM)	Mookkanthinai (IM) and Karumsamai (LM)
3.	Thirupulli	Sundangikaizhvaragu (FM)	Koranthinai (IM), Sadansamai (LM) and Thirigulasamai (LM)
4.	Gundani	Vellaperumsamai (LM) and Kattavettisamai (LM)	Panivaragu (CM) and Senthinai (IM)
5.	Selur	Perunkaizhvaragu (FM) and Palanthinai (IM)	Malliasamai (LM) and Perunthinai (IM)

Source: FM-Finger millet, LM-Little millet, IM-Italian/Foxtail millet, CM-Common/Proso millet and KM-Kodo millet.

The survey consisted of four parts. The first part consisted of the socio-economic characteristics of the households. The second part of the questionnaire consisted of the land-use pattern of the farmers. Moreover, there is information regarding crops that were cultivated by the farmers in the area. The third part consisted of the choice experiment (CE) survey and the fourth part was the CV survey. The CE results are not discussed in this chapter. Farmers were informed about the minor millet crops in Kolli Hills and worldwide. The minor millets are being replaced by more profitable crops and thus the number of farmers planting minor millet landraces and the areas being planted within the Kolli Hills, have been slowly declining over the years. If this trend continues, it is possible that one day these landraces would disappear from the production systems in the Kolli Hills, and that it will no longer be possible for farmers to obtain seed of those lost landraces; thus, there is a need for conservation of these millet varieties. Farmers were told to ensure that they will be cultivating millets over the coming years. The CV cards for MPV and LPV were shown and farmers were asked whether they were willing/not willing to participate in this conservation programme. If they chose to participate in the programme, they were asked to plant a specific landrace and cultivate over a specific number of years. They were also told to store 3 kg of quality seed at home for the next production season and for doing this they would be offered a reward.

Three CV cards were used for both MPV and LPV in the survey; the first card with initial bid price, second card with lower price than initial price and the third card with higher price than initial price. In the survey, two CV cards were shown to the farmers and were asked whether they were willing to participate in the conservation programme. Respondents were presented with the initial bid prices, and following their initial response were given a new price offer. Lower price was offered if their initial response was 'yes' and a higher price was offered if their initial response was 'no'. The attributes used in the CV cards are given in Table 9.4.

Results and Discussions

Descriptive Statistics

The descriptive statistics are reported in Table 9.5. The average household size in the study area is 4.4 members and 87 per cent of

Table 9.4:
The attributes used in the CV card

S. No.	*Attributes*	*Description*
1.	Landrace	Any specific landrace will be asked to cultivate by the surveyed farmer household (landrace differ between the households)
2.	Area	Area to be cultivated, 10 cents as a pure crop or 15 cents as a mixed crop
3.	Contract length	Three types of contract length is used in CV card, they are 1 year, 2 years and 3 years (any one contract length is given to each households)
4.	Support	Cash support is given to both MPV and LPV (50% will be paid in the beginning of contract and 50% upon successful completion)

Source: Household Survey, 2010.

the households are headed by males. Only 43 per cent of the heads of household are literate and most households depend on agriculture (67.6 per cent) for their livelihood. According to this survey, the average area of cultivated land during 2009 was 2.6 acres per household, with 12.3 per cent of the land devoted to millet cultivation with a mean yield of 234 kg per acre. About 45.4 per cent of the households are engaged in participatory organizations such as self-help groups (SHGs) and farmers' organizations, 89 per cent of the households keep their savings in banks, post offices and life insurance corporations (LIC), while 34 per cent of the households have taken loans during the year 2006–08, through banks, private money lenders, family friends and large-scale multi-purpose societies. The loans are largely used for household consumption rather than for agricultural purposes.

Seemingly Unrelated Bivariate Model

Seemingly Unrelated Bivariate Probit (SUBP) regression was used to estimate the determinants of willingness to participate in millet conservation of both MPVs (model 1) and LPVs (model 2)

Table 9.5:
Descriptive statistics of the survey samples

Household Social and Economic Characteristics	*Mean (S. D.)*
Age of the head of household	44.59 (11.32)
Household size	4.36 (1.70)
Number of males >14 years old	1.70 (0.85)
Number of females >14 years old	1.55 (0.72)
Number of Children ≤14 years old	1.11 (1.09)
Total cultivated land during 2009 (acres)	2.60 (1.68)
Millet cultivated land during 2009 (acres)	0.32 (0.38)
Millet yield per acre (in kg) during 2009	234
	Percentage
Distribution of sample between zones	
Zone 1: (Devanur)	19.8
Zone 2: (Alathur)	19.4
Zone 3: (Thirupulli)	21.1
Zone 4: (Gundani)	18.6
Zone 5: (Selur)	21.1
Male headed household	86.6
Literate of the head of household	42.7
Employment of the head of household	
Agriculture	67.6
Other than agriculture	32.4
Household organizational participation like SHGs, farmers' club, etc.	45.4
Household savings in banks, post office, LIC, etc.	88.8
Household taken loan during (2006–08)	34.4

Source: Household Survey, 2010.

in the Kolli Hills. The model estimates are given in Table 9.6. The robustness check was carried out and found that the data used in the model is robust.

The initial response in case of both MPVs and LPVs is significant with the farmers responding positively to the compensation offered, while the follow-up response results suggest the significant impacts of bid value for both MPVs and LPVs are in different direction.

Table 9.6:
Seemingly unrelated bivariate probit

	Coefficient (S.E.)			
	Model 1 for MPV		*Model 2 for LPV*	
Variable	*Response 1*	*Response 2*	*Response 1*	*Response 2*
Bid price (₹)	0.0030*** (0.0003)	0.0009* (0.0005)	0.0018*** (0.0002)	-0.0004 (0.0003)
Millet land (acre)	-0.4822* (0.2509)	-0.2702 (0.2385)	-0.4308* (0.2547)	-0.1579 (0.2235)
Millet yield (kg/acre)	0.0010 0.0011	0.0020* (0.0011)	0.0006 (0.0011)	0.0020** (0.0010)
Household size (no.)	-0.0703* (0.0421)	-0.0300 (0.0380)	-0.0036 (0.0381)	0.0333 (0.0359)
Age of household head (years)	0.0061 (0.0067)	0.0024 (0.0060)	-0.0070 (0.0059)	-0.0043 (0.0056)
Sex of household head (male=1)	0.2169 (0.2109)	0.1731 (0.1872)	-0.1254 (0.1910)	-0.1760 (0.1826)
Education of household head (years)	-0.0365* (0.0218)	-0.0257 (0.0196)	-0.0285 (0.0199)	0.0109 (0.0186)
Organization participation (SHGs, farmers' clubs, etc.)	0.5519*** (0.1454)	0.3226** (0.1344)	-0.0105 (0.1294)	-0.0992 (0.1233)
Intercept	-0.7790* (0.4291)	-0.0501 (0.4004)	-0.6871* (0.3944)	0.4037 (0.3947)
Log likelihood	-489.1666		-582.8664	
rho	0.1727 (0.1402)		-0.1148 (0.1218)	
Wald $\chi^2(16)$	111.49***		76.58***	
No. of observation	453		453	

Source: Household Survey, 2010.
***, ** and * indicate significance at 1, 5 and 10 per cent, respectively.

The negative value for LPVs shows that the probability of participation is low even with the higher compensation, this result reflects from Zone 1 (Devanur) where Kodo millet (LVP) was traditionally grown and farmers have indicated a strong dislike for the cultivation of its landrace due to low consumption value. The influence of the factor area under millet cultivation is negative for MPVs and LPVs, which reflects the fact that the farmers are shifting from their traditional cultivation of millets to other commercial crops. These results are in line with the findings of King et al. (2009). Millet yield per acre has positive influence, with farmers preferring varieties with higher productivity.

Farmers with larger household sizes are found not to be more likely to undertake millet cultivation and this is also in line with findings of previous studies. Better educated household heads hold preferences for other crops rather than millets. Nevertheless, larger families and better educated household heads have a positive response to the follow-up bid for LPVs, if offered higher compensation. The age of the household head is taken as a proxy for millet farming experience and it is found that their compensation to participate in LPVs is higher than MPVs. The farmers involved in organizational participation (e.g., SHGs, farmers' association) have a positive response to MPVs (significant) and negative response to LPVs in the millet conservation programme. Such a finding is also the result of the fact that in order to generate market linkages for minor millets, MSSRF has actively promoted SHGs among the millet-growing communities.

WTA Respondents

In order to estimate the degree of heterogeneity of WTA compensation across households, six household profiles were generated (Table 9.7).

The first two profiles are associated with farmers who are cultivating millets and not cultivating millet, whereas the following two profiles are associated with literacy levels. The last two profiles are associated with farmer status related to millet crop-related organizations participation such as SHGs and farmers' associations. The statistics related to these profiles are reported in Table 9.7. It was observed that 68.7 per cent of the farmers were cultivating millets in the study area, the literacy rate was similar for both millet and non-millet farmers' group, and organization participation

Table 9.7:
Household profiles used for WTA estimates

Profile	*Millet Farmers (%)*	*Non-millet Farmers (per cent)*
Average household	68.7	31.3
Profile 1: Millet farmers	100.0	0.0
Profile 2: Non-millet farmers	0.0	100.0
Profile 3: Literate	42.3	43.0
Profile 4: Illiterate	57.7	57.0
Profile 5: Organization participation	49.7	35.9
Profile 6: Non-organization participation	50.3	64.1

Source: Household Survey, 2010.

rates were higher for millet farmers. The SHGs are a common grass-roots institution through which development activities are implemented in many regions of India. Participation is voluntary, and the schemes are based on internal lending incentives (Gruere et al., 2009).

The WTA analysis estimates the welfare loss effectively when the respondents have limited knowledge about market conditions. The WTA of farmers who are willing to participate in the millet conservation programme is furnished in Table 9.8.

Millet farmers are willing to participate at higher compensation levels in the initial bid price offered, but they are still WTA a lower bid price than the initial compensation offered for both MPVs and LPVs. The same trend is followed by non-millet farmers, although they are willing to accept the higher compensation more than millet farmers. Literate farmers are willing to participate in LPVs' millet conservation programme with higher compensation than that of illiterate farmers, which is reflected in SUBP model. The farmers participating in millet-related organizations are willing to participate in the millet conservation programme at lower levels of compensation compared to non-organization participating farmers. The results suggest that the contingent valuation method used here seems to be an appropriate tool with which to reveal farmer participation decisions regarding a millet conservation programme.

Table 9.8:
Marginal WTA for the given profiles

	Average WTA Price (₹/acre)			
	MPV		*LPV*	
Profile	*Initial Bid*	*Final Bid*	*Initial Bid*	*Final Bid*
Profile 1: Millet farmers	4,728 (163.14)	3,403 (141.95)	7,406 (223.90)	6,494 (189.28)
Profile 2: Non-millet farmers	4,840 (253.69)	3,468 (208.49)	7,462 (317.02)	6,566 (328.27)
Profile 3: Literate	4,605 (213.12)	3,401 (198.08)	7,303 (295.30)	6,716 (270.67)
Profile 4: Illiterate	4,872 (179.01)	3,437 (143.26)	7,500 (232.69)	6,359 (202.54)
Profile 5: Organization participation	4,345 (196.67)	3,039 (178.98)	7,064 (295.87)	6,587 (259.08)
Profile 6: Non-organization participation	5,176 (185.71)	3,781 (148.28)	7,699 (226.93)	6,458 (212.11)

Source: Household Survey, 2010.
Note: WTA price indicates for millet cultivation in 1 acre as mono crop and 1.5 acres as inter/mixed crops; figures in the parentheses indicate standard error.

Conclusions

This chapter was developed based on a contingent valuation survey conducted in tribal farming communities in the Kolli Hills cultivating diverse millet varieties, which are under threat due to several factors. The study aims in facilitating the conservation of minor millets, leading to improved farmer livelihoods through the use of incentive mechanisms. The result suggests that the farmers are willing to accept less compensation for the varieties, which produce higher yield of MPVs and LPVs. The farmers involved in millet activities in SHGs and farmers' club are willing to accept lower level of compensation for MPVs and higher for LPVs than the farmer who does not participate in the organization. Given the farmers' willingness to participate in a millet compensation programme, it is clear that direct compensation mechanisms can be able to supplement returns so as to encourage the conservation of minor millets in a given year. Periodical re-assessment would nonetheless be needed in order to better understand the compensation demands of the farmers over time. Furthermore, this study shows that direct compensation incentive mechanisms may indeed be able to play a complementary role in the conservation of neglected landraces of millets relative to other types of intervention. These include community-based incentives and policies associated with market linkage development for millets in order to obtain higher prices for farmers, facilitating the availability of quality seeds, improving access to machinery for processing grains and the inclusion of millet in the local PDS.

References

Birol, E., Villalba, E.R. and Smale, M. 2009. 'Farmer Preferences for Milpa Diversity and Genetically Modified Maize in Mexico: A Latent Class Approach', *Environment and Development Economics*, 14(04): 521–40.

Desaigues, B. and Ami, D. 2001. 'An Estimation of the Social Benefits of Preserving Biodiversity', *International Journal Global Environmental Issues*, 1(1): 73–86.

Dupraz, P., Vermersch, D., De Frahan, H.B. and Delvaux, L. 2003. 'The Environmental Supply of Farm Households: A Flexible Willingness to Accept Model', *Environmental and Resource Economics*, 25(2): 171–89.

Freeman, A.M. 2002. *The Measurement of Environmental and Resource Values: Theory and Methods*. Washington, D.C.: Resources for the Future.

Gruere, G., Nagarajan, L. and King, E.D.I.O. 2007a. *Marketing Underutilized Plant Species for the Poor: A Case Study of Minor Millets in Kolli Hills, Tamil Nadu, India*. Report published by the Global Facilitation Unit for Underutilized Species (GFU). Rome, Italy: Biodiversity International.

———. 2007b. 'Collective Action and Marketing of Underutilized Plant Species: the Case of Minor Millets in Kolli Hills', Working Paper 69, Tamil Nadu, India, CAPRi.

———. 2009. 'The Role of Collective Action in the Marketing of Underutilized Plant Species: Lessons From a Case Study on Minor Millets in South India', *Food Policy*, 34(1): 39–45.

Horna, J.D., Smale, M. and Von-Oppen, M. 2005. 'Farmer Willingness to Pay for Seed-Related Information: Rice Varieties in Nigeria and Benin', EPTD Discussion Papers, 142, International Food Policy Research Institute (IFPRI).

King, E.D.I.O. 2015. 'Custodian Farmers of Nutri-millets in Kolli Hills, India: Approaches to Enhance Their Contribution', S. Sthapit, G. Meldrum, S. Padulosi and N. Bergamini (eds), *Strengthening the Role of Custodian Farmers in the National Conservation Programme of Nepal*. Proceedings of the national workshop 31 July to 2 August 2013, Pokhara, Nepal.

King, E.D.I.O., Kumar, N., and Padulosi, S. 2015. 'India: Community Seed Banks and Empowering Tribal Communities in the Kolli Hills', in R. Vernooy, P. Shrestha and B. Sthapit (eds), *Community Seed Banks Origins, Evolution and Prospects*. New York: Routledge, Earth Scan.

King, E.D.I.O., Bala Ravi, S. and Padulosi, S. 2013. 'Creating Economic Stake for Conserving the Diversity of Small Millets in Kolli Hills, India', in W.S. De Boef, A. Subedi, N. Peroni, M. Thijssen and E. O' Keeffe (eds), *Community Biodiversity Management: Promoting Resilience and the Conservation of Plant Genetic Resources*. New York: Earth Scan (Routledge).

King, E.D.I.O., Nambi, V.A. and Nagarajan, L. 2009. 'Integrated Approaches in Small Millets Conservation: A Case from Kolli Hills, India', *International Society for Horticulture Science*, 806(2): 79–84.

King, E.D.I.O., Swain, S. and Parida, A. 2014. 'Community Biodiversity Management: Strengthening Resilience of Family Farmers', DEEP ROOTS, FAO and Tudor Rose, pp. 97–100. Available at www.fao.org/3/a-i3976e.pdf

Kontoleon, A. and Swanson, T. 2003. 'The Willingness to Pay for Property Rights for the Giant Panda: Can a Charismatic Species Be an Instrument for Nature Conservation?', *Land Economics*, 79(4): 483–99.

Kumaran, M. 2004. 'Assessment of Development Interventions of M.S. Swaminathan Research Foundation in Kolli Hills Using Geographical Information Systems', Dissertation, Department of Rural Development, Gandhigram Rural Institute – Deemed University, Gandhigram, Tamil Nadu, India.

Kumar-Range, S. 2001. *Like Paddy in Rock: Local Institutions and Gender Roles in Kolli Hills*. Chennai, Tamil Nadu, India: M.S. Swaminathan Research Foundation (MSSRF).

M.S. Swaminathan Research Foundation (MSSRF). 2002. *Rural and Tribal Women in Agrobiodiversity Conservation*. Bangkok, Thailand: Food and Agriculture Organization (FAO) RAP Publication 2002/08.

Ndjeunga, J. and Nelson, C.H. 2005. 'Toward Understanding Household Preference for Consumption Characteristics of Millet Varieties: a Case Study From Western Niger', *Agricultural Economics*, 32(2): 151–65.

Pearce, D.W. and Moran, D. 2001. 'Handbook on the Applied Valuation of Biological Diversity', *Report prepared for Environment Directorate*, OECD, Paris.

Pradeep, V. and Rajasekeran, J. 2006. 'Classification and Characterization of Self Help Groups (SHG's) Enterprises in Kolli Hills Developed by MSSRF', Unpublished: Report submitted for Master of Arts in Social Works, Department of Social Work, The American College, Madurai, India.

Scarpa, R., Drucker, A., Anderson, S., Ferraes-Ehuan, N., Gomez, V., Risopatron, C.R. and Rubio-Leonel, O. 2003a. 'Valuing Animal Genetic Resources in Peasant Economies: The Case of the Box Keken Creole Pig in Yucatan', *Ecological Economics*, 45(3): 427–43.

Scarpa, R., Ruto, E.S.K., Kristjanson, P., Radeny, M., Drucker, A.G. and Rege, J.E.O. 2003b. 'Valuing Indigenous Cattle Breeds in Kenya: An Empirical Comparison of Stated and Revealed Preference Value Estimates', *Ecological Economics*, 45(3): 409–26.

10

Economic Analysis of Irrigation Institutions: A Case Study

Durba Biswas and L. Venkatachalam

The Issue

Empirical studies on natural resource management have demonstrated that institutions and institutional structures devised by individuals, groups and governments to organize human activities are found to influence the outcome of management of 'common pool resources' (CPRs) such as irrigation (e.g., Ostrom, 1994). As the new institutional economic theories postulate, those institutions contributing to sustainable management of CPRs are generally efficient in nature since only efficient institutions can survive by way of crowding out all the inefficient ones (Alchian and Demsetz, 1972), irrespective of the nature of social outcomes. The institutions, indeed, are not created for achieving socially efficient outcomes; rather, they may be designed to serve the purpose of individuals who have more bargaining powers (North, 1994a). The evolutionary process of institutions, as the extreme version of Coase theorem puts, explains why a particular type of institution that has come into being at a particular time period can be the most efficient in nature (Stigler, 1988). At initial stages of resource use, the 'spontaneous order' among the individuals carrying out 'purposeful act' brings self-enforcing institutions in an evolutionary process (Sugden, 1986), which are in many cases efficient in nature—

at least at individual or at group level. When the individual or group actions generate negative externality affecting the welfare of the third parties, the efficiency principle is not sacrificed because of the fact that mitigating the negative externality within the prevailing institutional domain is opportunistically costly. From the Coasian perspective, a higher level of transaction cost of controlling negative externality arises from the lack of well-defined property rights that hinder the costless negotiations between individuals in a society. In this case, the institutional options can be expanded by assigning well-defined property rights that minimize the transaction costs of renegotiations so that a new level of efficient equilibrium of resource use can be achieved (Coase, 1960). When the property rights are vaguely defined or when the transaction costs of renegotiations are prohibitively high, some argue that the direct intervention of the government is considered appropriate (Pigou, 1932). So, the central thesis of the new institutional economics is that a combination of market, firms and government is required for governing the resource use and a particular combination is Pareto optimal when the transaction costs of resource use is minimized; new forms of intermediary institutions (such as non-governmental organizations [NGOs]) can also emerge to reduce any residual transaction costs. Therefore, the 'unbounded rationality' strand of new institutional economics claims that with a given set of institutions the efficient institutions (or combination of such institutions) are frequently chosen from the choice set, by the individuals (Dixit, 2004).

In the case of irrigation water, the selfish maximizing individuals are found to design their own efficient institutions collectively (Ostrom, 1990) in order to achieve those 'joint benefits' from irrigation management, which could *not* be achieved by their individual efforts alone (Wade, 1988). In many countries where such collective action does not emerge to maximize the joint benefits, the government takes initiative to bring such actions through institutional arrangements such as forming water user associations (WUAs). Each association is not only governed by the well-specified formal rules of the games but also by those informal constraints (North, 1991) that are site-specific in nature and therefore, there is an interplay between these two forms of institutions that makes the difference in the collective outcomes. This leads to a fundamental question, namely why only few such efforts succeed while many other fail to bring in the desired outcomes? In other words, if efficient institutions outperform inefficient institutions, then how one could explain the existence of inefficient institutions in the irrigation management systems in different river basins especially in the Indian context? One possible explanation would be that the nature of the institutions as well as the 'interaction' between them may not be conducive for brining cooperation among the group members to achieve collective benefits. When 'outside' institutional constraints are imposed on the existing institutional rules, the institutions may compete with each other to generate undesirable outcomes (Easterly, 2008; see also Dixit, 2004; North, 1994b); this may lead to set-in of spiralling disequilibrium in the system, thereby increasing the social costs. Sometimes, even with the same set of institutions the institutional outcomes may differ across regions due to differences in the transaction cost. The 'top-down' approach of introducing WUAs in many of the canal systems in India did not produce any substantial additional pay-offs to the users (Marothia, 2005); rather, they contributed, along with various other factors, towards destabilizing some of the prevailing institutions—such as village *panchayat*s—which managed the irrigation water traditionally more efficiently (Mahapatra, 2007).

Conventional neoclassical economic paradigm assumes that the rational individuals in a relatively larger group may not have adequate incentive for nurturing cooperation to sustain the resource use because of high level of uncertainty involved in predicting the behaviour of other members in the group. Thus, the resulting Nash equilibrium is 'prisoner's dilemma' in nature, where even though everyone would benefit from cooperation, no one would prefer to cooperate. Olson (1971) suggests that smaller groups, where the transaction cost of monitoring the behaviour of the members is minimum, are capable of managing the CPRs more successfully.[1]

[1] However, why such kind of groups did not emerge at the very beginning itself is a question for further research.

In the absence of external intervention, the cooperation among the group members is found to be brought about by the institutions devised by the groups themselves; these institutions are influenced by the intrinsic as well as the instrumental motives of the members, such as 'spontaneous order' (Sugden, 1989), 'reciprocal behaviour' (Cárdenas, 2009; Cárdenas and Ostrom, 2004) and the norm of 'tit-for-tat' (Axelrod, 1984). When these motives in many cases do not necessarily work towards achieving cooperation, how to make the individuals to cooperate in a commons context is still a major challenge in both theoretical as well as in empirical literature. As public choice theory suggests, the external institutions imposed either to supplement the prevailing institutions or to replace them can be designed by those special interest groups (such as politicians and bureaucrats) in the government in order to maximize their own private benefits, jeopardizing the cooperative behaviour of the group members by increasing the transaction costs of such cooperation (Brady, 2000). More empirical studies are required on how the receiving parties adopt strategies in terms of either lobbying or credible threats to the policymaking bodies so that more group-oriented policies can be introduced, when the transaction cost of doing so is low. On the other hand, behavioural economics views the expected level of cooperation to depend on how boundedly rational the individuals[2] are and whether their cognitive abilities allow them to optimize on the perceived transaction costs (Camerer et al., 2003). In reality, even the small groups where the transaction cost of uncertainty is negligible also fail to sustain the resource use efficiently. So, apart from the transaction costs argument there may be other factors that may influence the institutional outcomes in a particular context and this issue will have to be empirically investigated. In this chapter, we make an attempt to 'qualitatively' analyse the institutional arrangements for water management and their performance in the Malaprabha river basin, Karnataka, India.

[2] For example, if the individuals are 'docile' then their behaviour would reflect high degree of altruism and therefore, would bring in more cooperation (see Knudsen, 2003).

The Institutions at State Level

Until the late 1980s, irrigation development in India was based on the notion that difference between the actual irrigated area and the potential irrigated area was due to physical scarcity of water and therefore, the water resource development was tightly linked to the infrastructural development. As infrastructure required huge amount of investment, the irrigation development and water management were handled mainly by the state agencies setting the stage for 'path dependency' that guided irrigation management in the subsequent periods. At the state level, additional efforts were made in the command area of the irrigation projects to achieve improved water management and increased agricultural development in an integrated manner. For example, the *Command Area Development Authority* (CADA) in Karnataka during the 1980s was created towards this end. In order to fill-in the gap between irrigation potential created and potential utilized, the CADA programme was aimed at enhancing land development as it is a key factor in efficient utilization of irrigation facilities.

With the passage of time, however, most part of readily available 'cheap' water sources was harnessed and all possible least-cost options to augment water resources were utilized, especially in peninsular India. In the early decades, the dams were basically built to counter vagaries of monsoon and to facilitate self-sufficiency in food production in order to reduce high level of poverty. The irrigation water was highly subsidized with a view to generate large-scale positive externalities through increased food production and reduced poverty. The underlying assumption was that the demand for water for food is highly inelastic in nature and in order to keep the price of the food at lower level a large scale agricultural subsidy, including irrigation subsidy, was justified. The policies based on this kind of assumption failed to understand the fact that subsidized irrigation would lead to inefficiency in water use and would not generate adequate resource for reinvestment; the resulting indiscriminate use of water also led to inequality among the farmers since rich farmers extracted more amount of water, adversely affecting the profitability of the small and marginal farmers. So, agricultural policies in general and irrigation policies in particular during the initial period were dominated by the supply-side-oriented approach in which the government agents determined almost all the components of these policies neglecting completely the preferences of the farmers. In the early 1990s, a new policy paradigm emerged wherein water was recognized as a 'scarce and precious national resource', which had to be conserved, planned and developed in an integrated manner (National Water Policy, 1987 and 2002). In this regard, the policy focus shifted towards institutional arrangements for managing water with more emphasis on the demand-side aspects of management where emphasis has been given to farmers' participation. *Participatory Irrigation Management* (PIM) (National Water Policy, 2002) is one such important institutional arrangement in the area of India's water policy. Karnataka State Water Policy (2002) also emphasized decentralized decision-making by way of creating *Water Users Cooperative Societies* (WUCSs) supported by the *Karnataka Neeravari Nigama Limited* (KNNL), CADA and *Water and Land Management Institutes* (WALMI). The new paradigm was aimed at transferring some of the important activities previously carried out by the government agents, such as operations and maintenance, water distribution and revenue collection, to the farmers' associations. The fundamental issue with this approach is that all the above activities to be carried out by the WUAs, according to economic principles, should have been earmarked on the basis of 'comparative advantage' of different agents in the organizational structure of irrigation management. This suggests that the government agents might have deliberately transferred these activities to the farmers in order to minimize the transaction costs of water management at the government level. However, the economic motive of the government could be assessed only in terms of costs and benefits of those activities retained by the government and that of those transferred to the farmers. For example, if the operation and maintenance activities provide more room for the government agents to seek rent, then the government agents would prefer to retain these activities with them. The way in which the government decentralized some of the activities raises the following questions: if water management by the farmers is transaction cost[3] minimizing, then why such kind of efficient management has not arisen in the first place itself? If the transaction cost minimization is an outcome of institutional process that evolves over a period of time, then what processes made the transaction cost of carrying out the above activities lower by the WUAs? Why such processes were absent when the same activities were carried out by the government agents? Is there any empirical evidence that shows that the decentralization of the above activities had minimized the transaction cost in absolute terms? Or, the decentralization mechanism just transferred the transaction costs from the government to the farmers without reducing the absolute size of it? Are the private benefits—occurring to government agents—of transferring the activities greater than social costs occurring to a large number of farmers? These are some of the questions that require empirical assessment but very difficult to answer due to practical difficulties.

The state government also had taken initiatives in addressing low water tariffs by introducing revised irrigation water rates in 2002. This revision came after a gap of 15 years (Table 10.2). The economic value of water is reflected in terms of two aspects: the actual cost of meeting the demand–supply gap both at the government as well as at the user level; and the users' marginal willingness to pay (WTP) for additional water over and above the cost of supply. If the water price is fixed on the basis of its marginal economic value, then the pricing mechanism, in principle, will reallocate the water to its most efficient use. If the price, on the other hand, is fixed arbitrarily by the government agencies by using non-scientific methods then one could expect no reallocation of water to take place; or even

[3] Although minimizing transaction cost is an important aspect, there are other objectives of decentralization such as more political and social power to the farmers so that they can exercise more control over the irrigation process. We, however, argue that in well-working institutions such as markets come into play, the farmers can trade among themselves efficiently and effectively.

if it takes place, it may not be socially efficient. The social cost of arbitrary pricing in the administered pricing regime will be greater than that of under a 'regulated market' regime. Moreover, economic theory suggests that inefficiency in water use would become dominant if the price fixed does not provide adequate incentives efficient use and disincentives for inefficient use (Gneezy and Rustichini, 2000). The price fixed should reflect the true opportunity cost of water use, in principle; the preferences of the users reflect the true opportunity cost of water and the price based on true preferences is expected to reallocate water in an efficient manner. Rather than government agents fixing the price arbitrarily, a conducive institutional arrangement has to be in place where the water transfer could take place on the basis of farmers' WTP and willingness to accept (WTA) compensation.

Although there has been emphasis on inclusive decision-making process at both national and state levels, the existing institutional arrangements can still be termed as to fall within the 'command and control' approach, which is a 'supply-side approach' in nature. The State Water Policy (2002) intends to make the allocation process more efficient within the command and control system and in this respect, it tries to integrate various interests and develop basin-level management unit. The centralized decision about the cropping pattern, penalty for crop violation and existing pattern of inter and intra-sectoral water allocation is an evidence for the continued supply-side policies pursued by the governments. Moreover, the proposed institutional arrangements in the State Water Policy (2002) were already tried somewhere else (such as River Basin Boards in Palar and Thambirabharani basins in Tamil Nadu) and they became dysfunctional (Venkatachalam, 2004). The fact is that an additional ineffective institution into the existing ones would cause more distortions. In order to make these institutions work effectively, a policy reform that includes appropriate incentives and disincentives to make the agents to produce desirable outcomes is warranted for. We will outline such a kind of reform in a later section.

Participatory Irrigation Management in Karnataka

The WUCSs, which are similar to WUAs, were initially introduced—as part of PIM—in Karnataka state in the late 1980s on a pilot basis by way of involving the farmers in managing water at canal level. After a decade-long 'successful' experimentation, formalization of PIM was recommended in 1999 and it was supported by the State Water Policy (2002) and the Irrigation Act (2000). The purpose of introducing PIM was embedded in the policy objective of 'efficient' management of water resources and resolving prolonged conflicts among various interest groups. In addition, the farmers were to be trained in administrative responsibilities, maintenance of canal and distributary procedures, and training other farmers to use water efficiently and economically (Table 10.1). WALMI and CADA have been responsible for dissemination of knowledge so that information externalities can benefit all farmers. As on February 2006, 2,321 WUCSs got registered in the state, with 1,304 of them taking over the management (Nayantara, 2006). An important point to be noted here is that if some institution is successful in some part of the system, the economic theory predicts that this institution would spontaneously spread in other parts of the system as well—provided the transaction cost of such institutional spread is low. The successful institution not moving to other areas suggests that *ceteris paribus*, the transaction cost involved in the movement is relatively higher. Apart from high level of transaction cost, there may be other reasons such as, site-specific socio-economic-political factors, which would also affect the movement of the successful institutions. At the group level, factors that include elite capturing, heterogeneity, inequality and other behavioural issues influence the level of acceptance of successful 'outside' institutions (Araral, 2009; Bardhan, 2001). So, the government's deliberate attempt to replicate the successful institutions in other parts of the state seems to be economically illogical as well as non-scientific in nature.

Table 10.1:
Hierarchical structure and main functions of PIM in Karnataka

Tiers	*Main Functions*
Water Users Apex Level Federation	1. Make recommendation to the State Government on the policies to be adopted and the guidelines to be formulated regarding construction, maintenance and regulation of irrigation work. 2. The Water Users Apex Level Federation may give directions to the Water Users Project Level Federation, Water Users Distributary Level Federation and the Water Users Society to carry out the purposes of this Act.
Water Users Project Level Federation	1. To prepare an operational plan based on its entitlement area, soil and cropping pattern at the beginning of each irrigation season. 2. To identify and prioritize the critical maintenance works those are to be carried out at project level. 3. To monitor the maintenance works being executed and ensure that they conform to prescribed standards. 4. To prepare water budgets and crop plans. 5. To promote economy in the use of water.
Water Users Distributary Level Federation	1. To prepare an operational plan based on its entitlement, area, soil and cropping pattern at the beginning of each irrigation season consistent with the operational plan prepared by the project-level federation. 2. To identify the critical maintenance work that are to be carried. 3. To monitor the maintenance works being executed and ensure that they conform to prescribed standards. 4. To monitor and regulate the use of water among various societies in its area of operation. 5. To undertake periodical social audit. 6. To promote economy in the use of water. 7. To prepare water budgets and crop plans.
Water Users Cooperative Society	1. Develop irrigation infrastructure by availing institutional finance. 2. Procure water in bulk on volumetric basis from the Irrigation Department or KNNL and distribute it to farmers. 3. Operate and maintain canals within its jurisdiction. 4. Collect water charges and service charges from the farmers. 5. Educate and train farmers to use water efficiently and economically. 6. Prepare water budget and financial budget for each irrigation season. 7. Resolve disputes among farmers. 8. Assist the Irrigation Department in implementing irrigation and drainage works. 9. Make and forward an audit.

Source: Nayantara (2006) and various government documents.

The government of Karnataka formalized PIM by amending the Karnataka Irrigation (Levy Water Rates) Rules in 2002, which guided the formation of four levels of PIM (NIVA-CISED, 2008) (Table 10.2). As the transaction cost theory suggests, the nature and size of the hierarchy of an institutional structure itself has to be determined by the size of the transaction cost associated with it. In other words, an efficient hierarchical structure is the one that minimizes the overall transaction cost. In certain cases, the activities that are earmarked for a particular organization in the hierarchy may be carried out at a lower cost by another organization in the same hierarchical structure. For example, irrigation infrastructure to be developed by the WUCS may be developed at a lower cost by Water Users Distributary Level Federation due to economies of scale. Similarly, some of the activities listed in the hierarchical structure can be carried out in a cost-effective manner by those institutions/organizations that are not included in the structure. For example, the dispute resolution can be effectively dealt with

Table 10.2:
Status of water rates (1985 and 2000)

		Previous Status (1985)	*Current Status (2000)*
S. No.	*Crops*	*Water Rate per Acre (in ₹)*	*Water Rate per Acre (in ₹)*
1.	Sugarcane	150.00	400.00
2.	Paddy	75.00	100.00
3.	Cotton	40.00	60.00
4.	Wheat	22.00	60.00
5.	Groundnut	24.00	60.00
6.	Sunflower	–	60.00
7.	Jowar, maize, navane, ragi	20.00	35.00
8.	Semi-dry crops	–	35.00
9.	Cereals	–	35.00
10.	Tobacco	24.00	35.00
11.	Other crops	–	35.00

Source: Karnataka Irrigation (Levy of Water Rates) (Amdt) Rules, 2002.
Note: For sunflower, cereals, semi-dry and other crops no water rates existed till 2000.

by the traditional farmers' communities in an 'informal manner', rather than through formal channels (Sokile and van Koppen, 2004). It should be noted that the individuals arrange to resolve their conflicts 'outside the formal dispute resolution mechanism' if the resulting pay-off is more under such kind of arrangements (Dixit, 2004). Similarly, the River Basin Boards, once created, can handle different activities under a 'single window system', avoiding a lengthy hierarchical structure required. In certain cases, appropriate market-based instruments (MBIs) with 'proper regulation' would resolve some of the problems that are costly to be resolved by other forms of institutions/organizations. For example, facilitating water transfer within a market-oriented framework could reallocate water in an efficient and environmentally friendly manner, without demanding huge infrastructural development such as, large dams. So, merely creating an institutional structure or replicating an institutional arrangement without proper scrutiny would in no way help improve the efficiency of water use and therefore, we doubt that such a structure created by the Karnataka government under the PIM approach is based on any sound principle of economic efficiency.

Role of WUCS in Karnataka

The WUCSs are the grass-root level institutions and as we have already mentioned they have various responsibilities, including operation and maintenance of the canal infrastructure within their jurisdiction. The WUCSs are also authorized to procure water on volumetric basis from the KNNL and distribute it to the farmers, conditional on the payment of water charges. A part of the revenue collected is retained by the WUCS for its various administration costs. Since most Dam projects like Malaprabha are largely gravity-fed canal irrigation systems, water rates are charged at a flat rate or a fixed charge (as opposed to marginal cost pricing). Under the flat rate system, the charges are based not on the amount of water used but on other aspects that include the land area cultivated, yield and type of the crop (Turner et al., 2004). The most common form of charging is based on land area, as this is easy to administer and suited to continuous flow of irrigation (Johansson, 2000). However, such a pricing technique is not based on actual water used, socio-economic status and farmers' WTP and is also not necessarily consistent with economic expectations and straightforward notions of price and costs (Turner et al., 2004). In Malaprabha basin, the revenue collection is quite low in absolute terms (Table 10.3). It should be noted that the farmers are willing to pay more for the improved irrigation supply as demonstrated by empirical studies in the Indian context (Biswas and Venkatachlam, 2015). It is, however, claimed that the low revenue collection is attributed to the unwillingness on the part of the officials to collect the revenue from the farmers. The alternative interpretation is that the farmers who are upset with the low level of service are not willing to pay even the

Table 10.3:
Year-wise demand for revenue raised and collection realized in Malaprabha dam project

Year	*Demand Raised (₹ in lakhs)*	*Amount Collected (₹ in lakhs)*	*Percentage to the Demand*
		1985 Rates	
1991–92	510.82	50.23	9.83
1992–93	471.42	39.34	8.34
1993–94	510.51	29.80	5.83
1994–95	517.64	25.40	4.90
1995–96	381.93	66.22	17.33
1996–97	325.18	51.03	15.69
1997–98	443.68	46.86	10.56
1998–99	211.17	120.89	57.24
1999–00	368.15	39.94	10.84
		2000 Rates	
2000–01	517.40	43.20	8.34
2001–02	341.49	15.14	4.43
2002–03	435.00	82.32	18.92

Source: KNNL, Belgaum.

existing level of tariff and therefore, the officials may be reluctant to collect the revenue from these dissatisfied farmers. In a later section, we will discuss how redesigning the existing institutions and introducing innovative institutions in the river basin would lead to improve the service delivery as well as increase the revenue.

As part of the activities to be carried out, the WUCSs are also required to maintain the canal infrastructure under their jurisdiction. The WUCS and the government entered into a Memorandum of Understanding in which the condition of canal network to be maintained, repair works to be carried out and amount of water each WUCS is entitled to are defined through negotiations. In principle, the KNNL has to undertake repair works of the canals before passing them onto the WUCS, but in most cases the responsibility of maintenance is passed onto the WUCS before such repairs are complete (Nayantara, 2006). The KNNL is also supposed to help the WUCS by providing technical assistance in terms of how the repair is to be undertaken. This is to be executed by way of holding meetings with WUCS' presidents and secretaries and the members of CADA and KNNL. These representatives of WUCS are to learn various aspects of efficient management of irrigation water and to disseminate the knowledge to other farmers; however, the field research carried out by the first author of this chapter suggests that in reality, not only that a very little knowledge is disseminated but also, even the limited knowledge disseminated does not get reflected in terms of improved management practices. In a nutshell, the KNNL's approach supports the view that the government is trying to pass its own transaction cost on to farmers under the umbrella of PIM.

Challenges of WUCS

In order to evaluate the functioning of the WUCS, we focus on the WUCS in the Malaprabha river basin in Karnataka. Malaprabha is an important tributary to the River Krishna, which originates in the Western Ghats. The Malaprabha dam was constructed in 1972 near Manoli in Belgaum District, Karnataka, to have a catchment area of 2,175.6 sq. km and total irrigable area of 220,028 ha (GoK, 1991). There are two major canals off taking from the dam site, the Malaprabha Left Bank Canal (MLBC) and the Malaprabha Right Bank Canal (MRBC), respectively. The MLBC was constructed after modification to the original plan in 1969 so that water could be supplied to more villages. As an extent of enforcement of PIM, by the year 2005–06, 236 WUCSs were functioning in the Malaprabha Project area (Nayantara, 2006); however, this does not indicate the success of PIM in the study region. Firstly, our qualitative assessment shows that the water use practices in WUCS' jurisdiction have not changed adequately. The design of the Malaprabha dam is to facilitate a fixed cropping pattern in terms of 40–20–40 for kharif, two-season and rabi crops, respectively. At any given time, only 60 per cent of the land area was to be cultivated while the remaining 40 per cent to be left uncultivated or to be coming under rain-fed crops (GoK, 1991). The crops to be cultivated are mainly irrigated-dry crops, including jowar, pluses and cotton. But, it was observed that there has been gross violation of this cropping pattern. For example, on both the MLBC and the MRBC, we observed that sugarcane, which is a highly water-intensive and a penal crop, is being widely cultivated (NIVA-CISED, 2008). In addition to this, it was also observed that the farmers along the main canals irrigate more than 60 per cent of their land area, which is a crop violation. The violations are widespread as there is hardly any mechanism available to check them. Indeed, a few farmers in the tail-end regions of MLBC admitted that they were unaware that their current practice of siphoning water directly from the main distributaries using diesel-powered pumps is illegal. Thus, this not only indicates that there is a poor communication between the government and the farmers but also that even if there is a communication, the monitoring and punishing the violators is an extremely costly affair. Currently, the WUCSs neither have control of the gates of the canal nor do they have measuring devices to monitor water discharge. Monitoring by KNNL officials could check the overuse of water (NIVA-CISED, 2008) but there is no incentive for these officials to do so. In short, the supply based on original plan is falling short of meeting the current demands.

The infrastructure maintenance is poor and can be attributed to lack of manpower and skilled workers to maintain the canal infrastructure. Though there is a large amount of money invested in the project,[4] the cost recovery is very poor.[5] This implies that there is very low level of water delivery service and funding may not be sufficient for actual improvements.[6] The government usually assumes that the infrastructure is in good condition and is ready to be handed over to the WUCS. However, based on the field survey of the tail-end regions of MLBC it was observed that the gates were rusted or broken, the sub-distributaries were choked with silt and rubble and were not conducive for efficiently transporting water to the fields. The WUCS feel that they are not trained enough to maintain the canals and hence, they recommend that the KNNL staff should take up the responsibility of maintaining the canals (Nayantara, 2006), which is a kind of reverting to the old practices. The essence of PIM rests on the participation of farmers in different forums such as training workshops organized by CADA and meetings between the WUCS representatives and KNNL staff. It can provide the necessary platform for the marginal and small farmers to express their needs and requirements. This is particularly important in terms of reducing inequity in water distribution. Under the Irrigation Act of 1995 (sub-sections 1-A and 1-B), the WUCS can be held legally responsible for not providing water on equitable basis. However, the WUCSs are entrenched in politics and the important positions in the WUCS offices are held by those few

[4] For Malaprabha river basin alone, the estimated cost for 2001 was ₹704 crore. For all the major and medium irrigation projects in the same year was ₹18,072 crore (GoK, 2003).

[5] The water rate collected in 2001–02 was ₹15.14 lakh, whereas the demand was ₹339.86 lakh.

[6] During the field survey, the officials stated that the last 6 km of the MLBC and 58th distributary of the MLBC are still under construction; however, water from the reservoir has not reached beyond the 51st distributary of MLBC since its inception and neither is there much probability of supply in the future, indicating the financially wasteful and politically motivated decisions of the government. Admittedly, according to the KNNL officials, if the water was managed efficiently, then there are high chances that water would reach beyond the 51st distributary but not up to the last distributary and extreme tail-end.

who are already powerful and have political support—as we have observed in the tail-end region of MLBC. The powerful farmers are the ones who can unrightfully take water from other farmers without much repercussion. Even if the small and marginal farmers want to raise their objection, they may get bogged down by the long process of justice. Even if there is platform for the small and marginal farmers, it is mostly on paper; the 'elite capturing' may also be a dominant issue under the PIM regime.

In the face of growing demand for water from other sectors in the basin, especially from urban areas, the opportunity cost of water used in the agriculture sector is increasing tremendously. Currently, the increasing demand for drinking water is being met by exploiting groundwater resources (NIVA-CISED, 2008). The Government of Karnataka is addressing the problem of water scarcity in Malaprabha river basin by proposing to undertake inter-basin water transfers, which involve transferring water from the west flowing *Mahadayi* river. If the proposal is followed through, it will add 7.56 TMC of water to the Malaprabha river. This proposal, however, is expected to submerge about 557.28 ha of forests and cultivable lands apart from settlements in the villages (Kohli, 2004). The proposal has faced criticisms from media and the environmental lobby since the ecological, social and livelihood consequences of such diversions could not be properly accounted for. Also, the Mahadayi enters Goa where it is known as *Mandovi* and hence there are inter-state political issues to be addressed for passing the proposal. Currently, both the states are caught in an inter-state conflict over the issue. No doubt that the additional water in Malaprabha river will reduce the drinking water crisis in Hubli–Dharwad substantially; however, the implication of the net benefits from the project (which has not been estimated scientifically so far) will be different if one takes into account the social cost of the diversion as well. Although this issue is not directly related to irrigation, it shows that water currently available in the Malaprabha river is not adequate to meet the demands for water from various sectors. So, without improving the irrigation efficiency with adequate incentives and disincentives bringing additional water to the basin would be another form of wasting public resources.

The qualitative analysis of the existing institutions reveals that the PIM in Karnataka has not performed satisfactorily. We found that most of the success in peninsular India is reported by the case studies focusing on few successful cases of decentralized water management institutions; there are a large number of failure cases, which have not been reported adequately. The replication of few successful cases has not been succeeded in producing the expected outcomes. This is because there is no clear mechanism in place to link the performance with the incentives. As economic theory suggests, inefficiency would be the dominant outcome if the current water rates are different from the true scarcity value of water (Meinzen-Dick and Mendoza, 1996). Even with perfectly working institutions, one cannot guarantee efficient use of water as water might still be allocated from one low value use to another low value use, rather than from low value use to a high value use. This implies that simply imposing an outside institution into existing ones will not produce expected results; rather, they may even make the things worse. Now the important issue is how to design the institutions that make the reallocation of water more efficient? As we have already argued, the new institutional arrangements with appropriate incentives and disincentives embedded in the preferences of the users will have to be designed and implemented in the river basin. For example, water allocation should be based mainly on the farmers' WTP and WTA values by retaining the decentralized decision-making framework. The authors, based on the field research in the Malaprabha basin, estimated the economic value[7] of improvements in canal water supply in the tail-end region of MLBC for the year 2005–06. The farmers were willing to pay an average amount of ₹223 per acre per year in case water for 30 additional irrigation during a cropping season is made available to them and more than 74 per cent of the farmers stated that they would use

[7] These values can be derived using valuation techniques available in the economic valuation literature. These methods are broadly classified into Revealed Preference methods and Stated Preference methods. In a study conducted by the authors in the tail-end region of the MLBC, a stated preference method was used—Contingent Valuation Method. The economic value of an improvement in canal water supply in terms of additional 30 irrigations between August till February each year was estimated.

the additional water to cultivate maize. Also, up to 50 per cent of the farmers interviewed were willing to pay at least ₹173 for the improvement in canal water supply, which is about 4.9 times higher than the current water rates. How to translate this WTP value into practice? In the following section, we present the outline of an alternative, market-based institutional arrangement that could be introduced for addressing the water scarcity and water reallocation in the Malaprabha river basin in the coming years.

Introducing Market-based Instruments as an Alternative Institutional Arrangement: A Case for Tradable Water Rights

In recent times, it is recognized that the command-and-control (CAC) policies, such as the ones operating in Karnataka, do not produce desired results in the irrigation sector. These CAC policies and institutional rules are based on what the government agents think is appropriate in terms of water pricing and allocations. These policies do not take into account the behaviour of the farmers, influenced by the underlying socio-economic and institutional factors and therefore, there is a huge gap between what the farmers prefer to have from the projects and what the officials want to deliver out of them (Venkatachalam, 2008). As the Austrian school of economic thought suggests, the process of discovering the farmers' preferences is a costly affair to the governments and therefore, the governments very often adopt 'rule of thumb' about farmers' preferences while formulating social policies. As the supply-side policies do not yield any expected results in terms of efficient, equitable and sustainable use of irrigation water, there is a need to look at various other institutional paradigms that can help in achieving these objectives.

Of late, there has been a consciousness among many countries to shift from CAC-type policies and rules to more flexible MBIs in reallocating water not only within the agriculture sector but also across agriculture and non-agriculture sectors. One of the more commonly used MBIs in case of irrigation water is the tradable water rights. In the literature, there is argument in favour of introducing markets for irrigation water for inducing economic efficiency and allocation efficiency (Griffin, 1998; Holden and Thobani, 1996; Venkatachalam, 2008). The argument is based on the success of formal water markets under similar scarcity conditions in Australia, Chile, Mexico and South Africa in ensuring efficient and sustainable water use in irrigation. Conversely, it has been argued that administrative allocation of water even with adequate institutions in place may lead to inefficient water use (Holden and Thobani, 1996; Thobani, 1997). Also, there are existing groundwater markets that have emerged when the state-operated water supply systems fail to meet the increasing demand. However, in case of groundwater markets in India, they are purely private markets without being adequately regulated by the state. Such markets may be detrimental especially to the poor, in case the groundwater market is controlled by the monopoly seller (Mienzen-Dick and Menzoa, 1996); with proper regulation in place, the markets are capable of producing better results than the ones produced under the CAC policies.

There are numerous empirical evidences that show how informal water markets emerged to play a major role in water allocation during the period of scarcity (Schoengold and Zilberman, 2007). The most basic requirement in terms of creating markets for a scarce commodity is to establish property rights (Nabli and Nugent, 1989). The MBIs in case of canal irrigation can be in terms of 'tradable water rights'. Under the tradable water rights system, the willing sellers would be willing to sell excess amount of water from the quota allotted to them while the willing buyer can buy this excess water from the sellers at a market determined price; the market determined price is fixed at that point where the marginal WTP and marginal WTA converge. However, a centralized authority such as a river board or even existing authority such as KNNL, is required to coordinate the activities of sellers and buyers in order to avoid any adverse consequences of water sale. The water authority is responsible for the initial allocation of water rights, based on land size/crop being cultivated by the farmers. The right to trade water is purchased from the central authority; in the case of poor farmers, these rights can be initially assigned on the basis of their WTP values, which may even be zero. This is an important step towards achieving efficient management as the farmers can then trade amongst themselves to reallocate the water in a more efficient way. This would not only give incentive for the farmers to reduce wastage of water but also remove the burden of monitoring their water use. This incentive-based system would influence the farmers to adopt conservation strategies so as to generate surplus water for sale. The needy farmers, on the other hand, would be able to buy that amount of water that they require for cultivation; the water transfer occurs without a huge amount of investment, which would be economically burdensome in the absence of tradable water rights.

There is an argument that in the Indian context, existence of large-scale informal water extracting activities and small land holdings would hinder the effectiveness of water transfer through formal markets (Shah and van Koppen, 2006). Rosegrant and Binswanger (1994) argue that rather than issuing tradable permits to the individual farmers, these permits can be issued among the already established WUAs, which can trade these permits among themselves through market negotiations. This not only would save resources on establishing new institutions for facilitating water trade but also would reduce the transaction cost of monitoring water use, since peer monitoring is possible among the farmers within the WUAs. But one may argue that introducing the tradable permits within the WUAs, which have already failed in many basins, may not yield any productive results. The point to be noted here is that the tradable water rights system brings in innovative incentive mechanism into the operation of WUAs and therefore, one can expect this system to improve the performance of the WUAs. In many river basins, the informal WUAs are more effective and the formal system can be strengthened with ingredients from these informal associations in order to produce better outcomes (Sokile and van Koppen, 2004). Another argument that can come up against the implementation of tradable permits is that initially, the government would have to invest vast amount of its financial resources. However, the past trend in financial investment and grants to the major and the medium irrigation projects across the country and in Karnataka suggests that the financial commitments[8] are already very high and therefore, commitment of financial resources will not be an additional burden for implementing tradable water rights (Meinzen-Dick and Mendoza, 1996). The experiences from other developing countries have shown that with the introduction of tradable water rights, the poorer farmers could also be benefited, bringing equity among the farmers (Meinzen-Dick and Mendoza, 1996). Appropriate institutional arrangements can be made to include the landless farmers as well in the tradable water rights scheme, in case the landless will be benefited from being included.

Conclusion

In this chapter, we have discussed certain institutional issues involved in managing surface water—especially in the context of water-scarce Malaprabha river basin in India. We have seen that the wisdom of water management based on the supply-side-oriented approach gradually moving towards a demand-side-oriented approach by way of decentralizing the management decisions. However, this demand-side approach did not produce any concrete results since this approach is only partially implemented and that too, within the already existing inefficient CAC method. As part of this so-called demand-side approach, the Government of Karnataka has adopted the principle of PIM by involving farmers in the decision-making process by way of creating the WUCS. However, our qualitative analysis suggests that the PIM has not achieved its primary objective of increasing water use efficiency because of the fact that the demand-oriented approach has not been adequately supported by other efficient institutions such as

[8] For the financial year 2004–05, the Malaprabha River Project was allotted ₹113 crore. In the Ninth Plan, the financial outlay of almost ₹13,277 crore for all the major and medium projects in Karnataka.

the MBIs. The failure of the PIM and the WUCS demonstrates that continued 'top-down approach' in which imposing outside institutions into existing ones would produce results that are economically distortive in nature. When new institutions are introduced, they destabilize the existing institutions—that may be relatively inefficient but working smoothly at the local or regional level; when the new institutions also fail, it may generate a non-linear impact in the system because of multiple institutional failures. Hence, we proposed an alternative institutional arrangement, which moves away from the current CAC regime towards a market-based tradable water rights system. Introducing 'market-based tradable water rights system' with appropriate regulation for water allocation will produce improved results. Though there are problems with the tradable water rights system (Bauer, 1997), there are indeed many advantages to it: (i) the existing institutions such as WUCS can be effectively used for facilitating water transfer and therefore, there is no additional cost involved in creating new institutions under the tradable water rights regime; (ii) since the water allocation takes place on the basis of WTP and WTA values of the buyers and sellers, respectively, the water is always transferred from low value use to high value use; and (iii) since even the small farmers can participate in the water trade, equity issues can be effectively addressed. Any kind of institution will tend to fail, if they are not properly regulated. The success or failure of innovative institutions like tradable water rights depends mainly on how effectively the institutions are governed by the governments, the NGOs and the user associations, apart from the individual users participating in the process.

References

Alchian, A.A. and Demsetz, H. 1972. 'Production, Information Costs, and Economic Organization', *American Economic Review*, 62(5): 777–95.

Araral, E. 2009. 'What Explains Collective Action in the Commons? Theory with Econometric Results from the Philippines', *World Development*, 37(3): 687–97.

Axelrod, R. 1984. *The Evolution of Cooperation*. New York: Basic Books.

Bardhan, P. 2001. 'Water Community: An Empirical Analysis of Cooperation on Irrigation in South India', in M. Aoki and Y. Hayami (eds), *Communities and Markets in Economic Development* (pp. 247–64). Oxford: Oxford University Press.

Bauer, C.J. 1997. 'Bringing Water Markets Down to Earth: The Political Economy of Water Rights in Chile, 1976–1995', *World Development*, 25(5): 639–56.

Biswas, D. 2008. 'Willingness to Pay for Improvements in Irrigation Water: The Case of Malaprabha Basin, Karnataka, India', *Review of Development and Change*, 13(2): 181–201.

Brady, G.L. 2000. 'Applying Public Choice to Environmental Policy', in G. Tullock, A. Seldon and G. L. Brady (eds), *Government Failure: A Primer in Public Choice* (pp. 117–26). Washington, D.C.: CATO Institute.

Camerer, C.F., Loewenstein, G. and Rabin, M. 2003. *Advances in Behavioral Economics*. NJ: Princeton University Press, USA.

Cárdenas, J.-C. 2009. 'Experiments in Environment and Development', *Annual Review of Resource Economics*, 1(1): 157–82.

Cárdenas, J.-C. and Ostrom, E. 2004. 'What Do People Bring into the Game: Experiments in the Field about Cooperation in the Commons', CAPRi Working Papers 32, International Food Policy Research Institute (IFPRI), Washington, D.C.

Coase, R. 1960. 'The Problem of Social Cost', *Journal of Law and Economics*, 31(October): 1–44.

Dixit, A.K. 2004. *Lawlessness and Economics: Alternative Modes of Governance*. Princeton University Press.

Easterly, W. 2008. 'Institutions: Top Down or Bottom Up?' *American Economic Review (Papers and Proceedings)*, 98(2): 995–99.

Gneezy, U. and Rustichini, A. 2000. 'Pay Enough or Don't Pay at All', *Quarterly Journal of Economics*, 115(3): 791–810.

Government of Karnataka (GoK). 1991. *The Malaprabha Dam Project*, KNNL Belgaum.

———. 2003. Annual Report 2002–2003, Water Resources Department.

Holden, P. and Thobani, M. 1996. 'Tradable Water Rights: A Property Rights Approach to Resolving Water Shortages and Promoting Investment', Policy Research Working Paper No. 1627, World Bank, Washington, D.C.

Johansson, R.C. 2000. 'Pricing Irrigation Water: A Literature Survey', World Bank Policy Research Working Paper No. 2449, Washington, D.C.

Knudsen, T. 2003. 'Simon's Selection Theory: Why Docility Evolves to Breed Successful Altruism', *Journal of Economic Psychology*, 24(2): 229–44.

Kohli, K. 2004. 'Diverting a River, West to East', *India Together*, Available at: http://www.indiatogether.org/2004/mar/env-tailend.htm (accessed on 20 October 2014).

Mahapatra, S.K. 2007. 'Functioning of Water Users Associations or Pani Panchayat in Orissa: Principle, Procedure, Performance and Prospects', *Law, Environment and Development Journal*, 3/2: 126–147. Available at http://www.lead-journal.org/content/07126.pdf (accessed on 30 March 2010).

Marothia, D. 2005. 'Institutional Reforms in Canal Irrigation System', *Economic and Political Weekly*, 40(28): 3074–84.

Meinzen-Dick, R. and Mendoza, M. 1996. 'Alternative Water Allocation Mechanisms: Indian and International Experiences', *Economic and Political Weekly*, 31(13): A25–A30.

Nabli, Mustapha K. and Nugent, Jeffrey B. 1989. 'The New Institutional Economics and its Applicability to Development', *World Development*, 17(9): 1333–47.

Nayantara, S.N. 2006. 'Participatory Approach in Water Resources Management: Role of Water Users Groups in Dharwad and Belgaum districts [Malaprabha left & right bank canal]', Unpublished.

NIVA-CISED. 2008. 'Institutional Analysis of Participatory Irrigation Management in the Malaprabha River Basin, Karnataka, India'. CISED-NIVA, Policy Brief No. 02-2008. http://www.malaprabha.org/publications/.pdf (accessed on 15 May 2009).

North, D.C. 1991. 'Institutions,' *Journal of Economic Perspectives*, 5(1): 97–112.

———. 1994a. 'Institutional Competition'. Available at http://129.3.20.41/eps/eh/papers/9411/9411001.pdf (accessed on 17 March 2010).

———. 1994b. 'Economic Performance through Time', *American Economic Review*, 84(3): 355–67.

Olson, M. 1971. *The Logic of Collective Action: Public Goods and the Theory of Groups*. Cambridge, MA: Harvard University Press.

Ostrom, E. 1990. *Governing the Commons: The Evolution of Institutions for Collective Action*. New York: Cambridge University Press.

———. 1994. *Neither Market Nor State: Governance of Common-Pool Resources in the Twenty-First Century*. Washington, D.C: International Food Policy Research Institute..

Pigou, A.C. 1932. *The Economics of Welfare*, 4th edition. London: Macmillan and Co.

Rosegrant, M.W. and Binswanger, H.P. 1994. 'Markets in Tradable Water Rights: Potential for Efficiency Gains in Developing Country Water Resource Allocation', *World Development*, 22(11): 1613–25.

Schoengold, K. and Zilberman, D. 2007. 'The Economics of Water, Irrigation, and Development', *Handbook of Agricultural Economics*, 3: 2933–77.

Shah, T. and Koppen, B. 2006. 'Is India Ripe for Integrated Water Resources Management? Fitting Water Policy to National Development Context', *Economic and Political Weekly*, 41(31): 3413–21.

Sokile, C.S. and Koppen, B. 2004. 'Local Water Rights and Local Water User Entities: The Unsung Heroines of Water Resource Management in Tanzania', *Physics and Chemistry of the Earth*, 29(15–18): 1349–56.

Stigler, George J. 1988. *Memoirs of an Unregulated Economist*. New York: Basic Books.

Sugden, R. 1986. *The Economics of Rights, Co-operation and Welfare*. Oxford: Basil Blackwell.

———. 1989. 'Spontaneous Order', *Journal of Economic Perspectives*, 3(4): 85–97.

Thobani, Mateen. 1997. 'Formal Water Markets: Why, When, and How to Introduce Tradable Water Rights', *The World Bank Research Observer*, 12(2): 161–79.

Turner, K., Georgiou, S., Clark, R., Brouwer, R. and Burke, J. 2004. *Economic Valuation of Water Resources in Agriculture: From the Sectoral to a Functional Perspective of Natural Resource Management*. Rome: Food and Agriculture Organization of the United Nations.

Venkatachalam, L. 2004. 'Sources of Government Failure and the Environmental Externality: Analysis of Groundwater Pollution in Tamil Nadu, India', *Water Policy*, 6(5): 413–26.

———. 2008. 'Market-Based Instruments for Water Allocation in India: Issues and the Way Forward', In: 'Managing Water in the Facecae of Growing Scarcity, Inequality and Declining Returns: Exploring Fresh Approaches, Proceedings of the 7th Annual Partners' Meet, IWMI-TATA Water Policy Programme, Hyderabad, pp. 498–512.

Wade, R. 1988. *Village Republics: Economic Conditions for Collective Action in South India*. Cambridge: Cambridge University Press.

11

Improving Tiger Conservation in India

Zareena Begum I. and Amanat K. Gill

Introduction

From more than 100,000 in the early 1900s, the population of tigers has dwindled to less than 3,200 today. The Bali tiger became extinct during the 1930s, followed by the Caspian tiger in 1970s and the Javan tiger a decade later. Six species of tiger, namely Bengal, Indochinese, Amur, South China, Malaysian and Sumatran, survive, scattered throughout eastern Russia, Indochina, the Indian subcontinent and Southeast Asia, and have been classified as endangered by International Union for the Conservation of Nature (IUCN). Tigers have undergone a serious range collapse and today occupy only 7 per cent of their historic range.

Tiger is an umbrella species for the conservation of the biota of a majority of the eco-regions in Asia. Its role as a top predator is vital in regulating and perpetuating ecological processes and systems. Monitoring tiger population is equivalent to monitoring the health of the ecosystems, which the tigers inhabit. India is home to over 50 per cent of the world's wild tigers in spite of having a growing human population of over a billion. It is also one of the world's fastest growing economies. It is with full recognition of these challenges that India is committed to conserving its tigers and their habitats. India plays a vital role in accomplishing the objectives of the Global Tiger Recovery Plan that was ratified at the meeting of world leaders held at St. Petersburg in 2010.

The plight of the Indian tigers came to light, when a census conducted in 1972 revealed the existence of only 1,827 tigers in the wild. This resulted in the initiation of 'Project Tiger' in 1973, which sought to conserve tigers with the establishment of tiger reserves. Today, there exist a total of 39 tiger reserves with a population of 1,706 tigers. Currently tigers occur largely in the forest areas of 17 states in India. Nagaland, Meghalaya, Tripura and Haryana have reports of occasional tiger occurrence. The distribution of tigers and their density in these forests vary on account of several ecological and anthropogenic factors like forest cover, terrain, natural prey availability, presence of undisturbed habitat and the quality of managerial efforts taken towards protection.

The main threats faced by wild tigers today is poaching to feed the illegal trade in skins and bone, depletion of natural prey and habitat destruction and fragmentation. Despite the prohibition of international trade in tiger parts and its products, with the listing of the tiger in Appendix I of UN Convention on International Trade in Endangered Species (CITES) in 1975, the lucrative trade in tiger parts still continues. The number of poached tigers between 1994 and 2011 is 936, but this does not even begin to indicate the gravity of the problem since most of the poaching goes undetected. With the demand for tiger products miniscule in India, most of the poaching is carried out to meet the demand overseas especially in China, where tiger bone is used in traditional oriental medicine, wine, etc., and tiger skin is used in home décor, taxidermy and bribery. Much of the tiger poaching is done by tribal population who know their forests well. They are usually paid a meagre amount, their hunting talents and knowledge is exploited by greedy traders.

Despite a country-wide increase of 20 per cent in tiger population, from 1,411 in 2006 to 1,706 in 2010, there has been a decline of 12.6 per cent in tiger occupancy from connecting habitats, from 93,697 km^2 in 2006 to 81,881 km^2 in 2010. The existence of migration corridors between reserves is essential to enhancing the conservation potential by increasing the viability and resilience of the wild tiger population by overcoming the genetic consequences of an inbred tiger population as a result of isolated tiger reserves. Habitat destruction and associated natural prey decline, as well as hunting of prey species, forces tigers into conflict with local communities and the vicious cycle of human–predator conflict.

The protected areas (PAs) in India are comparable to small islands in a vast sea of ecologically unsustainable land uses of varying degrees. To ensure that these natural systems continue to provide ecosystem services and remain repositories of biodiversity for future generations, it is essential to (i) protect them from human impacts, and (ii) maintain natural areas of sufficient size so as to allow for ecosystem processes to occur. Tigers need large areas of undisturbed habitats to sustain tigers in the long run. This dilemma can be addressed by managing these 'small' tiger populations as meta-populations. By permitting tigers to migrate between reserves, the long-term persistence of individual populations is enhanced. The 'tiger bearing forests' need to be fostered with protection as well as restorative inputs to ensure their source and corridor value for demographic and genetic viability of tiger populations. Tigers are a conservation-dependent species requiring connected forests with good prey and a fair interspersion of undisturbed breeding areas.

This study contributes to the debate about tiger farming by using a bio-economic model of wild tiger population dynamics, trade and habitat to analyse the potential of heightened anti-poaching enforcement and/or liberalization of the captive tiger breeding industry to prevent extirpation of wild tigers. A major conclusion is that anti-poaching and trade ban enforcement must be increased to seemingly unattainable rates if extirpation of wild tigers is to be prevented, but that a captive breeding industry and/or effective transfer payments from rich countries to poor ones for protecting the habitat could potentially prevent the extirpation of wild tigers.

The fate of the wild tiger population is modelled by a tiger survivability function that is derived from economic principles. The survivability function is a differential equation that maps the tiger population, the rate of poacher detection, the output of tiger farms, the stigma effect, available habitat and other relevant variables to the rate of change in the wild tiger population. Using the survivability function, we determine for any combination of parameters whether the tiger population will reach a stable positive equilibrium or go extinct. The model makes no distinction between poachers and farmers, except that the ability to sell farmed animals increases the supply of tigers while also shifting out the demand function, which is taken to be downward sloping. We estimate the current levels of all of the parameters and then calculate how much each must change, *ceteris paribus*, to prevent wild tigers from becoming extinct.

Literature Review

Tiger Research and Conservation Needs

Following pioneering work by Schaller (1967), researchers have tried to understand the ecology, behaviour and more recently, macro-ecology and evolutionary patterns of tigers (Karanth and Chellam, 2009). While a number of scientific studies have discussed aspects like the number of tiger sub-species (Kitchener, 1999; Luo et al., 2004; Mountfort, 1974), conservation priority has shifted to remnant landscapes and populations (Walston et al., 2010b; Wikramanayake et al., 2011). Recent reviews of the science on tiger conservation and biology include Seidensticker et al. (1999), Karanth (2003, 2006), Tilson and Nyhus (2010) and Seidensticker (2010), and this section relies heavily on these papers. The IUCN estimates there to be about 2,150 breeding tigers in protected 'source sites' and about 4,000 individuals spread across 13 countries across Asia: Bangladesh, Bhutan, Cambodia, China, India, Indonesia, Lao PDR, Malaysia, Myanmar, Nepal, Russia, Thailand and Vietnam (Chundawat et al., 2011; Jhala et al., 2011; Walston et al., 2010a). North Korea may also have a small number of tigers. Importantly, there has been a sharp decline in the historic range of tigers over time (Dinerstein et al., 2007; Sanderson et al., 2006). Many authors have identified the various factors that are affecting tiger populations, summarized in Table 11.1 using the Driver Pressure-Status-Impact-Response (DPSIR) framework (European Environment Agency, 1999). This framework considers a causal chain between the 'Drivers' (D) of change, which create 'Pressures' (P) on the environment because of activities, affecting the 'Status' (S) of the system. The changes in 'Status' (S) then have 'Impacts' (I) on the system, and desirable 'Responses' (R) can be identified for policymakers (Elliott, 2002) (for example on the use and criticism of the framework, refer Atkins et al., 2011; Jago-on et al., 2009; Ojeda-Martínez et al., 2009; Svarstad et al., 2008). Although our DPSIR analysis omits many nuances of the complex challenges facing tiger conservation, it is clear that the emphasis of the tiger conservation literature and actions has been on securing habitat and providing adequate protection to tiger populations. Other strategies, for example, artificial breeding of tigers or reintroduction, have also been discussed by authors (Gratwicke et al., 2008; Kirkpatrick and Emerton, 2010; Lynam, 2010; Mitra, 2006, 2005; Morell, 2007). Yet, PAs emerge as the central requirement for tiger conservation (Table 11.1).

Protected Areas Are Key

The requirement for PAs is reinforced by several factors. The tiger requires large areas of habitat to maintain minimum viable populations. This is due to the relatively high food intake, up to 3000 kg of wild ungulate meat for an average male tiger per year, which necessitates individuals to establish ranges of up to several hundred square kilometres across the landscape, to secure prey resources, and to find undisturbed places for breeding (Karanth et al., 2004; Karanth and Stith, 1999). Additionally, scientists have justified the establishment of large PAs because (i) they translate into the conservation of a host of associated species in a wide variety of ecosystems (Karanth, 2003; Linkie, 2007; Seidensticker, 2010; Walston et al., 2010b) and (ii) such areas provide essential ecosystem services such as water regulation for a large part of the globe (Wikramanayake et al., 2011). Many authors have emphasized the protection of the wide variety of tiger habitat across ecosystems, rather than focussing specifically on genetic variation within tiger

Table 11.1:
Drivers–pressure–status–impact–response (DPSIR) analysis of the challenges facing tiger conservation

Challenges for Tiger Conservation	*Drivers*	*Pressure*	*Status*	*Impacts*	*Responses*
Poaching-related challenges	Tiger body parts are used for traditional medicine and other practices in China and other Asian countries. (Kenney et al., 1995; Project Tiger, 2005)	Trade is officially banned by China, yet continues illegally and provides an incentive for poaching of tigers. (Nowell and Ling, 2007)	Tiger populations are highly sensitive to poaching. Poaching can lead to extinction. (Chapron et al., 2008; Kenney et al., 1995)	Tigers are known to have become locally extinct from at least two Protected Areas in India. (Ali, 2009; Project Tiger, 2005)	Markets for tiger body parts have to be closed. Tigers have to be strictly protected against poaching. (Abbott and Kooten, 2011; Damania and Bulte, 2007)
Reduction in prey	Many local communities traditionally depend on forests and livestock for subsistence and livelihoods. (Davidar et al., 2010; Gadgil and Thapar, 1990; Persha et al., 2011; Project Tiger, 2005)	(a) Poaching of prey populations by local communities is reported. (b) Domestic livestock of local communities are known to ecologically compete with ungulates (tiger prey), causing ungulate populations to decline. (Carbone and Gittleman, 2002; Damania et al., 2003; Karanth et al., 2004; Karanth and Stith, 1999; Madhusudan, 2004; Sanderson et al., 2006)	Ecological models suggest that an average tiger requires about 50 ungulates/year. Prey density affects tigers' breeding rates, and is a key determinant of tiger populations. (Carbone and Gittleman, 2002; Damania et al., 2003; Karanth et al., 2004; Karanth and Stith, 1999)	Tiger populations directly depend upon prey density, and hence are affected by the presence of livestock populations. Loss of prey can also exacerbate the vulnerability to poaching. (Dinerstein et al., 1997; Karanth et al., 2004; Karanth and Stith, 1999; Sunquist et al., 1999)	A viable population of about 75–100 tigers (including >25 breeding females) would need 500–2,500 km^2 of 'forests relatively free of incompatible human uses'. These large areas of tiger habitats with sufficient prey availability have to be legally protected. (Jhala et al., 2008; Karanth and Gopal, 2005; Karanth et al., 2004; Karanth and Stith, 1999)

(Table 11.1 Contd)

(Table 11.1 Contd)

Challenges for Tiger Conservation	*Drivers*	*Pressure*	*Status*	*Impacts*	*Responses*
Habitat depletion	With rising populations and increasing resource consumption, human enterprise and demands from natural resources are expanding. (Vitousek et al., 1997)	Changing land-use patterns and resource extraction (such as logging, mining and urbanization) by various agencies have been major causes of deforestation and loss of habitat. (Barbier, 2001; Butler and Laurance, 2008; Rudel, 2007)	The range of tigers in 2006 was about 7% of their historical range. In the years 1997–2006 alone, the area with wild tigers shrunk by 41%. (Dinerstein et al., 2007; Dinerstein et al., 1997; Sanderson et al., 2006; Wikramanayake et al., 1998, 1999)	Loss of habitat is a major challenge for tiger conservation; we must focus on specific regions and connectivity between small and large habitat fragments. (Linkie et al., 2006; Loyola et al., 2009)	Key Sites: (a) Nearly 76 units of Tiger Conservation Landscapes across the range have been identified, 33 in India. (b) There are 42 source sites, where the tiger populations have the potential to repopulate larger landscapes. 18 sites are in India. (c) In addition, landscapes level interventions are important to secure corridors. (Sanderson et al., 2006, 2010; Walston et al., 2010a; Wikramanayake et al., 2011)
Summary	(a) Traditional livelihoods (use of livestock, use of forests for subsistence). (b) Urban growth and demands of economic and infrastructure development (logging, mining, infrastructure projects, etc.).	Human activities involve direct or indirect interaction with tigers or their environment, creating active or passive pressures on tiger populations.	Tiger numbers and their ranges have reduced to historic lows.	(a) Anthropogenic disturbances affect tigers and reduce numbers. (b) Active pursuit and destruction of habitat reduce tiger populations.	Sufficient areas need to be procured and protected for conservation of remaining tiger populations. Viable tiger populations need relatively large areas of contiguous habitat, which require immunity from anthropogenic disturbances.

Source: Created by the authors from the present study.

populations (Chundawat et al., 2008; Dinerstein et al., 1997, 2006; Sanderson et al., 2006). However, this approach has led to conservation efforts spreading 'thin' across the landscape (Sanderson et al., 2006; Walston et al., 2010b). As a result, more recently the scientific emphasis has been on the protection of tiger ranges that are already protected and have the best chance of restoring tiger populations, coupled with the landscape perspective, managing populations in the core areas, buffer zones and corridors in a mosaic of land-use patterns (Seidensticker, 2010; Wikramanayake et al., 2011). Therefore, the emphasis on habitats that are already designated PAs has only increased (Karanth and Chellam, 2009; Sanderson et al., 2006; Walston et al., 2010b; Wikramanayake et al., 2004). However, despite the scientific evidence in support of formal and exclusive PAs, tigers have recently become locally extinct from two Tiger Reserves in India: Sariska and Panna (Ali, 2009; Project Tiger, 2005). In the following section, we examine the problems of the exclusive PA approach, which can help us understand some of the challenges facing tiger conservation.

India and Its Protected Areas

India offers a unique and important context within which to understand the challenges associated with tiger conservation. India is thought to have the largest population of wild tigers across the global range of the species, with about 1,410 individuals estimated in 2006 (range 1,165–1,655, excluding the population in Indian Sunderbans) (Jhala et al., 2008). More recent surveys conducted between 2009 and 2010 estimate wild tiger populations in India at 1,706 with a range of 1,571–1,875 (Ministry of Environment and Forests et al., 2011). Although the reliability of these numbers remains debated (Karanth et al., 2011), the population represents more than half the extant genetic diversity of tigers worldwide (Mondol et al., 2009). A recent study that compiled various sources of data identified only five sites in the world that contained tiger populations close to their estimated carrying capacity, and all of these are in India (Walston et al., 2010a). India also has a strong commitment to tiger conservation, demonstrated by its large financial contribution to conservation efforts (Walston et al., 2010b). While many other tiger range countries are dealing with challenges of development and stable governments, India can claim to be a liberal and open democracy (Guha, 2007) where successive legitimate governments since the 1970s have encouraged or tolerated the conservation of tigers. Also, India has experienced a high degree of economic growth in the last two decades. Therefore, it is likely that India's experiences with establishing and managing PAs offer insights and lessons that will be relevant across various contexts in conservation science.

The Institutional Context

The modern network of PAs in India was significantly strengthened with the enactment of the Wild Life (Protection) Act 1972. This Act (including the amendments) prescribes many categories of PAs, including Tiger Reserves, National Parks and Wildlife Sanctuaries, together covering nearly 5 per cent of India's geographic area (Wildlife Institute of India, 2007). National Parks and Wildlife Sanctuaries are managed by the state governments, and out of these, 39 PAs are designated Tiger Reserves, managed by a federal authority, the National Tiger Conservation Authority (Damayanti, 2007). These PAs remain exclusively controlled by distant authorities with no role for local communities in day-to-day management activities (Badola, 1999). This approach to conservation management has also been referred to as the 'preservationist', 'authoritarian conservationist' or the 'exclusionary' approach in the literature.

The most common recommendation for preventing extirpation of wild tigers is to increase enforcement of the trade bans, while opposing tiger farming on the grounds that farmed output removes the stigma of using tiger-based products and facilitates the laundering of illegal tiger parts. The so-called 'stigma effect' (Fischer, 2004) postulates that the demand for illegal wildlife products falls when trade is banned. Proponents of tiger farming and trade in tiger parts, on the other hand, favour a supply-side approach to conservation, arguing that a captive breeding industry could meet all demand for tiger products, thereby eliminating illegal killing of wild tigers and preventing their extinction.

Domestication of Tigers and Tiger Trade

With more than 100,000 tigers at the beginning of the twentieth century, the population of tigers has fallen to fewer than 3,200 today. Across their range, tigers are seriously threatened by poaching to feed the illegal trade in skins and bones, habit destruction and decline in natural prey populations. Tigers (*Panthera tigris*) have been listed in Appendix I of the UN CITES since 1975, with the exception of the Siberian sub-species, which was added in 1987. All international trade in tiger parts and products is strictly prohibited but the demand for tiger bone for traditional medicines and the burgeoning market for skins continues, and a recent analysis by TRAFFIC reveals that on an average, a minimum of 104 tigers have entered trade every year between 2000 and 2010. In India, home to nearly half of the world's remaining wild tiger population, the current population is officially estimated to be 1706 (Ministry of Environment and Forests (MoEF)) as compared to 40,000 in the beginning of the twentieth century. At this rate, wild tigers are faced with a future of being confined to a small number of isolated reserves and as captured animals in zoos and private holdings (EIA, 2010).

The illegal trade in poached skins between India, Nepal and China is the most significant immediate threat to the continued existence of the tiger in the wild. While the gravity of the situation has been recognized and plenty of information is already available, the lucrative illegal trade continues. The fundamental reason being, that the governments in question have failed to implement an adequate enforcement response at the domestic and regional levels. Wild life crime remains a low priority in terms of political commitments and investment, and is rarely subjected to sustained and specialized enforcement effort (EIA and WPSI, 2006). In the early 1990s, China emerged as a major importer and consumer of tiger bone and an exporter of tiger bone products, surpassing Thailand and Indonesia as the primary supplier to markets in South Korea and Japan. China's growing domination of the marketplace coincided with reports of increased tiger poaching in India, starting in the late 1980s (EIA, 1996).

In 1993, following intense international pressure, China introduced a domestic trade ban on the sale of tiger parts and derivatives. This was aided by donors and non-government organizations launching global campaigns to engage the practitioners of Traditional Asian Medicines, working together to promote alternatives. Despite the official move-away from patented and packaged tiger bone medicines, tigers continued to be poached in India.

In December 1999, the illegal tiger trade again exploded onto the international agenda with the seizure in India of a large consignment of skins: three tigers, 50 leopards and five otters in one truck in Ghaziabad, Uttar Pradesh. Weeks later, in January 2000, leads from this seizure resulted in a massive haul in the small town of Khaga, also in Uttar Pradesh, comprising four tigers, 70 leopards, 221 otter skins, 175 kg of tiger bone, 132 tiger claws and approximately 18,000 leopard claws. Not only was the skin trade escalating, there was clearly still demand for bones and other body parts. Information from both seizures suggested the old trade connections with Tibet and China were still flourishing (EIA and WPSI, 2006).

By the end of 2004, news was beginning to emerge that all the tigers in India's Sariska Tiger Reserve had been exterminated, while the loss of tigers in Panna Tiger Reserve was also reported (EIA and WPSI, 2006).

Although appeals by religious leaders and targeted outreach campaigns have reduced demand from the Tibetan community, without law enforcement operations targeting the criminals profiting from the trade, trafficking in Asian big cat skins and parts into China has continued via the same routes.

Importantly, there has been a clear shift in favour of meeting the demand for skins to be used as home décor, taxidermy and for bribery. Many skins are now sold with the head and paws intact, or backed onto cloth for display (EIA, 2009). According to traders selling skins in 2007–09, the primary buyers have also changed and are principally the mainland Chinese business elite, officials and the military. Investigations in 2009 revealed that tiger and leopard bones continue to flow into a network of dealers selling to mainland Chinese for medicinal purposes, with customers apparently purchasing the raw, authentic item over patented packaged products. Tiger bone is also increasingly used in tiger bone wine, marketed as a gift or 'tonic', with large volumes advertised openly at wildlife parks and tiger breeding centres.

EIA has identified the obstacles to enforcement as:

- Lack of understanding and capacity and unclear policies
- Lack of resources
- Lack of cooperation and trust
- Lack of motivation compounded by corruption and institutional weaknesses.

Some key recommendations by EIA are as follows:

- Secure greater involvement of police and custom officers in tiger and other Asian big cat conservation
- Reduce demand for tigers and other Asian big cat parts
- Expand the use of intelligence-led enforcement in combating tiger trade
- Improve international cooperation to disrupt transnational criminal networks
- Reform of judicial processes
- Increase resources to combat wildlife crime
- Improve the motivation of enforcement personnel
- Tackle corruption in wildlife crime.

The most common recommendation for preventing the extinction of wild tigers is to increase enforcement of the trade bans, while opposing tiger farming, which sprung up following China's domestic trade ban on tiger products and its derivatives, on the grounds that farmed output removes the stigma of using tiger-based products and facilitates laundering of illegal tiger parts. On the other hand, proponents of tiger farming and permitting the sale of captive breeding farms favour a supply-side approach to conservation, arguing that a captive breeding industry could meet the demand for tiger products, thereby eliminating or reducing the illegal killing of wild tigers and aiding conservation.

Bulte and Damian (2005, 2007) assume imperfect competition to demonstrate theoretically that multiple equilibria are possible in a game between organized criminal poaching gangs and domestic wildlife farms. In their model, it is not possible to determine unambiguously whether products from captive-bred wildlife will increase or decrease harvests of wild animals. If poachers and farmers compete on the basis of quantity (Cournot competition), the solution to the game leads to higher populations of wild tigers, but if competition is on the basis of price (Bertrand competition), wild stocks are reduced. However, as Singh and Vives (1984) demonstrate, the poacher and farmer are unlikely to compete on the basis of price since they both can do better if they compete on the basis of quantity when the goods they market are substitutes, that is, the Cournot outcome dominates the Bertrand outcome, if wild and farmed products are substitutes, and especially if demand is linear (as assumed by Damian and Bulte).

The model used by Abbott and Kooten (2011), to evaluate the potential of permitting the sale of domesticated tiger products, indicates that, in the absence of the required institutions or effective community-based resource management regimes that inhibit illegal takings, the sale of tiger products from tiger farms could reduce poaching sufficiently to enable wild tigers to reproduce faster than they are killed. In the absence of other measures (additional food or habitat), a combination of increased enforcement and legal sales offers the best chance of wild tiger survival. However, the loss of quality habitat makes it difficult to design an effective strategy for saving wild tigers.

Their simulation results assume that anti-poaching enforcement efforts and the demand for poached tigers will be unaffected if tiger farming is legitimized, other than through the 'stigma effect' (which postulates that the demand for wildlife products falls when trade is banned) that causes the demand to shift outwards if trade is permitted. However, these assumptions can be debated on the following grounds (Kirkpatrick and Emerton, 2010):

- Legalization of farmed tigers increases the demand for poached tigers because farmers will purchase them to increase their captive stocks.
- Legalization of farmed tigers increases poaching because it is much cheaper to poach a tiger than to raise one in captivity; thus, producers of tiger products purchase poached animals and sell them as if they were raised in captivity.
- Since, there will be legal as well as illegal supply of tigers, it will be harder to recognize poached tigers and the effectiveness of anti-poaching efforts will be reduced.

These would be warranted if tiger farming was unregulated with many competitive firms. However, if tiger farming is concentrated in a single or a very small number of regulated monopolistic firms, these concerns may not materialize, since there is an added incentive to defend property rights, which could lead to greater anti-poaching enforcement to protect their profits. To help ensure that poached wild tigers are not laundered into the stock of captive-bred tigers, an animal registration system similar to the one used for cattle in Europe and North America can be adopted (Abbott and Kooten, 2011).

Community-based Wildlife Management

The plight of the Indian wild tigers came to light, when a census conducted in 1972 revealed the existence of only 1,827 tigers as compared to approximately 40,000 tigers in the early 1900s, which led to the launch of 'Project Tiger' in 1973. The various reasons responsible for the fall in the tiger population were:

- shrinkage of tiger habitat
- excessive disturbance in tiger habitat
- depletion of tiger prey
- poaching of tigers
- poisoning for the protection of cattle.

'Project Tiger' targeted conservation of tigers by the creation of tiger reserves. The tiger reserves followed a 'core–buffer' model, wherein tiger reserves are divided into two zones—the 'core' area, which is devoid of human interference and the 'buffer' area, which is subjected to conservation-oriented land use. One major drawback of this 'fines and fences' approach to conservation was that it led to the displacement of people from the land that was traditionally theirs. 'Project Tiger' suffers from various other problems as well—delayed and inadequate funds, poaching, grazing, encroachment and inadequately trained and insufficient number of field staff (Khandelwal, 2005).

Most of the national parks, where tigers breed, are small and the land-use changes, resulting in the destruction of migration corridors between reserves, threatening to increase reserve and population isolation. Both site-level protection and landscape-scale interventions, to maintain habitat corridors, are essential, in order to maintain the viability and resilience of wild tiger population by managing tigers as meta-populations. Source sites alone do not have the potential to meet the range-wide goal of doubling the population, effective protection of tigers and prey at the current range-wide reserve system is essential. The tiger's ecological and demographic requirements, and genetic consequences of isolated tiger populations, demand a landscape approach that goes beyond reserve boundaries (Wikramanayake et al., 2010).

In response to the recognized failure of top-down approaches to development, and ecological limits of fortress conservation, community-based conservation (CBC) has become the trademark of the 'new conservation' approach, which is now unfolding across Africa. CBC shifts the focus of conservation from nature as protected exclusively by the state, to nature as managed through inclusive, participatory, community-based approaches. Its premise was that giving local people a stake in wildlife would increase their incentive to conserve it. This would therefore make wildlife an important engine of local economic development. CBC seeks to create a synthesis between conservation and development (Igoe, 2004).

A study, carried out by Sara Tynnerson (2009), of the 'Burunge Wildlife Management Area in Tanzania', revealed that while gains for the local communities were not clear, gains for wildlife were more evident. Both species numbers and individuals increased, but at the same time there was also an increase in conflicts between locals and wildlife. Officials in Babati District claim that the project has been a success. Positive effects for the people have been that the villages have more money for development, people have been employed in the tourism and handicraft industries, and people are proud of the project and benefit from tourism. Positive effects for wildlife from the project have been an increase in wildlife and occurrence of wildlife in new places. Also, the community has more knowledge about wildlife and there is less poaching. Some negative aspects in the area include some illegal grazing and poaching, mostly by Maasai (semi-nomadic tribals). There have been conflicts between wildlife and farmers, with elephants, zebras and bushpigs raiding fields, and lions killing livestock. At the moment, there is no compensation for the farmers who get their fields destroyed or lose their livestock.

Bulte and Horan (2003) developed a model of open-access wildlife exploitation, habitat conservation and agriculture, in which farmers may either hunt for wildlife or grow crops. They showed that increasing wildlife conservation may well be Pareto-superior to equilibria in which agriculture dominates.

A bio-economic model, formulated by Fischer et al. (2005) to analyse community incentives for wildlife management before and after CAMPFIRE, a programme which was created to institute sustainable management practices for wildlife, land and other natural resources by rural communities in Zimbabwe in 1989, showed that resource sharing with local communities can have ambiguous effects on both conservation incentives and welfare. Two agents influence the wildlife stock: a parks agency, which determines hunting quotas, and a local community, which chooses to either collaborate with or discourage poachers from outside the area. Wildlife generates economic benefits both from the sale of hunting licenses and from non-consumptive tourism; however, it also intrudes on the agricultural rents of the local community. Since a larger wildlife stock reduces agricultural returns, the community will engage in anti-poaching efforts only if they reap benefits from wildlife activities. The conservation incentives depend critically on three factors: the type of resource activity that generates the shared profits, the extent to which these shared profits outweigh agricultural losses from additional wildlife, and the way that the parks agency responds to profit sharing and whether the community internalizes this response.

Evidence from some areas in Zimbabwe indicates that poaching was rampant prior to CAMPFIRE. Post CAMPFIRE, poaching has been drastically reduced in some areas as the neighbouring communities started reaping economic benefits from legal wildlife utilization and consequently began to make public arrests of commercial poachers (Child et al., 1997). However, in other areas, poaching subsided only temporarily with CAMPFIRE and then bounced back after a few years.

Objective

Based upon the literature reviewed, the following objectives are set for the present research work:

- To theoretically analyse the impact of permitting sales from captive-tiger breeding farms, in China, on the population of wild tigers in India. More specifically, parameterization of the tiger survival functions in the context of India.
- To show how the application of Community-Based Wildlife Management (CBWM), in the 'buffer' zone of a tiger reserve

and in migration corridors between tiger reserves in India, would aid tiger conservation and would also result in the existence of a viable and resilient wild tiger population.

Domestication of Tigers

The illegal trade in poached skins between India, Nepal and China is the most significant immediate threat to the survival of tigers in the wild. Even though international trade in tigers has been prohibited since 1975 with the listing of the species under Appendix I of CITES, with the exception of the Siberian sub-species which was added in 1987, and China has imposed a domestic ban on trade in tiger parts and its derivatives in 1993, the lucrative trade in tiger parts still continues.

The domestic ban on trade in tiger parts in China coincided with the onset of domestication of tigers with the establishment of tiger breeding facilities. In recent years, captive breeding of tigers has accelerated to the point where the captive tiger population exceeds 4,000. Tiger farming can be looked upon as a supply-side approach to conservation of wild tigers, which seeks to eliminate or reduce the illegal killing of wild tigers and aid their survival by meeting all the demand for tiger products.

It is a common knowledge that organized criminal networks are attracted to wildlife crime because it offers high profits with little risk of detection and prosecution. The presence of captive-bred tigers would result in an increase in the total supply of tiger products, thus, reducing their price and making poaching a less profitable enterprise. However, the introduction of farmed tigers in the market would reduce the 'stigma effect' associated with the prohibition of tiger trade.

It is argued that the costs of raising tigers in captivity are considerable due to which the farmers are unable to undercut suppliers of illegal wildlife products. However, the costs of processing and marketing poached animals, such as the payment of bribes, opportunity cost of conviction etc., are underestimated. The existence of tiger farms despite a trade ban indicate that the associated costs of captive tiger breeding may not be burdensome and there may be benefits specific to tiger farming, like paid public viewing.

Despite the outlawing of killing tigers in India in 1972 and the prohibition of international trade in tiger parts in 1975 under CITES, poaching of tigers continues at an alarming rate in India. With the demand for tiger products miniscule in India, poaching is carried out mainly to meet the demand outside the Indian borders, particularly China. With the supply from captive-breeding farms meeting the demand for tiger products, poaching in India is expected to fall with the legalizing of sale of tiger products from captive-tiger farms.

Using the mathematical bio-economic model developed by Abbott and Kooten to evaluate whether domestication of tigers would aid conservation, we try to evaluate the potential of this domestication of tigers in East Asia to support conservation in India.

Bio-economic Model of Tiger Exploitation

The forgoing model neglects the dynamics of tiger reproduction, habitat loss and so on. A bio-economic analysis begins by supposing that the population of wild tigers x is characterized by the following single-species growth function with Allee effect:

$$G(x(t)) = gx(t)\left[\frac{x(t)}{m} - 1\right]\left[1 - \frac{x(t)}{m}\right] \quad (1)$$

where m is the minimum viable population, K is the population carrying capacity and g is the intrinsic growth rate.

The harvest function is given by a square-root variant of the standard constant returns to scale Schaefer production function:

$$H(x, L_P) = \theta x^{1/2} L_P^{1/2} \quad (2)$$

where, θ is the catchability coefficient and L_P is the fraction of time spent on poaching.

The expected payoff to the poacher from both legitimate activities and poaching is

$$E[u(x, L_P)] = (1 - \pi)[w(1-L_P) + p\theta x^{1/2} L_P^{1/2}] + \pi[w(1-L_P) - \epsilon] \quad (3)$$

where, π is the probability of apprehension, p is the price of tiger parts, w is the wage rate in other employment and ϵ is the penalty faced on apprehension.

The first term of equation (3) is the payoff to a poacher who avoids detection weighted by the probability of avoiding detection, while the second part is the payoff to a poacher who gets caught weighted by the probability of apprehension.

A rational expected utility maximizing poacher will choose L_P, such that the marginal benefit of time spent poaching is equal to its opportunity cost given by the wage rate.

$$\frac{1}{2}\theta x^{1/2} L_P^{1/2} (1-\pi) p = w \quad (4)$$

Solving for L_P and substituting in equation (2) gives us

$$L_P = \left[\frac{\theta(1-\pi)p}{w}\right]^2 \chi \quad (5)$$

$$H(x) = \frac{\theta^2 (1-\pi) x p}{2w} \quad (6)$$

$$\theta = \sqrt{\frac{2Hw}{(1-\pi)xp}} \quad (7)$$

Tiger Survivability Function

Whether tigers are likely to survive in the wild can be determined by the sign on the following differential equation:

The tiger survivability function is given by:

$$\frac{dx}{dt} = G(x) - H(x) = gx(t)\left[\frac{x(t)}{m} - 1\right]\left[1 - \frac{x(t)}{K}\right] - \frac{\theta^2(1-\pi)xp}{2w} \quad (8)$$

If it can be shown that the growth of wild tigers exceeds their (illegal) harvests, so that $\dot{x} > 0$, then tiger numbers will increase over time, while they will decline if $\dot{x} < 0$. Once the relations in equation (8) are appropriately defined, this differential equation can be thought of as a tiger survivability function. If demand is perfectly elastic so that p is fixed, the survival function can easily be parameterized. If demand is not perfectly elastic, then price is a function of output and we replace p with $p(h)$. As discussed later, the case where the output from tiger farms affects the price of tigers is the one of most interest, because, if this is not so, tiger farming has no effect on wild tigers and policymakers need to think of strategies to save wild tigers that are independent of decisions regarding the legitimacy of tiger farms.

The illegal supply of tigers is given by $(1 - \pi)h$,

$$S(p) = \frac{\theta^2(1-\pi)^2 xp}{2w} \quad (9)$$

Assuming a linear-derived demand function for wild tigers, $D(p) = \alpha - \beta p$, with $\alpha, \beta > 0$. Equating demand and supply and solving for price and substituting in equation (8) gives us,

$$\theta = gx(t)\left[\frac{x(t)}{m} - 1\right]\left[1 - \frac{x(t)}{K}\right] - \frac{\alpha\theta^2(1-\pi)x}{(1-\pi)^2\theta^2 x + 2w\beta} \quad (10)$$

With the inclusion of sale of captive-bred tigers, the supply of tigers changes to:

$$S(p) = \frac{\theta^2(1-\pi)^2 xp}{2w} + \Omega \quad (11)$$

If tigers are farmed, there will be some number Ω produced by the farms. The supply of tigers will differ from equation (8) because legal sales will need to be added to the illegal supply:

$$\dot{x} = gx(t)\left[\frac{x(t)}{m} - 1\right]\left[1 - \frac{x(t)}{K}\right] - \frac{(\alpha - \Omega)\theta^2(1-\pi)x}{\theta^2(1-\pi)^2 x + 2w\beta} \quad (12)$$

Partially differentiating equation (12) with respect to Ω gives the impact of sale of captive-bred tigers on the dynamics of tiger population, which is seen to be positive.

$$\frac{d\dot{x}}{d\Omega} = \frac{\theta^2(1-\pi)x}{\theta^2(1-\pi)^2 x + 2w\beta} > 0 \quad (13)$$

The direct effect of permitting the sale of farmed tigers, on the survival of wild tigers, is seen to be positive, that is, permitting sale of farmed tigers would lead to an increase in the rate of population growth of wild tigers. But the overall impact of sale of farmed tigers on the population of wild tigers is uncertain, and depends on whether supply of farmed tigers outweighs the stigma effect, which is given by the change in α due to the presence or absence of trade ban on tiger products. This can be shown by partially differentiating in equation (12) with respect to (α – Ω).

$$\frac{\partial \dot{x}}{\partial(\alpha - \Omega)} > 0 \, if \;\; \Omega > \alpha \quad (14)$$

$$\frac{\partial \dot{x}}{\partial(\alpha - \Omega)} > 0 \, if \;\; \alpha > \Omega \quad (15)$$

Tiger Survival Parameterization

From the theoretical model, we find that the rate of change in tiger population increases as a result of increased habitat, conservation payments, increased anti-poaching enforcement and a trade ban that operates through the stigma effect. But this says nothing about the survivability of wild tigers. If wild tiger populations are declining, an increase in these parameters might only reduce the rate of decline. Further, the effect of sales of captive-bred tigers is uncertain as it depends on the size of the stigma effect parameter (α) and the sales of farmed tigers (Ω). Therefore, we consider plausible parameter values to provide some notion of the potential impact of various policies on wild tiger populations (Table 11.2). Our model cannot take into account sub-species details regarding reproduction, habitat and minimum viable populations, because, while some sub-species and regional demand information is available, too much is lacking for such a detailed analysis.

In rainforests, tigers occur at densities of one to two tigers per 100 km^2 because of low prey densities; in other regions with higher prey densities and/or smaller tiger subspecies, habitat can support an average of as many as five adult tigers per 100 km (Save the Tiger, 2009). Dietary requirements, prey densities and other factors determine the size of habitat required to support tigers. Habitats can support an average of five adult tigers per 100 km^2, in areas with higher prey densities and/or smaller tiger sub-species (Sanderson et al., 2006). Tiger occupancy in India is 81,881 km^2 (WII, 2012); this habitat can support 4094 tigers.

To maintain a minimum viable population of six breeding females (perhaps as few as 20 animals total), reserves need to be a minimum of about 500 km^2 for Bengal tigers, since prey are generally abundant in their native habitat, to more than 2,000 km^2 for the Amur (Siberian) tiger. Thus, habitat and prey availability are important factors affecting wild tiger populations. With 39 tiger reserves in India (MoEF) and a minimum population of approximately 20 tigers in each to ensure survival (Sanderson et al., 2006) implies a minimum viable population of 780 tigers for India.

To determine the growth constant g, we need an estimate of the growth rate of a wild tiger population that is not subject to poaching. One such estimate is provided by Sanderson et al. (2006) who indicate that only 20 per cent of newborn tigers will have the

Table 11.2:
Parameterization of tiger survival

Parameter	*Description*	*Value*	*Estimation*
K	Carrying capacity	4,094	Habitats can support an average of 5 adult tigers per 100 km^2, in areas with higher prey densities and/or smaller tiger sub-species (Sanderson et al., 2006). Tiger occupancy in India is 81,881 km^2 (WII, 2010); this habitat can support 4094 tigers.
M	Minimum viable population	780	With 39 tiger reserves in India (MoEF) and a minimum population of approximately 20 tigers in each to ensure survival (Sanderson et al., 2006) implies a minimum viable population of 780 tigers for India.
P	Price of poached tiger	\$20 (local poachers); \$20,000 (organized gangs engaged in wildlife crime); \$56,000 (traders)	Local poachers' and organized gangs engaged in wildlife crime →WPSI, 2001. Traders in China →EIA, 2009 (see Appendix A11.1).
Π	Probability of apprehension	0.1	To reach an estimate of the magnitude of the poaching of tigers in India, the customs authorities multiply known offences by 10 to estimate the size of an illegal trade (WPSI, 2012). This implies a 0.1 probability of apprehension.
w	Wage rate in other employment	₹73.57 (≈\$1.5)	Based on the report, 'Wage Rates in Rural India, 2008–09', by the Labour Bureau, Ministry of Labour and Employment, Government of India, the average wage over the agricultural and non-agricultural occupations, and men, women and children is ₹73.57 (Appendix A11.2).
ϵ	Penalty	₹10,000 (≈\$200)	Wildlife (Protection) Act, 1972 [Amendment Act, 2002], Ministry of Environment and Forests (Appendix A11.3).

(Table 11.2 Contd)

(Table 11.2 Contd)

Parameter	*Description*	*Value*	*Estimation*
g	Intrinsic growth rate	0.087	Sanderson et al. (2006) estimated that only 20 per cent of newborns will have an opportunity to breed, annual reproduction averages 0.61 per young female and there are 2.5 females per male. This implies an intrinsic growth rate of 0.087 (0.2×0.61×2.5/3.5)
θ	Catchability parameter	0.3	Calculate using eq^n (7). H = 936 (WPSI) (see Appendix A11.4), x = 1706 (MoEF), p = \$20 (since poaching is undertaken by locals who have an intimate knowledge of the forests).
α	Demand intercept (measuring the stigma effect)	104	Using the demand function: $D(p) = \alpha - \beta p$. $D(p)$ = 104 (TRAFFIC → on an average a minimum of 104 tigers have entered trade every year between 2000 and 2010); p = \$56,000 (value of a tiger to the traders in China).

Source: Created by the authors from the present study.

opportunity to breed, annual reproduction averages 0.61 per young female, and there are 2.5 females per male. Then the growth constant is $g = 0.087$ (=0.2×0.61×2.5/3.5).

Economic data are even more difficult to find. Data from local poachers and organized gangs engaged in wildlife crimes (WPSI, 2001) and traders in China (EIA, 2009) (see Appendix A11.1) indicate that wild tigers were harvested in India at a value of \$56,000 per tiger. There is evidence that poachers working in the forest only receive about \$20 per tiger, but that those with highly sophisticated criminal gangs receive considerably more. We choose a price of p = \$20,000 per wild tiger, but also consider scenarios with lower prices to provide some notion of the directional effect of prices.

To reach an estimate of the magnitude of the poaching of tigers in India, the customs authorities multiply known offences by 10 to estimate the size of an illegal trade (WPSI, 2012). This implies a 0.1 probability of apprehension. Each tiger produces between

5 and 12 kg of dry bone (Ng and Nemora, 2007: 8); thus, 200 wild tigers would yield 1,000–2,400 kg of bone. Over the period from 1999 to 2005, an average of 60 kg of tiger bone was seized annually, or 2.5–6.0 per cent of the 1992 illegal harvest. We assume a baseline detection rate of $\pi = 0.1$, approximately halfway between 2.5 and 6 per cent.

Using the demand function: $D(p) = \alpha - \beta p$, $D(p) = 104$ (TRAFFIC: on an average a minimum of 104 tigers have entered trade every year between 2000 and 2010); $p = \$56{,}000$ (value of a tiger to the traders in China). To determine the stigma effect, it is necessary to know something about the demand function and sales of tigers before and after the Chinese domestic trade ban. Given that 23 tigers were marketed in shops in Indonesia (Ng and Nemora, 2007) and there might be 500 tigers in that country (Table 11.1), we get a poaching rate of 4.5 per cent. If this rate applied just before the trade ban when there were some 7,000 tigers, then 315 tigers would have been harvested and sold. After the ban, when there were an assumed 6,000 tigers, 104 would be sold.

Given the complexity of tiger protection, our results suggest that, because habitat is being eroded, neither legitimizing trade in products from captive-bred tigers nor increased enforcement is likely able to prevent wild tigers from being extirpated. Rather, a cocktail of policies will be needed to give wild tigers a chance of surviving. Clearly, if governance institutions found in developed countries (rule of law, low levels of corruption, etc.) characterized range states, the tiger would survive in the wild. These kinds of institutions lead to rates of detection that exceed those required to preserve wild tigers. Our results also indicate that conservation payments from rich countries to poor range states can be effective in protecting tigers, and that such payments need not be onerous. But again, lack of adequate institutions precludes writing enforceable contracts that protect habitat and prevent poaching of tigers.

In the absence of the required institutions or effective community-based natural resource management regimes that inhibit illegal takings, our results indicate that the sale of tiger products from tiger farms could reduce poaching sufficiently to enable wild tigers to reproduce faster than they are killed. In the absence of other measures (additional food or habitat), a combination of increased enforcement and legal sales offers the best chance of wild tiger survival. However, the loss of quality habitat makes it extremely difficult to design an effective strategy for saving wild tigers.

Community-based Wildlife Management

With an estimated 40,000 tigers at the beginning of the 20th century, the number of tigers in India continuously declined in the absence of legal constraints. The gravity of the situation was first realized when the first all-India tiger census revealed the existence of only 1,827 tigers in India. In order to combat the declining tiger population, the Government of India enacted the Wildlife Protection Act of 1972 and launched 'Project Tiger' in 1973.

Project Tiger seeks to conserve tigers by protecting their habitat and minimizing human interference with creation of tiger reserves. Launched with nine tiger reserves, Project Tiger currently has 39 tiger reserves under its umbrella, with four more in the process of being added to this count. It followed a 'core–buffer' model, wherein the 'core' area is devoid of any human presence or activity and the 'buffer' area is subjected to conservation oriented land use only.

Even though this traditional way of conserving tigers, through the creation of national parks and reserves known as the 'fences and fines', may have aided tiger conservation to a certain extent, it has also displaced communities from land that was traditionally theirs. While the wildlife, on the other hand, could roam freely in the surrounding areas, destroying crops and threatening livestock and people. Thus, the creation of national parks and reserves created a conflict between wildlife conservation and agricultural development.

CBWM seeks to resolve this problem by making tigers an important engine of economic development. It is based on the premise that giving local people a stake in tiger conservation would increase their incentives to conserve tigers. The core elements of CBWM are development, conservation and sustainable land use.

Migration corridors connecting reserves are essential to the conservation of tigers. Genetically, in most of the tiger reserves, the tiger population is too small to maintain long-term viability and persistence. Migration corridors maintain connectivity which allow greater gene flow between sub-populations and mitigate further inbreeding depression in these populations without the cost of translocations. Maintaining migration corridors between reserves is also necessary to achieve other important conservation targets, such as to increase the resilience of tiger populations and maintain the natural ecology and behaviour of tigers for long-term persistence.

A landscape approach to conservation that goes beyond reserve boundaries is vital to the long-term conservation of tigers (Wikramanayake et al., 2010). A possible step towards such conservation can be the protection of the migration corridors between reserves and the application of CBWM in these corridors as well as the 'buffer' zone in tiger reserves, as it would not only meet the tiger's ecological and demographic requirements, and avoid the genetic consequences of isolated tiger populations but also create a synthesis between conservation and development.

Communities when viewed as small and homogenous units are seen as better positioned to realize conservation goals, and as necessary allies in the expansion of conservation beyond national park boundaries and into human-inhabited rural landscapes (Igoe, 2004). Providing the right incentives, like sharing revenue from wildlife services, can induce communities to engage in conservation activities. In the absence of such incentives, the presence of tigers may be regarded as a menace by the local communities and they may be less inclined to alert the authorities to poachers and more likely aid the poachers or poison the carcasses of livestock killed by tigers. The anti-poaching effort exerted by the communities makes poaching more difficult and expensive since poachers cannot count on local support, thus aiding conservation through reduced poaching.

Using a model, devised by Fischer, Muchapondwa and Sterner to evaluate the incentives for wildlife management before and after CAMPFIRE, we can see that sharing revenue from non-consumptive wildlife services like benign tourism, between park agency and local communities provides an incentive to the local communities to engage in anti-poaching activities provided the share of revenue received by the communities is greater than the cost of anti-poaching activities, they engage in. The positive impact of an increase in anti-poaching activities on tiger conservation due to the contribution of the local communities is shown using the model, used in the previous chapter, devised by Abbott and Kooten to evaluate the impact of tiger farming on tiger conservation.

Model

The bio-economic model comprises one agent (a local community), one control variable (anti-poaching effort) and a stock variable (tiger biomass). Economic rents are generated from non-consumptive wildlife services, like tourism, which is distributed between the park agency and the local community, and from agricultural production, which solely benefits the community. It is assumed that the local communities do not benefit directly from poaching proceeds, rather they choose the degree to which they collaborate with or oppose poachers, based on their perception of the value of tigers to them.

The 'core' area of the national reserve is devoid of human interference, while the local community has user rights over the 'buffer' zone and the migrating corridors between reserves. The main agricultural alternatives outside the national park are livestock and crop production. The tigers tend to wander outside the park into the surrounding areas, threatening livestock. The ecological interaction between tigers and agricultural productivity is assumed to be unidirectional and is represented by a revenue function that is declining and convex in the stock of tigers (x), that is, $R'(x) < 0$ and $R'(x) > 0$.

The revenue from tourism is increasing in the stock of tigers, that is, $T'(x) > 0$; $T'(x) < 0$ and $T(0) = 0$. The local communities get a share of the profits from benign tourism (τ). We assume that τ is fixed through time and $0 < \tau < 1$. The remaining profit goes to the park agency.

The anti-poaching activities (A) undertaken by the community involve costs, like value of time lost, wages for private enforcement agents, and others, and is represented by a function that is increasing and convex in positive effort, that is, $C'(A) > 0$ and $C'(A) > 0$.

The community's utility function is the sum of revenues earned from agriculture and tourism minus the costs of undertaking anti-poaching efforts, that is,

$$V(x,A) = R(x) + \tau T(x) - C(A) \tag{16}$$

The local community maximizes the present value of its income by choosing A subject to the dynamics of the tiger population.

The growth in the stock of tigers is given by

$$\theta = G(x) - H(x,A) \tag{17}$$

where $G(x)$ is the natural growth function and $H(x,A)$ is the harvest function, representing the loss due to poaching. The harvest function is increasing in the stock of tigers and decreasing in anti-poaching effort, that is, $H_X(x,A) > 0$ and $H_A(x,A) < 0$. It is important to note that poaching will never be zero no matter how large A is, since a certain amount of poaching cannot be detected even with the co-operation of the local communities.

The current value Hamiltonian is

$$Y = V(x,A) + \mu[G(x) - H(x,A)] \tag{18}$$

The first-order condition with respect to anti-poaching effort is

$$-C'(A) + \mu[-H_A(x,A)] = 0 \tag{19}$$

The dynamics of the shadow value of the tiger stock to the community is defined by

$$\frac{\partial \mu}{\partial t} = -[R_x(x) + \tau T_x(x) + \mu(G'(x) - H_x(x,A))] \tag{20}$$

Steady state implies $\frac{\partial \mu}{\partial t} = 0$ and the shadow value of tiger equals

$$\mu^* = [R_x(x) + \tau T_x(x)] / [\delta - G'(x) + H_x(x,A)] \tag{21}$$

From equation (19), we see that anti-poaching effort is strictly increasing in the shadow value of tigers to the community, that is, $\frac{dA}{d\mu} > 0$, and from equation (21) we see that the equilibrium shadow value of tigers is unambiguously increasing in τ, that is, $\frac{d\mu}{d\tau} > 0$. Thus, anti-poaching effort is strictly increasing in τ, that is, $\frac{dA}{d\tau} > 0$.

The impact of anti-poaching on tiger population can be shown by:

$$d\theta/d\pi = \theta^2 xp/2w = \alpha\theta^2 x/[\theta^2(1 - \pi)^2 x + 2w\beta] > 0 \tag{22}$$

Hence, sharing tourism revenues increases anti-poaching efforts, which in turn imply an increase in the probability of apprehension (π), and thus, aid conservation.

Conclusion

Domestication of Tigers

The bio-economic model used for simulating the domestication of tigers scenario in India indicates that permitting sales from captive-bred tiger farms can aid the conservation of tigers. It has the potential to curb the illegal trade in tiger parts by meeting the demand for tiger parts. Patients who have been unable to obtain their medicines legally have no choice but to go to illegal channels for tiger bones. If legal channels exist and patients can legally get tiger bone for their medicine, the motivations to purchase tiger bones from illegal sources can be minimized. Also, an increase in supply can also lower the price of tiger products. Thus, it can result in compressing the huge profits made by smugglers and poachers and poaching of tigers is less attractive. This type of approach has successfully worked in the conservation of certain endangered species, like crocodiles in 1970s and vicuna in 1988.

To date, conservation measures have focused on curbing demand for tiger parts, by combating poaching and securing the tiger's habitat. Unfortunately, the efforts in these areas have not borne fruit, since poaching is still rampant and the tiger habitat is eroding due to the human pressures. Management of the supply side of trade in tigers and their parts remains largely unexplored.

However, permitting sales of captive-bred tiger farms alone is not sufficient, it must be complemented by increased enforcement to ensure that the parts being sold are indeed from captive tigers and that poached tigers are not 'laundered' into the stock of captive-bred tigers. A possible solution to this could be enforcing an animal registration programme similar to the one implemented in Europe and North America for cattle. To increase the effectiveness of legalizing sales from tiger farms, we can introduce the incentive to defend property rights by granting exclusive rights to certain farmers to manage tiger farms and sell tiger products. However, the loss of tiger habitat makes the designing of an effective strategy for the survival of tigers in the wild very difficult.

Community-based Wildlife Management

A CBWM programme wherein the local communities share the revenue generated by non-consumptive wildlife services, like tourism, leads to increase in anti-poaching effort undertaken by the communities. Since the poachers base their decisions regarding the harvest on the amount of effort exerted and the cost of undertaking poaching activities, an increase in anti-poaching activities by the local communities will curtail poaching, as it is costlier for them to undertake such activities and the effort required is higher as well. But we must keep in mind that the success of such a programme is contingent upon the additional revenues generated from wildlife services being higher than the cost of intrusion, that is, $\tau T'(x) > -R'(x)$, for if it is not so then the local communities have no incentive to carry out anti-poaching activities as it is costlier for them to do so. The success of CBWM in aiding conservation depends upon the design of the revenue sharing system; the revenue earned by the local communities from wildlife services must be higher than the cost of anti-poaching effort exerted and the cost of intrusion.

A way forward from the current 'fences and fines' can be the implementation of CBWM in the buffer zone of a tiger reserve and in the migration corridors between reserves. This will not only solve the field staff shortage faced by the tiger reserves under 'Project Tiger', but will also provide the community an incentive to engage in anti-poaching activities and since tigers will no longer be looked at as pests but as an asset. Since local people and tribesmen are usually hired by the organized criminal gangs engaged in wildlife crime to carry out poaching, the increase in anti-poaching activities by the local communities and the refusal to engage in poaching by the locals would increase the cost and effort faced by the organized criminals and make poaching less attractive as not only will the costs increase but the risk as well since the probability of apprehension will increase as well. Also, maintaining and protecting the migrating corridors between reserves is essential for the long-run survival of the existing wild tiger population, as they increase the viability and resilience of the tigers by overcoming the genetic consequences of an in-bred tiger population, which would result due to isolated reserves and populations, and it would also reduce the translocation cost.

Appendix A11.1

Table A11.1:
Indian tiger trade value in China

Item	*Price Range*
Full tiger skin	Approx. $11,764–$22,058
Tiger teeth	Approx. $661 [1 tiger → 30 teeth]
Tiger bone	Approx. $882–$1,176 per kg [1 tiger → 12 kg]

Source: EIA (2009).

Appendix A11.2

WAGE RATES IN RURAL INDIA (2008–09) *Labour Bureau, Ministry of Labour and Employment, Government of India, 2010*

Table A11.2a:
All-India annual average daily wage rates in agricultural occupations during the year 2008–09 (occupation-wise)

(in ₹)

Occupation	*Men*	*Women*	*Children*
Ploughing	102.90	55.43	–
Sowing	90.00	65.00	48.91
Weeding	80.15	68.02	49.46
Transplanting	83.28	71.43	52.51
Harvesting	87.05	71.58	50.49
Winnowing	81.23	65.08	43.40
Threshing	85.06	67.66	46.06
Picking	81.10	66.37	45.78
Herdsman	53.48	41.32	36.22
Well-digging	116.28	63.47	–
Cane crushing	87.27	61.23	–

Table A11.2b:
All-India average daily wage rates in non-agricultural occupations during the year 2008–09 (occupation-wise)

(in ₹)

Occupation	Men	Women	Children
Carpenter	144.60	–	–
Blacksmith	107.21	–	–
Cobbler	79.59	–	–
Mason	160.30	–	–
Tractor driver	113.13	–	–
Sweeper	63.40	63.42	–
Unskilled labourer (un-specified)	86.43	65.66	42.03

Source: Labour Bureau, Ministry of Labour and Employment, Government of India, 2010.

Appendix A11.3

WILDLIFE (Protection) ACT, 1972
[Amendment Act, 2002]

Ministry of Environment and Forests, Government of India

- An offence involving a species listed in Schedule I or Part II of Schedule II, or an offence committed within a sanctuary or natural park, attracts a mandatory prison term of three years, which may extend to seven years. Mandatory fine of ₹10,000. For subsequent offence, the prison term remains the same, mandatory fine of at least ₹25,000.
- An offence committed inside the core area of a Tiger reserve, attracts a mandatory prison term of three years, extendable to seven years and a fine of ₹50,000 extendable to ₹2 lakh. In case of subsequent conviction of this nature, there is an imprisonment of at least seven years and a fine of ₹5 lakh, which may extend to ₹50 lakh.

Source: Wildlife (Protection) Act, 1972, Amendment Act, 2002.

Appendix A11.4

Table A11.3:
India's tiger poaching crisis

Year	*Poaching and Seizures*
1994	95
1995	121
1996	52
1997	88
1998	39
1999	81
2000	52
2001	72
2002	46
2003	38
2004	38
2005	46
2006	37
2007	27
2008	29
2009	32
2010	30
2011	13
TOTAL	**936**

Source: WPSI (2011).

References

Abbott, B., Cornelius, G. and Kooten, V. 2011. 'Can Domestication of Wildlife Lead to Conservation? The Economics of Tiger Farming in China', *Ecological Economics*, 70(4): 721–28.

Ali, F.M. 2009. 'Indian Tiger Park "Has No Tigers"', BBC News, Bhopal.

Atkins, J.P., Burdon, D., Elliott, M. and Gregory, A.J. 2011. 'Management of the Marine Environment: Integrating Ecosystem Services and Societal Benefits with the DPSIR Framework in a Systems Approach', *Marine Pollution Bulletin*, 62(2): 215–26.

Badola, R., 1999. 'People and Protected Areas in India', *Unasylva*, 50: 67.

Barbier, E.B. 2001. 'The Economics of Tropical Deforestation And Land Use: An Introduction to The Special Issue', *Land Economics*, 77(2): 155–71.

Bulte, E.H. and R. Damian. 2005. 'An Economic Assessment of Wildlife Farming and Conservation', *Conservation Biology*, 19(4): 1222–33.

———. 2007. 'The Economics of Wildlife Farming and Endangered Species Conservation', *Ecological Economics*, 62: 461–72.

Bulte, E.H. and Horan, R.D. 2003. 'Habitat Conservation, Wildlife Extraction and Agricultural Expansion', *Journal of Environmental Economics and Management*, 45(1): 109–27.

Butler, R.A. and Laurance, W.F. 2008. 'New Strategies for Conserving Tropical Forests', *Trends in Ecology & Evolution*, 23(9), 469–472.

Carbone, C. and Gittleman, J.L. 2002. 'A Common Rule for the Scaling of Carnivore Density', *Science*, 295: 2273–76.

Chapron, G., Miquelle, D.G., Lambert, A., Goodrich, J.M., Legendre, S. and Clobert, J. 2008. 'The Impact on Tigers of Poaching Versus Prey Depletion', *Journal of Applied Ecology*, 45: 1667–74.

Child, B., Ward, S. and Tavengwa, T. 1997. 'Zimbabwe's CAMPFIRE Programme: Natural Resource Management by the People', *IUCN-ROSA Environmental Issues Series No. 2. Harare, Zimbabwe: World Conservation Union–Regional Office for South Africa.*

Chundawat, R.S., Habib, B., Karanth, U., Kawanishi, K., Ahmad Khan, J., Lynam, T. et al. 2008. *Panthera Tigris*. IUCN. 2009. IUCN Red List of Threatened Species, Version 2009.1.

———. 2011. *Panthera Tigris*. IUCN. 2011. IUCN Red List of Threatened Species. Version 2012.1.

Damania, R. and Bulte, E.H. 2007. 'The Economics of Wildlife Farming and Endangered Species Conservation. *Ecological Economics*', 62(3): 461–72.

Damania, R., Stringer, R., Karanth, K. and Stith, B. 2003. 'The Economics of Protecting Tiger Populations: Linking Household Behavior to Poaching and Prey Depletion', *Land Economics*, 79(2): 198–216.

Damayanti, E.K. 2007. *Legality of National Parks and Involvement of Local People: Case Studies in Java, Indonesia and Kerala, India*. Thesis, Graduate School of Life and Environmental Sciences. University of Tsukuba, Japan.

Davidar, P., Sahoo, S., Mammen, P.C., Acharya, P., Puyravaud, J.-P., Arjunan, M., Garrigues, J.P. and Roessingh, K. 2010. Assessing the Extent and Causes of Forest Degradation in India: Where Do We Stand? *Biological Conservation*, 143(12): 2937–44.

Dinerstein, E., Loucks, C., Heydlauff, A., Wikramanayake, E., Bryja, G., Forrest, J. et al. 2006. *Setting Priorities for the Conservation and Recovery of Wild Tigers: 2005-2015. A User's Guide*. Washington, D.C., New York: WWF, WCS, Smithsonian and NFWF-STF.

Dinerstein, E., Loucks, C., Wikramanayake, E., Ginsberg, J., Sanderson, E., Seidensticker, J. et al. 2007. 'The Fate of Wild Tigers', *BioScience*, 57(6): 508–14.

Dinerstein, E., Wikramanayake, E., Robinson, J., Karanth, U., Rabinowitz, A., Olson, D. et al. 1997. *A Framework for Identifying High Priority Areas and Actions for the Conservation of Tigers in the Wild*. Washington, D.C.: World Wildlife Fund-US and Wildlife Conservation Society.

Elliott, M. 2002. 'The Role of the DPSIR Approach and Conceptual Models in Marine Environmental Management: An Example for Offshore Wind Power', *Marine Pollution Bulletin*, 44: iii–vii.

Fischer, C. 2004. 'The Complex Interactions of Markets for Endangered Species Products', *Journal of Environmental Economics and Management*, 48(2): 926–53.

European Environment Agency. 1999. *Environmental Indicators: Typology and Overview*. Copenhegan: European Environment Agency.

Environment Investigation Agency (EIA). 1996. 'The Political Wilderness: India's Tiger Crisis', EIA, London.

———. 2009. 'A Deadly Game of Cat and Mouse: How Tiger Criminals give China the Run-around', EIA, London.

———. 2010. 'Enforcement not Extinction: Zero Tolerance on Tiger Trade'.

EIA and Wildlife Protection Society of India (WPSI). 2006. 'Skinning the Cat: Crime and Politics of the Big Cat Skin Trade', EIA, London and WPSI, India.

Fischer, C., Edwin, M. and Thomas, S. 2005. 'Bioeconomic Model of Community Incentives for Wildlife Management Before and After CAMPFIRE'. Resources for the Future. Discussion Paper 05–06.

Gadgil, M. and Thapar, R. 1990. 'Human-ecology in India: Some Historical Perspectives', *Interdisciplinary Science Reviews*, 15(3): 209–23.

Gratwicke, B., Bennett, E.L., Broad, S., Christie, S., Dutton, A., Gabriel, G. et al. 2008. 'The World Can't Have Wild Tigers and Eat Them, Too', *Conservation Biology*, 22(1): 222–23.

Guha, R. 2007. *India after Gandhi: The History of the World's Largest Democracy*. New York: Macmillan.

Igoe, J. 2004. *Conservation and Globalization: A Study of National Parks and Indigenous Communities from East Africa to South Dakota*. Belmont, CA, USA: Thomson/ Wadsworth.

Jago-on, K.A.B., Kaneko, S., Fujikura, R., Fujiwara, A., Imai, T., Matsumoto, T. et al. 2009. 'Urbanization and Subsurface Environmental Issues: An Attempt at DPSIR Model Application in Asian Cities', *Science of the Total Environment*, 407(9): 3089–104.

Jhala, Y.V., Gopal, R. and Qureshi, Q. 2008. Status of Tigers, Co-predators and Prey in India. National Tiger Conservation Authority, Ministry of Environment and Forests, Government of India and the Wildlife Institute of India, Dehradun, 164.

Jhala, Y.V., Qureshi, Q., Gopal, R. and Sinha, P.R. 2011. *Status of the Tigers, Copredators, and Prey in India, 2010*. National Tiger Conservation Authority.

Govt. of India, New Delhi, and Wildlife Institute of India, Dehradun. Karanth, K.K., Curran, L.M. and Reuning-Scherer, J.D. 2006. 'Village Size and Forest Disturbance in Bhadra Wildlife Sanctuary, Western Ghats, India', *Biological Conservation*, 128: 147–57.

Karanth, K.U. 2003. 'Tiger Ecology and Conservation in the Indian Subcontinent', *Journal of the Bombay Natural History Society*, 100(2, 3): 169–89.

———. 2006. *Tiger Tales: Tracking the Big Cat across Asia*.New Delhi, New York: Penguin Books.

Karanth, K.U. and Chellam, R. 2009. 'Carnivore Conservation at the Crossroads', *Oryx*, 43: 1–2.

Karanth, K.U. and Gopal, R. 2005. 'An Ecology-based Policy Framework for Humanetiger Coexistence in India', in R. Woodroffe, S. Thirgood and A. Rabinowitz (eds), *People and Wildlife: Conflict or Coexistence?* (pp. 373–87). New York: Cambridge University Press.

Karanth, K.U., Gopalaswamy, A.M., Kumar, N.S., Delampady, M., Nichols, J.D., Seidensticker, J., Noon, B.R. and Pimm, S.L. 2011. 'Counting India's Wild Tigers Reliably', *Science*, 332: 791.

Karanth, K.U., Nichols, J.D., Kumar, N.S., Link, W.A. and Hines, J.E. 2004. 'Tigers and Their Prey: Predicting Carnivore Densities from Prey Abundance'. *Proceedings of the National Academy of Sciences of the United States of America*, 101: 4854–58.

Karanth, K.U. and Stith, B.M. 1999. 'Prey Depletion as a Critical Determinant of Tiger Population Viability', in J. Seidensticker, S. Christie and P. Jackson (eds), *Riding the Tiger: Tiger Conservation in Human-dominated Landscapes* (pp. 100–13). Cambridge, UK: Cambridge University Press.

Kenney, J.S., Smith, J.L.D., Starfield, A.M. and McDougal, C.W. 1995. 'The Long-term Effects of Tiger Poaching on Population Viability', *Conservation Biology*, 9(5): 1127–33.

Khandelwal, V. 2005. *Tiger Conservation in India*. Institute Paper, Centre for Civil Society, Delhi.

Kirkpatrick, R.C. and Emerton, L. 2010. 'Killing Tigers to Save Them: Fallacies of the Farming Argument', *Ecological Economics*, 36: 655–59.

Kitchener, A.C. 1999. 'Tiger Distribution, Phenotypic Variation and Conservation Issues', in J. Seidensticker., S. Christie and P. Jackson (eds), *Riding the Tiger: Tiger Conservation in Human-dominated Landscapes* (pp. 19–39). Cambridge, UK: Cambridge University Press.

Linkie, M. 2007. 'The Value of Wild Tiger Conservation', *Oryx*, 41(4): 415–16.

Linkie, M., Chapron, G., Martyr, D.J., Holden, J. and Leader-Williams, N. 2006. 'Assessing the Viability of Tiger Subpopulations in a Fragmented Landscape', *Journal of Applied Ecology*, 43(3): 576–86.

Loyola, R.D., Oliveira-Santos, L.G.R., Almeida-Neto, M.r., Nogueira, D.M., Kubota, U., Diniz-Filho, J.A.F. and Lewinsohn, T.M. 2009. 'Integrating Economic Costs and Biological Traits Into Global Conservation Priorities for Carnivores', *PLoS ONE*, 4(8): 6807.

Luo, S.-J., Kim, J.-H., Johnson, W.E., Walt, J.v.d., Martenson, J., Yuhki, N., Miquelle, D.G. et al. 2004. 'Phylogeography and Genetic Ancestry of Tigers (*Panthera tigris*)', *PLoS Biology*, 2: 442.

Lynam, A.J. 2010. 'Securing a Future for Wild Indochinese Tigers: Transforming Tiger Vacuums into Tiger Source Sites. *Integrative Zoology*, 5(4): 324–34.

Madhusudan, M.D. 2004. 'Recovery of Wild Large Herbivores Following Livestock Decline in a Tropical Indian Wildlife Reserve', *Journal of Applied Ecology*, 41(5): 858–69.

Ministry of Environment and Forests, GoI, *Wildlife Institute of India, National Tiger Conservation Authority, 2011*. India Tiger Estimate 2010.

Ministry of Labour and Employment. 2012. Wage Rates in Rural India (2008–2009). http://labourbureau.nic.in/Wage_Rates_Rural_India_2008_09.pdf (accessed on 10 March 2012).

Ministry of Law and Justice. 2012. The Wildlife (Protection) Amendment Act, 2002, available at http://www.moef.nic.in/legis/wildlife/wild_act_02.htm (accessed on 10 March 2012).

Mitra, B. 2006. 'Sell the Tiger to Save It', *New York Times*, p. 19.

Mitra, B.S. 2005. 'How the Market Can Save the Tiger', *Far Eastern Economic Review*, 168: 44–47.

Mondol, S., Karanth, K.U., and Ramakrishnan, U. 2009. 'Why the Indian Subcontinent Holds the Key to Global Tiger Recovery'. *PLoS Genet*, 5: -1000585.

Morell, V. 2007. 'Wildlife Biology: Can the Wild Tiger Survive?', *Science*, 317: 1312–1314.

Mountfort, G. 1974. 'International Efforts to Save the Tiger from Extinction', *Biological Conservation*, 6: 48–52.

Mushove, P. and Vogel, C. 2005. 'Heads or Tails? Stakeholder Analysis as a Tool for Conservation Area Management', *Global Environmental Change*, Part A 15: 184–198.

Nowell, K. and Ling, X. 2007. *Taming the Tiger Trade: China's Markets for Wild and Captive Tiger Products since the 1993 Domestic Trade Ban*. Hong Kong, China: TRAFFIC East Asia.

Ng, J. and Nemora. 2007. *Tiger Trade Revisited in Sumatra, Indonesia*. Petaling Jaya, Selangor, Malaysia: TRAFFIC Southeast Asia.

Ojeda-Martínez, C., Giménez Casalduero, F., Bayle-Sempere, J.T., Barbera Cebrián, C., Valle, C., Luis Sanchez-Lizaso, J., Forcada, A., Sanchez-Jerez, P., Martín-Sosa, P., Falcón, J.M., Salas, F., Graziano, M., Chemello, R., Stobart, B., Cartagena, P., Pérez-Ruzafa, A., Vandeperre, F., Rochel, E., Planes, S. and Brito, A. 2009. 'A Conceptual Framework for the Integral Management of Marine Protected Areas', *Ocean & Coastal Management*, 52: 89–101.

Persha, L., Agrawal, A. and Chhatre, A. 2011. 'Social and Ecological Synergy: Local Rulemaking, Forest Livelihoods, and Biodiversity Conservation', *Science*, 331(6024): 1606–08.

Project Tiger. 2005. *Joining The Dots: The Report of the Tiger Task Force Union Ministry of Environment and Forests*. New Delhi: Government of India.

Rudel, T.K. 2007. 'Changing Agents of Deforestation: from State-initiated to Enterprise Driven Processes, 1970–2000', *Land Use Policy*, 24(1): 35–41.

Sanderson, E., Forrest, J., Loucks, C., Ginsberg, J., Dinerstein, E., Seidensticker, J. et al. 2006. *Setting Priorities for the Conservation and Recovery of Wild Tigers: 2005–2015. The Technical Assessment*. New York, Washington, D.C.: WCS, WWF, Smithsonian, and NFWF-STF.

———. 2010. 'Setting Priorities for Tiger Conservation: 2005-2015', in R. Tilson, and P.J. Nyhus (eds), *Tigers of the World: The Science, Politics, and Conservation of Panthera Tigris* (second ed., pp. 143–73). London, Burlington, San Diego: Academic Press.

Schaller, G.B. 1967. *The Deer and the Tiger: A Study of Wildlife in India*. Chicago: University of Chicago Press.

Seidensticker, J. 2010. 'Saving Wild Tigers: A Case Study in Biodiversity Loss and Challenges to be Met for Recovery Beyond 2010. *Integrative Zoology*, 5(4): 285–99.

Seidensticker, J., Christie, S. and Jackson, P. 1999. *Riding the Tiger: Tiger Conservation in Human-dominated Landscapes* (pp. xix, 383).Cambridge, UK: Cambridge University Press.

Singh, N. and Vives, X. 1984. 'Price and Quantity Competition in Differentiated Duopoly', *Rand Journal of Economics*, 15(4): 546–54.

Sunquist, M., Karanth, K.U. and Sunquist, F. (1999). 'Ecology, Behaviour and Resilience of the Tiger and Its Conservation Needs', in J. Seidensticker, S. Christie and P. Jackson (eds), *Riding the Tiger: Tiger Conservation in Human-dominated Landscapes* (pp. 5–18). Cambridge, UK: Cambridge University Press.

Svarstad, H., Petersen, L.K., Rothman, D., Siepel, H. and Watzold, F. 2008. 'Discursive Biases of the Environmental Research Framework DPSIR', *Land Use Policy*, 25(1): 116–25.

Tilson, R. and Nyhus, P.J. 2010. *Tigers of the World: The Science, Politics, and Conservation of Panthera tigris* (second ed., p. 522). London, Burlington, San Diego: Academic Press.

Tynnerson, S. 2009. 'Community Based Wildlife Management: Its Role in Conservation and Development', Bachelor Thesis. Soderton University College, School of Life Sciences.

Vitousek, P.M., Mooney, H.A., Lubchenco, J. and Melillo, J.M. 1997. 'Human Domination of Earth's Ecosystems', *Science*, 277(5325): 494–99.

Walston, J., Karanth, U.K. and Stokes, E.J. 2010a. *Avoiding the Unthinkable: What Will It Cost to Prevent Tigers Becoming Extinct in the Wild?* New York: Wildlife Conservation Society.

Walston, J., Robinson, J.G., Bennett, E.L., Breitenmoser, U., da Fonseca, G.A.B., Goodrich, J. et al. 2010b. 'Bringing the Tiger Back from the Brink e the Six Percent Solution', *PLoS Biol*, 8, 1000485.

Wikramanayake, Eric, Dinerstein, E., Seidensticker, J., Lumpkin, S., Pandav, B., Shrestha, M. et al. 2011. 'A Landscape-based Conservation Strategy to Double the Wild Tiger Population',*Conservation Letters*, 4(3): 219–27.

Wikramanayake, E., Dinerstein, E., Robinson, J.G., Karanth, K.U., Rabinowitz, A., Olson, D. et al. 1999. 'Where Can Tigers Live in the Future? A Framework for Identifying High-Priority Areas for the Conservation of Tigers in the Wild', in J. Seidensticker, P. Jackson, and S. Christie (eds), *Riding the Tiger: Tiger Conservation in Human-dominated Landscapes* (pp. 255–72). Cambridge, U.K.: Zoological Society of London; Cambridge University Press.

Wikramanayake, E., McKnight, M., Dinerstein, E., Joshi, A., Gurung, B. and Smith, D. 2004. 'Designing a Conservation Landscape for Tigers in Human-Dominated Environments', *Conservation Biology*, 18(3): 839–44.

Wikramanayake, E.D., Dinerstein, E., Robinson, J.G., Karanth, U., Rabinowitz, A., Olson, D. et al. 1998. 'An Ecology-based Method for Defining Priorities for Large Mammal Conservation: The Tiger as Case Study', *Conservation Biology*, 12: 865–78.Wildlife Institute of India. 2007. *Protected Area Database*. ENVIS. Wildlife and Protected Area.

———. 2012. 'Status of Tigers, Co-predators and Prey in India, 2010'. Available at http://www.projecttiger.nic.in/whtsnew/Tiger_Status_oct_2010.pdf (accessed on 1 March 2012).

Wildlife Protection Society of India (WPSI). 2012. 'Tiger Poaching Statistics'. Available at http://www.wpsi-india.org/statistics/index.php (accessed on 10 March 2012).

———. 2012. 'Update on the Trade in Tiger Parts'. Available at http://www.axxel.it/tiger/Tiger7.html (accessed on 10 March 2012).

SECTION II

Development

12

Importance of Excess Female Mortality in Explaining Lowness of the Sex Ratio in India

*D. Jayaraj**

Introduction

'Lowness' and the declining trend in the weight of women in India's population have received considerable attention of scholars (see, for example, Visaria, 1971; Mitra, 1979; Sen, 1987, 1990, 1992, 2003; Klasen and Wink, 2002a, 2002b; Mayer, 1999). The consensus, until the early 1990s (Sen, 1990, 1992), was that the 'lowness' and the declining trend in the weight of women in India, respectively, were largely due to 'excess mortality' of women vis-à-vis men and its exacerbation over time. Excess female mortality, in turn, was attributed to, '... the relative neglect of females, especially in health care and medical attention' (Sen, 1990: 2). However, there seems to have been a shift in this line of reasoning since the beginning of the twenty-first century. Attention appears to have shifted from mortality differentials or 'low' relative survival advantage of

*Acknowledgements: This chapter draws heavily on and should be seen as a companion piece to 'Exploring the Importance of Excess Female Mortality and Discrimination in "Natality" in Explaining the "Lowness" of the Sex Ratio in India', *The Developing Economies*, Vol. 47(2). The author is very grateful to S. Subramanian for the discussions with him, over a long period of time on the subject of the chapter, and the comments on an earlier version of the chapter were extremely useful.

women vis-à-vis men as an explanation for the observed lowness of the weight of women in India's population to discrimination in natality (particularly before birth).

This shift is reflected in the considerable growth of literature on the subject of sex-selective abortion in India (see, for example, Westley, 1995; Sudha and Rajan, 1999; Clark, 2000; Ganatra et al., 2001; Arnold et al., 2002; Mehra, 2003; Retherford and Roy, 2003; Bhagat, 2004; Glenn, 2004; *Middle East Times*, 2005; Agnivesh et al., 2005; Boseley, 2006; Schultz, 2006; Gentleman, 2006; Jha et al., 2006; Baldauff, 2006; Patel, R., 2007; Patel, T., 2007; Unisa et al., 2007; Balakrishnan, 2013). The works cited earlier include articles that bear titles such as '10 Million Girl Foetuses Aborted in India', '7000 Unborn Girls Die From Sex-Selective Abortions Daily in India', 'Millions of Abortions of Female Fetuses Reported in India', 'Missing: 50 million Indian girls', 'India's Baby Girls Decimated Through Infanticide or Abortion' and 'India's 70 Million Missing Women: Female Feticide'. The growth of literature on sex-selective foeticide, and the titles referred to above appear to suggest that the problem of 'lowness' of the weight of women in India's population is, largely, attributable to the 'lowness' of the female-to-male ratio (FMR) at birth. There is a tendency to attribute the latter, largely, to sex-selective abortion or female foeticide.[1]

The previously mentioned tendency seems to have emerged from conflating the causes for the 'lowness' and the declining trend of the FMR in India. In this context, it seems important, as Sen (1987) had argued, to distinguish the trend from the 'lowness' of the FMR. To quote Sen (1987: 60), '...the lowness of that ratio [female-to-male ratio] has to be distinguished from the declining *trend* [emphasis in original] of the ratio'. The causes for the observed trend and the 'lowness' of the FMR in a population may differ. It is possible, while the observed 'lowness' of the FMR is explained by excess female mortality, the trend in FMR is accounted for by the trend in FMR

[1] For example, in an article in *Humanist News*, titled 'Female foeticide in India', Indu Grewal and J. Kishore (2004) state: 'Female foetuses are selectively aborted after pre-natal sex determination, thus avoiding the birth of girls. As a result of selective abortion, between 35 and 40 million girls and women are missing from the Indian population'. They also indicate that, 'The United Nations has expressed serious concern about the situation'.

at birth. Thus, there is a case for distinguishing the trend from the 'lowness' of the FMR, and maintaining the two as distinct analytical categories. However, it needs to be stated that the attempt in this chapter is restricted[2] to accounting for the 'lowness' of the share of women in India's population at two points of time, that is, in 1991 and 2001. To this end, first the constituent elements of the weight of women or sex ratio of a population are identified in the next section. The section 'Accounting for the 'Lowness' of the Sex Ratio of a Population' details the accounting procedure adopted. The choice of the 'norm', and the rationale attending such choice of the 'norm' employed to assess the 'lowness' of the weight of women in India's population are provided in the section 'On the Choice of the "Norm"'. Sources of data employed are discussed in the section 'Sources of Data and the Method Employed to Generate the Time Series on Sex Ratio at Birth in India'. The results of the accounting exercise are provided and discussed in the section Results and Discussion. The final section concludes the chapter.

Identifying the Constituent Elements of the Sex Ratio of a Population[3]

There are two widely employed measures of weight of women (or sex ratio) in a society. First is the FMR (denoted as S), and the other is the female headcount ratio, which is the proportion of women in the total population in a society (denoted as F). These measures are defined, respectively, as:

$$S=(P^f/P^m)*1000 \quad (1)$$

[2] In this context, it may be noted that Jayaraj and Subramanian (2007) have attempted to decompose the changes in the sex ratio in India between 1961 and 1971 and 1981 and 1991 into that attributable to trends in relative survival advantage of females and sex ratio at birth.

[3] This section relies heavily on, and is largely a reproduction of, the previous section in the study by Jayaraj and Subramanian (2007).

where P^m and P^f, respectively, are the total male and female population in a society; and

$$F = P^f / P \tag{2}$$

where P^f and P, respectively, are female and total population in a society. It may be added here that, in this note, unless stated explicitly, the female headcount ratio will be employed as the measure of the sex ratio of a population.

The sex ratio of a population at any particular point of time can also be written as a weighted—the weight is the proportion of the total population in each age—sum of age-specific Fs. Accordingly, F can be written as:

$$F_t = \sum_{a=0}^{\bar{a}} \varphi_t(a) F_t(a) \tag{3}$$

where t signifies time, a represents age, ā is the age of the oldest person in the society, φ is the proportion of the population, and F is the female headcount ratio. From equation (3), it is clear that the sex ratio of a population at any point of time depends on the age-specific sex ratios and the age structure of the population at that point of time.

$F_t(a)$ is the ratio of females born t–a years ago who have survived to age a to total persons born t–a year ago who have survived to age a. Accordingly, $F_t(a)$ can also be written as: $[B^f_{t\text{-}a}(1-q^f_t(a))]/[B_{t\text{-}a}(1-q_t(a))]$, where B^f_{t-a} and $B_{t\text{-}a}$, respectively, are the total number of females and the total number of persons born t–a years ago, and $q^f_t(a)$ and $q_t(a)$, respectively, are the proportions of females and persons born t–a years ago who have died before reaching age a. Notice that $(1-q^f_t(a))$ and$(1-q_t(a))$, respectively, are the survival ratios of females and of all persons born t–a years ago to age a. The ratio defined as: $r_t(a)=(1-q^f_t(a))/(1-q_t(a))$ is called 'the ratio of relative survival advantage of females' of age a at the time t. It may also be noted that B^f_{t-a}/B_{t-a} is the female headcount ratio at birth t–a years ago, which will be denoted as F^0_{t-a}. For future reference, it may be noted that $r_t(a)$ could also be written as: $F_t(a)/F^0_{t-a}$. From the previous discussion, it is clear that equation (3) can be written as follows:

$$F_t = \sum_{a=0}^{\bar{a}} \varphi_t(a)[r_t(a)F^0{}_{t-a}] \qquad (3')$$

From equation (3'), it is clear that the sex ratio of a population at any particular point of time is determined by three factors: the age structure ($\varphi(a)$), the ratio of relative survival advantage of females ($r(a)$) or excess female mortality, and the trend in sex ratio at birth ($F^0{}_{t-a}$). It may be noted here that the observed age structure at a particular point of time captures the impact of the past history of demographic development experienced by a population. Relative survival advantage ratio of females at age *a* accounts for mortality differentials experienced by females of a birth cohort at different points of time in their life between birth and reaching age *a*. For example, $r(5)$ at time *t* captures the mortality differentials experienced by females born *t*–5 years ago at: (1) infancy *t*–5 years ago, (2) the age interval 0–1 *t*–4 years ago, (3) the age interval 1–2 *t*–3 years ago, (4) the age interval 2–3 *t*–2 years ago, (5) the age interval 3–4 *t*–1 year ago and (6) the age interval 4–5 in year *t*. Similarly, the sex ratio of a population at a particular point of time is influenced by the trend in sex ratio at birth over a long period (the length of which depends on the age of the oldest birth cohort present in the population) of time. Thus, the sex ratio of a population at a particular point of time encapsulates the prior histories—the history of demographic development, the cumulative history of discrimination in survival experienced by females (history of 'excess' female mortality), and the history of sex ratio at birth—in three variables.

Accounting for the 'Lowness' of the Sex Ratio of a Population

To account for the 'lowness' of the sex ratio of a population by its constituent elements, one needs to find answers to a series of counterfactual questions. While posing the counterfactual questions, it is important to take into account the levels of demographic and economic developments experienced by the population. The development experience is largely reflected in the age structure (Klasen and Wink, 2002a, 2002b) of the population. Thus, given the levels of demographic and economic developments reached, to account for the 'lowness' of the sex ratio in India, answers need to be found for the following counterfactual questions. The basic question that needs to be answered is: what would be the sex ratio in India in the absence of discrimination against females? To answer this question, one needs to find answers to the following queries. They are: (i) What would be the age structure of India's population if females have not been discriminated against? (ii) What would be the sex ratio in India corresponding to the age structure that would obtain in the absence of 'excess' female mortality? and (iii) What would be the sex ratio of India's population if there have been no abnormalities in the trend in the sex ratio at birth?

The questions posed previously are easily answered if one could find a population that experiences comparable levels of economic and demographic developments but, unlike in India, does not discriminate against its females. In this connection, Klasen and Wink (2002a) have pointed out that in every known society women experience discriminations against them in one form or another. Thus, it is extremely difficult to identify a society where there exists no discrimination against females in all spheres of life. However, it appears to me that it is reasonable to assume that in the developed countries discrimination against women does not affect their survival chances in any age. Accordingly, to judge the performance of India at any particular age, the observed sex ratio of that age in any one of the developed countries could be employed as the 'norm'. However, the overall performance of India could not be judged employing the overall sex ratio of the population of any one of the developed countries. The developed countries have reached much higher levels of economic and demographic developments compared to India. Consequently, the age structures of the populations in the developed countries differ vastly from that of India's. For this reason, the overall sex ratios of the developed countries need to be corrected to correspond to the age structure[4] of India's population.

It is possible to derive the 'norm' for the overall sex ratio by combining the age structure of India and the sex ratios in each age *a* of a developed country. However, the observed age structure of India's population itself is a product of overall mortality pattern, which is contaminated by 'excess' female mortality. For this reason, the age structure of India needs to be corrected for 'excess' female mortality. In what follows, the procedure employed to arrive at the corrected age structure of India's population is explained.

Employing the sex ratio in each age *a* of a developed country, indexed as *j*, the population share in each age, corrected for 'excess' female mortality in India, at time *t*, is obtained as follows. It is important to note here that the subscript *t*, which represents time, will be suppressed whenever the context presents no ambiguity. Notice, as indicated earlier, that $F(a)$ is the product of two ratios: $F^0_{t\text{-}a}$, the sex ratio at birth *t–a* years ago and $r(a)$, 'the ratio of relative survival advantage of females' at age *a*. Combining information on the sex ratio at birth in India and $r(a)$ of the developed country *j*, the expected sex ratio at time *t* for each age *a* in India, could be obtained as:

$$ {}^{i}F^{*}(a)=[{}^{i}F^{0}_{t\text{-}a}\,{}^{j}r(a)] \tag{4} $$

where ${}^{i}F^{*}(a)$ is the expected sex ratio at age *a* for India, and ${}^{j}r(a)$ is the relative survival advantage ratio at age *a* for the selected developed country. Notice here that the expected sex ratio in India in each age *a* is estimated employing the sex ratio at birth, ${}^{i}F^{0}_{t-a}$, for India. In other words, ${}^{i}F^{*}(a)$ is the sex ratio that would obtain in age *a*, given the sex ratio at birth in India *t–a* years ago, in the absence of discrimination against females in survival. Employing

[4] There appears to be a statistically significant positive relationship between age and relative survival advantage of females in the developed countries. The positive relationship between age and relative survival advantage of females suggests that as the share of the population in the upper end of the age spectrum increases, the sex ratio of the population is likely to increase. This impact could be termed as 'longevity' effect or demographic development effect.

the expected sex ratio and the number of males present in each age, the expected number of females to be present in each age *a* in India at time *t* is obtained as:

$$ {}^{i}P^{*f}(a) = [{}^{i}F^{*}(a){}^{i}P^{m}(a)]/[1-{}^{i}F^{*}(a)] \tag{5} $$

where ${}^{i}P^{*f}(a)$ and ${}^{i}P^{m}(a)$ are, respectively, the female population expected to be present and male population observed to be present in age a in India, and ${}^{i}F^{*}(a)$ is as defined earlier. Now, the expected share of the population in each age *a* at time *t* could be estimated as:

$$ {}^{i}\varphi^{*}(a)= [({}^{i}P^{*f}(a)+{}^{i}P^{m}(a))/({}^{i}P^{*f}+{}^{i}P^{m}] \tag{6} $$

where ${}^{i}\varphi^{*}(a)$ is the expected share of the total population in age *a*, and ${}^{i}P^{*f}$ is the total female population expected to be present in India. Notice here that $\sum_{a=0}^{\bar{a}} {}^{i}\varphi^{*}(a)$ is the age structure that would obtain in the absence of 'excess' female mortality in India.

Now it is easy to derive the overall sex ratio 'norm', denoted as $\hat{F}$, by combining ${}^{i}\varphi^{*}$(a) and ${}^{j}F(a)$, as follows:

$$ \hat{F} = \sum_{a=0}^{\bar{a}} {}^{i}\varphi^{*}(a)\,{}^{j}F(a) \tag{7} $$

Notice that ${}^{j}F(a)$, the sex ratio at age a for country *j*, could also be written as a product of two quantities as: ${}^{j}F(a) = [{}^{j}F^{0}_{t-a}\,{}^{j}r(a)]$. Notice also that the sex ratio at birth in the developed country is not affected by pronounced son preference. Accordingly, $\hat{F}$ is the overall sex ratio of India's population that would be obtained in the absence of abnormality in the sex ratio at birth and 'excess' female mortality. To put it differently, given the level of demographic development achieved, $\hat{F}$ is the sex ratio that would be obtained in India in the absence of discrimination against females. Thus, the 'lowness' of $\hat{F}$ in relation to ${}^{j}F$ (the population sex ratio of country *j*) is attributable only to differences in age structures or differences in the levels of demographic developments of the two populations.

Similarly, the female headcount ratios,[5] that accommodates only for abnormality in sex ratio at birth and only for 'excess' female mortality or 'lowness' of the relative survival advantage in India, respectively, are derived as:

$$F^{sb} = \sum_{a=0}^{\bar{a}} {}^{i}\varphi^{*}(a)[{}^{j}r(a)\,{}^{i}F^{0}{}_{t-a}] \qquad (8)$$

and

$$F^{r} = \sum_{a=0}^{\bar{a}} {}^{i}\varphi^{*}(a)[{}^{i}r(a)\,{}^{j}F^{0}{}_{t-a}] \qquad (9)$$

where F^{sb} and F^{r}, respectively are the overall sex ratios obtained allowing for abnormality in sex ratio at birth and the 'lowness' of the relative survival advantage of females in India. Notice that the F^{sb} is arrived at combining corrected age structure and sex ratios at birth for India, and the relative survival advantage ratios of country *j*. As noted earlier, $\hat{F}$ is obtained by combining the corrected age structure of India, and the sex ratio at birth and the relative survival advantage ratio of country *j*. Accordingly, the difference between $\hat{F}$ and F^{sb} is attributable only to abnormalities in the observed trend in sex ratio at birth in India. Similarly, F^{r} is derived by combining the corrected age structure and relative survival advantage ratios of India with the sex ratios at birth for country *j*. Thus, the difference between $\hat{F}$ and F^{r} is attributable only to 'lowness' of the relative survival advantage ratios or 'excess' female mortality in India.

Now, it is possible, employing ${}^{i}F$, $\hat{F}$, F^{r}, F^{sb} and ${}^{j}F$ to quantify the extent of the 'lowness' of the sex ratio in India attributable to young

[5] The construction of the female headcount ratios adjusted for age structure, relative survival advantage of females and the sex ratio at birth is, somewhat, similar to the procedure adopted by Dreze and Sen (1995). They apply the age-structure of 1901 to the female-to-male ratio of 1981 to obtain the age-structure adjusted female-to-male ratio in 1981 in India. Here, the age-structure adjusted for 'excess' female mortality in India at time t is applied to the sex ratio in each age *a* of the population for country *j* at time *t*. This procedure helps to arrive at the age-structure adjusted headcount ratio of females which is employed to judge the contribution by young age structure of India to the observed 'lowness' of the sex ratio in India at a particular point of time.

age structure or 'lowness' of demographic development, 'lowness' of the ratio of relative survival advantage or 'excess' female mortality and abnormality in sex ratio at birth. It needs to be noted that the extent of 'lowness' of the observed sex ratio in India is assessed by estimating the number of 'missing' women. 'Missing' women is the count of women required to make the sex ratio in India equal to that of country *j*. Thus, the total number of 'missing' women is estimated as:

$$\text{TMW}=[({}^{j}F\,{}^{i}P^{m})/(1-{}^{j}F)]-{}^{i}P^{f} \tag{10}$$

where TMW is the total number of missing women in India; ${}^{i}P^{m}$ and ${}^{i}P^{f}$, respectively, are observed total male and female populations in India; and ${}^{j}F$ is the population sex ratio of country *j*. The total number of 'missing' women (TMW) could be decomposed into four components. They are missing due to (i) young age structure or 'lowness' of demographic development, (ii) 'lowness' of the ratio of relative survival advantage of females or 'excess' female mortality, (iii) abnormality in sex ratio at birth in India vis-à-vis country *j*, and (iv) 'missing' due to the interaction effect of age structure, 'excess' female mortality and sex ratio at birth differences. The last term is hard to interpret. However, since this term usually accounts for a very small proportion of TMW, its contribution may be neglected.

The estimation of the numbers of 'missing' women attributable to young age structure, abnormality in sex ratio at birth, 'excess' female mortality and the interaction effect at a point of time in India is detailed further. 'Missing' women accounted for by longevity or age structure impact, denoted as MW^{a}, is obtained as:

$$\text{MW}^{a} = [({}^{j}F\,{}^{i}P^{m})/(1-{}^{j}F)] - [(\hat{F}\,{}^{i}P^{m})/(1-\hat{F})] \tag{11}$$

The numbers of 'missing' women attributable to (i) the 'lowness' of the relative survival advantage ratio in India, MW^{r}, and (ii) abnormality in the sex ratio at birth in India, MW^{sb}, respectively, are obtained as follows:

$$\text{MW}^{r} = [(\hat{F}\,{}^{i}P^{m})/(1-\hat{F})] - [(F^{r}\,{}^{i}P^{m})/(1-F^{r})] \tag{12}$$

and

$$MW^{sb} = [(\hat{F}\ {}^{i}P^{m})/(1-\hat{F})] - [(F^{sb}\ {}^{i}P^{m})/(1-F^{sb})] \quad (13)$$

Given, TMW, MW^a , MW^r , and MW^{sb}, the 'missing' women attributable to the complex interaction of age structure, relative survival advantage, and sex ratio at birth, denoted as IMW, is obtained as a residual as follows: $IMW= [TMW-(MW^a + MW^r + MW^{sb})]$. Given, the decomposition procedure, in what follows, the selection of the 'norm' or the country employed to assess the 'lowness' of the sex ratio in India is discussed.

On the Choice of the 'Norm'

As indicated earlier, I believe that in none of the developed countries discrimination against females results in excess female mortality. Accordingly, one could employ the sex ratio of any one of the developed countries as the 'norm'. However, in order to decompose the extent of 'lowness' of the sex ratio in India into the four components, listed previously, data on: (i) annual time series on the sex ratio at birth of all the age cohorts that constitute the population, and (ii) age-specific sex ratios of the population present at a point of time are required. Data on both the variables could be easily accessed only for the two countries, Japan and Finland. An examination of the age distributions of sex ratios of the populations of both the countries indicates the presence of abnormalities at the upper end of the age spectrum. Such abnormalities[6] are probably attributable to the impact of the First and the Second World Wars (see, in this connection, Klasen and Wink, 2002a). For this

[6] An examination of the age–sex ratio curves (not provided here, but will be made available on request) for Japan, for the year 1990, and Finland, for the year 1991, show that there exist some abnormalities in the distributions of sex ratios across age in these countries. In the age–sex ratio curve for Japan, there exists a hump in the age range 65–75 years. In the case of Finland, one observes that the age–sex ratio curve displays very steep increases after age 65 years.

reason, age-specific sex ratios of these two countries, for which requisite data are available, could *not* be employed as 'norms'. Sweden, a country known for its neutrality[7] during the First and Second World Wars, appears to be a better candidate. However, for Sweden, while age-wise data on sex ratios are available on the Internet, time series data on sex ratio at birth are not easily accessible.

To overcome the problems of non-accessibility of data and hence the choice of the country, the following procedure has been employed. The FMR employed—employed to estimate the number of 'missing' women in China, South Asia, West Asia and North Africa—by Sen (1990) at 1.05 (or 1,050[8] females per 1,000 males) has been adopted as the 'norm' to judge the 'lowness' of the overall sex ratio of India's population. This adoption solves the problem with respect to the overall sex ratio 'norm'. However, to effect the decomposition suggested earlier, data on age-specific sex ratios, age structure and sex ratio at birth are required. As mentioned earlier, the age distribution of the sex ratio in Sweden does not display any abnormality. However, the overall sex ratio of Sweden's population is observed to be lower than the 'norm' adopted here. For this reason, the distribution of the sex ratio across age in Sweden needs to be adjusted in such a way that the overall sex ratio is at 0.5122 (corresponding to an FMR of 1050) $= \sum_{a=0}^{\bar{a}} {}^{s}\varphi^{*}(a)\,{}^{s}F^{*}(a)$. Notice here that a represents age, $\bar{a}$ indicates the age of the oldest person, superscript s represents Sweden, superscript * indicates that the variable

[7] It appears that Swedish men took part in the Second World War, but since the country itself had maintained neutrality, the impact of World Wars on the overall sex ratio and the age structure of Swedish population appears to be relatively small. Accordingly, the age–sex ratio curve, examined for the year 1991, for Sweden does not display the presence of any significant abnormality.

[8] I do *not* believe that the overall sex ratio of Sweden is affected by gender discrimination in survival. Accordingly, the overall sex ratio of that country could be employed as the 'norm'. However, since Sen (1990) suggests that the female-to-male ratio in populations where men and women receive similar care is observed to be around 1.05, while this is questionable, has been adopted here as the 'norm'. It may also be noted that the objective in this paper is to identify the contributions of the constituent elements of the sex ratio to the 'lowness' of the sex ratio in India, and not obtaining an accurate estimate of 'missing' women in India.

is adjusted to make the overall sex ratio equal to 0.5122, φ is the proportion of the population and F is the female headcount ratio. Notice that the adjusted age distribution rather than the observed one for Sweden is employed. This change in the use of the variable is necessitated by the correction made to the distribution of females in each age a for Sweden to make the overall sex ratio to correspond to the 'norm' adopted. Notice also that, as in the previous section, subscript t has been suppressed.

To arrive at the adjusted age-specific sex ratios and the adjusted age structure, first, the total number of women expected to be present at time t to make the population sex ratio of Sweden equal to 0.5122 has been estimated as: ${}^{s}W^{*}= [(0.5122\,{}^{s}P^{m})/(1-0.5122)]$, where ${}^{s}W^{*}$ and ${}^{s}P^{m}$, respectively, are the total number of women expected to be present, and the total number of males reported to be present in Sweden. Employing ${}^{s}W^{*}$, the number of females expected to be present in each age a in Sweden has been estimated as: ${}^{s}P^{*f}(a) = ({}^{s}\varphi^{f}(a)\,{}^{s}W^{*})$, where ${}^{s}\varphi^{f}(a)$ is the share of total females in each age a in Sweden. Now, it is easy to estimate the corrected sex ratio in each age a at the time t in Sweden as: ${}^{s}F^{*}(a) = ({}^{s}P^{*f}(a)/({}^{s}P^{*f}(a)+{}^{s}P^{m}(a))$. Employing the estimated number of females expected to be present in each age in Sweden, the corrected population share in each age a is obtained as: ${}^{s}\varphi^{*}(a) = [{}^{s}P^{*f}(a)+{}^{s}P^{m}(a)]/[{}^{s}P^{m}+{}^{s}W^{*}]$. Thus, the corrected population share and corrected sex ratio in each age a for Sweden at time t have been obtained. It may also be noted, as mentioned earlier, that data on the sex ratio at birth are not easily accessible for Sweden. To overcome this difficulty, the data on sex ratio at birth for Finland are employed as a proxy for sex ratio at birth in Sweden. Accordingly, the ratio of relative survival advantage of females in each age, a, in Sweden has been obtained as: ${}^{s}r^{*}(a) = {}^{s}F^{*}(a)/{}^{f}F^{0}_{t-a}$, where ${}^{f}F^{0}_{t-a}$ is the sex ratio at birth for Finland. Notice here that in accordance with the fact that age-specific sex ratios of Sweden have been corrected, ${}^{s}F^{*}(a)$ instead of ${}^{s}F(a)$ has been employed in computing ${}^{s}r^{*}(a)$.

Finally it needs to noted that the variables ${}^{j}F(a)$, ${}^{j}r(a)$ and ${}^{j}F^{0}_{t-a}$ have been replaced, respectively, by ${}^{s}F^{*}(a)$, ${}^{s}r^{*}(a)$ and ${}^{f}F^{0}_{t-a}$ in all the relevant equations in the section 'Accounting for the 'Lowness' of the Sex Ratio of a Population'. Similarly the variable ${}^{j}F$ has been replaced by the overall sex ratio 'norm' at 0.5122, that corresponds to an FMR of 1.05 employed by Sen (1990), in the equation used for estimating TMW.

Sources of Data and the Method Employed to Generate the Time Series on Sex Ratio at Birth in India[9]

It may be recalled that the decomposition exercise requires: (i) time series data on sex ratio at birth for Sweden and India, and (ii) sex ratio in each age for the years 1991 and 2001 for the two countries. As noted earlier, time series data on the sex ratio at birth for Sweden are not easily accessible. Hence the time series data (available at http://www.joensu.fi/statistic/lin/alho/7_3_Sex_ratio.html), based on Statistics Finland, for Finland are employed as a proxy for the time series on sex ratio at birth for Sweden. Data on sex ratio at birth in India are not available. For this reason, Jayaraj and Subramanian (2007) had resorted to estimating the sex ratio at birth for the years 1901 to 1991 employing an indirect method. The procedure employed by them is described further.

In order to construct an annual time series on sex ratios at birth for India, Jayaraj and Subramanian (2007) had resorted to the 'reverse survival method'. To employ the reverse survival method, an annual time series on the male and female populations less than a year old and the annual time series on male and female infant mortality rates are required. A brief account of the data sources and assumptions employed by them to construct the annual time series data on sex ratio at birth for India are provided here.

It is important to note, in this context, that the construction of the time series on male and female populations less than a year old had been complicated by over-time changes in the territorial boundaries of India. Independence obtained in 1947 occasioned a change in the boundary of India. Changes were effected to the

[9] This section too relies heavily on Jayaraj and Subramanian (2007).

territories of states in 1956 as a result of reorganization of states within the country. The coverage of census operations, which differed over time, affected the geographical unit of India for which the time series could be constructed. To be more precise, census was not conducted in 1981 and 1991, respectively, in the states of Assam and Jammu and Kashmir. For these reasons, to make the inter-temporal comparisons consistent, Jayaraj and Subramanian (2007) had left out of reckoning the states of Assam and Jammu and Kashmir from India as constituted at the time of independence. They had employed data available in Census of India (1961a), which permit the reconstruction of over-time state-wise estimates of male and female populations for the geographical unit of 'India' as defined, excluding the states of Assam and Jammu and Kashmir from post-1947 India.

Jayaraj and Subramanian (2007) had constructed the annual time series data on male and female populations less than a year old along the following lines. They had employed data on the proportions of males and females less than a year old available for each of the Census years 1901, 1911, 1921 and 1931 in Census of India 1931. For the years 1941 and 1951, these proportions were computed making use of the data from Census of India 1951a and b. Absolute number of males and females less than a year old had been obtained by application of the proportions to the total populations as recorded in the relevant censuses. For the years 1961, 1971, 1981 and 1991, the male and female populations less than a year old had been obtained from the corresponding censuses for these years by aggregating the relevant population totals across the states of the Indian Union. These data had been employed to compute the annual compound growth rates of females less than a year old and males less than a year old for each decade between one Census year and the next. Computed annual compound growth rates had been used to estimate the less-than-one-year female population and the less-than-one-year male population in each of the nine years between a pair of successive census years. In this manner, they had constructed an annual time series of the female and male populations of age less than one year from 1901 and 1991. Employing the same procedure, we extend the coverage to include the decade between 1991 and 2001. For the year 2001, the single year age returns are available for all-India (including the states of Assam and Jammu and Kashmir) in Census of India (2001). However, for the two states Assam and Jammu and Kashmir, single year age returns of male and female populations are not available. Hence, the total female and male populations of Assam and Jammu and Kashmir have been subtracted, respectively, from the all-India total female and male populations. Thus, the total female and male populations of India excluding Assam and Jammu and Kashmir have been obtained. The age distributions of females and males, respectively, for all-India have been employed to obtain, respectively, the age distributions of female and male populations for India excluding Assam and Jammu and Kashmir. It needs to be noted here that the Indian census data suffer from considerable age misreporting and age less than one year (frequently referred to as age zero) is unlikely to be an exception to the rule.

The time series on male and female infant mortality rates had been constructed largely from data generated by the Civil Registration System (CRS), published in different sources for different periods. The CRS, as noted by Visaria (1971), suffers from incomplete registration of births and deaths. Visaria also notes that the extent of such under-registration varies across both regions and the sexes. Since there is no other alternative, as Jayaraj and Subramanian observe, one is constrained to use the data provided based on the CRS. Further, for the years 1901–47, and for want of an alternative, they had employed figures of infant mortality valid for British India as valid for 'India'. They also note that, despite their best efforts at accessing direct statistical sources or compilations made by other researchers, they were unable to obtain infant mortality figures for 11 specific years in the 90-year time series from 1901 to 1991: the gaps for these 11 years were filled in by resorting to simple linear interpolation. The time series on female and male infant mortality rates generated by them have been extended to cover the period from 1991 to 2001. For the first five years in the decade of 1991–2001, data on female and male infant mortality rates have been obtained from the annual publication titled 'Vital Statistics of India', based on CRS. For the years 1996–2001, required data on infant mortality rates based on CRS could not be obtained. For this reason, the data gaps in infant mortality rates have been filled by resorting to linear extrapolation. Specifically, the estimated trend lines, respectively, of female and male infant mortality rates for the period 1976–95 have been extrapolated to obtain data on, respectively, male and female infant mortality rates for the years 1996–2001. The specific assumption made in this context needs to be noted. It is assumed that the trends in infant mortality rates of only the recent past (i.e., the trend in the two decades that precede the year 1996) determine the levels of infant mortality rates in the years 1996–2001. The sources of data employed by Jayaraj and Subramanian (2007) and the additional sources employed in this chapter are provided in Appendix A12.1.

Results and Discussion

The attempt in this chapter has been to explore the importance of 'excess' female mortality and abnormality in the sex ratio at birth in explaining the 'lowness' of the sex ratio of India's population in 1991 and 2001. In this context, it has been identified that demographic development that gets reflected in longevity and fertility are important factors affecting the level of the sex ratio of a population. Age structure captures the impact of demographic development. Accordingly, attempt has been made to identify the contributions by the young age structure, abnormality in sex ratio at birth and 'lowness' of relative survival advantage of females to TMW in India. To this end, data on the age distributions of the populations of Sweden and India in 1991 and 2001, and the time series data on the sex ratio at birth for Finland and India for the period 1901 and 2001 have been employed. It may be noted here that data on these variables are not provided here, but will be made available on request. Notice also that the population distributions are truncated at age 90 years. A truncation necessitated by the fact that it is possible to construct the sex ratio at birth series for India only since 1901. The birth cohort of 1901, the first birth cohort in the time series, constitutes the age cohort of 90 in 1991. To make the comparison of the results between 1991 and 2001 consistent, the age distribution in 2001 is also truncated at age 90 years. This truncation is likely to be of little consequence. For the attempt, here is to get a quick fix on the broad orders of magnitude of the contributions of the constituent elements of the sex ratio of a population to the observed 'lowness' of the overall sex ratio in India. Moreover, the age interval [0, 90] accounts for as much as 99.37 and 99.63 per cent of the total populations in India, respectively, in 1991 and 2001. The share of the relevant age interval in the estimated (estimated adjusting the female population in such a way that the overall sex ratio corresponds to the 'norm' at 0.5122) total population of Sweden in the years 1991 and 2001, respectively, are at 99.63 and 99.43 per cent. The overall sex ratio 'norm' at 0.5122 becomes 0.5113 and 0.5108, respectively, for the years 1991 and 2001 because of the truncation of the age distribution of the populations at 90 years of age.

Data on $\hat{F}$, F^r, F^{sb}, ${}^sW^*$, and male and female populations of India and Sweden in the age range [0, 90] are provided in Table 12.1 for the years 1991 and 2001. Table 12.2 presents the estimates on TMW, MW^a, MW^r, MW^{sb} and IMW, for the years 1991 and 2001. It may be recalled that (1) $\hat{F}$, given the levels of demographic and economic developments achieved, is the population sex ratio that would be obtained in India in the absence of discrimination against females; (2) F^r is the sex ratio that would be obtained in India if only the impact of 'excess' female mortality is present and (3) F^{sb} is the sex ratio that would be obtained in India if only the abnormality in sex ratio at birth is present. ${}^sW^*$ is the total number of women expected to be present in Sweden to make the FMR equal to 1050. TMW is the total number of missing women in India. MW^a, MW^r and MW^{sb} are the estimated number of missing women accounted for, respectively, by young age structure or 'lowness' of the demographic development; 'excess' female mortality or 'lowness' of the relative survival advantage of females and abnormality in sex ratio at birth in India. IMW is the estimated number of 'missing' women accounted for by the complex interaction of variations in the three factors: age structure, sex ratio at birth and relative survival advantage of females and it is hard to interpret this term.

Table 12.1:
Data on population and sex ratios

	Population of Sweden (in the age range 0 and 90)		*Population of India (in the age range 0 and 90)*			*Population Sex Ratio*			
Year	*Females*	*Males*	*Females*	*Males*	${}^{s}W^{*}$	*'norm'*	$\hat{F}$	F^{r}	F^{sb}
1991	4,349,823	4,262,564	390,381,220	420,599,135	4,484,154	0.5113	0.4984	0.4757	0.5036
2001	4,462,763	4,396,154	477,088,079	511,113,669	4,628,867	0.5108	0.4992	0.4803	0.5008

Source: Provided in Appendix A12.1.

Notes: (1) ${}^{s}W^{*}$ is estimated in relation to the total population and not the population in the age range [0, 90].

(2) The population sex ratio 'norm' differs from 0.5122 because of the truncation of the distribution of population at age 90.

Table 12.2:
Estimates on 'missing' women

Year	*Total 'Missing' Women:* **TMW**	*'Missing' Women Attributable to Age Structure Difference:* **MM^a**	*'Missing' Women Attributable to 'Excess' Female Mortality:* **MW^r**	*'Missing' Women Attributable to Abnormality in Sex Ratio at Birth:* **MW^{sb}**	*'Missing' Women Attributable to interaction Effect:* **IMW**
1991	49,687,852 (100.00)	22,219,863 (44.72)	36,242,793 (72.94)	–8,874,270 (–17.86)	99,466 (0.20)
2001	56,547,433 (100.00)	24,112,648 (42.64)	37,110,156 (65.63)	–3,136,331 (–5.55)	–1,539,040 (–2.72)

Source: As in Table 12.1.
Note: Figures in parentheses are the per cent contribution by the relevant factor to TMW.

The numbers presented in Tables 12.1 and 12.2 are, largely, self-explanatory. Hence, only the important points that emerge are highlighted here. Notice that $^{s}W^{*}$ for the years 1991 and 2001, respectively, are estimated to be at 4,484,154 and 4,628,867. But the actual number of women reported to be there in Sweden in 1991 and 2001, respectively, are at 4,373,496 and 4,500,683. Simple calculations, based on the numbers presented previously, suggest that there were 110,658 (4,484,154–4,373,496) and 128,184 (4,628,867–4,500,683) women 'missing' in Sweden, respectively, in the years 1991 and 2001. These numbers suggest that between 1991 and 2001 the count of 'missing' women had increased in Sweden!

The figures provided in parentheses in Table 12.2 indicate the contribution of each factor to total estimated number of 'missing' women in India in the age range [0, 90]. The numbers in column 1 suggest that the absolute number of missing women has increased from around 50 million in 1991 to 56.5 million in 2001. Notice here that the population sex ratio 'norm' employed at 0.5113 and 0.5108, respectively, for the years 1991 and 2001 are substantially higher than the $\hat{F}$ values, at 0.4984 and 0.4992 for the respective years. If $\hat{F}$ is employed to estimate (the difference between TMW and MM^a) the number of 'missing' women, the count turns out to be around 27.5 and 32.4 million, respectively, in 1991 and 2001. These figures are much lower than TMW for the respective years. Since the difference between TMW and (TMW–MM^a) is attributable to young age structure of India's population, the latter estimates are preferable. Even the preferred estimates suggest that the problem of 'missing' women is vast in India.

While the absolute number of 'missing' women has increased between 1991 and 2001, the ratio of 'missing' women (TMW) to total enumerated women in the appropriate age range has registered a marginal decline[10] from 12.73 to 11.85 per cent. This decline is in accordance with the marginal increase (FMR increased from 929 to 933) observed in the sex ratio of India's population between 1991 and 2001. Accordingly, the results suggest that *the observed increase* between 1991 and 2001 in TMW, as Sen (2003) has observed, is attributable to population growth effect and, probably, to the declining trend in sex ratio at birth.

In this connection, digressing a little bit from the results presented in this paper, attention is drawn to the results presented in Jayaraj and Subramanian (2007). Their results indicate that while the decline in the sex ratio of India's population between 1961 and 1971 is, almost exclusively, attributable to deterioration in relative survival advantage of females, the decline between 1981 and 1991 is, largely, explained by the declining trend in the sex ratio at birth. The questions that arise, in this context, are: (i) Is the declining trend in the sex ratio at birth unique to India? (ii) How much of the declining trend in the sex ratio at birth could be attributed to foeticide? It appears that the declining trend is not unique to India. Declining trends in sex ratio at birth had occurred in countries such as England and Wales (Moore, 1958) and Sweden (Johansson and Nygren, 1991). Data[11] available (not reported here, but will be made available on request) for Finland suggest that the FMR at birth: (i) was in the region of 980–90 (very close to the range observed for India at the beginning of the 20th century) in the early 1750s; (ii) declined to a low figure of 931 in 1911 (close to the figure esti-

[10] The decline is from 7.04 per cent to 6.80 per cent when 'missing' women are estimated employing $\hat{F}$ as the appropriate 'norm'.

[11] Available at http://www.joensu.fi/statistic/lin/alho/7_3_Sex_ratio.html, are based on Statistics Finland employed here.

mated for India in 1991) and (iii) experienced a marginal recovery since 1911, and at present is observed to hover around 950. Time series data,[12] available for Japan from 1872 to 2002, interrupted for three years 1944, 1945 and 1946 too display a significant[13] declining trend. Thus, it appears that the declining trend in the sex ratio at birth is not unique to India and it had occurred in other countries, which are not known to have pronounced son preference, too. It is possible that such declining trends have been mediated by 'benign' factors related to development: both economic and demographic. More specifically, improvements in maternal healthcare and nutritional status of women could have contributed to the declining trend in sex ratio at birth both in India and elsewhere (see, on this line of reasoning, Schultz, 1918; Jayaraj and Subramanian, 2004). In the absence of reliable data on sex ratio at birth and on sex-selective abortion, it is hard to quantify the extent of the influence of discrimination in natality on sex ratio at birth in India. Often the sex ratio of the age group 0–4 or 0–6 is employed as a proxy for sex ratio at birth. Sex ratio of the age group 0–6 observed to be around 927 is considered to be low (Sen, 2003) compared to the norm employed at 950. In this connection, it needs to be noted that the data on sex ratio at the lower end of the age spectrum (of age group 0–4 or 0–6) appear to suffer from progressive deterioration in the count of the population. The progressive deterioration could be understood by comparing the population in the age group 0–4 in a census with the enumerated population in the age group 10–14 in the next census (notice that population censuses are conducted in India at the start of each decade since 1901). Such comparisons over successive pairs of censuses starting from 1961 indicate the following. In India, as constituted excluding the states of Assam and Jammu and Kashmir, the population of males enumerated in 10–14 in successive censuses of the pairs: 1961, 1971; 1971, 1981; 1981, 1991 and 1991, 2001, respectively, exceeded that

[12] Available at www.stat.go.jp/data/chouki/zuhyou/02-21.xls, Statistics and Information Department, Minister's Secretariat, Ministry of Health, Labour and Welfare, Japan are used describe the trend.

[13] The estimated linear trend co-efficient of female-to-male ratio at –0.1159 is statistically significant at 1 per cent level.

of the population in the age group 0–4 in the previous census by a factor of, respectively, 8.7, 16.13, 20.45 and 24.40 per cent. These figures for girls are observed to be at 0.00, 7.63, 11.05 and 17.11. These numbers clearly suggest that the undercount of both boys and girls increased over time in the age group 0–4. The implications of such progressive undercount to the declining trend and 'lowness' of the sex ratio of the age group 0–4 or 0–6 at a particular point of time is difficult to assess. However, the evidence provided above on the progressive undercount of the population, particularly at the lower end of the age spectrum, indicates the need for validating the population census data for internal consistency. It needs to be emphasized here that these issues are brought to attention *not* to discredit the notion that female foeticide is prevalent in India, but to indicate that it is hard to quantify its significance. It is probable that the influence of this phenomenon on the trend and the 'lowness' of the sex ratio at birth is limited (see, for example, Bhat, 2002).

Getting back to the numbers presented in Table 12.2, the results indicate that, despite the fact that the sex ratio at birth appears to be declining in India almost since the early 1930s (see, in this context, Jayaraj and Subramanian, 2004), the sex ratio at birth effect on TMW in India is negative. In other words, the history of sex ratio at birth holds up the population sex ratio in India. Accordingly, even as late as in 2001, discrimination in natality (attributed largely to foeticide) has not contributed to 'missing' women in India. However, the negative contribution, which was around 18 per cent in 1991, has declined to 5.55 per cent. This decline suggests that the sex ratio at birth, if the declining trend in it is not halted, will emerge[14] as an important candidate for explaining the 'lowness' of the overall sex ratio in India in the near future.

[14] See, in this connection, Probst (2009: 9), who states that,

> Due to technological progress, techniques for pre-conceptual and prenatal sex determination become cheaper and more accurate; at the same time, the general income level rises. Thus, these methods become more and more affordable for the middle and lower class, providing people the opportunity to act according to their reproductive preferences.

Thus, with technological progress, sex-selection techniques will become more affordable and will become an important determinant of missing women in India in the future.

The numbers presented in Table 12.2 suggest that, even in the latest census year 2001, the effect of the history of 'excess' female mortality accounts for around 66 per cent of the total 'missing' women or 'lowness' of the sex ratio of India's population. Also, it is important to note that the contribution of 'excess' female mortality to TMW has declined from around 73 in 1991 to around 66 per cent[15] in 2001. The results in Anderson and Ray (2010, 2012) assume salience in this context. They identify that vast majority of missing women in India are of adult age; and further, Anderson and Ray (2012) identify that respiratory and infectious diseases are important sources of excess female mortality in India. An important source of respiratory infection is likely to be indoor air pollution caused by burning unclean fuel for cooking. Access to clean fuel for cooking is likely to reduce indoor air pollution[16] and hence reduce respiratory diseases. Provision of clean drinking water and sanitation facilities, particularly toilets, may help to reduce the incidence of infectious diseases.

The results presented in this chapter and by Anderson and Ray (2010, 2012) suggest that subtle forms of discrimination throughout the life span of women persists and continues to have large impact on the 'lowness' of the sex ratio in India. This implies that there is a case for not neglecting or diverting attention from subtle forms of discrimination that affect the relative survival chances of women in India.

[15] It is possible that the importance of excess female mortality in explaining the count of missing women in India at 66 per cent in 2001 has declined between 2001 and 2011. The decline is likely to be of the order of 10 percentage points (notice here that between 1991 and 2001, the importance of excess female mortality had declined by 7 percentage points: from 73 per cent in 1991 to 66 per cent in 2001). It is also likely that the contribution of history of sex ratio at birth to missing women has gone up and probably contributes to around 10 per cent (note here that the contribution of history of sex ratio at birth to missing women in India was negative and stood at 5.55 per cent in 2001). Thus, excess female mortality is likely to be an important factor in explaining the 'lowness' of the sex ratio in India even in the present context.

[16] See, Isara and Aigbokhaode (2014), who argue that indoor air pollution from cooking is an important source of respiratory morbidity and mortality. It is important to note that in India, as late as in 2005–06, 74 per cent of rural households did not have access to clean fuel (Jayaraj and Subramanian, 2010).

The results also suggest that the contribution of young age structure or 'low' demographic development to TMW in India in 2001 was around 43 per cent. The importance of age structure in accounting for the 'lowness' of the weight of women in India's population suggests that the well-being of both the overall population and, probably, that of the population at the upper end of the age spectrum needs to be considerably improved.

Concluding Observations

The objective of this chapter has been to identify the relative importance of discrimination in natality and excess female mortality in accounting for the 'lowness' of the sex ratio in India. 'Lowness' of the sex ratio was sought to be quantified by estimating the number of 'missing' women in India. The contributions of young age structure or 'lowness' of demographic development, abnormality in sex ratio at birth and 'excess' female mortality to the count of missing women in India in 1991 and 2001 have been estimated. The results indicate that the contribution of 'excess' female mortality to the count of 'missing' women is observed to be around 66 per cent in 2001. It is important to note here that expectation of life at birth differential in India has switched in favour of females since the mid-1980s. Despite such a switch, 'lowness' of the relative survival advantage of females emerge as the single most important determinant of the deficit of women in India in 2001. Notice here that while the switch in the expectation of life at birth is of recent vintage (since mid-1980s onwards) the 'missing' women is accounted for by the history of relative survival (dis)advantage experienced by women over a period of nine decades from 1911 to 2001.

The results also suggest that the contribution of abnormality in sex ratio at birth to the count of 'missing' women is negative. However, as pointed out earlier, the trend in the sex ratio in the recent period is explained largely by the trend in sex ratio at birth. Thus, as Sen (1987) had argued, it is important to draw a distinction between level (stock) and trend (flow) in the FMR. Distinguishing the trend from the level not only has intrinsic merit but also has practical utility. In the present case, policy formulations based on an analysis of the trend or changes over time will result in focussing, somewhat, exclusive attention on the declining trend in sex ratio at birth, which may lead to the neglect of '… social practices that lead to excess female mortality [which] are far more subtle and widespread …' (Dreze and Sen, 1995: 144) that still persist.

The results also suggest that a little more than two-fifths of the 'lowness' of the sex ratio in India is attributable to the age structure, which is relatively dense in young age groups in India. This result points to the importance of demographic development in determining the sex ratio of a population. To put it differently, elimination of discrimination against females while is a necessary condition to arrive at the level of the sex ratio employed as the 'norm', that in itself may not be sufficient. In India, expectation of life at birth must increase and fertility must fall to levels achieved in the developed countries.

Persistence of the importance of excess female mortality as an important cause of missing women in India suggests that discrimination in intra-family allocation of resources continues to exert its influence on the survival chances of women. This implies that there is a case for attending to improving the well-being of the population in general, and that of women in particular. Specifically, there is a case for exerting pressure on the state to improve the availability of infrastructural facilities (or basic amenities) such as roads, hospitals, schools, protected drinking water, clean fuel and public transport. More importantly, there is a case for maintaining pressure on the state to provide for social security measure such as widow pension, and free healthcare for women. Provision of housing, with proper ventilation and toilet facilities, extending the coverage of LPG use for cooking to the rural areas need to be given priority to reduce the influence of respiratory and infectious diseases-induced excess female mortality.

Appendix A12.1: Sources of Data

Data Sources for the Less-than-one-year-population Series

Census of India, 1931, Volume I: With Complete Summary of Tribal Life and System. Gyan Publishing House, Delhi.
Census of India, 1951a, paper No.3 of 1954, Age Tables – 1951 Census.
Census of India, 1951b, Volume I, India, Part II – A – Demographic Tables. Registrar General, India. New Delhi.
Census of India, 1961a, Volume I, Part II-A (i) General Population Tables. Office of the Registrar General, India. Ministry of Home Affairs, New Delhi.
Census of India, 1961b, paper No. 2 of 1963, Age Tables. Registrar General of India, New Delhi.
Census of India, 1971, series I, Paper 3 of 1977, Age Tables. Demography, Office of the Registrar General, India. New Delhi.
Census of India, 1981, Social and Cultural Tables, Table C5. Registrar General, India. New Delhi.
Census of India, 1991, Single Year Age Returns (Table C5). Available on Floppy Diskette. Registrar General of India. New Delhi.
Census of India, 2001, Single Year Age Returns (Table C13) for India, Available at: http://www.censusindia.net/results/C_Series/c13_India.pdf

Data Sources for the Infant Mortality Series

Agnihotri, S.B. (2001). 'Declining Infant and Child Mortality in India: How Do Girl Children Fare', *Economic and Political Weekly*, 36(3): 228–33.
Chandrasekhar, S. (1972). *Infant Mortality, Population Growth and Family Planning in India*, George Allen & Unwin Ltd., London.
Mitra, A. (1978). *India's Population: Aspects of Quality and Control*, (Volume Two), A Family Planning Foundation/ICSSR Book, Abhinav Publications, New Delhi.
Statistical Abstract Relating to British India. (1919). *(From 1907–08 to 1916–17)*, published by his Majesty's Stationery Office, London.
Statistical Abstract for British India (1928). *with Statistics, where available relating to certain Indian states from 1917–18 to 1926–27*, Department of Commercial Intelligence & Statistics, Government of India, Central Publication Branch, Calcutta.
Statistical Abstract for British India (1932): *with Statistics, where available relating to certain Indian states from 1920–21 to 1928–29*, Department of Commercial Intelligence & Statistics, Government of India, Central Publication Branch, Calcutta.
Statistical Abstract for British India (1939): *with Statistics, where available relating to certain Indian states from 1929–30 to 1938–39*, Department of Commercial Intelligence & Statistics, India.

Vital Statistics of India (based on Civil Registration System), for the various years since 1966 to 1991, Registrar General, India, Ministry of Home Affairs, New Delhi.
Vital Statistics of India (based on the Civil Registration System), for the years 1992–1995, Registrar General, India, Ministry of Home Affairs, New Delhi.

Data Sources for Sex Ratio at Birth for Finland and Japan

http://www.joensu.fi/statistic/lin/alho/7_3_Sex_ratio.html.
http://www.stat.go.jp/data/chouki/zuhyou/02-21.xls.

Data Sources on the Distribution of Population by Age/Age-group

Sweden: SCB Statistics Sweden; Population Statistics, Available for the period 1860-2006 on the Internet, which could be accessed by entering the search on the Google as: Population of Sweden 1860-2006.
Census of India, 1961b, paper No. 2 of 1963, Age Tables. Registrar General of India, New Delhi.
Census of India, 1971, series I, Paper 3 of 1977, Age Tables. Demography, Office of the Registrar General, India. New Delhi.
Census of India, 1981, Social and Cultural Tables, Table C5. Registrar General, India. New Delhi.
Census of India, 1991, Single Year Age Returns (Table C5, Available on Floppy Diskette. Registrar General of India, New Delhi.
Census of India, 2001, Single Year Age Returns (Table C13), Available at:http://www.censusindia.net/results/C_Series/c13_India.pdf.

References

Anderson, S. and Ray, D. 2010. 'Missing Women: Age and Disease', *Review of Economic Studies*, 77: 1262–1300.
Anderson, S. and Ray, D. 2012. 'The Age Distribution of Missing Women in India', *Economic and Political Weekly*, XLVII(47&48): 87–95.
Agnivesh, S., Mani, R. and Koster-Lossack, A. 2005. 'Missing: 50 Million Indian Girls', *Herald Tribune*, Friday, 25 November. http://www.qern.org/blog/missing-50-million-indian-girls-iht/ (accessed September 2015).
Arnold, F., Kishor, S. and Roy, T.K. 2002. 'Sex-Selective Abortions in India', *Population and Development Review*, 28(4): 759–85.

Balakrishnan, S. 2013. 'India's 70 Million Missing Women: Female Feticide', *SoroptivoiceBlog*. Available at http://www.soroptimistinternational.org/blog/post/437-indias-70-million-missing-women-female-feticide (accessed 2 April 2015).

Baldauff, S. 2006. 'India's "Girl Deficit" Deepest Among Educated: Study: Sex-Selective Abortion Claims 500000 Girls a Year', *The Christian Science Monitor*. Available at http://www.csmonitor.com/2006/0113/p01s04-wosc.html (accessed 3 March 2007).

Bhagat, R. 2004. ' Slaughter in the Womb', *Business Line*, Financial Daily from the Hindu group of publications, Friday, 17 December.

Bhat, Mari P.N. 2002. 'On the Trail of 'Missing' Indian Females, Published in two Parts: I: Search for Clues; and II: Illusion and Reality', *Economic and Political Weekly*, 37(51 & 52): 5105–18 and 5244–63.

Boseley, S. 2006. '10 Million Girl Foetuses Aborted in India', *The Guardian*. Available at http://www.guardian.co.uk/india/story/0,,1682102,00.html (accessed 4 April 2007).

Clark, S. 2000. 'Son Preference and Sex Composition of Children: Evidence From India', *Demography*, 37(1): 95–108.

Dreze, J. and Sen, A. 1995. *India: Economic Development and Social Opportunity*. New Delhi: Oxford University Press.

Ganatra, B., Hirve, S. and Rao, V.N. 2001. 'Sex-Selective Abortion: Evidence from a Community-based Study in Western India', *Asia-Pacific Population Journal*, 16(2): 109–24.

Gentleman, A 2006. 'India's Lost Daughters: Abortion Toll in Millions', *International Herald Tribune*, Tuesday, 10 January. Available at http://www.jatland.com/forums/showthread.php?t=11494 (accessed 15 March 2007).

Glenn, D. 2004. 'A Dangerous Surplus of Sons?: Two Political Scientists Warn that Asia's Lopsided Sex Ratios Threaten World Peace', *The Chronicle of Higher Education*, 50(34): 14–16. http://chronicle.com/free/v50/i34/34a01401.htm (accessed 20 May 2008).

Grewal, I. and Kishore, J. 2004. 'Female Foeticide in India', *Humanist News*, International Humanist and Ethical Union. http://www.academia.edu/9650454/Female_Foeticide_in_India (accessed September 2015).

Isara, A.R. and Aigbokhaode, A.Q. 2014. 'Household Cooking Fuel Use among Residents of a Sub-Urban Community in Nigeria: Implications for Indoor Air Pollution', *The Eurasian Journal of Medicine*, 46(3): 203–08.

Jayaraj, D. and Subramanian, S. 2004. 'Women's Wellbeing and the Sex Ratio at Birth: Some Suggestive Evidence From India', *Journal of Development Studies*, 40(5): 91–119.

———. 2007. 'The Welfare Implications of a Change in the Sex-Ratio of a Population', mimeo.

———. 2010. 'A Chakravarty-D'Ambrosio View of Multidimensional Deprivation: Some Estimates for India', *Economic and Political Weekly*, XLV(6): 53–65.

Jha, P., Kumar, R., Vasu, P., Dhingra, N., Thiruchelvam, D. and Moineddin, R. 2006. 'Low Male-to-Female Sex Ratio of Children Born in India: National Survey of 1.1 Million Households', *Lancet*, 367(9506): 211–18.

Johansson, Sten and Nygren, Ola 1991. 'The Missing Girls of China: A New Demographic Account', *Population and Development Review*, 17(1): 35–51.

Klasen, S. and Wink, C. 2002a. 'A Turning Point in Gender Bias in Mortality? An Update on the Number of Missing Women', *Population and Development Review*, 28(2): 285–312.

———. 2002b. 'Missing Women: A Review of the Debates and an Analysis of Recent Trends', June 2002. Available at http://ssrn.com/abstract=321861 (accessed 11 March 2007).

Mayer, P. 1999. 'India's Falling Sex Ratios', *Population and Development Review*, 25(2): 323–43.

Mehra, B. 2003. 'Sex Selective Abortion in India'. Available at http://beloo-mehra.sulekha.com/blog/post/2003/04/sex-selective-abortion-in-india.htm (accessed 11 March 2007).

Middle East Times. 2005. 'India's Baby Girls Decimated Through Infanticide or Abortion', AFP, 13 October 2005. http://www.island.lk/2005/10/15/features4.html (accessed September 2015).

Mitra, A. 1979. *Implications of Declining Sex Ratio in India's Population*. Bombay: Allied Publishers.

Moore, P.G. 1958. 'Variations in the Sex Ratio at Birth', *Journal of the Institute of Actuaries*, 84(1): 92–96.

Patel, R. 2007. 'The Practice of Sex Selective Abortion in India: May You Be the Mother of a Hundred Sons'. Available at http://gi.unc.edu/research/pdf/abortion.pdf (last accessed on 20 February 2007).

Patel, T. (ed). 2007. *Sex Selective Abortion in India: Gender, Society and New Reproductive Technologies*. New Delhi: SAGE Publications.

Probst, W. 2009. 'The Missing Women Phenomenon in India: Causes and Effects', *Journal of Young Investigators*, November 2009, Available at http://www.jyi.org/issue/the-missing-women-phenomenon-in-india-causes-and-effects/ (accessed 21 August 2012).

Retherford, R.D. and Roy, T.K. 2003. 'Factors Affecting Sex-Selective Abortion in India', *National Family Health Survey Bulletin*, Number 17, January 2003: 1–4. Available at http://www.eastwestcenter.org/fileadmin/stored/pdfs/NFHSbull017.pdf (accessed September 2015).

Schultz, A. 1918. 'Studies in the Sex-Ratio in Man', *Biological Bulletin*, 34(4): 257–75.

Schultz, G. 2006. '7000 Unborn Girls Die From Sex-Selective Abortion Daily in India'. https://www.lifesitenews.com/news/7000-unborn-girls-die-from-sex-selection-abortion-daily-in-india (accessed September 2015).

Sen, A. 1987: *Commodities and Capabilities*. New Delhi: Oxford University Press.

———. 1990. 'More Than 100 Million Women Are Missing', *New York Review of Books*, 37(20). http://www.nybooks.com/articles/archives/1990/dec/20/more-than-100-million-women-are-missing/ (accessed September 2015).

———. 1992. 'Missing Women', *British Medical Journal*, 304: 586–87.

———. 2003. 'Missing Women—Revisited' (Editorial), *British Medical Journal*, 1297–98. http://www.ncbi.nlm.nih.gov/pmc/articles/PMC286281/pdf/bmj32701297.pdf (accessed September 2015).

Sudha, S. and Rajan, I. 1999 'Female Demographic Disadvantage in India 1981–1991: Sex Selective Abortion and Female Infanticide', *Development and Change*, 30(3): 585–618, Special Issue on Gendered Poverty and Well-being.

Unisa, S., Pujari, S. and Usha, R. 2007. 'Sex Selective Abortion in Haryana: Evidence From Pregnancy History and Antenatal Care', *Economic and Political Weekly*, 42(1): 60–66.

Visaria, P. 1971. 'The Sex Ratio of the Population of India', *Census of India 1961*, Monograph No. 10, New Delhi, Office of the Registrar General of India, Ministry of Home Affairs.

Westley, S. 1995. 'Evidence Mounts for Sex-Selective Abortion in Asia', *Asia-Pacific & Population Policy*, No. 34, May-June 1995: 1–4. http://scholarspace.manoa.hawaii.edu/bitstream/handle/10125/3935/p%26p034.pdf (accessed September 2015).

13

Subsidized Credit vs Public Works Programme in Rural India

*Kausik Chaudhuri and Debanjali Dasgupta**

Introduction

Eradication of poverty has been one of the persistent objectives in developing countries despite the impressive aggregate growth performance in recent years. The government in developing countries therefore initiates various income-enhancement programmes for the poor. India has not been an exception in this regard. The income-enhancement programmes can differ in genre: either the self-employment programmes or the wage employment programmes (public works programmes). The benefits accruing to the poor from these programmes can be classified into direct transfer benefits (short run income gains to the poor from being employed), indirect transfer benefits (benefits accruing to the village community in terms of the infrastructure) and stabilization benefits (wages earned through these programmes provide a stream of income for the rural poor so that they are not forced to sell off their assets and stability is also ensured through a guaranteed earning even in the lean season).

Both the wage employment programmes (like the public works programme) and the self-employment programmes in principle

*IGIDR, Mumbai, India. E-mail: debbie2704@gmail.com

targeted the poorest of the poor, precisely the below poverty line (BPL) households. However, the exact manner in which the programme was made to reach the targeted population differs across the programmes. The wage employment programmes encouraged *self-targeting* (voluntary participation) by setting the wages below the market wages and the payment of wages were contingent on fulfilling of the work requirement. The self-employment programmes have selected its beneficiaries. For example, in the self-employment programmes like the Integrated Rural Development Programme (IRDP) in India, beneficiaries were to be selected from among the low-income households as recorded in the household register maintained by the *gram panchayat* (the lowest tier of elected organization). The beneficiaries were to be selected in the open *gram sabha* (general meetings of the *gram panchayat*) to limit the inset of corrupt practices.

Being multi-dimensional in nature, poverty alleviation requires integrated and coordinated effort. To achieve this, various poverty alleviation programmes have been implemented in India. Prudent attempts have been made throughout the decades of planning in structuring programmes that could attend to the various dimensions of poverty reduction like income enhancement, income maintenance, provision of food and nutritional security, access to basic minimum services like sanitation, health, education and natural resource management and livelihoods.

The 'target-based' approaches to poverty alleviation can be structured either as a self-employment programme or as a wage employment programme. The self-employment programmes were introduced at the national level in the late 1970s. Initially, these programmes aimed at providing subsidized credit and infrastructure to small and marginal farmers and to agricultural labourers. In the 1980s, the focus of these programmes was extended to also target the scheduled castes (SCs), the scheduled tribes (STs) and the rural artisans. One of the largest self-employment programmes, the IRDP uses a mix of subsidy and institutional credit from the formal financial system. The pattern of subsidy allowed 25 per cent to the small farmers, 33.33 per cent to the marginal farmers, agricultural labourers and the rural artisans and 50 per cent to the SC and ST families and the physically challenged. The overall responsibility of the policy formulation, monitoring, evaluation and the release of the central share of the funds lies with the Ministry of Rural Employment, Government of India. At the district level, the programme was being implemented by the District Rural Development Agencies. The wage employment programmes, on the other hand, have attempted to generate economic assets in a labour-intensive way. The programme assures the rural poor of getting employment during the lean agricultural season and also during natural calamities like floods and droughts. The National Rural Employment Programme and the Rural Landless Employment Guarantee Programme were started in the sixth and the seventh plans. They were merged as the Jawahar Rojgar Yojana (JRY) in April 1989. The JRY was revamped from 1999 as the Jawahar Gram Samridhi Yojana (JGSY). This restructuring has aimed at creation of rural economic infrastructure while employment generation became a secondary objective. The Employment Assurance Scheme (EAS) launched in 1993 serves the purpose of offering employment in the form of manual work in the lean agricultural season. The Food for Work (FFW) programme was started in 2000–2001 as a component of *EAS* in eight notified drought-affected states of Chhattisgarh, Gujarat, Himachal Pradesh, Madhya Pradesh, Orissa, Rajasthan, Maharashtra and Uttaranchal. This programme meant to augment food security though wage employment. In September 2001, the JGSY, EAS and the FFW programme were revamped and merged into the Sampoorna Gramin Rozgar Yojana. Generation of wage employment, creation of durable infrastructure in the rural areas and granting food and nutritional security to the rural poor continued to be the prime objective of this programme.

One issue still remains: evaluation of the two types of programme regarding the impact effects acknowledging the difference in targeting mechanism.[1,2] Our chapter is an attempt in this

[1] A judgemental conclusion about the performance of any of the programmes and declaring them as a 'success' or a 'failure' is not what we aim at.

[2] There could be two kinds of ill-targeting: first one relates to the *E-error* measuring the proportion of the non-poor among the total participants. The other is the *F-error* that refers to the proportion of the poor, which have been left out from the programme. The

direction. We believe that we have made a significant contribution in the existing literature by evaluating the impact effects of these two types of programmes using household-level data from India. Propensity score matching technique has been used to arrive at the impact estimates (see Markus, 2004; Hirano et al., 2003; Ichimura et al., 2001; Heckman et al., 1997, 2004).[3] Tritah (2003) has investigated the effect of food subsidies on poverty in India using propensity score matching technique. We consider three outcome variables: annual household consumption expenditure, annual household food expenditure and household annual purchases from the public distribution system (PDS). We use consumption expenditure poverty for three reasons: first, it measures the command a household has over goods and services that are inputs into their welfare. Second, there is a strong theoretical basis for it as an indicator of current welfare. Third, it is perhaps the most common indicator of welfare used in poverty analysis.

Our results show that the self-employment programme has a positive and a significant impact effect for the entire sample while a negative (although statistically insignificant) for the targeted sub-sample population. The impact estimates of the public works programme are seen to be positive and significant only for the targeted sub-sample population, that is, the sub-sample comprising only of the 'below poverty line' households.

The rest of this chapter is organized as follows: in the next section, we briefly describe the estimation methodology. The section 'Data and Variables' introduces our data along with the salient features, and the successive section reports our empirical results. The final section concludes with policy prescriptions.

---

other is the *F-error* that refers to the proportion of the poor, which have been left out from the programme.

[3] For a variety of assessments using Propensity Score Matching, see Jalan and Ravallion (2003), Sianesi (2004), Dahejia and Wahba (2002), Heckman et al. (1997).

Estimation Methodology

In a randomized experiment, it can be assumed that the covariates and the unobservable do not differ in a systematic way between the treated and the non-treated groups. Given the absence of experimental data and the assignment to treatment is non-random, one needs to consider the factors that influence the treatment status to assess the treatment impact. This is accomplished through the creation of comparison or control groups that are subsequently compared with the treatment group that are similar in covariates to the treatment group. The only difference between the two groups is in terms of programme participation. In a case like this, the difference in the 'outcome values' between the two groups can be attributed to programme participation.

We use 'Propensity Score' as defined by Rosenbaum and Rubin (1983)[4] to obtain the impact estimates of a programme. The matching estimators can be obtained using matching on the estimated propensity scores instead of matching on the covariates. However, this would only work provided the conditional independence and the balancing property assumption (which requires that the mean propensity scores should be identical across the treatment and the control groups) have been satisfied. We create sub-groups to study participants who are similar across a broad range of characteristics and then compare the outcomes of those who have participated in the intervention versus those who did not. We assume that given any value of propensity score, the sub-group of participants to a treatment would have the same joint distribution as the untreated in all the covariates that were used to estimate the propensity score.[5] We impose the common support condition. It takes the local averages of the comparison group observations near each treated

[4] For further development, see Heckman et al. (1997).

[5] However, an estimate of propensity score is not enough to obtain an estimate of the 'average treatment effect on the treated'. This is because that propensity score is a continuous variable and so the probability of observing two units with exactly the same score is zero.

observation to construct the counterfactual for that observation. We test for the balancing property assumption and it has been satisfied.

Various matching methods have been proposed in the literature: the Kernel, the Nearest Neighbour, the Mahalanobis and others.[6] We use Kernel method of matching. This is because that with about 5 per cent of the sample being an IRDP beneficiary and 3 per cent of the sample being a public work participant, the ratio of control observation to the treatment observation is large. In such a situation, the Kernel matching is a good option (Frolich, 2004). However, the Kernel weight function is sensitive to the chosen bandwidth. We have used a bandwidth equal to 0.1. There are two reasons behind the choice of this bandwidth. First, an inspection of the data (both visual as well as an assessment of the distribution of the propensity scores) helped us in making a choice of the bandwidth. Second, given the fact that we have a large set of control given our treatment set (both in case of the IRDP as well as the public works) and due to ill-targeting, the magnitude of the E-errors and F-errors are large, we did not expect a problem of inability to find a counterfactual with a relatively small bandwidth.[7] In order to be able to obtain a confidence interval on the estimated average treatment effect, we use bootstrapping methods to calculate the standard errors by re-sampling of the data (with replacement). We use 100 replications for our exercise. How good is our quality of matching? The *t*-tests show matching significantly reduces the bias in unmatched sample means for almost all the variables and a joint-test provides evidence in favour of good matching. As a robustness

[6] The different methods of matching differ in terms of the weights that they assign to the various control observations in order to create the counterfactual.

[7] It is, however, acknowledged that the ideal manner in which the optimal bandwidth needs to be selected is by minimizing the mean square errors or a leave-one-out method (Frolich, 2004). A possible extension of this part of the work will be to analyse in detail the optimal band width and contribute significantly to the existing research on bandwidth selection. However, given that we have studied the data well before making the choice of the bandwidth, we do not expect the optimal bandwidth to be drastically different from that selected by us. Although we have also experimented with other bandwidths, our results remain qualitatively the same as reported in the chapter.

check, we also compute the impact estimates using radius matching and our results qualitatively remain the same.

We did not use regression-based approach (e.g., Instrumental Valuable Regression or Heckman Sample Selection Model) as the outcome for the same person for the two states: receiving and not receiving the treatment cannot be observed. Our emphasis is not on the determinants of the participation in the IRDP/public works programme. Instead, we are interested in sieving out the treatment impact by means of creation of virtual counterfactuals.[8]

Data and Variables

The National Sample Survey Organization set up in 1950 provides household level data in successive rounds. A stratified sampling design was adopted for the selection of the first-stage sampling units (FSUs). The FSUs were villages for the rural areas. Large FSUs were further subdivided into hamlet groups. These were grouped into two segments and the ultimate stage units were selected independently from each of these segments by the method of circular systematic sampling. We have used NSS data-55th Round collected in 1999/2000 for our analysis. We have chosen to work with the 55th round of the NSS when the 61st round has also been in the public domain. The NSS 55th round data has asked questions on both IRDP and public works beneficiary, whereas the same was not there for the IRDP participation in NSS 61st round. For our analysis, we have used annual household consumption expenditure, household annual food expenditure and household annual value of purchases from the PDS as the outcome variables.[9] The PDS provides rationed amounts of food items like rice, wheat, sugar and non-food items like kerosene to the rural as well as to the urban population at below market prices through the fair price shops. We include the value of purchases from the PDS as an outcome variable

[8] The difference-in-difference estimator could have been used if we had data available over two time periods.

[9] We would like to mention that all our variables are log-transformed.

to examine whether any substitution exists between PDS purchases and non-PDS purchase once items from both the sources become affordable to the poor due to enhanced income from programme participation. Our data are based on a 30-day recall period as NSS in their report (Number 457) adduces higher errors for 7-day recall as against based on 30-day recall. The survey is confined to a single time period and asks whether any sort of IRDP assistance received during the last five years or did they participate in public works programme for at least 60 days in preceding year of the survey. It does not indicate when the IRDP loan has been sanctioned to the household.

Our sample data show that 5.2 per cent of the population has received IRDP assistance out of which only 24.14 per cent are from the eligible group. On the other hand, about 3 per cent of the population has participated in the public works programme out of which 30.14 per cent are from the poorest strata of the population (below the poverty line). Around 26 per cent of the IRDP beneficiaries in the population belong to the general category, while almost 74 per cent comprises the SC, ST and other backward caste (OBC) household. In case of the participation in the public works programmes, almost 71 per cent of the participation is from the backward section of the society. We find that the participation from non-Hindu is relatively quite meagre. Among the different household types, we find that the agricultural sector has more IRDP beneficiaries than the non-agricultural sector. More specifically, 35 per cent of the IRDP beneficiaries are agricultural labourers while, 33 per cent are self-employed in agriculture. Almost 14 per cent of the IRDP beneficiaries are self-employed in the non-agricultural sector, while, 9 per cent each belong to the categories 'other labour' and 'others'. Not very different is the composition of the public works participants with respect to 'household type'. Around 66 per cent of the public works participants belong to the agricultural sector (37 per cent are agricultural labourers, while 27 per cent are self-employed in agriculture). In the non-agricultural sector, almost 12 per cent each are 'self-employed in non-agriculture' and 'other labour', while the remaining 10 per cent belong to the category 'others'. Participation in a public works programme and bagging an IRDP loan is more for 'male household heads'.

As a first step for computing the impact estimates, we use a probit model to determine the probability of participation in the IRDP or in the public works programme.[10] We use various demographic variables as the first set of control variables. The ratio of dependents in the household is defined as the total proportion of dependents (less than or equal to 14 years of age and greater than or equal to 60 years) per household. The total number of working children in the household counts the total number of children in the household within the age group of 1–14 years involved in any kind of economic activity. We also control for household size and proportion of females among the adults of the household, age, gender, religion, marital status and social group of the head of the household.

The income and wealth status of the household has been controlled. Land irrigated measured in hectares captures the irrigated land of the household that the household posses. We used controls for the major source of lighting (electricity, kerosene, oil, gas, candle, etc.) and cooking (electricity, LPG, coal, coke, firewood, gobar gas, dung cake or charcoal) in the household. Income sources of the household have also been controlled for specifically if the household receives any rental income, income from remittances, income from interests and dividends, wage/salary income, pension income. A BPL dummy has been created, which takes the value '1' if the household is a BPL household and takes the value '0' otherwise. Poverty line has been defined based on the national poverty line. We also created a dummy variable that takes the value '1' if the household possesses a kitchen garden and '0' otherwise. The working status of the household head is being controlled: a dummy variable that takes the value '1' if the head is working (engaged in any economic activity) and takes the value '0' otherwise. Agricultural household dummy variable takes the value '1' if the household

[10] We would like to mention here that a very small percentage of households (less than 1 per cent) in our sample were both IRDP beneficiaries and public work participants. We have excluded them from the analysis.

is an agricultural household and takes the value '0' otherwise.[11] Dummy variable to control for the literacy status of the head of the household has been included in the analysis. The literacy levels considered are illiterate, educated up to the primary level, educated to more than primary and less than secondary level, educated to higher secondary level or above. We control for the occupational status of the household: self-employed in non-agricultural activities, self-employed in agricultural activities, agricultural labour and other labour. Amount of land owned by the household has been controlled for.[12] The number of meals per day taken by each member of the household on an average is considered. This variable takes the value '1' if the number of meals taken by each member of the household per day is greater than 2 and takes the value '0' otherwise. Finally, we also included regional dummies to control for the unobserved effects at the regional level.[13] Tables 13.1 and 13.2 represent the summary statistics for some of the selected variables.

Empirical Results

We divide this into two sections. The first section highlights the results from the probit estimates and in the second section, we report the average treatment effects for all-India.

[11] By agricultural household, we mean that the major share of income of that household would be from agricultural activities, whether the members of the household are self-employed or wage employed in agriculture.

[12] While deciding upon the classes of land owned, the distribution of rural poor across land owned has been considered. An attempt has been made via the use of this variable to separate out the rich from the ordinary. That is the reason why we have not used the variable 'land possessed' although the observations available on 'land possessed' are greater than that of 'land owned'. 'Land possessed' comprises land-owned plus land leased in plus land encroached minus land leased out. A rich household owning a huge plot of land, most of which is leased out will have a small entry for land possessed and may fall in the same class as that of a poor household owning negligible amount of land.

[13] One may argue that in absence of control for village level factors our results could lead to omitted variable bias in the propensity score estimates. We believe that the control for regional dummies to some extent address this bias.

Table 13.1:
Distribution of IRDP beneficiaries and public work participants

	IRDP Beneficiaries	*Public Work Participants*
Distribution in the Population		
Percentage of beneficiaries in the population	5.2	3.05
Percentage of beneficiaries from the BPL	24.14	30.15
Distribution according to Social Caste (expressed in percentage terms)		
Scheduled tribe	12.47	17.54
Scheduled caste	27.71	24.28
OBC	33.73	29.62
General caste	26.07	28.55
Distribution according to Religion (expressed in percentage terms)		
Hindu	83.33	86.64
Muslim	9.91	9.77
Christian	1.68	1.82
Others	5.07	1.77
Distribution according to Household Occupation (expressed in percentage terms)		
Self-employed in non-agriculture	14.00	12.05
Agricultural labour	34.46	38.22
Other labour	9.34	12.70
Self-employed in agriculture	33.24	27.46
Others	8.96	9.56
Distribution according to Gender of Household Head (expressed in percentage terms)		
Male household head	91.6	93.1
Female household head	8.4	6.9

Source: National Sample Survey and authors' calculation.

Table 13.2:
Descriptive statistics of outcome variables

	APL Households	*BPL Households*
Household size	4.796	5.837
Annual household consumption expenditure (in ₹)	32,277.55	18,419.48
Annual household food expenditure (in ₹)	18,845.14	12,175.43
Total annual value purchases from public distribution system (in ₹)	762.57	639.65

Source: National Sample Survey and authors' calculation.

Determinants of IRDP and Public Works Programme Participation

Table A13.1 highlights the effect of the control variables on the probability of the household being an IRDP beneficiary. The results indicate that with an increase in the number of working children, the probability of being an IRDP beneficiary significantly increases. Greater the number of working children in a household, the more acute is the poverty status of the household. The adult female proportion is significant and positive. The dependency ratio and the size of the household though yield expected signs, are not significant. The probability of receiving IRDP assistance is higher if the household belongs to the category of 'others' as compared to the Hindu households. We also find that the Muslims and the Christians also have a significant lower probability of receiving the assistance (as compared to the base category 'others'). The social group dummies also have the expected sign since the IRDP intends to reach out to the minority social groups. The marital status and the age of the head of the households are found to be insignificant.

Able to access electricity as a primary source of lighting has a significantly smaller probability of receiving assistance. As compared to the household not owning any amount of land, the households owning land (true for all the classes) have a greater probability of receiving assistance. This differential impact is, however, only significant for the households owning land between 0 and 6 hectares. The households whose head earns income from other sources have a significant higher probability of receiving IRDP assistance compared to others. This may be due to the perception of the bank officials that the households with earning heads are less likely to default as compared to the households with non-earning heads. The households receiving pension income and income from remittances have a lower probability of receiving IRDP loans. The effect is, however, significant only for the latter. The households receiving rental income and income from interests and dividends have a significantly greater probability of receiving the loans.

The BPL dummy has a negative insignificant coefficient. The sign of the dummy captures the ill-targeting of the programme.

In terms of occupational status and education of the households, our results imply that education plays no significant role in obtaining an IRDP loan. The agricultural labour has a greater probability of bagging the assistance as compared to those self-employed in agriculture. The 'other labour' (mainly comprising the unskilled labour of the non-agricultural sector) has significantly greater probability of receiving assistance as compared to those who are self-employed in agriculture.

Table A13.2 displays the results for the participation decision in the public works programme. A household is said to participate in the public works programme if at least one member of the household has participated in any public works programme (at least 60 days in the past year).[14] The sample data show that the larger sized households have a significantly higher probability of participating in the programme. Higher the dependency ratio and the proportion of adult females in the household, smaller is the participation probability of the household.[15] The sign of these two coefficients may seem to be contrary to the expectations. But, it has been seen that the wages offered in the public works programmes are usually so low that the extremely impoverished households often do not find any incentive to participate. The probability of receiving IRDP assistance is significantly higher if the household belongs to the category of 'Hindu' or 'Christian' as compared to the others. We also find that the Muslims and the Christians also have a significant lower probability of receiving the assistance (as compared to the base category 'others'). The social group dummies also have the expected sign since the IRDP intends to reach out to the minority social groups. The marital status and the age of the head of the households are found to be insignificant.

We obtain that chronically food-deficient households have a significantly higher probability of participating. Households that

[14] Note here that the objective of several public works programme was to provide 50–100 days of gainful employment to at least one member of the rural poor households.

[15] Both these variables had been primarily included to assess the poverty status of the household.

do not have any lighting arrangement as well as the households that have the common (to rural area) mode of lighting (like candle, gas and others) have a significantly higher probability of participation as compared to the households that have electricity as the primary source of energy for lighting. Households not owning any land are seen to have a higher probability in participating. Among the landowners, the owners of smaller holdings have a significantly higher probability of participation. Households having received wage income, income from other agricultural activities, income from interest and dividends have a significantly a greater probability of participation.

In terms of occupational status and education of the households, our results imply that education plays no significant role in participating in a public works programme. On the other hand, all occupation has a lower probability of participating in the programme compared to the 'other labours' category. We note that the 'other labour' mainly comprises the unskilled labour of the non-agricultural sector.

All-India Impact Estimates

The entries in Table 13.3 are of the Average Treatment Effect on the Treated (at the all-India level). The impact effect of IRDP for all the outcome variables is positive for the entire sample and negative for the BPL households. Kurian (1987) reports about 84 per cent of the households have enjoyed a positive increment in income after a period of two years amongst the IRDP beneficiaries. Guhan (1986) has concluded that IRDP has channelled funds in an unprecedented scale to generate supplementary income for the poor in the rural areas all over India; however, the extent to which it has actually been able to create additional income for the targeted poor has been limited. Our results (especially that pertaining to the BPL sub-population) seem to be in line with the criticisms inflicted on the performance of the IRDP programme. Dreze (1990) postulates that only one among the eight households in the poorest deciles

Table 13.3:
Average treatment effects of the treated, all-India

	Whole Sample		*Below Poverty Line Households*	
	IRDP	*Public Works*	*IRDP*	*Public Works*
Annual household consumption expenditure	0.032** (0.049)	–0.018 (0.141)	–0.039 (0.156)	0.025** (0.040)
Annual household food expenditure	0.023* (0.083)	–0.005 (0.671)	–0.023 (0.387)	0.036*** (0.008)
Value of annual household purchases from PDS	0.009 (0.713)	0.043* (0.098)	–0.001 (0.990)	0.162*** (0.000)

Source: Authors' estimates.

Notes: The impact estimates are obtained from Kernel matching. The values in parentheses are the *p*-values based on bootstrapped standard errors with 100 replications. ***Significance at 1 per cent level, **significance at 5 per cent level and *significance at 10 per cent level.

received any benefit from the IRDP. The results of his study show that within two years, only about 5 per cent of the IRDP beneficiaries have been able to cross the poverty line. Paul (1998) has compared the poverty indices before and after the programme and concludes that over the period of two years, the level of poverty among IRDP families declined by 22 per cent with 7 per cent of the families crossing the poverty line. The probable reason could be the fact that some of the IRDP assets distributed to the poor are of low quality and defective which even cease to be operative after some time. The positive impact effects for the entire sample could be due to the fact that the financially better off IRDP beneficiaries (of a decent proportion in the sample) by pecuniary influence are able to access the technically sound and the operative assets, which have brought an increment in their income.

While studying the impact estimates of the public works programme, it needs to be kept in mind that public works reach out at an individual level unlike the IRDP that reach out at the household level. Our data, however, do not contain any information on the number of members of a particular household who have participated in the programme. Hence, our data treat all the households who have participated in the public works programme homogeneously not differentiating between the participant households in terms of the number of participating members. The all-India results for the impact effects of the public works programme are quite encouraging. The results show positive and significant effects on Annual Household Consumption Expenditure and Annual Household Expenditure on Food for the BPL households, while negative (although insignificant) impact effects for the whole population. The poorest of the poor have benefited significantly from participation in the public works programme, but the households that did not belong to the poorest strata and yet participated in the public works programme could have performed better elsewhere (as indicated by the negative ATT). This was exactly what the public works was designed to achieve. We also see that for the BPL group the impact estimate for the outcome variable 'annual purchases from the PDS' are also positive and significant. Our results are in line with the report by Acharya and Panwalker (1988). They have compared the wage income of a sample of 100 employment guarantee scheme participants (households) with that of 100 non-participants and concluded that the average annual wage income of the participant households was meagrely higher to that of the non-participant households.[16] We perform a sensitivity exercise using radius matching to obtain the impact estimates. The results are reported in Table 13.4. The estimates remain qualitatively the same.

Conclusion

This chapter estimates the impact effects for the 'average treatment effect on the treated' for the IRDP and the public works programme using data from 15 major states in India. We consider three outcome variables: annual household consumption expenditure, annual household food expenditure and household annual purchases from the PDS. The results show that the IRDP has a

[16] Other studies on public works programmes include Datt (1994), Mukherjee (1997) and Panda et al. (2005).

Table 13.4:
Evidence from alternative matching estimates

		Kernel Matching Estimates		*Radius Matching Estimates*	
	Outcome Variables	*ATT*	*p-value*	*ATT*	*p-value*
IRDP as the treatment variable, all sample households	Annual household consumption expenditure	0.032**	0.049	0.046***	0.000***
	Annual household food expenditure	0.023*	0.083*	0.025**	0.024
	Value of annual household purchases from PDS	0.009	0.713	0.024	0.357
Public work as the treatment variable on only the targeted population, the sample BPL households	Annual household consumption expenditure	0.034*	0.087*	0.029*	0.071
	Annual household food expenditure	0.044***	0.009***	0.039**	0.016
	Value of annual household purchases from PDS	0.153**	0.005***	0.185***	0.000

Source: Authors' estimates.
Notes: The caliper has been chosen to be of width 0.0002 units.
***Significance at 1 per cent level, **significance at 5 per cent level and *significance at 10 per cent level.

positive and a significant impact effect for the entire sample while a negative and a statistically insignificant effect on the targeted sub-sample. Contrary to this and relatively more encouraging are the impact estimates related to the public works programme. The impact estimates are seen to be positive and significant only for the poorest strata of the sample, that is, the sub-sample comprising only the 'below poverty line' households.

Our obtained result has important policy implications. We find that at the all-India level, the results point favourably at the reach and impact of the public works programme as compared to the IRDP. The government budgetary allocations for these two programmes are different and should be considered while drawing any comparisons. Nevertheless, we believe that the estimated impact effects of the programme make very interesting contributions to the existing literature apart from being able to provide precise impact estimates of the programme intervention. This chapter in some way could speak to contemporary debates in India with regard to, for example, microfinance and the National Rural Employment Guarantee Act in India. Microfinance programme has been activated to reach the poor communities with access to financial services that are sustainable over time and to those who have little or no access to formal credit or savings services. On the other hand, the National Rural Employment Guarantee Act aims at enhancing the livelihood security of people in rural areas by guaranteeing hundred days of wage-employment in a financial year to a rural household whose adult members volunteer to do unskilled manual work. Our result implies that a proper implementation of the National Rural Employment Guarantee Act could bring fruitful objective in eradicating poverty. Although our analysis is limited to India, we believe that it could also draw attention to the international policymakers for similar programme design in other developing countries.

Table A13.1:
Determinants of IRDP loan beneficiary (probit model)

Dependent Variable: Household Has IRDP Loan	*Coefficient*	*Standard Error*	*P-value*
Demographic and Social Characteristics			
Dependency ratio	0.063	0.062	0.314
Total working children	0.093	0.051	0.067*
Household size	0.007	0.005	0.137
Adult female proportion	0.167	0.099	0.094*
Hindu religion dummy	–0.489	0.055	0.000***
Christian religion dummy	–0.540	0.130	0.000***
Muslim religion dummy	–0.508	0.071	0.000***
Schedule tribe dummy	0.116	0.051	0.024***
Schedule caste dummy	0.139	0.041	0.001***
Other backward caste dummy	0.036	0.032	0.258

(Table A13.1 Contd)

(Table A13.1 Contd)

Dependent Variable: Household Has IRDP Loan	*Coefficient*	*Standard Error*	*P-value*
Dummy if head of the household is married	-0.025	0.088	0.778
Dummy if head of the household is widow, divorcee or separated	-0.005	0.097	0.962
Dummy if the age of the head is between 18 and 60 years	0.311	0.325	0.339
Dummy if the age of the head is above 60 years	0.289	0.327	0.375
Economic Characteristics			
Land irrigated	-0.003	0.008	0.694
Meals per day dummy (base is less than two meals)	0.033	0.029	0.257
Household belongs to below poverty line dummy	-0.016	0.036	0.663
Household has a kitchen garden dummy	0.043	0.036	0.237
Household owns land less than 6 hectares (base is no land)	0.272	0.142	0.056*
Household owns land between 6 and 34 hectares (base is no land)	0.202	0.173	0.242
Household owns land more than 34 hectares (base is no land)	0.136	0.179	0.446
Household uses common source like coal, coke for cooking (no arrangement as base)	-0.149	0.388	0.700
Household uses source like kerosene, electricity for cooking (no arrangement as base)	-0.410	0.376	0.275
Household uses oil, gas or candle as source of lighting (no lighting as the base)	-0.238	0.178	0.181
Household uses electricity as source of lighting (no lighting as the base)	-0.407	0.179	0.023**
Head of the household earns income from economic activity	0.026	0.058	0.652
Head of the household earns income from other sources	0.141	0.082	0.085*
Source of income is non-agriculture (base agriculture)	0.042	0.042	0.317
Source of income is rental activity (base agriculture)	0.216	0.106	0.042**

(Table A13.1 Contd)

(Table A13.1 Contd)

Dependent Variable: Household Has IRDP Loan	*Coefficient*	*Standard Error*	*P-value*
Source of income is from remittances (base agriculture)	–0.172	0.052	0.001**
Source of income from interest and dividends (base agriculture)	0.132	0.068	0.053**
Source of income from pension (base agriculture)	–0.027	0.076	0.725
Household Occupation and Education			
Self-employed in non-agriculture (base self-employed in agriculture)	–0.038	0.054	0.485
Agricultural labourers (base self-employed in agriculture)	0.001	0.038	0.980
Other labour (base self-employed in agriculture)	0.144	0.066	0.029**
Others (base self-employed in agriculture)	0.001	0.050	0.990
Head of the household has education less than primary (illiterate is base)	0.010	0.033	0.754
Head of the household has education more than primary (illiterate is base)	0.022	0.036	0.538
Head of the household has education more than secondary (illiterate is base)	–0.065	0.056	0.253

Source: Authors' own estimates.

Notes: *P*-values are based on robust standard errors adjusted for heteroskedasticity and clustering at the village level. *Significance at the 10 per cent level, **significance at the 5 per cent level and ***significance at the 1 per cent level. We have also included region dummy (NSS divides India in 88 regions). The estimates for the regional dummies are not reported.

Table A13.2:
Determinants of public works beneficiary (probit model)

Dependent Variable: Household is involved in Public Works Programme	*Coefficient*	*Standard Error*	*P-value*
Demographic and Social Characteristics			
Dependency ratio	–0.125	0.055	0.023**
Total working children	0.072	0.043	0.096*
Household size	0.016	0.004	0.000***

(Table A13.2 Contd)

(Table A13.2 Contd)

Dependent Variable: Household is involved in Public Works Programme	*Coefficient*	*Standard Error*	*P-value*
Adult female proportion	−0.200	0.079	0.011**
Other religion dummy	−0.206	0.078	0.009**
Christian religion dummy	0.030	0.073	0.680
Muslim religion dummy	−0.057	0.0403	0.155
Schedule tribe dummy	0.304	0.037	0.000**
Schedule caste dummy	−0.027	0.032	0.398
General caste dummy	0.006	0.036	0.870
Dummy if head of the household is married	0.051	0.080	0.524
Dummy if head of the household is never married	−0.020	0.038	0.606
Dummy if the age of the head is between 18 and 60 years	0.050	0.160	0.753
Dummy if the age of the head is above 60 years	0.037	0.163	0.818
Economic Characteristics			
Meals per day dummy (base is less than two meals)	−0.097	0.024	0.000***
Household belongs to below poverty line dummy	−0.017	0.028	0.548
Household owns no land (base is more than 34 hectares)	0.124	0.109	0.255
Household owns land less than 6 hectares (base is more than 34 hectares)	0.109	0.053	0.040**
Household owns land between 6 and 34 hectares (base is more than 34 hectares)	0.218	0.109	0.044**
Household uses common source like coal, coke for cooking (no arrangement as base)	0.293	0.214	0.171
Household uses source like kerosene, electricity for cooking (no arrangement as base)	0.239	0.217	0.272
Household uses oil, gas or candle as source of lighting (electricity as the base)	0.181	0.025	0.000***
Household uses electricity as no source of lighting (electricity as the base)	0.375	0.147	0.011**
Head of the household earns income from economic activity	0.031	0.050	0.539

(Table A13.2 Contd)

(Table A13.2 Contd)

Dependent Variable: Household is involved in Public Works Programme	*Coefficient*	*Standard Error*	*P-value*
Head of the household earns income from other sources	0.172	0.065	0.008**
Source of income is wage-income (base agriculture)	0.257	0.029	0.000***
Source of income is non-agriculture (base agriculture)	–0.081	0.042	0.050**
Source of income is rental activity (base agriculture)	0.024	0.099	0.809
Source of income is from other than agriculture (base agriculture)	0.139	0.046	0.002**
Source of income from interest and dividends (base agriculture)	0.108	0.066	0.100*
Source of income from pension (base agriculture)	0.075	0.068	0.273
Household Occupation and Education			
Self-employed in agriculture (base other labour)	–0.111	0.059	0.060**
Agricultural labourers (base other labour)	–0.168	0.040	0.000**
Self-employed in agriculture (base other labour)	–0.175	0.044	0.000***
Others (base other labour)	–0.169	0.051	0.001**
Head of the household has education less than primary (illiterate is base)	0.003	0.033	0.920
Head of the household has education more than primary (illiterate is base)	0.003	0.031	0.919
Head of the household has education more than secondary (illiterate is base)	0.050	0.040	0.210

Source: Authors' own estimates.

Notes: *P*-values are based on robust standard errors adjusted for heteroskedasticity and clustering at the village level. *Significance at the 10 per cent level, **significance at the 5 per cent level and ***significance at the 1 per cent level. We have also included region dummy (NSS divides India in 88 regions). The estimates for the regional dummies are not reported.

References

Acharya, S. and Panwalker, V.G. 1988. 'The Employment Guarantee Scheme in Maharashtra: Impact on Male and Female Labor', *Regional Research Paper*. Bangkok: Population Council.

Dahejia, R. and Wahba, S. 2002. 'Propensity Score Matching Methods for Non Experimental Causal Studies', *Review of Economics and Statistics*, 84(1): 151–61.

Datt, G. 1994. 'Poverty Alleviation through Rural Public Works: The Experience of Maharashtra's Employment Guarantee Scheme', *Indian Journal of Labour Economics*, 37(4): 659–72.

Dreze, J. 1990. 'Poverty in India and IRDP Delusion', *Economic and Political Weekly*, 25(39): A95–104.

Frolich, M. 2004. 'Finite Sample Properties of Propensity Score Matching and Weighting Estimators', *Review of Economics and Statistics*, 86(1): 77–90.

Guhan, S. 1986. 'Rural Poverty Alleviation in India: Policy, Performance and Possibilities', reproduced in S. Subramanian (ed.), *India's Development Experience: Selected Writings of S. Guhan* (pp. 5–46). New Delhi: Oxford University Press, 2001.

Heckman, J. and Lozano, S.N. 2004. 'Using Matching, Instrumental Variables and Control Functions to Estimate Economic Choice Models', *Review of Economics and Statistics*, 86(1): 30–57.

Heckman, J., Ichimura, H. and Todd, P. 1997. 'Matching as an Econometric Evaluation Estimator: Evidence from a Job Training Programme', *Review of Economic Studies*, 64(4): 605–54.

Hirano, K., Imbens, G. and Ridder, G. 2003. 'Efficient Estimation of Average Treatment Effects using Propensity Score', *Econometrica*, 71(4): 1161–89.

Ichimura, H. and Taber, C. 2001. 'Propensity Score Matching with Instrumental Variable', *American Economic Review*, 91(2): 119–24.

Jalan, J. and Ravallion, M. 2003. 'Does Piped Water Reduce Diarrhea for Children in Rural India?', *Journal of Econometrics*, 112(1): 153–73.

Kurian, N.J. 1987. 'IRDP, How Relevant Is It?', *Economic and Political Weekly*, 22(52): A161–76.

Markus, F. 2004. 'A Note on the Role of Propensity Score for Estimating Average Treatment Effects', *Econometric Reviews*, 23(2): 167–74.

Mukherjee, A 1997. 'Public Works Programmes: Some Issues', *Indian Journal of Labour Economics*, 40(2): 289–302.

Panda, M., Mishra, S., Kamdar, S. and Tondare, M. 2005. 'Evaluation of Food-for-Work (FFW) Component of Sampoorna Grameen Rozgar Yojana (SGRY) in Selected Districts of Maharashtra', mimeo, Indira Gandhi Institute of Development Research, India.

Paul, S. 1998. 'The Performance of Integrated Rural Development Programme in India: An Assessment', *Developing Economies*, 36: 117–31.

Rosenbaum, P.R. and Rubin, D.B. 1983. 'The Central Role of the Propensity Score in Observational Studies for Causal Effects', *Biometrika*, 70(1): 41–55.

Sianesi, B. 2004. 'An Evaluation of the Swedish System of Active Labor Market Programs in the 1990s', *Review of Economics and Statistics*, 86(1): 133–55.

Tritah, A. 2003. 'The Public Distribution System in India: Counting the Poor from Making the Poor Count', mimeo, Universit ́e des Sciences Sociales, Toulouse, France.

14

Budgetary Allocation on Education: A Study of Inter-state Imbalances

C. Bhujanga Rao and D.K. Srivastava

Introduction

There are considerable inter-state disparities in government resources devoted to education across states in India. These disparities arise because of (i) difference in fiscal capacity and (ii) differences in priority attached to education by the respective governments. While India's demographic dividend is currently unfolding, it has a significant inter-state dimension. In order to exploit the demographic dividend fully, states with relatively higher share of working age population in total population need to devote larger resources to education in particular and human resource development in general so as to make their young population employable. If states with a larger working age population happen also to be the states with low per capita resource allocation, the potential benefit of the demographic dividend would remain largely under-utilized.

In this chapter, we analyse the pattern of inter-state imbalances in education and its implications. The analysis pertains to the period from 1993–94 to 2011–12 covering 28 states before the 29th state of Telangana was formed from Andhra Pradesh.[1] States are classified into two groups. Group 1 comprises Andhra Pradesh, Bihar, Chhattisgarh, Goa, Gujarat, Haryana, Jharkhand,

[1] Andhra Pradesh was divided on 2 June 2014 and a new state of Telangana was created. This became the 29th State of India.

Karnataka, Kerala, Madhya Pradesh, Maharashtra, Odisha, Punjab, Rajasthan, Tamil Nadu, Uttar Pradesh and West Bengal. Group 2 consists of Arunachal Pradesh, Assam, Himachal Pradesh, Jammu and Kashmir, Manipur, Meghalaya, Mizoram, Nagaland, Sikkim, Tripura and Uttarakhand. These two groups of states were until recently referred to as general and special category states. But since the Planning Commission, which has used this nomenclature, does not exist in its old form and the Finance Commission has also discontinued with this distinction, we shall refer to these as group 1 and group 2 states for analytical purposes. The latter group contains states that are relatively smaller and generally characterized by large hilly terrains and other cost disadvantages.

Various aspects of inter-state inequality have been examined by many authors, for example, Barro (1991), Nagaraj et al. (1998), Govinda Rao et al. (1999), Shand and Bhide (2000), Ahluwalia (2000, 2002), Kurian (2002), Rao and Dev (2003), Dholakia (2003), Shetty (2003), Bhattacharya and Sakthivel (2004), Krishna (2004), Chaudhuri (2004), Pal and Ghosh (2007) and Acharya and Sahoo (2012). Many of these studies observed that the regional disparity in India has widened especially during the 1990s. But overall the findings have been mixed. As argued earlier, inter-state disparities in fiscal capacity proxies by per capita Gross State Domestic Product (GSDP) translate into disparities in the allocation of government resources to education.

This chapter is organized as follows. The next section deals with the trends of per capita GSDP in both sets of states. The successive section discusses the methodology. The section 'Inter-state Imbalance in Education' highlights the pattern of inter-state imbalances in education expenditure. Here we analyse whether a state's deficiency relative to the average is due to its lower fiscal capacity or due to that of lower priority that it attaches to the concerned service relative to the average. The final section summarizes the findings.

Trends in Income of States

To capture changes in the inter-state profile of economic activities, we look at both the GSDP growth rates and per capita GSDP.

Central Statistical Organization compiles the GSDP series supplied by the state, which are based on the primary data of production and prices collected by the concerned state statistical departments.[2] Tables 14.1 and 14.2 show the trend growth rates of GSDP at 2004–05 prices for the two groups of states for three periods: 1993–94 to 1999–2000, 2000–01 to 2009–10, and 2010–11 and 2011–12. Among group 1 states, low-income states like Chhattisgarh, Bihar, Odisha and Uttar Pradesh, and surprisingly Punjab registered a growth rate below 5 per cent per annum during the period 1993–94 to 1999–2000. Four states namely Andhra Pradesh, Kerala, Haryana and Jharkhand showed a growth rate of 5–6 per cent. Three states namely Madhya Pradesh, Tamil Nadu and Maharashtra registered growth rates of 6–7 per cent while the remaining five states (West Bengal, Gujarat, Rajasthan, Karnataka and Goa) showed a growth rate of more than 8 per cent, Rajasthan and Karnataka grew at 8–9 per cent and Goa grew at rate of 9.8 per cent per annum.

In the second period from 2000–01 to 2009–10, Uttar Pradesh and Madhya Pradesh registered the lowest growth rate among group 1 states, while Punjab, Jharkhand and West Bengal achieved a growth rate of about 5–6 per cent. Two states (Rajasthan and Karnataka) achieved a growth rate of 7–8 per cent. Five states (Andhra Pradesh, Kerala, Goa, Tamil Nadu and Chhattisgarh) grew at a rate of 8–9 per cent, while the remaining four states (Haryana, Odisha, Maharashtra and Gujarat) accounted for over 9 per cent growth per annum. Gujarat was the highest with little above 10 per cent.

In the third period, which covers only two years (2010–11 to 2011–12), Karnataka, Odisha, Jharkhand, West Bengal and Maharashtra show a growth of less than 5 per cent per annum, while two states (Rajasthan and Uttar Pradesh) grew at 5–6 per cent per annum. Punjab and Chhattisgarh achieved a growth rate of 6–7 per cent and the remaining states achieved a growth rate of

[2] There are a lot of measurement problems particularly that of value added component. A consistent longtime series on Gross State Domestic Product is not available due to frequent changes in the base years. To arrive at a long series for each of the states from 1993–94 to 2011–12, a simple splicing technique has been used. This basically takes care of the price indexation and leaves the product basket as constant.

Table 14.1:
Trend growth rates of GSDP at constant prices (2004–05)

(per cent)

Sl. No.	States	1993–94 to 1999–2000	2000–01 to 2009–10	2010–11 to 2011–12	1993–94 to 2011–12
Group 1					
1.	Andhra Pradesh	5.24	8.35	7.51	7.16
2.	Bihar	3.93	6.22	10.29	6.09
3.	Chhattisgarh	3.00	8.74	6.98	5.87
4.	Goa	9.77	8.19	20.21	7.83
5.	Gujarat	7.66	10.54	7.66	7.91
6.	Haryana	5.76	9.06	8.03	7.98
7.	Jharkhand	5.93	6.42	4.49	5.04
8.	Karnataka	8.55	7.82	3.69	7.21
9.	Kerala	5.24	8.06	7.96	6.89
10.	Madhya Pradesh	6.16	6.28	9.69	5.33
11.	Maharashtra	6.22	9.29	4.82	7.23
12.	Odisha	4.14	9.14	3.78	6.49
13.	Punjab	4.86	6.29	6.52	5.43
14.	Rajasthan	8.25	7.15	5.17	6.39
15.	Tamil Nadu	6.25	8.62	7.39	7.05
16.	Uttar Pradesh	4.58	6.05	5.57	5.07
17.	West Bengal	7.20	6.54	4.72	6.40
	17 States	**6.06**	**7.98**	**6.35**	**6.64**
Group 2					
1.	Arunachal Pradesh	2.84	8.12	4.49	6.50
2.	Assam	1.95	4.98	5.33	4.04
3.	Himachal Pradesh	6.98	7.75	7.31	7.22
4.	Jammu and Kashmir	5.10	5.45	7.95	5.03
5.	Manipur	5.86	6.08	9.79	5.12
6.	Meghalaya	6.75	7.13	12.58	6.96
7.	Mizoram*		7.43	-2.55	
8.	Nagaland	4.67	7.43	8.32	7.19
9.	Sikkim	6.35	11.43	10.77	9.96
10.	Tripura	8.42	7.87	8.69	8.21
11.	Uttarakhand	2.87	12.74	9.36	9.10
	11 States	**4.21**	**7.26**	**7.48**	**6.20**
	All-India (GDP)	**6.66**	**7.83**	**6.69**	**7.04**

Source (Basic Data): Central Statistical Organization.
Note: * Constant GSDP data for Mizoram is not available for the period 1993–94 to 1999–2000.

Table 14.2:
Ranking of the states according to growth rate ranges

Growth Rates (per cent)							
Rank	*Below 5*	*Rank*	*Between 5 and 6*	*Rank*	*Between 6 and 7*	*Rank*	*Above 7*
1993–94 to 2011–12							
Group 1 (17)							
		25	Jharkhand	19	Bihar	12	Tamil Nadu
		24	Uttar Pradesh	18	Rajasthan	11	Andhra Pradesh
		22	Madhya Pradesh	17	West Bengal	9	Karnataka
		21	Punjab	16	Odisha	7	Maharashtra
		20	Chhattisgarh	14	Kerala	6	Goa
						5	Gujarat
						4	Haryana
*Group 2 (10)**							
27	Assam	26	Jammu and Kashmir	15	Arunachal Pradesh	10	Nagaland
		25	Jharkhand	13	Meghalaya	8	Himachal Pradesh
		23	Manipur			3	Tripura
						1	Sikkim

Source: Table 14.1.
Note: *For Mizoram constant prices data with 1999–2000 base is not available for the period 1993–94 to 1999–2000.

above 7 per cent per annum. Goa achieved a growth rate of 20 per cent and Bihar little above 10 per cent.

In the case of group two states, four states namely Assam, Arunachal Pradesh, Nagaland and Uttarakhand observe growth rate of less than 5 per cent per annum during the years 1993–94 to 1999–2000. Two states namely Jammu and Kashmir and Manipur registered a growth rate of 5–6 per cent, while three states namely Sikkim, Meghalaya and Himachal Pradesh grew at 6–7 per cent and Tripura at 8.4 per cent.

In the second period (2000–01 to 2009–10), Assam registered the lowest rate followed by Jammu and Kashmir and Manipur.

Five states (Himachal Pradesh, Tripura, Nagaland, Mizoram and Meghalaya) achieved a growth rate of 6–7 per cent. The remaining three states accounted for above 7 per cent. The highest growth rate of 12.7 per cent was achieved by Uttarakhand followed by Sikkim (11.4 per cent).

In the third period (2010–11 to 2011–12), two states namely Mizoram and Arunachal Pradesh growth rate was below 5 per cent followed by Assam. Two states (Himachal Pradesh and Jammu and Kashmir) achieved a growth rate of 7–8 per cent, while Nagaland and Tripura grew 8–9 per cent. Two states (Manipur and Uttarakhand) grew at 8–9 per cent while Sikkim and Meghalaya achieved 10 per cent growth rate per annum.

The second period (2000–01 to 2009–10) is the period of highest GSDP growth for the average of the two groups and almost all the individual states. This is also the period of high growth of GDP.

Table 14.2 shows the ranking of the 28 states and categorizing the states for the overall period (1993–94 to 2011–12) according to growth rates below 5 per cent, between 5–6 and 6–7 per cent, and above 7 per cent per annum.

Table 14.3 presents summary indicators of disparity in comparable per capita GSDP over the period 1993–94 to 2011–12.

The ratio of maximum (Punjab) to minimum (Bihar) per capita GSDP fell from 5.46 in 1993–94 to 4.24 in 1995–96 and thereafter fluctuated between 5 and 6 but declined to 4.07 in 2000–01. Thereafter, this ratio increased to 5.33 in 2005–06 and since then has been fluctuating in the range of 4.93–5.89. The ratio of average per capita GSDP to minimum per capita GSDP has ranged from 2.80 to 4.06 over the period 1993–94 to 2011–12. The coefficient of variation has increased in the range of 31 per cent in the first seven years (1993–94 to 1999–2000) declined in the next two years and rose to a maximum of 39.04 per cent in 2011–12.

Table 14.4 shows the inter-state pattern of per capita GSDP at 2004–05 prices for the 28 states for the period 1993–94 to 2011–12. For convenience three-year averages have been taken. Thus, 1994–95 refers to the three year average of 1993–94 to 1995–96; 1997–98 refers to three-year average of 1996–97 to 1998–99 and so on. In group 1 states, it is observed that Bihar has the lowest

Table 14.3:
Indicators of inter-state inequality: Based on per capita GSDP at factor cost at 2004–05 prices

Years	*Ratio of Max (excluding Goa)/ Minimum*	*Ratio of Average/ Minimum*	*Coefficient of Variance (per cent)*
1993–94	5.46	3.45	30.70
1994–95	5.08	3.30	31.01
1995–96	6.24	4.06	31.74
1996–97	5.37	3.51	31.94
1997–98	5.85	3.86	31.42
1998–99	5.71	3.80	31.65
1999–2000	6.17	4.00	31.27
2000–01	4.07	2.68	29.09
2001–02	4.54	3.01	28.56
2002–03	4.31	2.80	29.99
2003–04	4.98	3.21	29.74
2004–05	4.81	3.09	30.22
2005–06	5.33	3.40	32.64
2006–07	5.22	3.20	33.70
2007–08	5.50	3.32	34.44
2008–09	4.93	3.12	34.02
2009–10	6.18	3.35	37.50
2010–11	5.87	3.17	38.02
2011–12	5.89	3.07	39.04

Source (Basic Data): Central Statistical Organization.
Note: Refers to all states excluding Goa.

per capita income over the entire period from 1993–94 to 2011–12, while Goa accounts for the highest per capita income over the period. The next highest income is accounted by Punjab, a maximum of ₹17,423 in 1994–95, which rose to ₹30,459 in 2000–01. However, thereafter Haryana accounted for the maximum per capita income reaching a level of ₹116,284 in 2011–12. The average per capita income of sixteen states (excluding Goa) has gone up from ₹11,518 in 1994–95 to about ₹70,049 in 2011–12. These figures are at current prices.

Table 14.4:
Per capita GSDP of 28 states (three-year averages) current prices (2004–05 base year series)*

(₹)

Sl. No.	States	1994–95	1997–98	2000–01	2003–04	2006–07	2009–10	2011–12
Group 1								
1.	Andhra Pradesh	10,608	14,854	20,010	25,574	37,791	59,218	77,780
2.	Bihar	5,648	7,638	7,677	8,270	10,786	17,667	24,696
3.	Chhattisgarh			14,614	19,226	28,783	42,854	56,514
4.	Goa	24,039	40,331	54,893	73,760	110,298	174,098	240,440
5.	Gujarat	15,018	21,871	24,594	33,723	51,473	75,912	100,662
6.	Haryana	15,102	21,175	27,984	37,652	54,949	89,282	116,284
7.	Jharkhand			14,479	18,103	23,844	34,039	42,745
8.	Karnataka	11,044	16,387	21,834	26,543	40,780	60,210	76,148
9.	Kerala	12,718	19,208	24,947	32,489	46,421	68,016	90,088
10.	Madhya Pradesh	9,000	12,057	14,450	16,433	21,353	32,458	41,872
11.	Maharashtra	17,098	23,444	28,820	36,402	55,273	80,108	103,498
12.	Odisha	8,066	10,726	13,136	17,367	26,909	41,948	52,241
13.	Punjab	17,423	23,741	30,459	35,143	47,839	69,790	86,698
14.	Rajasthan	9,653	14,343	16,679	19,338	26,861	41,903	60,492
15.	Tamil Nadu	13,367	19,701	24,932	30,243	46,794	73,059	98,556
16.	Uttar Pradesh	7,341	10,172	11,679	13,620	18,184	26,653	33,797

(Table 14.4 Contd)

(Table 14.4 Contd)

Sl. No.	*States*	*1994–95*	*1997–98*	*2000–01*	*2003–04*	*2006–07*	*2009–10*	*2011–12*
17.	West Bengal	9,174	13,628	18,143	22,678	30,736	45,311	58,711
State Avg. Per Capita GSDP (excluding Goa)		11,518	16,353	19,652	24,550	35,548	53,652	70,049
Group 2								
1.	Arunachal Pradesh	12,872	16,021	20,539	26,150	35,837	58,104	77,131
2.	Assam	8,710	11,006	14,089	17,497	22,498	32,113	40,890
3.	Himachal Pradesh	12,623	18,897	26,811	34,059	45,119	69,277	94,127
4.	Jammu and Kashmir	10,359	13,877	18,810	23,714	30,256	43,048	57,755
5.	Manipur	9,476	13,249	16,036	18,625	24,160	30,336	39,258
6.	Meghalaya	10,949	14,941	19,692	24,883	34,295	50,262	65,171
7.	Mizoram	12,592	16,825	21,642	26,642	32,755	48,845	59,312
8.	Nagaland	13,856	16,931	19,715	24,139	27,780	48,274	66,664
9.	Sikkim	11,759	16,322	20,651	27,751	38,223	92,564	144,352
10.	Tripura	7,626	12,085	18,723	24,407	31,581	43,855	54,859
11.	Uttarakhand			18,631	24,575	40,260	71,976	97,594
State Avg. Per Capita GSDP		11,082	15,015	19,576	24,767	32,978	53,514	72,465
All-India		10,409	15,084	19,484	24,446	35,119	52,613	69,100

Source (Basic Data): Central Statistical Organization (2015) and Chand (2015), Data Bank NIPFP.

Notes: *1994–95 refers to average of 1993–94 to 1995–96; 1997–98 refers to average of 1996–97 to 1998–99: 2000–01 refers to average of 1999–00 to 2001–02; 2003–04 refers to average of 2002–03 to 2004–05; 2006–07 refers to average of 2005–06 to 2007–08; 2010–11 refers to 2008–09 to 2011–12 and 2011–12 refers to 2011–12.

In group 2 states the highest per capita income is accounted by Nagaland in 1994–95, Himachal Pradesh in 1997–98 to 2006–07 and thereafter Manipur, while the lowest income in 1994–95 was of Tripura, from 1997–98 to 2006–07 it was Assam and during 2009–10 to 2011–12 it was Manipur. The average per capita income of 11 states has risen from ₹11,082 to ₹72,465 during the period 1993–94 to 2011–12, while at the all-India level the per capita income increased from ₹10,409 to ₹69,100 in the same period.

Table 14.5 shows the per capita income of states as percentage to the average of 16 group 1 states (excluding Goa) and to the average of 11 group 2 States. This enables us to capture the states that are improving their performance above the states' average in the two categories. It is seen that generally Bihar, Jharkhand, Rajasthan, Madhya Pradesh and Uttar Pradesh have shown a continuous deterioration over the years. While for Odisha there has been a decline initially but with some fluctuation around the trend. In the case of Andhra Pradesh and Karnataka, they have moved above the average, while West Bengal showed reaching the average but declined from 2006 to 2007 onwards and Chhattisgarh is slowly inching towards the average.

In the case of group 2 states, Assam, Jammu and Kashmir, Manipur and Nagaland have been deteriorating over the years, while Uttarakhand, Arunachal Pradesh, Himachal Pradesh and Sikkim have moved above the average. Meghalaya has shown deterioration from 2008–09 onwards and Tripura from 2005–06 onwards.

We note that periods when the national growth is high, it uplifts all states but differentially. Some of the states that have done well in growth and per capita GSDP are not known to have performed equally well on education, for example, Punjab and Gujarat. One reason for this could be the relatively lower priority attached to education in budgetary allocation. The role of this factor can be brought out using the methodology proposed further.

Table 14.5:
Per capita GSDP as percentage of averages for group 1 (17 states) and group 2 (11 states)

(per cent)

Sl. No.	States	1994–95	1997–98	2000–01	2003–04	2006–07	2009–10	2011–12
Group 1								
1.	Andhra Pradesh	92.10	90.83	101.82	104.17	106.31	110.38	111.04
2.	Bihar	49.03	46.70	39.07	33.69	30.34	32.93	35.26
3.	Chhattisgarh	0.00	0.00	74.37	78.31	80.97	79.87	80.68
4.	Goa	208.70	246.62	279.32	300.45	310.28	324.50	343.25
5.	Gujarat	130.38	133.74	125.15	137.36	144.80	141.49	143.70
6.	Haryana	131.11	129.49	142.40	153.37	154.58	166.41	166.00
7.	Jharkhand	0.00	0.00	73.68	73.74	67.07	63.44	61.02
8.	Karnataka	95.88	100.20	111.10	108.12	114.72	112.22	108.71
9.	Kerala	110.41	117.46	126.94	132.34	130.58	126.77	128.61
10.	Madhya Pradesh	78.14	73.73	73.53	66.94	60.07	60.50	59.78
11.	Maharashtra	148.44	143.36	146.65	148.27	155.49	149.31	147.75
12.	Odisha	70.03	65.59	66.84	70.74	75.70	78.19	74.58
13.	Punjab	151.26	145.17	154.99	143.15	134.57	130.08	123.77
14.	Rajasthan	83.80	87.71	84.87	78.77	75.56	78.10	86.36

15.	Tamil Nadu	116.05	120.47	126.86	123.19	131.64	136.17	140.70
16.	Uttar Pradesh	63.73	62.20	59.43	55.48	51.15	49.68	48.25
17.	West Bengal	79.64	83.34	92.32	92.37	86.46	84.45	83.81
State Avg. Per Capita GSDP (₹)		11,518	16,353	19,652	24,550	35,548	53,652	70,049
Group 2								
1.	Arunachal Pradesh	116.15	106.70	104.92	105.58	108.67	108.58	106.44
2.	Assam	78.60	73.30	71.97	70.65	68.22	60.01	56.43
3.	Himachal Pradesh	113.90	125.85	136.96	137.51	136.81	129.46	129.89
4.	Jammu and Kashmir	93.47	92.42	96.08	95.75	91.75	80.44	79.70
5.	Manipur	85.50	88.23	81.91	75.20	73.26	56.69	54.18
6.	Meghalaya	98.80	99.50	100.59	100.47	103.99	93.92	89.94
7.	Mizoram	113.63	112.06	110.55	107.57	99.32	91.27	81.85
8.	Nagaland	125.03	112.76	100.71	97.46	84.24	90.21	92.00
9.	Sikkim	106.11	108.70	105.49	112.05	115.90	172.97	199.20
10.	Tripura	68.81	80.49	95.64	98.55	95.76	81.95	75.70
11.	Uttarakhand	0.00	0.00	95.17	99.22	122.08	134.50	134.68
State Avg. Per Capita GSDP (₹)		11,082	15,015	19,576	24,767	32,978	53,514	72,465

Source: (*Basic Data*): Table 14.4.
Note: Goa has been excluded in the group 1 states.

Methodology

The analysis of per capita expenditure for any service can be formulated as the priority that an *i*th state imparts for a service and the size of budget that *i*th state allocates to that service.

Per capita expenditure (revenue and capital) for a service can be written as

$$(\text{PCE} / \text{AE}) = (\text{TE} / N) \tag{1}$$

where

PCE: per capita expenditure on a particular service
AE: average expenditure on a particular service
TE: total expenditure on a particular service
TTE: total expenditure of a state
N: Population of a state

Per capita revenue expenditure for a state can be formulated as:

$$(\text{TE} / N)_i = (\text{TE} / \text{TTE})_i * (\text{TTE} / N)_i \tag{2}$$

Or

$$te = p_i * \text{tte}_i$$

The per capita expenditure is derived by multiplying the priority of a state to a particular service with the size of the budget. The average ($_a$) for the 16 states (excluding Goa) is arrived as

$$(\text{TE} / N)_a = (\text{TE} / \text{TTE})_a * (\text{TTE} / N)_a \tag{3}$$

Thus, $[(\text{TE}/N)_i / (\text{TE} / N)_a] = [p_i / p_a] * [\text{tte}_i / \text{tte}_a]$

Similarly, the average ($_a$) for 11 group 2 states is arrived. For further details refer to an earlier paper by Rao and Srivastava (2009).

Inter-state Imbalance in Education

In this section, the profile on inter-state imbalances in education is examined. By education we refer to education, sports, art and culture, which encompasses, elementary education, secondary education, university and higher education, adult education, language development, technical education, sports and youth services and art and culture. This analysis looks at the deficiency in fiscal capacity relative to the average and deficiency in the priority accorded to the sector as possible causes of relatively low per capita expenditures on education. The priorities of the states in education and the size of expenditure among the various states are analysed.

Table 14.6 shows the per capita total expenditure (revenue and capital) of education for the period 1993–94 to 2011–12 for group 1 and group 2 states. In the year 1994–95 (the average of three years 1993–94 to 1995–96) for group 1 states, the maximum expenditure on education was incurred by Goa (₹880), followed by Kerala (₹442) and the minimum expenditure was incurred by Bihar (₹186). In the year 2011–12, the maximum expenditure on education was incurred by Goa (₹5,704) followed by Kerala (₹2,738) and the minimum expenditure was incurred by Bihar (₹1,037). Maharashtra also incurred an expenditure of ₹2,645 during this year.

In the case of group 2 states, the maximum education expenditure incurred by Mizoram (₹999) and the minimum by Assam (₹366). Sikkim also incurred a per capita expenditure of ₹961. In 2011–12, Sikkim accounted for maximum expenditure (₹8,954) and Assam for minimum expenditure (₹1,992). Also Mizoram accounted a per capita expenditure of ₹6,058.

Table 14.7 shows the ranking of the states as per their per capita revenue expenditure on education for three year averages centred in the years 1994–95, 1997–98, 2000–01, 2003–04, 2006–07, 2009–10 and 2011–12.[3] Over the years, Uttar Pradesh had the second lowest

[3] Chhattisgarh, Jharkhand and Uttarakhand came into existence in November 2000; as a consequence the data available for the financial year 2000–01 is partial. Also, for this year it is a two year average for the new states, that is, average of 2000–01 and 2002–03 centred on 2000–01.

Table 14.6:
Per capita total expenditure on education (three year averages)*

(₹)

Sl. No.	States	1994–95	1997–98	2000–01	2003–04	2006–07	2009–10	2011–12
Group 1								
1.	Andhra Pradesh	229	319	479	563	747	1,126	1,767
2.	Bihar	186	248	418	384	557	3,295	1,037
3.	Chhattisgarh			227	443	698	1,679	1,996
4.	Goa	880	1,414	1,781	2,152	2,678	4,611	5,704
5.	Gujarat	363	535	689	713	901	1,481	2,103
6.	Haryana	309	488	649	699	1,011	2,040	2,478
7.	Jharkhand			470	589	821	1,242	1,302
8.	Karnataka	314	457	635	713	1,033	1,636	2,102
9.	Kerala	442	584	814	957	1,197	1,791	2,738
10.	Madhya Pradesh	205	288	399	381	526	951	1,369
11.	Maharashtra	369	532	904	943	1,165	1,996	2,645
12.	Odisha	244	357	497	510	686	1,373	1,636
13.	Punjab	368	591	756	823	910	1,332	1,838
14.	Rajasthan	305	446	587	613	802	1,367	1,704
15.	Tamil Nadu	337	517	704	684	946	1,684	2,310

16.	Uttar Pradesh	190	283	358	377	583	882	1,297
17.	West Bengal	247	349	591	559	735	1,299	1,777
State Avg. Per Capita GSDP (excluding Goa)		293	428	574	622	832	1573	1881
Group 2								
1.	Arunachal Pradesh	855	1,136	1,204	1,725	2,458	4,551	5,461
2.	Assam	366	469	692	825	959	1,449	1,992
3.	Himachal Pradesh	570	952	1,457	1,587	2,110	3,389	4,475
4.	Jammu and Kashmir	473	636	863	951	1,270	2,215	3,194
5.	Manipur	686	1,037	1,334	1,359	1,795	2,132	2,576
6.	Meghalaya	530	689	1,010	1,141	1,429	2,286	3,887
7.	Mizoram	999	1,363	2,137	2,361	3,081	4,667	6,058
8.	Nagaland	763	791	1,060	1,057	1,407	2,613	3,756
9.	Sikkim	961	1,680	2,499	3,117	4,125	7,422	8,954
10.	Tripura	519	755	1,280	1,597	1,562	2,385	3,000
11.	Uttarakhand			548	1,215	1,651	2,829	3,585
State Avg. Per Capita GSDP		672	951	1,280	1,540	1,986	3,267	4,267

Source (Basic Data): Reserve Bank of India (RBI), Study of State Finances, various years and Central Statistical Organization.

Notes: * 1994–95 refers to average of 1993–94 to 1995–96; 1997–98 refers to average of 1996–97 to 1998–99: 2000-01 refers to average of 1999–2000 to 2001–02; 2003–04 refers to average of 2002–03 to 2004–05; 2006–07 refers to average of 2005–06 to 2007–08; 2010–11 refers to 2008–09 to 2011–12 and 2011–12 refers to 2011–12.

Table 14.7:
Ranking of states as per capita total expenditure on education

Rank	2000–01	2003–04	2006–07	2009–10	2011–12
28	Chhattisgarh	Uttar Pradesh	Madhya Pradesh	Bihar	Bihar
27	Uttar Pradesh	Madhya Pradesh	Bihar	Uttar Pradesh	Uttar Pradesh
26	Madhya Pradesh	Bihar	Uttar Pradesh	Madhya Pradesh	Jharkhand
25	Bihar	Chhattisgarh	Odisha	Andhra Pradesh	Madhya Pradesh
24	Jharkhand	Odisha	Chhattisgarh	Jharkhand	Odisha
23	Andhra Pradesh	West Bengal	West Bengal	West Bengal	Rajasthan
22	Odisha	Andhra Pradesh	Andhra Pradesh	Punjab	Andhra Pradesh
21	Uttarakhand	Jharkhand	Rajasthan	Rajasthan	West Bengal
20	Rajasthan	Rajasthan	Jharkhand	Odisha	Punjab
19	West Bengal	Tamil Nadu	Gujarat	Assam	Assam
++18	Karnataka	Haryana	Punjab	Gujarat	Chhattisgarh
17	Haryana	Gujarat	Tamil Nadu	Karnataka	Karnataka
16	Gujarat	Karnataka	Assam	Chhattisgarh	Gujarat
15	Assam	Punjab	Haryana	Tamil Nadu	Tamil Nadu
14	Tamil Nadu	Assam	Karnataka	Kerala	Haryana
13	Punjab	Maharashtra	Maharashtra	Maharashtra	Manipur
12	Kerala	Jammu and Kashmir	Kerala	Haryana	Maharashtra
11	Jammu & Kashmir	Kerala	Jammu & Kashmir	Manipur	Kerala
10	Maharashtra	Nagaland	Nagaland	Jammu and Kashmir	Tripura
9	Meghalaya	Meghalaya	Meghalaya	Meghalaya	Jammu and Kashmir
8	Nagaland	Uttarakhand	Tripura	Tripura	Uttarakhand
7	Arunachal Pradesh	Manipur	Uttarakhand	Nagaland	Nagaland

(Table 14.7 Contd)

(Table 14.7 Contd)

Rank	*2000–01*	*2003–04*	*2006–07*	*2009–10*	*2011–12*
6	Tripura	Himachal Pradesh	Manipur	Uttarakhand	Meghalaya
5	Manipur	Tripura	Himachal Pradesh	Himachal Pradesh	Himachal Pradesh
4	Himachal Pradesh	Arunachal Pradesh	Arunachal Pradesh	Arunachal Pradesh	Arunachal Pradesh
3	Goa	Goa	Goa	Goa	Goa
2	Mizoram	Mizoram	Mizoram	Mizoram	Mizoram
1	Sikkim	Sikkim	Sikkim	Sikkim	Sikkim

Source: See Table 14.6.

expenditure on education (1994–95, 1997–98, 2000–01, 2009–10 and 2011–12), except in 2003–04 when it was the lowest and in 2006–07 the third lowest. Among the low income states (Bihar, Odisha, Madhya Pradesh, Rajasthan and Uttar Pradesh) Rajasthan has higher per capita expenditure on education. It is having higher expenditure than West Bengal except for the years 2000–01 and 2011–12. The per capita expenditure in the case of Punjab fluctuated between 11th and 22nd ranks, Maharashtra fluctuated between 10th and 14th ranks, and Haryana fluctuated between 12th and 18th ranks. Kerala has generally occupied the 12th rank in 1997–98, 2000–01 and 2006–07 and in the 11th rank in 1994–95, 2003–04 and 2011–12 and 14th rank in 2009–10. Andhra Pradesh has generally occupied 22nd rank in 1994–95, 1997–98, 2003–04, 2006–07 and 2011–12. In 2000–01, it ranked 23rd and 25th in 2009–10.

Sikkim has the highest per capita expenditure on education from 1997–98 to 2011–12 (except in 1994–95 when it was in 2nd position), followed by Mizoram and Goa ranking between 2nd and 3rd. In 1994–95 Mizoram has highest per capita income; Goa has been the third highest in 1994–95, 2000–01 to 2011–12, and second highest in 1997–98.

Table 14.8 shows the summary indicators of disparity in comparable per capita expenditure on education over the period 1993–94 to 2011–12. As the per capita expenditure on education by the state

Table 14.8:
Disparities in per capita education among the states

Years	*Ratio of Maximum to Minimum Per Capita Expenditure on Education*	*Ratio of Average to Minimum Per Capita Expenditure on Education*	*Coefficient of Variation (per cent)*
Group 1			
1993–94	2.50	1.65	27.18
1994–95	2.47	1.58	26.81
1995–96	2.22	1.53	26.58
1996–97	2.31	1.60	26.04
1997–98	2.26	1.60	28.27
1998–99	2.89	1.98	29.54
1999–2000	2.46	1.75	26.45
2001–02	2.88	1.72	31.19
2002–03	2.64	1.71	30.93
2003–04	2.63	1.69	29.90
2004–05	2.80	1.84	29.41
2005–06	2.36	1.64	25.14
2006–07	2.12	1.48	24.21
2007–08	2.36	1.64	25.16
2008–09	2.66	1.68	29.95
2009–10	2.65	1.71	28.14
2010–11	2.85	1.96	26.33
2011–12	2.64	1.81	26.53
Group 2			
1993–94	2.84	1.80	31.73
1994–95	2.62	1.80	32.42
1995–96	2.82	1.90	32.80
1996–97	3.33	2.07	37.69
1997–98	2.96	2.01	33.08
1998–99	4.47	2.01	49.43
1999–00	3.45	1.97	39.44
2001–02	3.96	2.03	45.81
2002–03	3.97	1.94	45.02

(Table 14.8 Contd)

(Table 14.8 Contd)

Years	*Ratio of Maximum to Minimum Per Capita Expenditure on Education*	*Ratio of Average to Minimum Per Capita Expenditure on Education*	*Coefficient of Variation (per cent)*
2003–04	3.63	1.79	43.48
2004–05	3.77	1.89	43.99
2005–06	4.40	2.05	48.51
2006–07	4.28	2.07	47.28
2007–08	4.23	2.09	44.70
2008–09	4.77	2.29	51.37
2009–10	5.31	2.44	52.00
2010–11	5.19	2.10	55.29
2011–12	4.50	2.14	45.87

Source (Basic Data): Reserve Bank of India (RBI), Study of State Finances, various years and Central Statistical Organization.

Notes: Disparity in per capita income for the year 2000–01 is not shown in both general and group 2 states as the expenditure for Chhattisgarh, Jharkhand and Uttarakhand was for only part of the financial year. These states were formed in November 2000. Prior to this they were part of Madhya Pradesh, Bihar and Uttar Pradesh, respectively. From 2001–02 general category states are 17 and group 2 states are 11 in number.

of Goa is way above group 1 states, Goa has been excluded while analysing the disparities in per capita expenditure on education. For group 1 states, the ratio of maximum (Kerala) to minimum (Bihar) fell from 2.50 in 1993–94 to 2.22 in 1995–96 and rose to 2.89 in 1998–99 (maximum refers to Punjab) and thereafter fluctuated between 2.12 and 2.85 over the period 1999–00 to 2011–12. Also, the states' accounting for maximum and minimum has changed. The ratio of average per capita revenue expenditure on education to minimum also followed a similar pattern. The coefficient of variation has fallen during the first four years (1993–94 to 1996–97); rose in the next two years and thereafter the coefficient has varied between 24 and 30 per cent. By all the three indicators, no reduction in the extent of disparity in the per capita expenditures is visible. For group 2 states, the disparity is higher than group 1 states. Sikkim has the highest per capita expenditure for the period 1995–96 to 2011–12, except for 2008–09 to 2010–11. Mizoram has the highest expenditure for the period 1993–94 to 1996–97.

The minimum per capita expenditure was incurred by Assam for the entire period (1993–94 to 2011–12) and the coefficient of variation is much higher than group 1 states.

Table 14.9 presents the share of per capita expenditure of each state on education to the average per capita expenditure of the 16 states (excluding Goa) in group 1 states. This enables us to see whether low incomes states are trying to attain the average performance of the states. States that show less than average priority for education are Andhra Pradesh, Bihar, Madhya Pradesh, Odisha, Uttar Pradesh, and West Bengal, where the share of per capita expenditure was lower than the 16 states average while for West Bengal in 2000–01 it was above the 16 states average but fell over time. In the case of new states created in the year 2000–01, the share of per capita expenditure was lower than the average for all the years except for Chhattisgarh in 2009–10 and 2011–12. In the case of Rajasthan which was above the average from 1993–94 to 2001–02, fell below the 16 states average over the period 2002–03 to 2011–12.

In the case of group 2 states, 6 out of 11 states were below the 11 states average over the entire period 1993–94 to 2011–12. The states are Assam, Jammu and Kashmir, Meghalaya, Nagaland (except for the three-year average 1993–94) and Uttarakhand, and Tripura except for the years 2002–03 to 2004–05. Manipur was above the 11 states average for the years 1993–94 to 2002–03, thereafter fell below the average. Arunachal Pradesh fell below the 11 states average in 1999–2000 to 2001–02.

Another way to look at the performance of the states is to plot the scatter of priority and capacity ratios for each of the years. Here, we plot the scatter for the year 2011–12. All those states that are spending more than the average share of revenue expenditure on education to total revenue expenditure show priority in spending on education. Similarly, states that are providing more than the average states in total revenue expenditure are creating higher capacity in education services.

Figures 14.1 and 14.2 show the performance of states in terms of capacity ratio and priority ratio for the year 2011–12 for group 1 and group 2 states. Odisha, Rajasthan and Uttar Pradesh slipped

Table 14.9:
Share of per capita expenditure on education to average (16 states) expenditure on education of group 1 states and to average (11 states) of group 2 states

(per cent)

Sl. No.	States	1994–95	1997–98	2000–01	2003–04	2006–07	2009–10	2011–12
Group 1								
1.	Andhra Pradesh	78.10	74.60	83.53	90.59	89.75	79.47	93.94
2.	Bihar	63.24	57.90	72.79	61.70	66.96	56.10	55.12
3.	Chhattisgarh	0.00	0.00	39.60	71.21	83.90	118.45	106.11
4.	Goa							
5.	Gujarat	123.64	125.04	120.04	114.64	108.28	104.50	111.79
6.	Haryana	105.36	113.92	113.20	112.45	121.43	143.93	131.71
7.	Jharkhand	0.00	0.00	82.03	94.65	98.59	87.65	69.23
8.	Karnataka	106.84	106.75	110.69	114.69	124.13	115.44	111.72
9.	Kerala	150.76	136.38	141.89	153.90	143.84	126.40	145.56
10.	Madhya Pradesh	69.79	67.26	69.51	61.26	63.20	67.13	72.80
11.	Maharashtra	125.86	124.29	157.61	151.57	139.95	140.87	140.57
12.	Odisha	83.21	83.35	86.63	81.96	82.40	96.89	86.99
13.	Punjab	125.43	138.08	131.88	132.26	109.30	93.98	97.72
14.	Rajasthan	103.93	104.08	102.39	98.60	96.38	96.44	90.56

(Table 14.9 Contd)

(Table 14.9 Contd)

Sl. No.	*States*	*1994–95*	*1997–98*	*2000–01*	*2003–04*	*2006–07*	*2009–10*	*2011–12*
15.	Tamil Nadu	114.77	120.74	122.66	109.95	113.64	118.85	122.81
16.	Uttar Pradesh	64.80	66.13	62.50	60.69	69.98	62.22	68.94
17.	West Bengal	84.26	81.48	103.06	89.88	88.25	91.67	94.44
State Avg. Per Capita GSDP (₹)		293	428	574	622	832	1,417	1881
Group 2								
1.	Arunachal Pradesh	127.20	119.49	94.01	112.06	123.78	139.29	127.98
2.	Assam	54.49	49.35	54.06	53.57	48.29	44.37	46.68
3.	Himachal Pradesh	84.72	100.10	113.80	103.07	106.21	103.74	104.87
4.	Jammu and Kashmir	70.30	66.91	67.41	61.78	63.96	67.79	74.85
5.	Manipur	102.02	109.08	104.19	88.28	90.37	65.26	60.36
6.	Meghalaya	78.90	72.41	78.87	74.13	71.94	69.96	91.09
7.	Mizoram	148.61	143.34	166.91	153.36	155.10	142.84	141.98
8.	Nagaland	113.57	83.19	82.81	68.66	70.85	79.97	88.03
9.	Sikkim	142.92	176.69	195.16	202.46	207.69	227.19	209.85
10.	Tripura	77.28	79.43	99.99	103.70	78.66	72.99	70.31
11.	Uttarakhand	0.00	0.00	42.79	78.92	83.14	86.60	84.01
State Avg. Per Capita GSDP (₹)		672	951	1280	1540	1986	3,267	4267

Source (Basic Data): Reserve Bank of India (RBI), Study of State Finances, various years and Central Statistical Organization.

Figure 14.1:
Performance of Group 1 states in terms of capacity and priority ratio: 2011–12

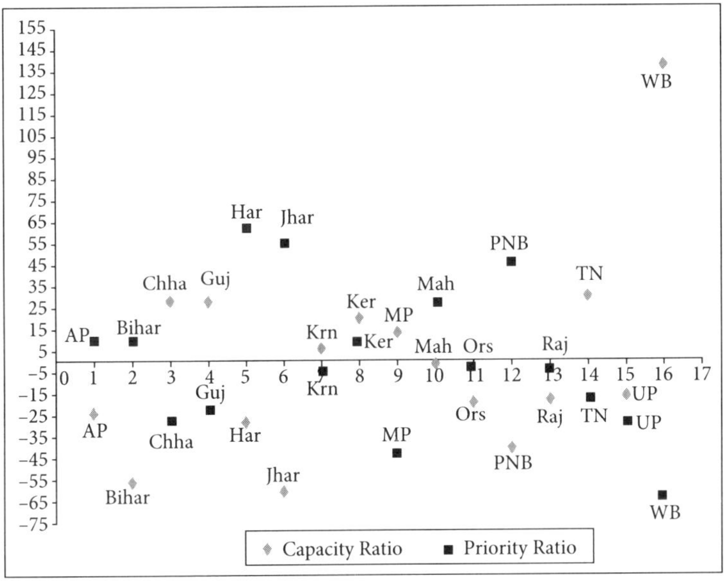

Source: GoI, Central Statistical Organisation, various years.

to lower than 16 states average in terms of their priority and capacity ratio in education (see Figure 14.1). Bihar's priority ratio is above the 15-state average but capacity is below 50 per cent of the average. The other low income states Chhattisgarh and Madhya Pradesh slipped below the 16 states average in terms of their priority in education but in terms of capacity ratio are above 16 states average. Jharkhand has the second highest priority ratio among group 1 states but has the least capacity to undertake expenditure on education. Among the middle income states except for Kerala other states are not performing well. Andhra Pradesh has less than average capacity ratio, while Karnataka and Tamil Nadu have less than 16 states average priority ratio. Among high income states, Gujarat is not giving priority to education. Haryana has the highest priority among group 1 states for education but has low capacity to undertake the expenditure on education. Also, Punjab and to an extent Maharashtra are spending less on education.

Figure 14.2:
Performance of Group 2 states in terms of capacity and priority ratio: 2011–12

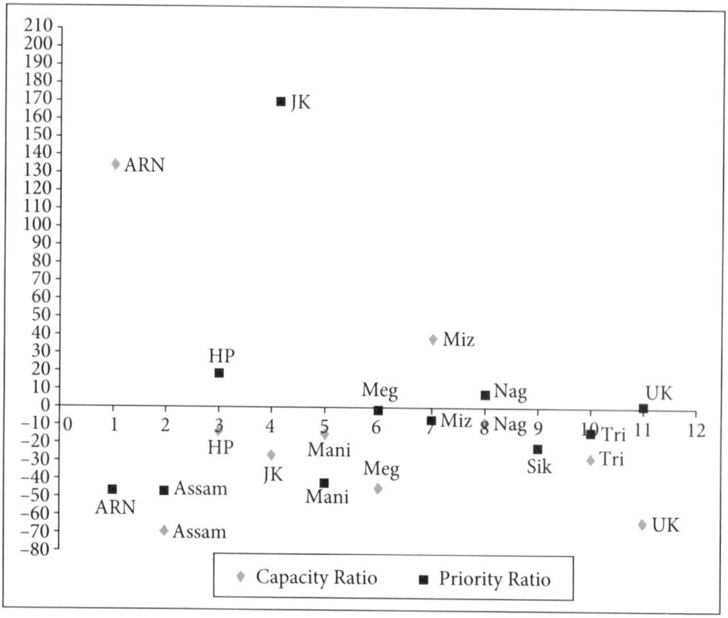

Source: GoI, Central Statistical Organisation, various years.

High-income states (Haryana, Maharashtra and Punjab) seem to allocate fewer resources on education (below the 16 states average). Gujarat, on the other hand, seems to have less priority in education.

In the case of group 2 states (see Figure 14.2), Arunachal Pradesh, Assam, Manipur, Mizoram, Sikkim and Tripura give less priority in education and are below the 11-states average though in terms of allocation of resources Arunachal Pradesh, Mizoram and Sikkim seems to be doing better.

Conclusions

From the analysis of GSDP, it appears that middle-income states like Andhra Pradesh, Kerala and Tamil Nadu have performed better in terms of their growth rates comparing between the periods (1993–2000 and 2001–10), while low-income states like Chhattisgarh, Jharkhand, Odisha, Uttar Pradesh and Bihar have also relatively improved. The high-income states have moved to higher growth levels. In group 2 states, except for Tripura, all states have performed well in terms of growth rates.

The analysis of per capita income of states as percentage to the average of the 16 states in group 1 states (excluding Goa) and to the average of 11 states in group 2 states enables us to capture the states that are improving their performance above the states average. It is seen that generally Bihar, Jharkhand, Rajasthan, Madhya Pradesh and Uttar Pradesh have shown a continuous deterioration over the years. While for Odisha there has been a decline initially but with some fluctuation around the trend. In the case of Andhra Pradesh and Karnataka, they have moved above the average, while West Bengal fell from the average since 2006–07 and Chhattisgarh is slowly inching towards the average. In the case of group 2 states, Assam, Jammu and Kashmir, Manipur and Nagaland have been deteriorating over the years, while Uttarakhand, Arunachal Pradesh, Himachal Pradesh and Sikkim have moved above the average. Meghalaya has shown deterioration from 2008–2009 and Tripura from 2005 to 2006 onwards.

The summary indicators of disparity in comparable per capita expenditure on education, namely the ratio of maximum to minimum, the ratio of average per capita expenditure on education to minimum, and the coefficient of variation over the period from 1993–94 to 2011–12 show no reduction in the extent of disparity in group 1 states, while the disparity is higher in group 2 states.

The analysis on education for the year 2011–12 shows that some of the low-income states like Odisha, Rajasthan and Uttar Pradesh slipped to below 16 states average in terms of their priority and capacity ratio. The other states like Chhattisgarh and Madhya Pradesh also slipped below the 16 states average in terms of their priority in education but in terms of capacity ratio they are above the 16 states average. Jharkhand has the second highest priority among group 1 states for education but has the least capacity to undertake the expenditure on education. The low-income states also happen to be the states with the largest share of working age population.

Among the middle-income states, except for Kerala other states are not performing well. High income states like Haryana, Maharashtra and Punjab allocate less resource to education (below the 16 states average) and Gujarat is giving less priority to education. As for group 2 states, Arunachal Pradesh, Assam, Manipur, Mizoram, Sikkim and Tripura give less priority to education and is below the 11 states average though in terms of allocation of resources Arunachal Pradesh, Mizoram and Sikkim seems to be doing better.

References

Acharya, D. and Sahoo, B.K. 2012. 'Constructing Macroeconomic Performance Index of Indian States using DEA', *Journal of Economic Studies*, 39(1): 63–83.

Ahluwalia, M.S. 2000. 'Economic Performance of States in Post-Reform Period', *Economic and Political Weekly*, 35(19): 1637–48.

———. 2002. 'State Level Performance Under Economic Reforms in India' in Anne O. Krueger (ed.), *Economic Policy Reforms and the Indian Economy* (pp. 91–125). New Delhi: Oxford University Press.

Barro, R.J. 1991. 'Economic Growth in a Cross Section of Countries', *Quarterly* Review *Journal of Economics*, 106(2): 407–43.

Bhattacharya, B.B. and Sakthivel, S. 2004. 'Regional Growth and Disparity in India: Comparison of Pre and Post-Reform Decades', *Economic and Political Weekly*, 29(10): 1071–77.

Bhujanga Rao C. and Srivastava, D.K. 2009. 'Inter-state Imbalances in Essential Services: Some Perspectives' in D.K. Srivastava, K.R. Shanmugam and C. Bhujanga Rao (eds), *Finance Commission Issues of the Southern States* (pp. 171–94). Chennai: Madras School of Economics.

Central Statistical Organisation, *Releases of State Gross State Domestic Product on 21.07.2010*, Department of Statistics, Government of India., and also on 27.02.2015. Available at http://mospi.nic.in/Mospi_New/site/inner.aspx?status=3&menu_id=82

Chand, D. 2015. Data Base at National Institute of Public Finance and Policy, New Delhi.

Chaudhuri, S. 2004. 'A Note on Sectoral Economic Growth in the States', *ICRA Bulletin Money and Finance*, 2(17): 63–89.

Dholakia, R.H. 2003. 'Regional Disparity in Economic and Human Development in India', *Economic and Political Weekly*, 38(39): 4166–72.

Krishna, K.L. 2004. 'Patterns and Determinants of Growth in Indian States', ICRIER Working Paper No. 144, pp. 1–37.

Kurian, N.J. 2002. 'Growing Inter-State Disparities', India 2001 a Symposium, January, New Delhi.

Govinda Rao, M., Shand, R.T. and Kalirajan, K.P. 1999. 'Convergence of Incomes across Indian States—A Divergent View', *Economic and Political Weekly*, 34(13): 27 769–78.

Nagaraj, R., Varouadakis, A. and Veganzones, M.A. 1998. 'Long Run Growth Trends and Convergence across Indian States', *OECD Technical Papers*, 131: 1–58.

Pal, P. and Ghosh, J. 2007. *Inequality in India: A Survey of Recent Trends*. Department of Economic and Social Affairs, United Nations, July.

Rao, C.H. and Dev, S.M. 2003. 'Economic Reforms and Challenges Ahead—An Overview', *Economic and Political Weekly*, 37(12) 1130–41.

Reserve Bank of India (RBI). 2004. *Handbook of Statistics on State Government Finances*. Mumbai.

———. 2010. *Handbook of Statistics on State Government Finances*. Mumbai.

———. 2013. *State Finances—A Study of Budgets*, 2009–10, 2010–11, 2011–12 and 2012–13.

Shand, R. and Bhide, S. 2000, 'Sources of Economic Growth—Regional Dimensions of Reforms', *Economic and Political Weekly*, 35(42): 3747–57.

Shetty, S.L. 2003, 'Growth of SDP and Structural Changes in State Economies: Interstate Comparisons', *Economic and Political Weekly*, 38(49): 5189–220.

15

Health Outcome Efficiency of the Indian States

J. Prachitha and K.R. Shanmugam***

Introduction

Health is a merit good. It can be excludable and rival. But the benefits of its consumption may extend beyond an individual who consumes it. In other words, the consumption of healthcare creates 'private gain' as well as 'social gain'. According to Grossman (1972), the social gain from consuming healthcare may be larger than the private gain. The Millennium Development Goals (MDGs) adopted by the United Nations in 2000 emphasized the greater significance of health in the overall development. Interestingly, three of the eight major MDGs (eight of the 18 targets and 18 of the 48 indicators) are health-related.[1]

*Research Scholar, Madras School of Economics, Chennai. E-mail: prachitha@mse.ac.in

**Professor, Madras School Economics, Chennai. E-mail: shanmugam@mse.ac.in (corresponding author)

[1] Goal 4—child mortality reduction; Goal 5—improving maternal health and Goal 6—combating HIV/AIDS, malaria and other diseases. These goals aim to reduce the mortality figures by two-thirds between 1990 and 2015 and to combat diseases like HIV/AIDS, malaria, tuberculosis, etc. by halting the incidence and reversing of the diseases.

Realizing its importance, governments in developed countries spend huge amounts in providing health services.[2] For instances, governments in UK, Denmark and New Zealand incur nearly 80 per cent of the total health expenditures (WHO, 2011). In developing nations, the share of public expenditure in total health expenditure remains low. According to the WHO database (2009), the public expenditure on health was 51.8 per cent of the total health expenditure in Indonesia, 50.3 per cent in China, 45.2 per cent in Sri Lanka, 44.8 per cent in Malaysia and 41.5 per cent in Singapore in 2009. In India, it was only 32.8 per cent, indicating larger dependency of the Indian health system on private funding.

India also compares poorly in terms of health outcomes. The life expectancy at birth (LEB) was 65 years in India in 2009 while it was 82 years in Singapore, 74 years in China and 73 years in Malaysia. Its infant mortality rate (IMR) was 50, while it was just two in Singapore, six in Malaysia and 13 in Sri Lanka. The under-5 mortality rate in India (66) was relatively high as compared to Singapore (3), Malaysia (6) and Sri Lanka (16) in 2009. Countries like Nepal and Bangladesh also have better health outcomes than India (WHO, 2011).[3]

Thus, evidences indicate that the healthcare services as well as the health outcome parameters in most of the countries including India are not at satisfactory levels. According to the WHO (2010), 'No country has yet been able to guarantee everyone immediate access to the services that might maintain or improve their health. They all face resource constraints of one type or another'. Therefore, it suggests that 'all countries can do something to improve the efficiency of their health systems, thereby releasing resources that could be used to cover more people, more services and more of the costs'. It further calls for equal attention on tracking the health outcomes.

According to WHO and UNICEF (2010), India is off-track in meeting MDG 4. Since the progress made by India so far is not

[2] Various external agencies including NGOs and foreign donors such as WHO also provide the health services. People also spend on their health.

[3] The LEB in Nepal was 67 years in 2009 and the IMR and U-5MR were 39 and 48, respectively. In Bangladesh, the LEB was same as that of India, while it fared better in terms of the mortality indicators. The IMR and U-5MR in Bangladesh were 41 and 52, respectively.

up to the mark, it is pushed to the 'insufficient progress' category. However, China, Nepal, Bangladesh and some African countries are on track in meeting the target by 2015. Low share of public expenditure on health could be a reason for poor performance of the health sector in India. There could be other reasons like public spending in-efficiency, regional inequalities in providing health services and others.

As health is a state subject, the state governments in India contribute more than 70 per cent of the total public expenses on health. The central government plays only a role of monitoring and facilitating the states by developing norms and regulations linking states with funding agencies and sponsoring various flagship schemes such as National Rural Health Mission, Integrated Child Development Scheme and Central Rural Sanitation Programme that are implemented by the states.

In this study, we provide the estimates of health outcome efficiency of the major Indian states, using the latest data available for the years 2004–05 to 2009–10. Studies by Jain (1985), Beenstock and Sturdy (1990), Kaur and Misra (2003) and Bhalotra (2007) have already emerged in the Indian context to analyse the impact of public expenditures in raising health outcomes (but not measuring efficiency). However, a few studies provide the estimates of health outcome efficiency of states in India. For instances, Kathuria and Sankar (2005) and Chakrabarti and Rao (2007) have measured the health outcome (measured by rural IMR) efficiency of various Indian states using the stochastic frontier model for panel data. Shetty and Pakkala (2010) have used the DEA approach to estimate the efficiency of the healthcare system in the Indian states considering IMR and LEB as health outcomes in 2001.[4]

A handful of studies also exist to measure the efficiency of health outcome or healthcare services in various nations. For instance,

[4] Purohit (2008) carried out a sub-state level (district level) analysis of health system efficiency for West Bengal considering life expectancy as the health output. Jat and Sebastian (2013) evaluate the efficiency of 40 public district hospitals for the year 2010 in Madhya Pradesh with special emphasis on maternal healthcare services using DEA method. The average efficiency estimated by them is 79 per cent and nearly 65 per cent of hospitals are found to be scale inefficient.

Kiadaliri, Jafari and Gerdtham (2013) provides a review of 29 studies in the field of hospital efficiency in Iran, while Varabyova and Schreyogg (2013) provide a comparison of efficiency of hospital sector for OECD nations during 2000–09. Spink and Hollingsworth (2009) provide cross-country comparisons of efficiency of health production using OECD and WHO data.

This study contributes to the literature in many ways. First, it uses the latest data available and provides the year-wise health outcome efficiency scores for the Indian states. Past studies on the topic used the data up to 2001. Second, after 2000, three major Indian states Uttar Pradesh, Madhya Pradesh and Bihar were bifurcated. This chapter covers not only the recent years, but also covers the newly created states, that is, it provides the efficiency scores for all major states, including the bifurcated states. Thirdly, it ranks the states based on their total health outcome performance while studies such as those done by Kathuria and Sankar (2005) rank them based on the rural health outcomes. Finally, this study compares its findings with that done by Chakrabarti and Rao (2007) (hereafter referred to as CR study).

This chapter proceeds as follows. The next section deals with the health system in India and provides the trends in the public spending on health and the status of health outcomes. Then, the methodology used in the study, the model, variables and data used are discussed. Finally, the last section presents the empirical results, concluding remarks and policy implications of the study.

Indian Health System

The 7th Schedule of the Indian Constitution entrusts the health responsibilities like public health service delivery, hospitals and sanitation to the states. Other responsibilities with wider ramifications at the national level are entrusted to both centre and states. The centre intervenes through financing key policies and schemes relating to family welfare, population control, medical education, prevention of food adulteration, quality control in manufacturing of drugs and others. According to NHA (2005, 2009), the private expenditure on health increased from ₹104,414 crore in 2004–05 (1 crore = 10 million) to ₹174,842 crore approximately in 2009–10.[5] Its share in total health expenditure declined from 81 per cent to 75 per cent between these years. Thus, the private expenditure on health has increased but its share declined (Table 15.1).

The share of public expenditure on health increased from 18.6 per cent in 2004–05 to 25 per cent in 2009–10. The per capita public expenditure on health (in 2004–05 prices) increased from ₹220 in 2004–05 to ₹366 in 2009–10, clearly indicating that the government has been spending increased amounts on health over the years.

Table 15.2 shows wide variations in the per capita health expenditure among the major state governments. Kerala spent ₹284 per head on public health in 2004–05 while Bihar spent only ₹70. In 2009–10, Kerala had the highest per capita public health expenditure of ₹394 while Bihar had the lowest of ₹105. Thus, the highest spending state's per capita expenditure on health is 3.8 times that of the lowest per capita spending state.

Table 15.2 also shows wider variations in providing health facilities such as community health centres (CHCs), primary health centres (PHCs) and the doctors at the state level in the years 2004–05 and 2009–10. In eight (Jharkhand, Kerala, Madhya Pradesh, Orissa,[6] Punjab, Rajasthan, Tamil Nadu and West Bengal) out of the 17 states, the number of PHCs declined from 2004–05 to 2009–10. In two states (Bihar and Maharashtra), the number of CHCs declined and in 10 states the number of doctors declined.

Many argue that health outcome depends on the availability of rural health infrastructure in the form of CHC and PHC. There are many health outcome indicators like LEB, the crude birth rate, the crude death rate and IMR. The UNDP uses the LEB[7] for computing

[5] The private sector health expenditure includes out-of-pocket (OOP) expenditure incurred by households for availing health care services, health expenditure through insurance mechanism and expenditure by corporate bodies on their employees and families.

[6] Recently the name Orissa has been changed as Odisha.

[7] LEB is available for four-year periods up to 2002–06. Thus, we are unable to use it for our analysis.

Table 15.1:
Health expenditures in India: Public and private

(₹ crore)

Details		*2004–05*	*2009–10*
Revenue account	State	18,456	38,301
	Centre	4,263	15,366
	Total	22,719	53,667
Capital account	State	1,161	4,034
	Centre	49	523
	Total	1,210	4,557
Total public expenditure	State	19,617	42,335
	Centre	4,311	15,889
	Total	23,928	58,224
Total private expenditure	Total	104,417	174,842*
Total health expenditure	Total	128,345	233,066
Share of public expenditure	Per cent	18.64	24.98
Share of private expenditure	Per cent	81.36	75.02
Population	Crore	108.9	117.82
Per capita public expenditure	Rupees	220	494
Per capita private expenditure	Rupees	959	1484
Deflator		1.00	1.351
Per capita public expenditure at 2004–05 prices	Rupees	220	366
Per capita private expenditure at 2004–05 prices	Rupees	959	1,098

Sources: Budget documents (various years) for the central government expenditures; state finances: A study of budgets, Reserve Bank of India (various years) for state government expenditures; National Health Accounts, 2009 for the private expenditures on health; national accounts statistics, central statistical organization, for population and deflator.

Note: *Projection based on the provisional figures provided in National Health Accounts, 2009.

the Human Development Index while IMR is popularly used as the health indicator. Many authors cite IMR as a good indicator of the degree of lack of availability of sanitation and safe water facilities, because of the susceptibility of infants to water-borne diseases. It

Table 15.2:
State-wise health facilities, medical officers/specialists and the per capita public expenditures on health

	2004–05				2009–10			
States	*CHC*	*PHC*	*Doctors*	*Per Capita Public Expenditure on Health (2004–05 prices)*	*CHC*	*PHC*	*Doctors*	*Per Capita Public Expenditure on Health (2004–05 prices)*
Andhra Pradesh	164	1,570	2,361	189	167	1,570	2,694	277
Bihar	101	1,648	1,694	70	70	1,863	1,669	105
Chhattisgarh	116	517	646	140	143	716	623	227
Gujarat	272	1,070	940	180	290	1,096	916	298
Haryana	72	408	911	174	107	441	583	301
Jharkhand	47	561	2,478	150	188	330	488	234
Karnataka	254	1,681	2,732	187	325	2,193	3,924	278
Kerala	106	911	1,031	284	233	813	1,896	394
Madhya Pradesh	229	1,192	888	139	333	1,155	786	174
Maharashtra	382	1,780	4,257	194	365	1,816	3,019	275
Orissa	231	1,282	1,788	163	231	1,279	1,543	204
Punjab	116	484	599	238	129	446	710	252
Rajasthan	326	1,713	2,087	178	368	1,504	2,255	245

Tamil Nadu	35	1,380	2,305	205	256	1,283	2,268	361
Uttar Pradesh	386	3,660	413	127	515	3,692	4,117	216
Uttaranchal	44	225	253	274	55	239	312	377
West Bengal	95	1,173	1,452	168	348	909	1,107	263
All States*	3,346	23,236	23,858	180	4,535	23,673	32,651	266

Source: Bulletin on Rural Health Statistics in India; RBI's State Finances: A Study of Budgets and; Central Statistical Organisation (various years).

Notes: Doctors refer to the medical officers and specialists in the PHCs and the specialists in CHCs.

'*'All States include the 17 major states as well as the special category states and the Union territories.

has also been characterized as an outcome variable summarizing multiple health and nutritional afflictions of very young children (Chelliah and Shanmugam, 2001).

Table 15.3 provides the state-wise IMR in various years. India's IMR declined from 58 in 2005 to 47 in 2010. If the reduction of IMR continues at its current rate, India is not likely to meet the MDG target of 28 in 2015. At state level, wide variations exist in IMR. Kerala ranked first in reducing IMR to 13 in 2010 followed by Tamil Nadu (24) and Maharashtra (28). Madhya Pradesh had the highest IMR of 62 followed by Orissa and Uttar Pradesh with 61 each in 2010.

Table 15.3:
State-wise IMR and its performance index

	2005		*2010*	
States	*IMR*	*PI*100*	*IMR*	*PI*100*
Andhra Pradesh	57	42	46	56
Bihar	61	37	48	53
Chhattisgarh	63	35	51	49
Gujarat	54	46	44	58
Haryana	60	38	48	53
Jharkhand	50	51	42	60
Karnataka	50	51	38	65
Kerala	14	95	13	96
Madhya Pradesh	76	19	62	36
Maharashtra	36	68	28	78
Orissa	75	20	61	37
Punjab	44	58	34	70
Rajasthan	68	28	55	44
Tamil Nadu	37	67	24	83
Uttar Pradesh	73	22	61	37
Uttaranchal	42	60	38	65
West Bengal	38	65	31	74
India	**58**		**47**	

Source: Sample Registration System Bulletin, Various Years.

Table 15.3 also shows the health performance index (PI), which is calculated using the formula: PI = $(IMR_{max} - IMR_{it})/ (IMR_{max} - IMR_{min})$, where IMR_{it} is the actual value of IMR for state *i* in time *t*, IMR_{max} is the highest IMR and IMR_{min} the lowest IMR over the years. The value of this index lies between 0 and 1. Higher the value, higher is the performance. That is, lower is the IMR. Kerala had the highest PI value of 96 while Madhya Pradesh had the lowest value of 36 in 2010. Since IMR is a negative indicator and inversely related to per capita income (Goldstein, 1985), PI is used as the health outcome indicator in our analysis in the fourth section of this chapter.

Methodology

The efficiency side of a policy design is concerned with making best use of the economic resources in any economic activity. Farell (1957) kick-started the modern efficiency measurement concepts for any decision-making units (DMUs) like firms, farms, hospitals and state governments. According to him, the economic efficiency of any DMU is the product of its technical efficiency (TE) and its allocative efficiency (AE). The AE reflects the ability of a DMU to use inputs in optimal propositions, given their respective prices/costs, while the TE reflects the ability of a DMU to obtain maximum output from a given set of inputs and technology. The major concern in TE analysis is whether the actual outcome generated could be achieved with less inputs or whether the same (given) inputs could produce better outcomes. Broadly, there are two approaches to estimate the efficiency: (i) mathematical approach or data envelopment analysis (DEA) and (ii) econometric or stochastic frontier approach (SFA).[8]

In this study, we employ the SFA for panel data to measure the efficiency of raising health outcomes in the major Indian states. The frontier function can be defined as maximum or potential outcome

[8] See Aigner et al. (1977), Meeusen and Broeck (1977), Battese and Coelli (1992), Greene (1993), Kalirajan and Shand (1994) and Kumbhakar et al. (1997) for complete review of various models in both approaches.

that a DMU (state government here) can produce with given level of inputs such as per capita income, per capita public expenditure on health and medical infrastructure facilities, and technology. The actual health outcome (Q_{it}) of a state i at time t can be written as:

$$Q_{it} = f(X_{it}; \beta) \exp(-u_{it}) \quad 0 \leq u_{it} \leq \infty; i = 1, \dots, n; t = 1, \dots, \mathrm{t} \quad (1)$$

where Q_{it} represents the actual health outcome, which is measured in terms of the PI relating to IMR (PI); X_{it} is a vector of determinants of health outcome such as per capita income and per capita health expenditure; β is a vector of parameters that describe the transformation process; $f(\,)$ is the potential performance function; u_{it} is one-sided non-negative residual term. If a state is inefficient (efficient) the actual outcome is less than (equal to) the potential outcome. Therefore, the ratio of actual and potential performance is a measure of TE. The residual term u_{it} is 0 when the state generates the potential outcome and is greater than 0 when the actual performance is below the frontier level. In general, the residual term and the state's efficiency are inversely related. The residual term is also referred to as the efficiency effect of the state. To capture the effects of omitted variables and measurement errors, a random noise v_{it} ($v_{it} \sim$ iid N $(0, \sigma_v^2)$) can also be included in equation (1) as:

$$Q_{it} = f(X_{it}; \beta) \exp(v_{it} - u_{it}) \quad (2)$$

Following Battese and Coelli (1995), the efficiency terms u_{it} are assumed to be independently distributed with a truncated (at zero) normal distribution and time-varying mean (i.e., $u_{it} \sim$ N (m_{it}, σ_u^2)). The state and time-varying mean, m_{it}, can be specified as:

$$m_{it} = Z_{it}\delta \quad (3)$$

where Z_{it} is a vector of endogenous variables associated with efficiency namely literacy rate and proportion of rural population. Thus, the efficiency terms are given by:

$$u_{it} = m_{it} + w_{it} \quad (4)$$

where w_{it} are unobserved id random variables ($w_{it} \sim N(0, \sigma_w^2)$ and $w_{it} \geq -m_{it}$). The truncation $w_{it} \geq -m_{it}$ guarantees that the efficiency terms are non-negative. The state-specific efficiency can be obtained using Jondrow et al.'s (1982) procedure, which has been subsequently generalized by Battese and Coelli (1988) for panel data models.

The maximum likelihood estimation (MLE) technique can be used to estimate simultaneously the frontier function and the inefficiency effect model. The likelihood function is parameterized in terms of variances in the model and the variance ratio $\gamma = \sigma_u^2/\sigma^2$, where $\sigma^2 = \sigma_v^2 + \sigma_u^2$. The γ shows the relative magnitude of the inefficiency variance to the total variance in the model and lies between 0 and 1. If it is 0, then the variance of the inefficiency effect is 0 and the model would reduce to the regular OLS model in which the variables in Z are included in the production function. In this case, δ cannot be identified. One can also test the null hypothesis that $\gamma = \delta_0 = \cdots = \delta_m = 0$ using the generalized likelihood ratio test statistic (a mixed χ^2 statistic).

Empirical Model and Data

We specify the following Cobb-Douglas form of the stochastic frontier production function for any given state i in period t as[9]:

$$\text{Ln (PI)}_{it} = \beta_0 + \Sigma\beta_j \, \text{Ln}X_{jit} + (v_{it} - u_{it}) \tag{5}$$

and inefficiency equation is specified as:

$$u_{it} = \delta_0 + \delta_1 \, \text{Ln (RPOP)}_{it} + \delta_2 \, \text{Ln (LIT)}_{it} + \delta_3 \, \text{(TIME)} + w_{it} \tag{6}$$

where RPOP is the proportion of rural population, LIT is the literacy rate and TIME is trend variable. The X_{jit} in (5) includes (i) two

[9] Initially we have tried many functional forms such as transcendental and CES. Finally, the Cobb-Douglas form is chosen as it best fits the data.

economic variables, namely per capita public health expenditures in 2004–05 prices (PCHEXP), per capita state income in 2004–05 prices (PCGSDP); (ii) three health infrastructure variables—number of CHCs, PHCs and the doctors and specialists (DOC) and; (iii) immunization variables, namely, proportion of children below one year receiving BCG vaccination (BCG) and proportion of children below one year receiving measles vaccination (MESL). All these variables are expected to have a positive impact on the health outcomes.

The data source for IMR is the Sample Registration System (SRS) Bulletin published by the Vital Statistics Division, Government of India. The IMR is used to calculate the performance indicator. The 'State Finances: A Study of Budgets' published by the Reserve Bank of India is the source for state-wise public health expenditure. Central Statistical Organization is the source for the per capita GSDP data. The health infrastructure data are obtained from various issues of the Rural Health Statistics Bulletin published by the Ministry of Health and the Family Welfare Statistics provided the data on immunization variables. The proportion of rural population and literacy rates are interpolated using the Census of India data for the years 2001 and 2011 due to non-availability of them during the study period. The final dataset used in this study is a balanced panel of 17 states for six years (2004–05 to 2009–10).

Thus, the total observations used in the empirical analysis are 102. The descriptive statistics of the study variables are shown in Table 15.4.

Empirical Results

Table 15.5 provides the empirical results. Column 1 of Table 15.5 provides the OLS estimation results of equation (5) for comparative purpose. As expected, the per capita income and per capita public expenditure on health have positive and significant impact on the health performance at 1 per cent level. The infrastructure

Table 15.4:
Descriptive statistics of the study variables

Variables	*Mean (S.D.)*	*Variables*	*Mean (S.D.)*
Performance indicator of health for IMR (PI)	52.26 (18.87)	Proportion of infants (below 1 year) received BCG vaccination (BCG)	103.79 (12.29)
Per capita income (PCGSDP) in 2004–05 prices	33,018.67 (13,262.37)	Proportion of infants (below one year) received measles vaccination (MESL)	94.96 (15.47)
Per capita heath expenditure (PCHEXP) in 2004–05 prices	217.82 (73.13)	Per cent of Rural population (RPOP)	71.68 (8.18)
Number of community health centres and primary health centres (CHCPHC)	1,437.30 (877.28)	Literacy rate (LIT) in percentage	70.63 (10.09)
Number of doctors and specialists in CHCs and PHCs (DOC)	1,601.19 (938.08)	Number of observations	102

Source: Computed by the authors.

variable—number of doctors also has a positive effect on the health performance. This effect is statistically significant at 1 per cent level.

The other infrastructure variable-number of CHCs and PHCs has a negative coefficient, and it is statistically significant at 5 per cent level. This is contrary to the expectation. However, the justification for the negative effect is that in many states, the number of PHCs exceeded the required level of 3.33 approximately per one lakh rural population suggested by the Ministry of Health. For example, the number of PHCs per one lakh of rural population in Karnataka, Tamil Nadu, Chhattisgarh, Orissa and Uttaranchal was 5.98, 4.10, 3.92, 3.83 and 3.45, respectively, in 2008–09. These were well above the prescribed norms. As expected, the immunization variable BCG has a positive and significant effect on the health performance at 5 per cent level. However, MESL has a negative and significant effect, which is contrary to our expectation.

Column 2 of Table 15.5 presents the MLE results. The results are more or less similar to what the OLS indicate in column 1 except a few changes in the significance level of parameters. Effects of the

Table 15.5:
OLS and ML estimates of stochastic frontier health performance and technical inefficiency models, major Indian states (2004–05 to 2009–10)

(Dependent Variable: Log of Performance Index for IMR)

Variables	*OLS* (1)	*MLE* (2)
Frontier Health Performance Model		
Constant	–1.1954	1.2802
	(–0.888)	(1.304)
Ln PCGSDP	0.3584	0.1578
	(5.110)***	(2.515)***
Ln PCHEXP	0.5755	0.4205
	(5.740)***	(4.708)***
Ln CHCPHC	–0.1175	–0.0487
	(–2.396)**	(–1.029)
Ln DOC	0.1379	0.101
	(3.132)***	(1.891)*
Ln BCG	0.8153	1.0313
	(2.117)**	(3.087)***
Ln MESL	–1.2374	–1.306
	(–5.140)***	(–5.113)***
Adjusted R^2	0.634	
Health Outcome Inefficiency Model		
Constant	–	0.4511
		(0.463)
Ln LIT	–	–0.7975
		(–6.055)***
Ln RPOP	–	0.8387
		(5.978)***
TIME	–	–0.0459
		(–2.004)***
Sigma-squared (σ^2)	–	0.0682
		(7.391)***
Gamma (γ)	–	0.9999
		(99029.437)***
Log-likelihood Function	–	16.974
LR test of the one-sided error (χ^2)	–	20.115
Number of iterations	–	19
Number of observations (*N*)	102	102
Mean efficiency	–	63.22

Source: Computed by Authors as explained in the text.
Note: *** indicates significance at 1 per cent level; ** at 5 per cent level and; * at 10 per cent level.

CHCs and PHCs turn out to be insignificant, while the effect of doctors is significant only at 10 per cent level.

Both per capita income and per capita public expenditure on health have positive and significant impact on health performance at 5 per cent level. The expenditure elasticity is 0.42, while the income elasticity is 0.16. Doctor variable is associated with a positive coefficient and significant at 10 per cent level. The BCG immunization also has a positive effect on the health performance, while the measles immunization continued to have negative effect on health outcome. The higher intercept value over the intercept value in OLS indicates that there is a Hicksian neutral technical shift in the performance function.

Results of the inefficiency model in column 2 indicate that the literacy rate is negatively associated with inefficiency, while the proportion of rural population is positively associated with inefficiency. Both effects are statistically significant at 1 per cent level. These results are as per the expectations. The time effect is negative and significant at 1 per cent level, indicating that the mean inefficiency has declined during the study period. This means that mean efficiency has improved over the years.

Both σ^2 and γ terms are positive and significant at 1 per cent level. The γ value of 0.99 indicates that about 99 per cent of the total variation in the performance is due to inefficiency. The average efficiency is estimated as 63.22 per cent indicating that, on an average, only about 63 per cent of the health outcome potentials are realized by states. In other words, on an average, the states can improve the performance more by 37 per cent, without additional resources. This result needs policy attention.

The state-wise and year-wise efficiency scores are shown in Table 15.6. Kerala has the highest mean efficiency score of 92.6 per cent followed by Tamil Nadu (83 per cent) and West Bengal (79.6 per cent). Orissa has obtained the lowest mean efficiency score (42.2 per cent). The other two poorer states in terms of efficiency levels are Madhya Pradesh and Rajasthan. In 10 out of 17 states, the average efficiency scores are less than the overall mean efficiency of 63.2 per cent. These states require special attention to improve the efficiency levels.

Table 15.6:
State-specific and time-specific health outcome efficiency values

States	*2004–05*	*2005–06*	*2006–07*	*2007–08*	*2008–09*	*2009–10*	*Mean 1*	*Mean 2 (CR study)*
Andhra Pradesh	54.50 (10)	56.5 (11)	58.56 (10)	54.41 (13)	56.94 (13)	60.32 (11)	56.87 (12)	75.0 (6)
Bihar	30.39 (16)	42.91 (15)	45.96 (14)	68.14 (6)	82.74 (4)	87.25 (1)	59.57 (11)	79.3 (5)
Chhattisgarh	57.15 (9)	62.67 (9)	63.59 (8)	67.37 (7)	65.99 (7)	68.54 (7)	64.22 (7)	33.9 (13)
Gujarat	63.27 (7)	61.80 (10)	61.92 (9)	61.24 (9)	62.64 (10)	56.61 (14)	61.25 (10)	69.9 (10)
Haryana	48.03 (11)	53.59 (12)	57.69 (11)	57.46 (10)	57.99 (12)	55.09 (15)	54.98 (13)	71.8 (9)
Jharkhand	43.09 (13)	79.54 (5)	57.06 (12)	62.25 (8)	61.37 (11)	73.27 (6)	62.76 (8)	79.3 (5)
Karnataka	57.53 (8)	64.92 (8)	63.64 (7)	56.81 (12)	62.89 (9)	65.38 (9)	61.86 (9)	73.7 (8)
Kerala	99.99 (1)	98.08 (1)	97.67 (1)	89.2 (1)	83.64 (3)	87.15 (2)	92.62 (1)	95.1 (1)
Madhya Pradesh	37.68 (15)	40.16 (16)	39.43 (16)	42.53 (15)	48.07 (15)	57.74 (13)	44.27 (16)	33.9 (13)

Maharashtra	76.36	84.16	84.84	81.11	74.35	68.35	78.20	90.2
	(4)	(2)	(2)	(4)	(6)	(8)	(4)	(2)
Orissa	27.58	38.55	38.07	39.43	45.70	63.82	42.19	23.0
	(17)	(17)	(17)	(17)	(17)	(10)	(17)	(14)
Punjab	67.07	71.3	71.78	76.70	75.55	79.27	73.61	88.2
	(6)	(7)	(5)	(5)	(5)	(3)	(5)	(4)
Rajasthan	38.29	43.07	46.13	46.25	47.74	51.55	45.50	64.0
	(14)	(14)	(13)	(14)	(16)	(16)	(15)	(11)
Tamil Nadu	86.08	79.07	82.24	85.53	86.26	78.75	82.99	74.5
	(2)	(6)	(3)	(2)	(2)	(4)	(2)	(7)
Uttar Pradesh	45.18	43.65	45.88	41.83	48.87	49.10	45.75	40.3
	(12)	(13)	(15)	(16)	(14)	(17)	(14)	(12)
Uttaranchal	78.35	82.62	68.04	57.27	65.44	59.36	68.51	40.3
	(3)	(3)	(6)	(11)	(8)	(12)	(6)	(12)
West Bengal	68.31	81.56	80.16	83.58	87.57	76.25	79.57	89.9
	(5)	(4)	(4)	(3)	(1)	(5)	(3)	(3)
Mean efficiency	**57.58**	**63.77**	**62.51**	**63.01**	**65.52**	**66.93**	**63.22**	**69.2**

Source: Computed by Authors as explained in the text.

Notes: The numbers in parentheses are the ranks of the states in terms of their performance.

Mean 1 is from the results in column 2 of Table 15.5.

The last column in the table contains the efficiency scores (ranks) obtained by Chakrabarti and Rao (2007). The newly formed states of Chhattisgarh, Jharkhand and Uttaranchal are assigned the same scores as that of Madhya Pradesh, Bihar and Uttaranchal, respectively.

It is also observed from Table 15.6 that over the study years, some states improve their efficiencies. Bihar obtained 16th rank in 2004–05 with efficiency score of 30.4 per cent and improved to first position with an efficiency score of 87.3 per cent in 2009–10. Chhattisgarh improved its position from 9 to 7, Jharkhand from 13 to 6, Madhya Pradesh from 15 to 13, Orissa from 17 to 10 while Punjab from sixth position to third position during the study period.

Table 15.6 also compares the efficiency scores estimated in our study with the scores estimated by CR study, which uses similar methodology and data during 1986–95. The efficiency scores (mean 1) of Andhra Pradesh, Bihar, Gujarat, Haryana, Karnataka, Maharashtra, Punjab, Rajasthan, Uttar Pradesh and West Bengal in our study are lower than that (mean 2) in CR study. In all other states, the efficiency scores are relatively high as compared to CR study. Accordingly, the ranks also changed. For instance, the rank of Andhra Pradesh declined from 6 in CR study to 12 in our study. Madhya Pradesh's rank declined from 13 to 16. The Spearman's rank correlation between the efficiency scores in our study and that of CR study is 0.98, indicating that our results are highly correlated to the results in CR study.

Concluding Remarks and Policy Implications

In this study, we have assessed the health outcome performance of 17 major Indian states using the stochastic frontier methodology for panel data during 2004–05 to 2009–10. Our findings are: (i) both state and central governments in India have been spending increased amounts on health in real terms over the years; (ii) during 2004–05 to 2009–10, the per capita public expenditures on health (2004–05 prices) increased from ₹220 in 2004–05 to ₹366 in 2009–10 and per capita public spending by all state governments increased from ₹180 to ₹266; (iii) in 8 out of 17 states, the number of PHCs declined, in two states the number of CHCs declined and in 10 states the number of doctors declined;

(iv) Although the health outcome indicator—IMR declined from 58 to 47, India is not likely to meet the MDG target of 28 in 2015; (v) wide variations exist among the states in terms of the health outcome indicator. For instance, in Kerala the IMR was 13 while it was 62 in Madhya Pradesh in 2010; (vi) per capita income and per capita public expenditure on health influence health performance indicator positively and significantly. Interestingly, the expenditure elasticity is estimated at 0.42 and the income elasticity is at 0.16; (vii) health outcomes are positively related to the availability of medical doctors/specialists and BCG vaccination of infants.

Our results also indicate that the health outcome efficiency increases with higher literacy rate as expected and decreases with higher proportion of rural masses. The mean efficiency is estimated at 63.22 per cent, implying that there is a greater scope for raising the health outcome performance of major Indian states, without additional resources. In 10 out of 17 states, the mean efficiency is below the average mean efficiency. These states need to follow the best practices adopted by other better performing states like Kerala to improve their performance. The mean efficiency has increased continuously over the study years from 57.58 per cent to 66.93 per cent. However, year-wise individual efficiency levels indicates that performance levels increase or decrease in some states.

It is interesting to notice that during the study period 2004–05 to 2009–10, Bihar improved its position from 16th rank to first rank. Jharkhand (which was bifurcated from combined Bihar state), also improved its position: 13th rank in 2004–05 to 6th rank in 2009–10. Madhya Pradesh and Chhattisgarh also slightly improved their positions: former from 15th to 13th position while the latter from 9th to 7th rank. But bifurcation seems to be not helping Uttar Pradesh and Uttaranchal states. Uttar Pradesh ranked 12th in 2004–05 and 17th in 2009–10. Uttaranchal's rank declined from 3rd to 12th.

As per the efficiency values in 2009–10, the bottom three states were Uttar Pradesh, Rajasthan and Haryana. These states need special attention. They need to use their resources efficiently to improve their health outcome performance.

The policy implications emerged out of the study are as follows. First of all, the major Indian states can reduce their existing resources (i.e., by cutting waste) to achieve the present level of health performance. Alternatively, they can increase their health outcome performances without additional resources, but employing the existing resources efficiently. The states can also improve their health performances by increasing their public (state government) expenditure on health and increasing the number of medical doctors/specialists in the CHCs and PHCs. They can also educate people and create health awareness among them to improve the health outcomes. Thus, both quantitative and qualitative efforts are needed to improve the health performance in India.

Although the results of this are interesting and provide meaningful policy implications, this study is not free from limitations. Firstly, studies like the one by Tandon et al. (2013) suggest the use of multiple health outcome indicators. But this study uses a single but a dominant indicator. Secondly, most existing studies employ the DEA approach and, however, this study employs the SFA. The DEA can also be used and results from DEA would have been compared with results of SFA in order to check the robustness of the results. Despite these limitations, we hope the findings of the study are useful to policymakers, researchers and other stakeholders to take appropriate strategies to improve the health outcome efficiency of major states in India and remove the regional imbalances.

References

Aigner, Dennis, C.A., Lovell, K. and Schmidt, P. 1977. 'Formulation and Estimation of Stochastic Frontier Production Function Models', *Journal of Econometrics*, 6(1): 21–37.

Battese, G.E. and Coelli, T.J. 1992. 'Frontier Production Functions, Technical Efficiency and Panel Data: With Application to Paddy Farmers in India', *Journal of Productivity Analysis*, 3(1–2): 153–69.

———. 1995. 'A Model for Technical Inefficiency Effects in a Stochastic Frontier Production Function for Panel Data', *Empirical Economics*, 20(3): 325–32.

———. 1998. 'Prediction of Firm Level Technical Efficiencies with a Generalized Frontier Production Function and Panel Data', *Journal of Econometrics*, 38(3): 387–99.

Beenstock, M. and Sturdy, P. 1990. 'The Determinants of Infant Mortality in Regional India', *World Development*, 18(3): 443–53.

Bhalotra, S. 2007. 'Spending to Save? State Health Expenditure and Infant Mortality in India', Institute for the Study of Labour Discussion Paper Series, IZA DP No. 2914.

Chakrabarti, A. and Rao, D.N. 2007. 'Efficiency in Production of Health: A Stochastic Frontier Analysis for Indian States', in A. Tavidze (ed.), *Global Economics: New Research* (pp. 105–28). New York: Nova Science Publications.

Chelliah, R.J. and Shanmugam, K.R. 2001. 'Some Aspects of Inter District Disparities in Tamil Nadu', Madras School of Economics, Working Paper No. 1, Madras School of Economics, Chennai.

Farell, M.J. 1957. 'The Measurement of Productive Efficiency', *Journal of Royal Statistical Society*, Series A (General), 120(3): 253–90.

Goldstein, J.S. 1985. 'Basic Human Needs: The Plateau Curve', *World Development*, 13(5): 595–609.

Greene, W.H. 1993. 'The Econometric Approach To Efficiency Analysis', in H.O. Fried, C.P.K. Lovell and S.S. Schmidt (eds), *The Measurement of Productive Efficiency: Techniques and Applications* (pp. 68–119). New York: Oxford University Press.

Grossman, M. 1972. 'The Demand for Health: A Theoretical and Empirical Investigation', Occasional Paper No. 119, NBER.

Jain, A.K. 1985. 'Determinants of Regional Variations in Infant Mortality in Rural India', *Population Studies*, 39: 407–24.

Jat, T.R. and Sebastian, M.S. 2013. 'Technical Efficiency of Public District Hospitals in Madhya Pradesh, India: A Data Envelopment Analysis', *Global Health Action*, 6(2, September 24): 17–42.

Jondrow, J.C.A., Lowell, K., Materow, I.S. and Schmidt, P. 1982. 'On the Estimation of Technical Inefficiency in the Stochastic Frontier Production Model', *Journal of Econometrics*, 19(2–3): 233–38.

Kalirajan, K.P. and Shand, R.T. 1994. *Economics in Disequilibrium: An Approach from the Frontier*. Delhi: Macmillan India Ltd.

Kathuria, V. and Sankar, S. 2005. 'Inter-state Disparities in Health Outcomes in Rural India: An Analysis Using a Stochastic Production Frontier Approach', *Development Policy Review*, 23(2): 145–63.

Kaur, B. and Misra, S. 2003. 'Social Sector Expenditure and Attainments: An Analysis of Indian States', *RBI Occasional Papers*, 24(1 & 2, Summer & Monsoon): 105–43.

Kiadaliri, A.A., Jafari, M. and Gerdtham, Ulf-G. 2013. 'Frontier-based Techniques in Measuring Hospital Efficiency in Iran: a Systematic Review and Meta-Regression Analysis', BMC *Health Services Research*, August 15, 13: 3–12. doi:10.1186/1472-6963-13-312.

Kumbhakar, S.C., Heshmati, A. and Hjalmarsson, L. 1997. 'Temporal Patterns of Technical Efficiency: Results from Competing Models', *International Journal of Industrial Organization*, 15(5): 597–616.

Meeusen, W. and Broeck, J. 1977. 'Efficiency Estimation and from Cobb-Douglas Production Functions with Composed Error', *International Economic Review*, 18(2): 435–44.

NHA. 2005. *National Health Accounts India 2001-02*. Government of India, New Delhi: National Health Accounts Cell, Ministry of Health and Family Welfare.

———. 2009. *National Health Accounts India 2004-05*. Government of India, New Delhi: National Health Accounts Cell, Ministry of Health and Family Welfare.

Purohit, B.C. 2008. 'Efficiency of the Healthcare System: A Sub-state level Analysis for West Bengal (India)', *RURDS*, 20(3): 212–25.

Shetty, U. and Pakkala, T.P.M. 2010. 'Technical Efficiencies of Healthcare System in Major States in India: An Application of NP-RDM of DEA Formulation', *Journal of Health Management*, 12(4): 501–18.

Spink, S.J. and Hollingsworth, B. 2009. 'Cross-country Comparisons of Technical Efficiency of Health Production: A Demonstration of Pitfalls', *Applied Economics*, 41(4): 417–27.

Tandon, A., Murray, C.J.L., Lauer, J.A. and Evans, D.B. 2013. 'Measuring Overall Health System Performance for 191 Countries', GPE Discussion Paper No. 3.

Varabyova, Y. and Schreyogg, J. 2013. 'International Comparisons of the Technical Efficiency of the Hospital Sector: Panel Data analysis of OECD Countries using Parametric and Non-Parametric Approaches', *Health Policy*, 112(1–2): 70–79.

WHO. 2010. *World Health Report—Health Systems Financing: The Path to Universal Coverage.* Switzerland: WHO Press.

———. 2011. *World Health Statistics 2011.* Switzerland: WHO Press.

WHO and UNICEF. 2010. *Countdown to 2015 Decade Report (2000–2010): Taking stock of maternal, newborn and child survival.* Switzerland: WHO Press.

WHO Database. 2009. Available at http://www.who.int/research/en/ (accessed October 2011).

16

The Software Sector in Bangalore and Hyderabad

V.N. Balasubramanyam and Ahalya Balasubramanyam

Introduction

Development economics is rife with controversies. The most recent one, albeit an age old one, revived by Jagdish Bhagwati (2010) in a lecture delivered in New Delhi, is on the primacy of growth as opposed to that of development. The debate coordinated by CUTS International, a non-governmental organization (NGO) in India, drew three broadly differing views: those that advocated the primacy of growth, those that saw growth as necessary but not sufficient for development and those that argued that investments in development, centring on education and health, should be the prime concern of policymakers.

The generally accepted view is that growth is necessary but not sufficient for promoting development objectives, including reduction of poverty, spread of literacy, reduction of infant mortality and increased participation of women in the labour force. Growth is necessary for the obvious reason that it is growth that provides the resources for investments designed to promote development, including health and education. Growth, though it provides investible resources, may not promote development in the absence of relevant institutions and political leadership that can identify and allocate resources to those areas that can maximize returns to investments. Growth is conditioned by the volume of resources available for investment, the quality of the available resources and the allocation of resources between sectors that maximize growth. It should though be emphasized that devoting a high proportion of a low volume of total resources to education and health may not achieve the sought after development goals, it may result in low growth of incomes and stagnation of the economy.

All this may be obvious and above controversy. That which is not often recognized though, is that the nature of growth and the rate of growth or rate of return to investments in growth are primarily conditioned by the resource endowments of the region and the initial structure of the economy of the region. Both the resource endowments and the structure of the economy are dictated by the history and geography of the region. Attempts at engineering the structure of the economy towards sectors and economic activity for which it is ill equipped, both because of the sort of endowments it possess and the institutions in place, are likely result in low social rates of returns to investments. Equally high levels of growth that yield high volumes of investible resources may not result in the promotion of development objectives in the absence of relevant institutions.

This chapter illustrates these and allied propositions drawing upon the growth and development experience of two major capital cities in south India: Bangalore the capital of Karnataka state and Hyderabad the capital city of the state of Andhra Pradesh (AP).[1] These two cities provide for a case study of the propositions discussed previously for a number of reasons. First, they illustrate the importance of institutions and the impact of history on the growth and development process. Second, they are geographically contiguous. Third, they are both home to the software sector with a number of firms clustered close together in specific regions of the two cities. Fourth, Bangalore is the capital city of a state that has achieved a relatively high growth rate of the state domestic product,

[1] Recently the name of Orissa has changed as Odisha and Andhra Pradesh has been bifurcated into Andhra Pradesh and Telengana.

whilst Hyderabad is the capital city of a state with relatively low growth rates. Fifth, AP despite its relatively low growth rate scores over Karnataka in the promotion of several development objectives including the reduction of poverty, especially so in rural areas.

The most significant of these features of the two cities that illustrates several of the growth and development propositions discussed earlier is the presence of software clusters in the two cities. The main argument of this chapter is that clusters have to evolve if they were to be effective engines of technological change and human capital formation, they cannot be superimposed on an economy that lacks the sort of institutions and resources for their promotion. The software cluster in Bangalore exemplifies the first sort whilst the Hyderabad cluster is an example of the second sort.

The second section of the chapter discusses the economics of clusters. The third section portrays the clusters in Bangalore and Hyderabad. The fourth section analyses the impact of the clusters on the economies of the two states.

The Economics of Clusters

The economics of location of economic activity and agglomeration dates back to Von Thunen (1826), the German economist who suggested that agricultural products that are perishable and have to be transported speedily to the market are produced nearer to the market than those goods that are bulky and much more durable. Based on a number of restrictive assumptions, the model outlines the location of economic activity around a central market based on transport costs.

The economics of clusters, much more broadly conceived than Von Thunen's location model, has had a revival with the birth of new growth models, new trade theories centred on imperfect competition, and economic geography models of agglomeration of economic activity. The new economic geography model of agglomeration developed by Krugman (2002) draws upon the work of Von Thunen and that of geographer Krugman's analysis incorporates both transport costs and wage rates; if transport costs outweigh labour costs, firms located in more than one place and labour is distributed amongst different locales, but as transport costs decline, firms located in low wage cost regions and export to the other regions. As agglomeration or clusters evolve in the low cost regions, real wages and employment increase.

A feature of the new geography models, as also of the new growth theory and new international trade theories, is the assumption of imperfectly competitive economic structures. Firms compete on the basis of product differentiation and can experience increasing returns to scale. These assumptions that reflect reality depart from the usual ones of perfect competition and constant returns to scale, typical of growth and trade models in vogue until the advent of the new growth theory and new trade theories in the 1990s. It is on the basis of these assumptions that the neo-classical theories of growth suggest that growth rates between the high- and the low-income regions would converge; high-growth regions with high capital-to-labour ratios would meet with diminishing returns, much more so than those regions endowed with relatively low amounts of capital relative to labour. The new growth theory contests the assumption of diminishing returns to capital that forms the basis of the neo-classical convergence thesis and argues that whilst diminishing returns may occur at the firm level, the industry or the region as a whole may experience increasing returns. This assumption of diminishing returns at the firm level but increasing returns at the industry level that confers decreasing costs in production on the firms that make up the industry is based on the existence of external economies or externalities in production. Externalities thus explain the presence of increasing returns at the industry level, though individual firms in the industry may be subject to diminishing returns. It is also possible for firms to experience increasing returns to scale if they operate in highly imperfectly competitive markets with each of the firms producing differentiated products.

The presence of externalities is intertwined with the formation of clusters. It is the presence of firms producing differentiated products in a given industry that generates externalities and externalities attract new firms and workers to the cluster and enhance it. Alfred Marshall (1907) recognized the importance of externalities in the development of industries. He categorized the economies arising from the increase in the scale of production of any goods into two categories: those that depended on the general development of the industry are external economies and those that depended on the enterprise and efficiency of individual enterprises are internal economies.

Marshall did not distinguish between pecuniary external economies and technological external economies; this distinction was developed later (Scitovsky, 1954). Technological externalities arise through the interdependence of firms based on non-market mechanisms, whereas pecuniary external economies arise through the market mechanism. Inventions and improved techniques of production that are often in the nature of non-rivalrous public goods, freely available to one and all, are in the nature of technological externalities. A reduction in the price of the final goods and/or increased price for inputs, as a consequence of the growth of the industry as a whole, are classed as pecuniary external economies.

It is noteworthy that both technological and pecuniary externalities arise from the growth of the industry or the general development of the industry, as Marshall puts it. Growth of the industry, needless to say, is dependent on growth in productive efficiency of the firms that constitute the industry, resulting from the differentiation of existing products, the invention of new products and growth in managerial efficiency, including marketing skills. In short, growth of the industry is dependent on the growth of human capital.

The issue then is whether or not clusters are suitable mechanisms to promote the growth and development of human capital. Specifically, can clusters be formed and promoted through public policy initiatives or are their birth and growth dependent on factors that are specific to geographical regions? Michael Porter, the Harvard management expert and economist, is known for his advocacy of clusters. As two of the critics of Porter's advocacy of clusters put it, 'as the celebrated architect and promoter of the idea, Porter has been consulted by policymakers the world over to help them identify their nations' or regions' key business clusters or receive his advice on how to promote them' (Martin and Sunley, 2003). There is nothing wrong in approaching Porter for advice on identifying potential clusters; the issue, however, is how to identify them. Porter and others (Basant, 2002; Porter, 1998) identify geographical proximity of firms, interconnections between firms and commonalities, and complementarities between firms as the key characteristics of clusters. Could all these features be developed with public investments or do clusters evolve in response to socio-economic and geographical factors specific to certain regions? The software clusters in the city of Bangalore in the state of Karnataka and the city of Hyderabad in the state of AP provide a case study for an analysis of this issue. It is also noteworthy that the software sector, because of its nature and characteristics, provides an ideal case study of human capital formation.

The Nature and Characteristics of Software Clusters

In many respects, the software sector is ideal for analyzing the contribution of clusters to the growth of human capital. The sector is human capital intensive in its production process, much more so than any other industry. A large part of the total expenditures of software-producing firms is made up of wages and salaries of the software engineers. Apart from buildings and hardware, the industry requires very little fixed physical capital.

Another feature of the software sector is the range and differentiated nature of products the industry produces. The firms in the industry produce a range of products including application software, system software and programming software. Besides, within each of these groups, individual firms are able to cultivate niche markets such as software for the banking industry, for education institutions and for the medical profession. Firms in the industry can thus be segmented on the basis of both the sort of specialist software they produce and the specific sector of the economy they cater to.

These features of the software sector are admirably suited to promote the growth and dissemination of human capital or human skills. The product and labour segmentation of the industry, described previously, suggest that the structure of the industry more or less resembles that of universities. Just as academic economists such as mathematical economists, trade specialists and labour economists specialize in specific areas within a discipline, software engineers too specialize in specific areas of a generic industry. Again, just as academics commune with each other and learn from each other, software engineers too benefit from each other's experience and training. This they do both through formal seminars and conferences organized by their trade associations such as the National Association of Software and Services Companies (NASSCOM) and the technology park administrators where the firms are located, and also through informal networks. Besides, just as academics move between universities in search of fame and fortune, software engineers too move between companies. The rate of such turnover of employees between firms depends not only on the salaries they receive, but also on the facilities for training, on-the-job learning and working conditions provided by the firms.

These and other features of the software industry suggests that the workers in the various firms are in the nature of what the 19th century Irish economist John Cairnes (1873) christened as non-competing groups. Cairnes's purpose in formulating the concept of non-competing groups was to argue that prices in the market are not always determined by pure competition; an element of rent enters the price formation process. Rents for specific groups are preserved because of non-competing nature of groups of labour. A feature of non-competing groups of labour is that there is very little vertical mobility of labour. Each labourer finds a niche depending on his/her education and social status and once the occupation is chosen, the labourer stays put in it. As Cairnes (1873) puts it 'The man who is brought up to be an ordinary carpenter, mason or smith, may go to any of these callings, or a hundred more, according as his taste prompts or the prospects of remuneration attracts him; but practically he has no power to compete in these higher departments of skilled labour for which a more elaborate education and larger training are necessary'. Software firms are non-competing in the sense that each of the firms has its niche products and customers, and hence do not compete with each other. Their employees though can exchange generic information relating to the industry and in so doing, enhance the productivity of the industry. It is thus that they generate technological externalities.

It is also the case that there are gradations of software firms ranging from those that produce application software to those that produce sophisticated programmes. These differing firms would be non-competing in the sense that Cairnes formulated the concept. However, as Cairnes himself noted, workers in a lower order firm may through sheer exertion, extraordinary energy and self denial can escape from the bonds of their original position. In other words, they can train themselves to graduate to firms producing superior products. It is also possible as Marshall (1907), building upon Cairnes' work, showed that each of the non-competing groups can institute specific training programmes that can result in pecuniary externalities and increasing returns.

It is these features of the software industry that promote the growth and dissemination of human capital. It is also these features of the industry, especially its human capital intensity and the structure of the industry which is diversified, but grounded in a common foundation of generic knowledge that contribute to the formation of clusters. Software firms tend to agglomerate in regions that are endowed with pools of trainable labour that they require. But then, as stated earlier, clusters, if they are to be successful in the building up of human capital and diffusing it, should evolve in a socio-economic climate that promotes their evolution; they cannot be instituted by policy dictate and incentives of various sorts. This is not to say that clusters do not require any form of external assistance at all; they do, but such external assistance alone cannot result in efficient clusters that are capable of promoting the generation and diffusion of human capital.

The Bangalore and Hyderabad Clusters

Origin and Growth

There are quite a few studies on the software industry in India (Arora, 2006; Atreye and Arora, 2002). The reference point of most of these studies is the software sector in Bangalore now known as the Silicon Plateau of India. Bangalore, the capital city of Karnataka with a population of around 9.6 million people, is known for its spacious gardens and salubrious weather. The city well known as the pensioner's paradise was to be transformed into the Silicon Plateau of India with the birth of the software industry in the city around the mid-1980s. Hyderabad, the capital city of AP with a population of 4 million (6.8 million people including metropolitan areas), was according to the biographer of the city Narender Luther (2000), conceived by its founder as a replica of heaven on earth. It is now home to bio-tech industries and a software cluster. The city of Bangalore is larger in size both by population and income than Hyderabad (Table 16.1).

State of Karnataka with Bangalore as the leading centre for the software industry heads the list of production and exports of software (Table 16.2).

Table 16.1:
Population and income

	Bangalore	*Karnataka*	*Hyderabad*	*Andhra Pradesh*	*India*
Population (millions)	9.58	61.13	4.01	84.86	1210
Density (per square mile)	4378	319	18,480	308	
Growth rate (2001–10)	46.68	15.67	21.74	11.10	17.64
Literacy rates	88.48	75.61	80.96	67.66	74.04

Source: Census of India; State Census, Government of India, Ministry of Home Affairs, 2011.

Table 16.2:
Number of institutions of higher education and number of engineering and polytechnic students, 2005–06

	University								
States/UTs	*Central*	*State*	*Deemed Universities*	*Institutions of National Importance*	*Research Institutions*	*Arts, Science and Commerce Colleges*	*Eng., Tech., and Arch., Colleges*	*Number of Engineering and Technical Students (Thousands)*	*Number of Engineering Students per 1,000 Population*
2	*3*	*4*	*5*	*6*	*7*	*8*	*9*	*10*	*11*
Andhra Pradesh	2	14	5	0	5	1603	278	379	4.9
Karnataka	0	16	7	0	1	930	134	265	5.1
Kerala	0	7	2	1	1	189	99	118	3.7
Maharashtra	1	19	20	1	54	1018	193	173	1.7
Tamil Nadu	0	17	16	2	1	693	269	504	8.1
Delhi	4	1	10	2	1	68	20	27	0.8
India	20	216	101	13	140	11,698	1562	2358	2.3

Source: Ministry of Higher Education, Government of India.

The birth of the software sector in Bangalore dates back to the mid-1980s when Texas Instruments, a 100 per cent export-oriented unit, set up shop in the city. The presence of Bangalore and the state of Karnataka at the head of the league tables of the industry cannot be dismissed either as a historical accident or a result of fortuitous circumstances. There is a long list of factors responsible for the emergence of Bangalore as the centre for the software industry in India. These include the Karnataka government's initiative in establishing a software technology park in 1977, reinforced by the Software Technology Parks Scheme of the Central government in the mid-1980s, the presence of a large number of science and engineering teaching and research institutions, the presence of a large number of public enterprises including Hindustan Machine Tools and Bharat Electronics, the contribution of the Indian Diaspora in the Silicon Valley in California to the growth of the sector, state support for infrastructure, the cultural ambience of the city of Bangalore and its salubrious weather (for a detailed review of the state support for the industry, see Basant, 2006).

The central government industries such as Hindustan Machine Tools, Bharat Electronics and Indian Telephone Industries Ltd established during the 1950s and the 1960s were all publicly owned. The choice of Bangalore for the location of these industries was dictated by strategic reasons of defence and security. There were also several hardware firms in the city, another proximate reason for software firms to gravitate to the region. Indeed, the presence of manufacturing firms of various sorts including Hindustan Aircraft Ltd and Mysore Electrical industries date back to the 1940s—the days of the British Raj. Thus Bangalore has had a history of being host to a varied set of industries.

One of the main reasons for the attraction of Bangalore as a locale for industries is the large number of scientists and engineers it produces, many more than most other states (Table 16.2). The tradition of higher education in science and engineering also dates back to the days of the Raj. The first of several engineering colleges that dot the city now was established by Vishweshvaraya, one of the top-level administrators (Dewan of Mysore state from 1912 to 1918) and an early advocate of industrialization during the days of the Raj, as early as 1917, when Mysore University was also established.

Karnataka has a total number of 20 universities, 152 engineering colleges, 114 medical colleges and 248 polytechnics. Bangalore is home to the reputable Indian Institute of Science, referred to as the Tata Institute after its founder Jamshedji Tata, established in 1909, known for its research in aeronautical engineering and the physical sciences. Besides the software industry, the city also hosts more than 90 of the 180 bio-tech firms in India. As Basant (2006) states, Bangalore is also home to a number of firms manufacturing machine tools, electronic equipment and bio-technology products. The educational and cultural ambience of the city, once known as the pensioner's paradise because of its salubrious weather and space, is succinctly captured by the well-known sociologist, the late M.N. Srinivas, in his introduction to a book on Bangalore (2000), where he says:

> Bangalore is intellectually vibrant, a multitude of institutions of higher learning and research providing homes for scientists and other specialists in a variety of fields. A perusal of the list of seminars, talks, discussions, plays, musical and other performances, exhibitions and religious events in the daily newspapers provide the curious reader with an idea of the city's deep interest in cultural and intellectual aspects of life.

Sunil Khilnani's (1998) observation that, 'Bangalore is a cosmopolitan city with a sizeable middle-income group whose incomes are derived not from land and inherited property, but from investments in education and the group actively encourages the pursuit of wealth based on education, enterprise and skill' echoes Srinivas's observation on Bangalore. This pursuit of education, especially engineering and medical education, also resulted in the large scale migration of educated Bangaloreans to the US and the UK during the decades of the 1960s and the 1970s. These professionals, unable to find suitable and remunerative jobs at home, migrated to the US and the UK, lured by the jobs on offer from the National Health Service for the medical graduates in the UK and the space programme in the US for the engineers. A number of these migrants were to actively participate in the birth and growth of the Silicon Valley software cluster in California. The Diaspora in the Silicon Valley has been a major factor in the growth of the software sector in Bangalore. These include both the to and fro migrants and those who have returned to Bangalore (see Balasubramanyam and Balasubramanyam, 2000). The Diaspora also contributes to the growth of the sector in yet another indirect fashion. Many of them head the operations of multinational firms in Bangalore; according to one source, 71 of the 75 multinationals in Bangalore Software Technology Park were headed by Indians who had lived and worked overseas, especially in the US (Basant, 2006). These Diaspora who head foreign firms in Bangalore and other locations could be a significant channel for the dissemination of human capital, and their expertise and knowledge of methods of operations and market intelligence would be of immense benefit to Indian firms. As Devesh Kapur (2010: 86), in his detailed study of India's Diaspora, states 'the diasporic networks act as reputational intermediaries and as credibility-enhancing mechanisms, which may be particularly important in economic sectors such as software, where knowledge, especially ex-ante knowledge of quality, is tacit'. Their cultural affinity to the Indian engineers and entrepreneurs is of course a major factor in the effective transmission of technology and know-how to the Indian engineers and firms (Wei and Balasubramanyam, 2006).

There is much to be said for each of these reasons that explain the birth and growth of the software sector in Bangalore. There is, however, a view, first expressed by the Economist magazine of London that the software sector in India in general has benefited from the benign neglect by the state. As the Economist puts it, the sector was left alone mostly because the policymakers did not understand the industry. This tongue in cheek comment may have a grain of truth. The industry may have escaped unnecessary bureaucratic rules and regulations such as the ones that prevailed during the Licence Raj. It has, however, received state support for setting up satellite facilities and benefited from state support for higher education (Balakrishnan, 2006; Basant, 2006). The contention of some writers, however, that the sector has vastly benefited from the state and in fact, from state regulation of industry may be an exaggeration. Allied to this view is the one that attributes the birth of the industry to the departure of IBM from India in the year 1973 because of its unwillingness to comply with the Foreign Exchange Regulation Act that required foreign firms to shed the majority of their equity in favour of local firms. The programmers who were made redundant by the departure of IBM are reported to have set up software firms. This view is contested by Rafiq Dossani (2006) who argues that it was domestic firms, often with the expertise provided by India's Diaspora in the developed countries that set up software firms and by 1981, there were 21 firms with annual exports of $4 million. Many of these firms later moved to Bangalore in the face of growing land values in Mumbai. Dossani also contests the often expressed view that state support was an essential significant factor in the growth of the software industry in India. He convincingly argues that the industry took birth and grew despite the hostile government policies towards private enterprise. All this suggests that Indian enterprise and expertise found a niche in the newly evolving IT industry, a novel and complex area of economic activity that may have flummoxed the bureaucrats as the economist suggests.

The large number of educational and research institutions in the city, the presence of a number of industries specializing in the production of machinery and equipment, the cultural ambience of the city and state support rather than interference all taken together do suggest that Bangalore has all the ingredients for a successful cluster capable of fostering human capital development. A study by Srinivas (1977) cited by Basant reports that all the domestic and foreign firms located in the software technology parks have had some form of contact with research laboratories or institutes in Bangalore. One-third of the firms surveyed by the author also stated that the institutes provided new ideas that helped them to design and invent new products.

A much more detailed study by Basant and Chandra (2006) based on a sample survey of institutions in Bangalore and Pune suggests that in the two cities there are a variety of linkages between the software and the pharmaceutical sectors and education institutions including labour market, product market and research links.

The labour market linkages are much more significant than the other sorts of linkages.

There are though those that argue that none of these reasons add up to much. They note that although Bangalore does possess a number of engineering institutions, the link between software firms and these institutions is not just weak, but absent. And the quality of education imparted in the institutions of higher learning in the state of Karnataka and in India in general leaves a lot to be desired (D'Costa, 2006). It is also argued that there is no collaboration between the software firms in the city and that the industry is much too heavily oriented towards export markets.

These observations on the structure of the industry and the nature of the education institutions are astute, but they need to be qualified in the context of the structure and stage of development of the Indian economy in general. The links between universities and the software firms are weak precisely because most, though not all, academic institutions in Bangalore lack a tradition of research and they are ill equipped to be trouble shooters or partners of software firms. But they do perform a significant service for the software firms; they produce engineering graduates who can be trained on the job, the so-called labour market linkages between education institutions and software clusters referred to earlier. They act as a filter; they sift the intelligent and capable students from the rest. They save the software firms considerable search costs. In fact, the engineering graduates who are successful in the interviews and tests administered by the software firms may be over-qualified for the jobs they are initially required to do. Their academic training in mathematics and engineering may be much more extensive and advanced than that required for the software industry. This may be no bad thing as these are the research-minded graduates capable of learning by doing and pushing the frontiers of knowledge. It may not be feasible to implement the Stanford/Silicon model in Bangalore, but there may be no need to do so. Software firms especially the large and reputable ones such as Infosys and Wipro, provide the sort of training the young graduates need. The cluster has evolved because of this sort of proximity of software firms to educational institutions in the city. Just as the Sheffield cutlery trade as Marshall (1907) noted 'is due chiefly to the excellent grit of which grindstone is made', software firms turn the engineering graduates into software engineers, the graduates are like the grit out of which grindstone is made. And when the industry took birth around the mid-1980s, most firms were producing products at the lower end of the range, over the years they have moved up the ladder.

There may not be much collaboration between software firms because they are in the nature of non-competing groups identified by Cairnes discussed earlier. Each of the firms has its own niche market, some specializing in software for banks, some in software for airlines, and some in software for health providers and so on. Such is the nature of the trade they ply that they neither collaborate nor compete with each other. This sort of lack of collaboration does not in any sense rule out the spread of external economies. In fact, most external economies are generated by the very presence of technology-intensive industries producing similar but not identical products and processes. Such externalities are generated in the software sector through informal networks of software engineers fostered by clubs, pubs and organized seminars and conferences. Bangalore, because of its ambience noted by the sociologist Srinivas, facilitates such informal networks. Much of the knowledge involved in software production is tacit knowledge, which can only be exchanged with face-to-face contacts between the engineers. This sort of communion between young software engineers is facilitated by the cultural ambience of Bangalore. Another channel for the spread of human capital via externalities is the turnover of personnel in the sector. This too occurs because of exchange of information about salaries and working conditions amongst the engineers in the industry. Such turnover, however, facilitates knowledge promotion, though it imposes costs on the software firms. Turnover of personnel that was fairly high in the initial years of the industry is now reported to have declined, mostly because of the efforts of the firms to retain the human capital they had trained.

In sum, Bangalore exhibits many of the socio-economic features to be found in the Silicon Valley in California. Saxenian's (1994) observations on the valley, though with some dilution, may not be too farfetched to describe the environment in Bangalore that promotes human capital dissemination:

> It is not simply the concentration of skilled labour, suppliers and information that distinguish the region. A variety of regional institutions—including Stanford University, several trade associations and local business organisations, and a myriad of specialised consulting, market research, public relations and venture capital firms—provide technical, financial, and networking services which the region's enterprises cannot afford individually. These networks defy sectoral barriers; individuals move easily from semiconductor to disk drive firms or from computers to network makers ... And they continue to meet at trade shows, industry conferences, and the scores of seminars, talks and social activities organised by local business organisations and trade associations. In these forums, relationships are easily formed and maintained, technical and market information is exchanged, business contacts are established and new enterprises are conceived. This de-centralised and fluid environment also promotes the diffusion of intangible technological capabilities and understandings.

To borrow Marshall's words, 'Bangalore's attractions to software firms may be summed up as it is all in the air'.

The Hyderabad Cluster

Both the city of Hyderabad and the state of AP of which it is the capital present a contrasting socio-economic picture to that of Bangalore and the state of Karnataka. Elsewhere, we refer to the model of development pursued by Karnataka as the elitist model and the one pursued by AP as the populist model (Balasubramanyam and Balasubramanyam, 2012). AP model of development reflects the state's comparative advantage and resource endowments centred on agriculture. The admirable Human Development Report for AP (2007) prepared by the Centre for Economic and Social Studies, located in Hyderabad, notes that AP was the first state to introduce the green revolution in agriculture. The growth in rice output following the introduction of the new rice varieties has justly earned the state the sobriquet 'rice bowl of India'. Another notable achievement of the state is its success in reducing the levels of poverty, especially rural poverty, which according to some estimates is about 10 per cent, a figure much lower than that in most states and substantially lower than in Karnataka estimated at 23.85 per cent (Dev and Ravi, 2007). That which is admirable about the state's record on poverty is that the reduction of poverty is largely a result of a state-wide rural poverty eradication programme based on social mobilization and empowerment of poor rural women. The programme aims at enhancing assets, capabilities and the ability of the poor to deal with shocks and risks. The record of the state in controlling the rate of growth of population is also far superior to that of most other states, again an outcome of the work of NGOs and women's self-help groups rather than the traditional route of promoting literacy amongst women. These and other achievements of the state are to be attributed to the tradition of a vigorous pursuit of equity through agitation for land reforms and land redistribution and struggle for the rights of the backward castes and communities. The success of AP demonstrates the significance of institutions is promoting development. The state owes the sort of rural institutions it has nurtured to the opposition too inequities in agriculture spearheaded by the Communist Party and other left-leaning parties in the state.

This tradition of struggle for equity in a largely agriculture-oriented state sets it apart from Karnataka that is dominated by high-tech industries and services that the state owes to its history in large part as stated earlier. It is for these reasons that the birth and growth of the IT sector in Hyderabad is somewhat of a superimposition on a city that lacked an inherent comparative advantage for growth of services and manufacturing. As the Human Development Report (2007) states, 'AP does not have a strong background and tradition of industrial development, like the neighbouring state of Tamil Nadu in terms of entrepreneurship, technical skills and infrastructure'.

It is against this background that the software cluster in Hyderabad should be assessed. The comparative advantage of the state of AP and its capital city lies in agriculture-based industries; the socio-political ambience of the state is centred on the pursuit of equity, especially promoting the economic interests and well-being of the socially disadvantaged. These facts were recognized by its political leaders on until the appearance of Chandra Babu Naidu on the political scene. Naidu, who was the chief minister of the state from 1995 to 2004, shifted the focus of economic policy from the pursuit of equity centred on the development of agriculture to one of growth centred on IT. The software sector took birth mostly because of his zeal for spreading IT throughout the state. It is a well-known fact that the software sector in Hyderabad owes a great deal to his zeal and perseverance. He had a planned strategy of development centred on information technology. An economist by training, he put the public finances of the state in order by raising the price of subsidized rice from ₹2 to ₹3.50 per kg, increasing tariffs on electricity and scrapping prohibition. Naidu's ardour for liberal economic policies and technology-led development centred on the private sector were instrumental in the generous provision of loans from the World Bank and the Department for International Development (DFID) of the UK to fund Naidu's technology-centred projects. The Bank is reported to have provided $266 million per annum during the late 1990s and the DFID provided another £230 million spread over three to four years. Such disbursements by external agencies directly to a state government by-passing the central government in Delhi, attests to the autonomy over policy Naidu exercised, mostly because of the number of seats his party held in the Lok Sabha, the lower house of the Indian Parliament. Naidu also managed to lure external investors such as Microsoft to establish research centres and a Business School in Hyderabad, linked to Kellogg Business School in the US. He bought the services of McKinley, the international management consultants to prepare a document titled Vision 2020 outlining the policies to be put in place to promote the development of AP. The consultants accorded information technology a major role in attaining his objective and he warmly embraced the recommendations of the consultants. The incentives provided for investment in the IT sector include non-applicability of labour laws, pollution control laws and statutory power cuts. Some of the other incentives provided are allotment of land, electricity, tariff rebate for small and medium enterprises, rebate on cost of land, physical infrastructure such as power, water, sewerage and roads and telecommunication infrastructure (Niranjana Rao, 2009). All this amounts to a sizeable package, but as Niranjana Rao notes, there is no estimate of the explicit and implicit subsidies given to the sector.

It is arguable if the software sector would have been established but for Naidu's active support and indeed zeal for turning Hyderabad into a centre for technology. Bangalore too did have state support, but not the sort of direct intervention of the state government in procuring external aid and assistance, nor did the sector receive the large volume of subsidies and fiscal exemptions that the sector in AP enjoys. Admittedly, the software sector in Hyderabad has registered impressive growth and its total exports of ₹325 billion in the year 2008–09 was surpassed only by Bangalore (₹703 billion) and Maharashtra (₹423 billion). The sector can also boast of an impressive growth performance and employment record. It is also noteworthy that a study by NASSCOM reports that Hyderabad scores over Bangalore and in fact over other software locations in the quality of its infrastructure. Whilst Hyderabad is ranked number one amongst the various locations of software firms in the country, Bangalore ranks number 6. It is a well-known and much lamented fact that the infrastructure in Bangalore, especially roads and power supply, are woefully inadequate. Software, however, is not a transport-intensive service and most companies in Bangalore have instituted emergency power supply facilities. The issue though is one of the capabilities of a cluster in generating externalities and promoting human capital development, without a heavy dependence on state subsidies.

The software sector in the two cities, one founded and formed by entrepreneurs with a relatively low level of state support and the other with substantial state support, open up several issues for analysis. The principal issue is whether a software cluster with extensive state support yields high rates of social dividends, principally the birth and growth of human capital necessary for growth and development of the region where the sector is located.

Implications of the Economics of Clusters for the Hyderabad and Bangalore Software Cluster

The essential features of successful clusters are that they evolve in response to market opportunities in specific regions that are capable of imparting a comparative advantage to specific industries or groups of firms. The import of the foregoing is that because of its history, its geographical location and its social and cultural ambience, Bangalore was an ideal locale for the software cluster. Although there is a software cluster in Hyderabad, it is not as vibrant as the Bangalore cluster. It is smaller in size judged by production and exports and its productive efficiency is not as high as that of the Bangalore cluster (Table 16.3).

The size of the sector in Bangalore, judged by the number of firms, number of employees, total production and exports, is much larger than that in Hyderabad.

Admittedly, Hyderabad too attracts its Diaspora to invest in the software sector. Indeed, the number of Andhra emigrants in the Silicon Valley is as high as one in four of all the immigrants from India. There are no data to show that a sizeable number have returned home to Hyderabad. Although there are no precise figures on the returning Diaspora to Bangalore, it is estimated to be around 3,000 per year. Also the state of Karnataka attracts a lot more immigrants from other parts of India than AP (Table 16.4).

Table 16.3:
Characteristics of software industry: Andhra Pradesh and Karnataka: 2008–09

	Andhra Pradesh	*Karnataka*	*All-India*
Units (2008–09)	1,408*	2,085	10,305
Software exports (₹ millions)	325,090	749,290	2,173,480(E)
Manpower (2008–09)			
Direct	251,786	554,000	2,200,000 (E)
Total investments (₹ millions)	37,390	30,000	

Source: Software Technology Parks of India (Annual Report various issues).
Note: Nearly 80 per cent of the exports of each of the two states are from their capital cities—Hyderabad and Karnataka.

Table 16.4:
In-migration into the four southern states (1991–2001)

	In-migration (0–9 years)					
	% Total Population	*Total*	*% Rural Population*	*Rural*	*% Urban Population*	*Urban*
Andhra Pradesh	**76,210,000**	**(number)**	**55,401,060**	**(number)**	**20,808,940**	**(number)**
Total	0.55	421,989	0.37	206,774	1.03	215,215
Northern	0.27	207,087	0.17	93,196	0.55	113,891
Southern	0.26	198,629	0.20	108,510	0.43	89,119
Karnataka	**52,851,000**		**34,889,471**		**17,961,529**	
Total	1.66	879,106	0.85	296,010	3.25	583,096
Northern	0.58	305,321	0.33	115,845	1.05	189,476
Southern	1.02	537,828	0.49	172,508	2.03	365,320
Kerala	**31,841,000**		**23,574,075**		**8,266,925**	
Total	0.74	235,087	0.58	136,878	1.19	98,209
Northern	0.14	45,441	0.09	21,639	0.29	23,802
Southern	0.55	175,143	0.46	108,986	0.80	66,157
Tamil Nadu	**62,406,000**		**34,922,002**		**27,483,998**	
Total	0.43	270,473	0.22	76,818	0.70	193,655
Northern	0.10	60,142	0.03	11,959	0.18	48,183
Southern	0.27	171,088	0.14	49,708	0.53	145,842

Source: Census of India, 2001.

The number of migrants into the urban areas of Karnataka (mostly Bangalore) is relatively high and this is mostly on account of the software sector. Bangalore has an advantage over Hyderabad in many other respects, including the longstanding presence of a number of higher education institutions. The institutions in Andhra are of a more recent vintage, mostly because the rulers of Hyderabad in the past took little interest in promoting education, though they were keen on the arts and architecture. Narender Luther, the historian of Hyderabad, writes that in the latter half of the 19th century 'The state did not do anything to impart education or to provide public health. Whatever schools existed was private, mostly denominational. The medium of instruction was mostly Persian and what was taught centred mostly around theology and writing of the script' (Luther, 2006). The now reputable Osmania University was set up in 1919 and until 1948, the medium of instruction in the university was Urdu and not English. This contrasts with the emphasis placed on education by the Maharajas and Dewans of Mysore, now Karnataka. Apart from several public and private schools, they were responsible for the setting up of the Engineering College and the University of Mysore as early as 1911.

All this is not to say that the city of Hyderabad is backward in any sense. It is just that its history and antecedents are different from that of Bangalore. Its comparative advantage in pharmaceuticals and science-based industries is well-known. The internationally known pharmaceutical firms in Hyderabad date back to the 1980s. The state of AP has well-known entrepreneurs in a variety of food products industries, most of them from the coastal areas. In general, the state's comparative advantage seems to rest in agro-industries and science-based industries such as pharmaceuticals, than in services. Indeed, judged by the number of enterprises or the gross value added per worker in the service sector, AP lags behind the other three southern states as well as most other states in India (Table 16.5).

Estimates of output and employment multipliers per unit increase in software output for a number of Indian states (Table 16.6) show that in the case of Karnataka, the output multiplier is high relative to the employment multiplier, whilst the reverse is the case in AP.

Table 16.5:
Service sector in India, 2006–07: Economic characteristics of enterprises

	Enterprises		*Workers*		*Gross Value Added (₹)*	
	Number	*%*	*Number*	*%*	*Per Enterprise*	*Per Worker*
High Performers						
Gujarat	68,261	5	152,042	5	152,737	68,824
Haryana	36,495	3	65,457	2	124,059	69,170
Maharashtra	138,363	11	434,821	15	264,970	108,343
Punjab	44,779	3	71,761	2	90,936	56,743
West Bengal	134,211	10	229,590	8	70,687	42,281
Average	**84,422**	**7**	**190,734**	**7**	**140,678**	**69,072**
Southern States						
Andhra Pradesh	111,674	9	294,690	10	183,210	86,414
Karnataka	46,635	4	430,982	15	1,761,753	335,079
Kerala	133,946	10	224,220	8	70,579	42,173
Tamil Nadu	137,098	11	266,065	9	103,298	53,673
Average	**107,338**	**8**	**303,989**	**11**	**529,710**	**129,335**
Others						
Bihar	69,417	5	103,722	4	62,050	41,077
Madhya Pradesh	64,985	5	117,872	4	64,187	35,109
Orissa	29,950	2	59,458	2	71,477	36,006
Rajasthan	55,315	4	92,188	3	83,318	49,994
Uttar Pradesh	219,192	17	342,688	12	60,468	41,586
Average	**87,772**	**7**	**143,186**	**5**	**68,300**	**40,754**
Average of 14 states	**92,166**	**7**	**206,111**	**7**	**225,981**	**76,176**
Total 14 states	1,290,321	100	2,885,556	100		
All-India	1,400,966		3,098,090		170,073	86,876

Source: NSS Reports No.528/ 529.

Table 16.6:
Software sector: Output multiplier and employment multiplier

State	*Output Multiplier*	*Employment Multiplier*
Delhi	1.41	2.35
Chandigarh	1.92	1.49
Maharashtra	3.22	0.32
Andhra Pradesh	1.15	3.87
Karnataka	1.45	0.23
Kerala	1.64	2.56
Tamil Nadu	1.46	0.67
Punjab	1.11	2.27
Haryana	1.62	2.00
Rajasthan	1.42	5.40
Uttar Pradesh	1.31	1.43
West Bengal	1.41	2.18
Orissa	1.38	4.34
Madhya Pradesh	1.84	5.45
Gujarat	2.25	1.30

Source: National Council of Applied Economic Research Development Report, 2002.

The NCAER study that has produced these interesting estimates argues that in the case of states where the output multiplier is higher than the employment multiplier, there are vertical linkages between software and other sectors, whilst in the case of states where the employment multiplier is higher, there are horizontal linkages. In other words, software is used in the production of goods and services. This may be so, but the high employment and low output multipliers also indicate low productive efficiency in the use of software in industries and sectors that are linked to the software sector.

The structure of AP's economy, its history and its institutions are very different from that of Karnataka. The sort of ingredients that Bangalore possesses for the development of the software cluster is largely absent in Hyderabad and so are the attributes needed for the generation of externalities in the sector discussed earlier.

The main difference between the cluster in Bangalore and the one in Hyderabad is that the former has evolved on the basis of the comparative advantage the city possesses for the birth and growth of an export oriented service industry, whereas the latter is sponsored and cultivated with substantial volumes of state investment.

In the absence of detailed data on the extent of state subsidies and assistance the Hyderabad and Bangalore clusters receive, the social rates of return to public funds invested in the two clusters cannot be estimated. One other piece of evidence in support of the hypothesis that the Bangalore software cluster may be superior to Hyderabad in productive efficiency and human capital formation is based on estimates of total factor productivity (TFP) and its components (Table 16.6 and Figure 16.1). There are a number of studies that estimate TFP for the aggregate manufacturing sector of India (Goldar, 2004; Ray, 2014), but virtually none for individual sectors such as software

The results shown in Table 16.7 and Figure 16.1 are based on estimates of Malmquist productivity indices for a small sample of software firms in Hyderabad and Bangalore for the years 2000–06. The Malmquist indices provide an estimate of TFP change and the factors contributing to the change in terms of technological change and technical efficiency change. Technical efficiency change or the ability of firms to extract the maximum amount of output from a given set of inputs is further sub-divided into pure technical change and scale efficiency change. The estimates shown in Table 16.7 suggest that (i) TFP for the sample of firms in the Bangalore cluster is higher than that for the firms in the Hyderabad cluster (ii) while there is not much to choose between the two clusters in terms of efficiency change or the optimal combination of inputs in response to input prices, much of the technical change in the case of the firms in the Bangalore cluster is on account of pure technical efficiency whilst it is pure scale effects or increased investments that contribute to technical change in the case of the Hyderabad firms. It is noteworthy that pure technical change is mostly on account of human skills. This piece of evidence again supports the hypothesis that knowledge formation and productivity growth tend to be relatively high in the Bangalore cluster.

Figure 16.1:
TFP change by type of firms

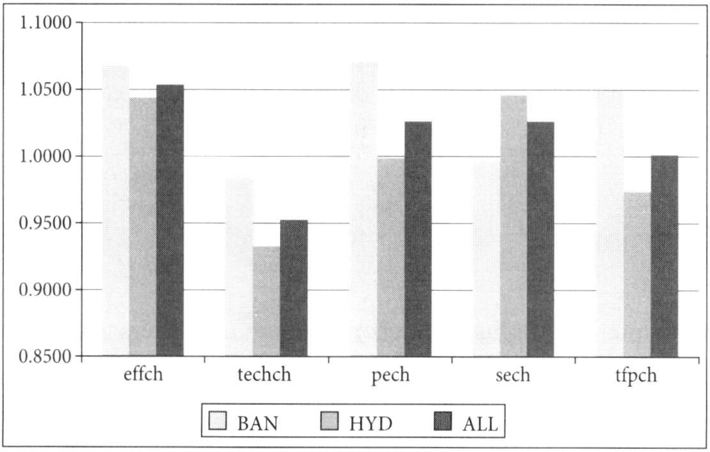

Source: Authors' estimates based on data for forms in Prowess database.

Table 16.7:
Total factor productivity change: Bangalore and Hyderabad firms

	BAN	*HYD*	*ALL*
effch	1.0668	1.0440	1.0530
techch	0.9837	0.9326	0.9520
pech	1.0710	0.9987	1.0260
sech	0.9961	1.0454	1.0260
tfpch	1.0495	0.9737	1.0020

effch: Efficiency change.
techch: Technological change.
pech: pure technical efficiency change.
sech: scale efficiency change.
tfpch: total factor productivity change.
BAN: Bangalore firms: number 27.
HYD: Hyderabad firms, number 16.

It should though be noted that these estimates of Malmquist productivity indices, while they do support the hypothesis argued in the chapter, are by no means conclusive. The number of firms in the Bangalore sample is only 16 and in the case of the Hyderabad sample 26. Also the data provided by Prowess do not include the number of employees, the wage bill data for each of the firms is used as a surrogate for labour inputs. Detailed analysis of human capital formation and efficiency change in the two software clusters requires not only statistical data on a sufficiently large sample, but also a set of case studies. This is the agenda for the next phase of research on the software clusters in the two cities.

Conclusions

This chapter has discussed the contribution of clusters to human capital formation in the context of the software firms located in Bangalore and Hyderabad. Analysis of clusters has a long history dating back to Marshall and Arrow followed by the work of Krugman and Porter. Transport costs, wage rates and interdependence of firms are cited to be the major factors promoting the growth of clusters. Transport costs do not play a major role in the formation of software clusters as the industry is not heavily dependent on transportable inputs nor does its output require cost-intensive transport facilities. A feature of the industry is its human capital intensity. Access to efficient, easily trainable labour, recognized by Marshall, is one of the factors that promote agglomeration of firms. The endowments of educated labour which is a historical inheritance, is one of the major factors that account for the Bangalore cluster. So also is the ambience of Bangalore that favours the location of software firms and the formation of the cluster. The nature of the industry and the cluster in Bangalore are ideally suited to generate the sort of technological externalities and to a lesser extent, pecuniary externalities discussed by Marshall and Krugman. The Hyderabad cluster, though has a recognizable presence, may not be in the same league as the one in Bangalore, mostly because of its history and the absence of a natural ambience required for the agglomeration of knowledge intensive software firms. Indeed, the software cluster is the result of heavy fiscal subsidies and the zest for spreading information technology facilities throughout the state of AP by its technocratic chief minister Chandra Babu Naidu.

Available data show that the Hyderabad cluster is not as vibrant as the Bangalore cluster despite the presence of a number of major players in the industry including foreign-owned firms.

The record of Hyderabad on development including reduction of poverty, however, is superior to that of Karnataka. One factor amongst others in its development record is the astute use of IT in promoting development objectives in the rural areas. Hyderabad could have had access to the sort of IT services it has deployed in the rural areas without the heavy investments in the software industry. Here again, importation of software services from more efficient producers may be much more welfare enhancing than producing it at home. AP is known for its village-level initiatives in utilizing the services of NGOs and micro-finance agencies. Its success in reducing the rate of growth of population and the level of poverty in the state are also notable achievements. It is worth pondering whether or not AP has deviated from its natural comparative advantage in agriculture and agro-based industries and ventured into software, where its advantages are not all that obvious. By the same token, it can be argued that Bangalore has stumbled on to the area of its comparative advantage by virtue of fortuitous circumstances. It is argued by Hyderabad-based economists that the crucial test of the benefits of the software sector in Hyderabad is its contribution to social development (Niranjana Rao, 2009; Ramachandriah, 2003). The sector appears to have passed this test, but the state could have allocated its resources much better by purchasing the IT services from the neighbouring state of Karnataka than producing it at home. The contrasting experience of the two states suggests that production of human capital should not be an end in itself, it has to be put to use in an imaginative manner to promote development objectives.

It should be noted that many of the propositions in the chapter, such as comparison of productivity of labour, rates of return to capital invested and TFP between firms located in Bangalore and Hyderabad, await statistical tests. Basant's study does compare the Bangalore cluster with that of other clusters and finds that the Bangalore cluster reaps several advantages over the others because of its proximity to customers, access to skilled labour, presence of hardware and software suppliers, better access to training facilities and access to R&D institutions. These are also the factors that have contributed to the superiority of the Bangalore cluster. It should, however, be noted that a definitive analysis of the proposition put generally that clusters are born and not made awaits a much more detailed statistical analysis. It is ironic that the data needed for such an analysis is not provided by the IT centres of Bangalore and Hyderabad or by the professional trade organization, NASSCOM.

References

Arora, A. 2006. 'The Indian Software Industry and its Prospects'. Available at SSRN: http://ssrn.com/abstract=964457 or http://dx.doi.org/10.2139/ssrn.964457 (accessed 21 February 2007).

Athreye, S. and Arora, A. 2002. 'The Software Industry in India's Economic Development', *Information and Economic Policy, El Selvier*, 14(2): 253–73.

Balakrishnan, P. 2006. 'Benign Neglect or Strategic Intent: Contested Lineage of Indian Software Industry', *Economic and Political Weekly*, 41(6): 3865–73.

Balasubramanyam, V.N. and Balasubramanyam, A. 2000. 'The Software Cluster in Bangalore', in J.H. Dunning, *Regions, Globalisation and the Knowledge-based Economy* (pp. 349–63). New Delhi: Oxford University Press.

———. 2012. 'Karnataka and Andhra Pradesh: The Disparate Twins', in K. Pushpangadan and V.N. Balasubramanyam (eds), *Growth, Development and Diversity: India's Record Since Liberalisation* (pp. 23–54). New Delhi: Oxford University Press.

Basant, R. 2002. *Knowledge Flows and Industrial Clusters: An Analytical Review of Literature* (pp. 1–80). Indian Institute of Management. Working Paper Number 2002-02-01, Indian Institute of Management, Ahmedabad.

———. 2006. 'Bangalore, Cluster: Evolution, Growth and Challenges Indian Institute of Management', Working Paper 2006-05-02, Ahmadabad.

Basant, R., ChandraBasant, R. and P. Chandra. 2004. 'Capability Building and Inter-Organizational Linkages in the Indian IT Industry: The Role of Multinationals, Domestic Firms and Academic Institutions, India', in A.D. Costa and E. Sridharan (eds), *The Global Software Industry: Innovation, Firm Strategies and Development* (pp. 193–219). London: Palgrave.

Bhagwati, J. 2010. 'Indian Reforms: Yesterday and Today', Hiren Mukherji Lecture Delivered at India's Lok Sabha.

Centre for Economic and Social Studies. 2007. 'Human Development', Report for Andhra Pradesh, Hyderabad.

Cairnes, J.E. 1873. *Essays in Political Economy*. London: Macmillan.

D'Costa, A.P. 2006. 'Exports, University-Industry Linkages, and Innovation Challenges in Bangalore, India', World Bank Policy Research Working Paper, 3387.

Dossani. 2006. 'Globalization and the Offshoring of Services: The Case of India', in S. Collins and L. Brainard (eds), *Offshoring White-Collar Work* (pp. 241–67). Washington, D.C.: Brookings Institution.

Goldar, B. 2004. 'Indian Manufacturing: Productivity Trends in the Pre and Post Reform Periods', Working Paper 137, Indian Council for Research in International Economic Relations, New Delhi.

Kapur, D. 2010. *Diaspora, Development and Democracy: The Domestic Impact of International Migration from India*. Princeton: Princeton University Press.

Khilnani, S. 1998. *The Idea of India*. London: Hamish Hamilton.

Krugman, P. 2002. *Development, Geography and Economic Theory*. Cambridge, MA: MIT Press.

Luther, N. 2006. *Hyderabad: A Biography*. New Delhi: Oxford University Press.

Marshall, A. 1907. *Principles of Economics*. London: Macmillan.

Martin, R. and Sunley, P. 2003. 'Deconstructing Clusters: Chaotic Concept or Policy', *Journal of Economic Geography*, 3: 5–35.

Niranjan Rao, C. 2009. 'Information Technology Sector in Andhra Pradesh', in S.M. Dev, C. Ravi and M. Venkatanarayana (eds), *Human Development in Andhra Pradesh: Experiences, Issues and Challenges* (pp. 170–78). Hyderabad: Centre for Economic and Social Studies.

Porter, M.E. 1990. *The Competitive Advantage of Nations*. New York: Free Press.

Ramachandriah, C. 2003. 'Information Technology and Social Development', in C.H. Hanumantha Rao and S. Mahendra Dev (eds), *Andhra Pradesh Development* (pp. 202–18). Hyderabad: Centre for Economic and Social Studies.

Ravi, C. and Dev, M. 2007. 'Poverty and Inequality: All India and States', *Economic and Political Weekly*, 42(6): 509–27.

Ray, S. 2014. 'What Explains the Productivity Decline in Manufacturing in the Nineties in India', Working Paper 289, Indian Council for Research in International Economic Relations, New Delhi.

Saxenian, A.L. 1994. *Regional Advantage*. Cambridge: Harvard University Press.

Scitovsky, T. 1954. 'Two Concepts of External Economies', *Journal of Political Economy*, 62(2): 143–51.

Srinivas, M.N. 2000. *Bangalore Scenes from an Indian City*. Bangalore: Gangaram Publications.

Srinivas, S. 1977. 'The Information Technology Industry in Bangalore: A mCase of Urban Competitiveness in India?' Paper Presented at the 5 Asian Urbanisation Conference, London.

Wei, Y. and Balasubramanyam, V.N. 2006. 'Diaspora and Development', *The World Economy*, 41(36): 3865–73.

About the Editors and Contributors

Editors

K.R. Shanmugam is a faculty member of Madras School of Economics since its inception in 1995. He is a member of Scientific and Technical Advisory Group of the CMPA, MoEF and GIZ. He is also a non-officio member of Central Direct Taxes Advisory Committee; non-officio member of State Planning Board of Government of Pondicherry; member of various committees of Government of Tamil Nadu; Academic Council Member of Central University of Tamil Nadu and Indian Institute of Finance. He held the position of Treasurer of Indian Econometric Society during 2001–06.

K.S. Kavi Kumar has been coordinating activities of Centre of Excellence in Environmental Economics (supported by the Ministry of Environment and Forests) at MSE for the past eight years. He is a member of the Expert Committee on Climate Change, MoEF&CC, GoI, and a member of State Environment Appraisal Committee (Tamil Nadu) and he has been working at MSE since 1999.

Contributors

Ishwarya Balasubramanian is a Research Scholar, Indira Gandhi Institute of Development Research, Mumbai.

Ahalya Balasubramanyam is Faculty, Department of Economics, Lancaster University Management School, Lancaster.

V. N. Balasubramanyam is Professor, Department of Economics, Lancaster University Management School, Lancaster.

Durba Biswas is an Independent Researcher based in New Delhi.

Debashis Chakraborty is Assistant Professor, Indian Institute of Foreign Trade, New Delhi.

Kausik Chaudhuri is Professor, Leeds University Business School, Leeds.

Sukanya Das is Assistant Professor, Madras School of Economics, Chennai.

Debanjali Dasgupta is a Research Scholar, Indira Gandhi Institute of Development Research, Mumbai.

Amanat K. Gill is an Independent Researcher based in Uttarakhand.

Haripriya Gundimeda is Professor, Department of Humanities and Social Sciences, Indian Institute of Technology Bombay, Mumbai.

Zareena Begum I. is Associate Professor, Madras School of Economics, Chennai.

D. Jayaraj is Professor, Madras Institute of Development Studies, Chennai.

Gaurav Joshi is with The World Bank, USA.

Kaliappa Kalirajan is Professor, Crawford School of Public Policy, Australian National University, Canberra, Australia.

Vinish Kathuria is Professor, Shailesh J. Mehta School of Management, Indian Institute of Technology Bombay, Mumbai.

E.D. Israel Oliver King is with the M.S. Swaminathan Research Foundation, Namakkal, Tamil Nadu, India.

Muthukumara Mani is Lead Economist, South Asia Region Office of the Chief Economists, The World Bank, USA.

Anil Markandya is Scientific Director, BC3 Basque Centre for Climate Change, Spain.

Sacchidananda Mukherjee is Associate Professor, National Institute of Public Finance and Policy, New Delhi.

Badri Narayanan G. is Research Economist, Center for Global Trade Analysis, Purdue University.

Thanh Nguyen is Rector, Hanoi University of Natural Resources and Environment, Hanoi, Vietnam.

Anubhab Pattanayak is Research Scholar, Madras School of Economics, Chennai.

J. Prachitha is an Independent Researcher based in Bangalore.

Prabhakaran T. Raghu is with the International Maize and Wheat Improvement Center (CIMMYT), New Delhi, India.

C. Bhujanga Rao is Assistant Professor, National Institute of Public Finance and Policy, New Delhi.

Aarsi Sagar is with The World Bank, USA.

D.K. Srivastava is Chief Policy Advisor, Ernst and Young, New Delhi and Former Director Madras School of Economics, Chennai.

Elena Strukova is with The World Bank, USA.

Anbumozhi Venkatachalam is with the Economic Research Institute for ASEAN and East Asia, Jakarta, Indonesia.

L. Venkatachalam is Associate Professor, Madras Institute of Development Studies, Chennai.

Brinda Viswanathan is Associate Professor, Madras School of Economics, Chennai.

Index